Locational Dynamics
of
Manufacturing Activity

Locational Dynamics
of
Manufacturing Activity

Edited by

LYNDHURST COLLINS

Department of Geography,
University of Edinburgh

and

DAVID F. WALKER

Department of Geography,
University of Waterloo, Canada

JOHN WILEY & SONS

LONDON · NEW YORK · SYDNEY · TORONTO

Library of Congress Cataloging in Publication Data:

Collins, Lyndhurst.
Locational dynamics of manufacturing activity.

1. Industries, Location of—Addresses, essays, lectures.
I. Walker, David F., joint author. II. Title.

HD58.C63   1974   338'.09   73–21939
ISBn 0 471 16582 4

Photosetting by J. W. Arrowsmith Limited and printed in Great Britain by J. W. Arrowsmith Limited, Bristol

Contributors

JEAN BASTIÉ   *University of Paris, France.*
JAMES H. BATER   *University of Waterloo, Ontario, Canada.*
JAMES B. CANNON   *Queens University, Ontario, Canada.*
GARTH CANT   *University of Canterbury, New Zealand.*
LYNDHURST COLLINS   *University of Edinburgh, Scotland.*
IRWIN FELLER   *Pennsylvania State University, U.S.A.*
JAMES M. GILMOUR   *McGill University, Quebec, Canada.*
ROGER HAYTER   *Memorial University of Newfoundland, Canada.*
E. FREDERICK KOENIG   *Ministry of State for Urban Affairs, Ottawa, Canada.*
GUNTER KRUMME   *University of Washington, U.S.A.*
WILLIAM F LEVER   *University of Glasgow, Scotland.*
JOHN S. LEWIS   *Statistics Canada, Ottawa.*
G. B. NORCLIFFE   *York University, Ontario, Canada.*
D. MICHAEL RAY   *Ministry of State for Urban Affairs, Ottawa, Canada, and University of Ottawa, Canada.*
DAVID F. WALKER   *University of Waterloo, Ontario, Canada.*
H. DOUGLAS WATTS   *University of Sheffield, England.*

Preface

Collections of original essays and readers of reprinted articles have the advantage of bringing together in single volumes a wide variety of approach, scholarship and intellectual viewpoints on selected topics. It is not surprising that many such volumes have been published in the last few years nor that reviews of these books within the geographic literature indicate that their contribution to undergraduate teaching has been considerable. This collection is designed primarily for the advanced student who is interested in industrial location. We believe that it helps to satisfy a need for more specialized books on particular aspects of this sub-field.

All the essays are research-oriented and many of them represent capsuled statements of larger ongoing research projects of the 1971–1973 period. For this reason some of the essays pose more questions than they attempt to answer. It is hoped, however, that these questions will provide a springboard for further enquiries. The primary aim of this volume then, is to present a cross section of research approaches—theoretical, methodological and empirical—concerned with the locational dynamics of manufacturing activity. Collectively, the essays consider the locational dynamics at the regional, urban and individual firm scale.

For the preparation of this volume the editors sincerely acknowledge the willing co-operation of the contributors who have shown through their immediate responses to deadlines from their locations around the world that distance is not an insuperable geographic concept. The maps were prepared for publication by Ray Harris and Alexander Bradley at the Department of Geography, University of Edinburgh. Finally, we wish to acknowledge the University of Edinburgh for providing leave of absence and the University of Waterloo for editing facilities.

Lyndhurst Collins
David F. Walker

Contents

ix

x

A Perspective

DAVID F. WALKER and LYNDHURST COLLINS

The geography of industrial activity and in particular that of manufacturing activity, has attracted in the last two decades an increasing amount of research interest. Although this research has advanced on several fronts much of the work has been linked by a common emphasis on problems relating to locational change. Locational change in this context relates not only to the change in location of industrial firms and factories but also to change in the spatial pattern of employment which is frequently used as a measure of industrial activity. It is convenient for the purpose of this volume to consider this concern with the 'dynamics' of manufacturing activity under three general headings which emphasize the approach rather than the content of the particular studies. The first section contains essays which essentially focus on theoretical and conceptual aspects of locational change though in most cases there is reference to specific area studies. Section two follows with four essays that elaborate behavioural and statistical procedures for describing, analysing, and forecasting manufacturing change through time. The third section comprises a selection of essays which consider particular examples of change in different contexts for regions, urban areas, and firms. A much larger selection of essays relating specifically to the firm is published in a companion volume *Location Decision and the Firm* (ed.) F. E. I. Hamilton.

It is recognized that within these broad divisions of approach—Theoretical and Conceptual, Methodological, and Empirical—there are subsets of more specialized approach which are well represented elsewhere in the literature. The aim of the present volume however, is not to provide a comprehensive collection of all possible approaches to the study of locational dynamics with respect to manufacturing activity, but rather to provide the reader with a summary of current and ongoing research interests which hopefully will stimulate further investigation.

The Process of Locational Change

An actual change in the locational pattern of manufacturing activity is the result of several processes which can act either singly, or together. In those areas or countries where there has been an observable change in manufacturing activity, measured in terms of say number of establishments (plants), a comparison of the map at two points in time will reveal one of three possible changes. In many western countries the most obvious change would be an enlargement or expansion of the previous pattern; in this, each node or concentration has become larger but the relative positions have remained the same. Second, there has been an internal change within the existing pattern whereby formerly large nodes have become smaller and smaller nodes larger, so that relative positions within the pattern have changed. Third, and possibly the least likely, is a complete change in the locational pattern; in this, former industrial areas have disappeared or almost disappeared and manufacturing is present in new portions of the map.

Each of these changes can be induced by several processes. The first, for example, may result from a positive birth/death differential of manufacturing establishments in all areas; the universal expansion may also result from the expansion of existing plants in the area either *in situ* or through the creation of local branch plants, alternatively branch plants from other areas or countries may be established. A less likely process, though one that is very much in evidence in certain countries, is the relocation into the nodes—lock, stock and barrel—of plants from outside the area.

The second change of pattern may also result from these processes, except that here there are both positive and negative birth differentials, and a situation in which some centres are highly preferred for both branch plants and the intra-regional relocation of plants.

Finally, the third major change will be influenced by all these processes but the former industrial areas will be marked by either negative birth/death differentials and/or net out-migration of manufacturing plants.

Within each of these broad changes however, there are likely to be marked internal structural changes, whereby particular industries (for example furniture and fixtures) will become more dispersed whereas the printing industry, for need of closer personal contacts and other agglomeration economies, may become more concentrated. The strength of linkages will vary through time (Bater essay) but the overall pattern of manufacturing activity may remain the same.

Measures of Locational Change

The measurement of manufacturing activity has been the central concern of numerous studies most of which are referenced in the work of Patni (1968) and Morrison, Scripter and Smith (1968). The aims of such studies have been either to provide an absolute measure of manufacturing activity for selected areas at one point in time, or to devise an index which provides a relative measure of the degree of concentration or localization of manufacturing activity for the particular areas. Much of the discussion relating to measurement techniques has concerned the choice of criteria for measuring manufacturing activity. Usually, however, the choice is constrained by available data.

A smaller segment of the literature has been concerned with the more difficult problem of locational change, that is with comparing the values of localization indices through time. This task has been hindered for two main reasons. First, significant changes in the spatial pattern of industrial activity usually take a long time to evolve but changes in the delimitation of the areal units (especially metropolitan areas in North America) for which data are collected are relatively frequent. Second, changes in the definitions of the components of industrial activity, such as the establishment and industrial categories (orders), make temporal comparisons extremely difficult (Gilmour, 1966). In those studies where comparisons have been made there have sometimes been conflicting results especially at the national and regional levels. Some studies, for example, have concluded that the observed trends indicate widespread decentralization whereas others, involving the same areal units, have concluded that the predominant trend is one of increasing concentration (Collins, 1972, pp. 77–78).

In addition to the measures of localization and concentration for 'all industries' there is a large family of indices for measuring specialization and diversification (Ferguson and Forer, 1973). Again most of these indices have been used for describing the pattern of industrial structure at one point in time though in some (Conkling, 1964) the indices have been employed for temporal comparisons. Such comparisons provide an indication of the change in amount of a particular industry relative to other industries for selected areal units and suggest a framework for examining aggregate patterns of locational change.

The increasing use of statistical techniques in recent years for measuring and describing changes in locational patterns of manufacturing activity is encouraging the adoption of methodologies developed in related disciplines. The use of three-mode factor analysis for example, has been transferred by Cant (1971) to the study of changes in the location of manufacturing employment in New Zealand (See Cant essay and also that of Koenig, Lewis and Ray). More recently Keeble (1972) has adopted the concept of the gravity model for describing and analysing the radial movement of manufacturing plants from London into the surrounding parts of S.E. England. The logical extension of these pursuits has been the development of forecasting models using procedures such as Markov chain analysis (Lever, 1972 and see Collins essay) and multiple regression analysis (Sant, 1974) for estimating the direction and amount of change in the spatial pattern of industrial activity. Although little used for such a purpose as yet, simulation models would seem to be appropriate also (Walker essay). No doubt many other techniques will eventually be discovered and applied in empirical studies designed to examine the relationships found to be of theoretical importance in industrial geography.

Theoretical and Conceptual Considerations

Location theory has been most fully developed in the context of static problems. This is understandable in view of the difficulties involved in understanding and predicting dynamic trends. Nevertheless, if location theory is to be really helpful, especially in the context of practical problems, the dynamics of locational change will require far more attention. A review of some of the major points covered in the literature provides a way of illustrating the current situation and a framework within which to view the contributions made here.

The simplest problems involving locational dynamics are those in which trends existing at a particular time continue in much the same way into a future time period. Growth of population is of special importance because of its relationship to demand. Thus a certain population growth implies a specific increase in demand and, consequently, increased outputs in the requisite manufacturing sectors. While other features will be responsible for spatial allocation, the overall demand conditions govern the *scale* of manufacturing activity. Viewed spatially, continuation of present population trends, normally means that differential growth rates will operate so that the absolute population size of cities will tend to converge or diverge over time.

The size of population, and therefore market, within an area is closely related to the threshold level at which production might be expected. The minimum profitable scale of operation is not the same for every manufacturing industry but, in general, such a level can be identified for a particular operation. Thus a minimum size of market is often a precondition for the development of an industry in a country, region, or town (Pred, 1965; Nourse, 1968, pp. 209–215; Lloyd and Dicken, 1972, pp. 110–126). Size of market cannot be equated exactly with size of population for three reasons. Firstly, socio-economic characteristics of populations may differ greatly, leading to variations in the type of goods demanded. Secondly, industries vary considerably in the extent to which they supply products to the final consumer market and in the degree to which they are market-oriented. Nevertheless, the trend is towards a greater degree of attraction to the market (Greenhut and Colberg, 1962, pp. 64–81; Haggett, 1965, pp.125–136). The third major consideration is the extent to which competition in manufacturing is not usually organized spatially in such a way that a manufacturer has a market area in which he is the exclusive supplier of certain products. More often several manufacturers, located in some cases quite close together, will compete over a very large area. Thus, market growth in an area may not call forth any substantial new manufacturing there. Despite all these qualifications, projection of market growth is very important in terms of measuring the relative attraction to industry. As a market becomes larger, so the distribution costs of servicing it from elsewhere increase in total: eventually, they may outweigh production cost advantages at other locations.

The establishment of empirical threshold levels, such that projections of manufacturing activity in particular regions or towns can be made, is difficult enough. But the impact of differential growth is more complex and far more difficult to understand. It has frequently been noted that once growth begins, the place where it starts has a tremendous ability to continue growing. This has been formalized into the principle of circular and cumulative causation by Myrdal (1963). In his work, Myrdal recognized that development problems frequently exhibit aspects of a vicious circle, and that as a result rich countries or regions tend to become richer and poorer ones even poorer. Thus 'in the normal case a change does not call forth countervailing changes but, instead, supporting changes, which move the system in the same direction as the first change but much further' (p. 13). Therefore, 'the play of the forces in the market normally tends to increase, rather than to decrease, the inequalities between regions' (p. 26). The initial reason for a start at a particular place may even have been fortuitous but the process, once begun, reinforces itself.

The way in which some of these forces operate is illustrated in a study of nineteenth-century urban growth in the United States (Pred, 1965). Pred discussed the process in relation to Figure 1.

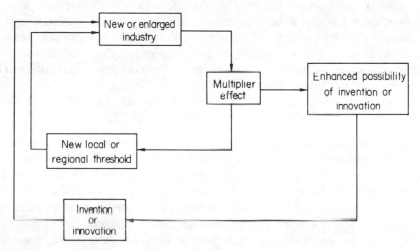

Figure 1. The circular and cumulative process of industrialization and urban size growth
Source: A. R. Pred (1966) *The Spatial Dynamics of U.S. Urban Industrial Growth, 1800–1914.* Cambridge, Mass.: M.I.T., p. 25

He distinguished two circular sequences of reactions. Firstly, the development of industry leads to increased population and income, which in turn stimulates further growth of the commercial and service sectors to satisfy the increased demands of the industrial workers and their families. The combined effect of such expansions may lead to other thresholds being attained, which allow further manufacturing growth and so continue the whole process. Such a sequence of events is normally termed the multiplier effect, and many empirical studies have attempted to calculate the extra jobs and income generated by one new manufacturing job (Miernyk, 1965, pp. 50–55; Nourse, 1968, pp. 163–176). Pred's second circular sequence propounds the view that an increase in manufacturing stimulates innovation and invention and thus makes further growth more likely. Improvements may be expected both in the technological and managerial realms and, as communications improve, will probably be disseminated more rapidly.

The increase in size of an urban concentration of industry also calls forth the whole range of cost advantages known as agglomeration economies. First recognized by Weber (1929, pp. 124–161), these factors are usually divided into three categories:

Scale Economies. These are the advantages accruing from large scale production in a single plant. Included here are the possibilities of buying and selling in multiples at reduced costs per unit, and economies frequently available as a result of specialization of machinery, labour or management which becomes more feasible as plant size increases.

Localization Economies. When a group of closely related plants cluster together, they frequently benefit through the common use of facilities and services needed by all of them (for example, transportation, vocational schools geared to their industry, machinery and tool production and service). In addition, they can specialize very narrowly to attain cheaper production but be close enough to suppliers and buyers to keep transportation costs to a minimum. Such clustering has been described in numerous studies (e.g. Wise, 1949; Hall, 1962, pp. 37–120; Bater and Walker, 1971).

Urbanization Economies. The urban area provides an overall level of service to all industry which tends to be proportionate to its size. Thus, as more and more plants concentrate in a city, the range and quality of service available to the manufacturer generally rises. In addition, larger centres often can provide more cultural, educational and other facilities which make them more attractive as places to live for the management and labour force.

Weber recognized that size of industrial concentration could also bring disadvantages (1929, pp. 131–134). Today, traffic congestion, pollution and high costs of land may be deterrents to manufacturing, especially in the core areas of large cities. The relative strengths of agglomerative and deglomerative forces are hard to evaluate and one of the major problems even with analyses of the contemporary scene is the lack of empirical evidence relating to these factors. In terms of projecting their likely importance in the future, there is very little basis from which to work. Nevertheless, one of the most dramatic, twentieth-century changes in the location of manufacturing activity—suburbanization—is closely related to the net balance of these factors (Reeder, 1954; Kerr and Spelt, 1958; Linge, 1963; Martin, J. E., 1966; and Cameron, 1972).

Within metropolitan areas, the result of suburbanization has been the development of 'doughnut' formations in which the city core areas of industrial activity have been greatly depleted, either through a high death rate or through significant outward movements to planned industrial parks and estates in the suburban fringe. In many cases this suburbanization process has been supplemented by an inward movement of plants—both relocations and branch plants—to suburban locations outside the metropolitan area. Studies of these changes have tended to focus on three main aspects. First, Reeder and Keeble (1968) have paid particular attention to the *direction* of movement which seems to have marked sectoral patterns. Second, Kerr and Spelt's study is one of the few in which the emphasis has been on appraising the *factors* which influence suburbanizing firms to locate in one particular sector as opposed to others. A third group of studies, has used total coverage data, as opposed to sample data used in the studies above for *measuring* the degree of suburbanization in terms of the establishment (Cameron, 1972; Collins, 1972; also see Bastié essay). In these studies the authors have attempted to separate the amount of locational change resulting from birth/death differentials, branch plant location, and net migration movements during a relatively short term period. Related to this approach are allocation models (W. A. Steger, 1965; Putnam, 1967) which have been used for prediciting spatial changes in the intra-urban employment structure.

The growth of an urban centre or a region may be expected to have an impact on other areas. Such growth attracts immigration and capital from elsewhere, which is likely to reduce the attractiveness of the supplying areas for further economic development. This is particularly true in view of the fact that migration tends to be selective, so that the younger and more able members of the population are most likely to move. Any area which is stagnating or declining finds it more and more difficult to maintain the quality of its infra-structure and services. These adverse effects can be expected to increase the costs of production for most manufacturing firms and reduce the likelihood of expansion in the manufacturing sector. They have been called 'backwash' effects by Myrdal (1963, pp. 27–31) and 'polarization' effects by Hirschman (1958, pp. 187–190).

Not all impacts from growing regions will be harmful to others. There may also be positive effects ('spread' or 'trickling down'). These are particularly related to the demands created in the growing regions for food and materials. If sufficient expansion in the primary sector takes place, a large enough population growth may be generated to encourage development in the manufacturing and commercial sectors and perhaps even begin a new growth cycle. A variant of this process is that described by the staple theory of economic growth (Gilmour essay). This describes how undeveloped areas are stimulated by external demand for 'staple' products (i.e. unprocessed or slightly-processed raw materials) which eventually may lead to a developed and growing economy. Today, however, there are few regions which are unsettled and yet have the potential to support large populations. Moreover, it is more and more difficult to compete in the world economy against established producers. Although there are exceptions, trading ties tends to make it difficult for countries and areas which are dependent on primary products to break out from this dependence. To do so requires capital and know-how which is rarely available except from areas with which they would later compete. If they have exceptional promise, the developed areas may invest but usually this is done with retention of ownership and control so that much of the benefit returns to the developed area (Levitt, 1970; Hymer, 1972). Within a country, these features have frequently led to the development of what has been called a core and periphery, or alternatively a heartland and hinterland. (Ray, 1972, pp. 46–54). In the heartland, family incomes and market potential are higher, unemployment is lower and manufacturing much more strongly developed. Frequently, the hinterland areas are controlled economically and politically by the heartland.

From these discussions of factors involved in regional and urban growth, it is clear that there are considerable interrelationships between numerous factors. The discussion to this point has focused on growth of population and markets, but this has already led to some consideration of cost factors, especially those associated with agglomeration economies. Cost factors loom large in the calculations used by manufacturers when locations are evaluated, and some consideration should be given to the possibility of their being modified independently of population change. Three categories of potential changes are discussed below.

Changes in Technology. Technical change is a day-to-day feature of most developed countries and, while most modifications are quite minor, major breakthroughs are not uncommon. In the context of urban growth, it has already been noted that invention and innovation are most likely to occur in existing industrial areas, but the application of new ideas will not necessarily benefit such established areas. In his essay, Feller reviews the literature on this topic and outlines its limitations. He suggests that four types of technological change should be distinguished:

(1) That which is 'site specific and enchances the competitiveness of a region's resources'. This mainly applies to the use and early processing of raw materials.
(2) That which reduces input costs and therefore widens an industry's market, allowing greater scale economies.
(3) That 'which provides the basis for a new footloose industry'.
(4) That which applies equally to all firms in an industry so that its effects depend upon the rate of adoption.

The locational effects of these different types of technological development are likely to be different. For example, the second type could encourage a reduction of the number of production sites so that some areas will decline (Gilmour essay), while the third type leads to the introduction of a new industry with its own locational requirements, leading to a completely new pattern of location.

A consequence of changing technology and the eventual development of new techniques and products is that over time products go through a cycle (Krumme and Hayter essay). The locational requirements of the experimental stage with its demands for highly skilled scientists and technicians are quite different from those which eventually will be needed if mass production is adopted. This poses problems both for towns and regions in that a logical location pattern may indicate separation of facilities but, unless there are several products at various stages of the product cycle, fluctuations at each separate location are likely to be severe. Because of the importance of large corporations in much research and development activity, the managerial policies pursued by them may be expected to have a considerable effect upon those future locational patterns which are closely associated with technological change.

Changes in Public Opinion. Industrial development takes place within a climate of public opinion expressed partly in terms of government policy and law. This climate is not the same everywhere and is subject to change. At the present time in many western countries, some of the negative aspects of growth are being recognized to a degree that has not been evident since the beginning of the industrial revolution. There is a growing dislike of road congestion, which is partly dependent on city size, and especially of pollution which frequently can be traced to manufacturing activity. It is no longer true that manufacturing will always be welcome because of the new jobs it brings; note for example the tremendous opposition from local inhabitants and environmentalists to the proposed industrial developments at Hunterston on the west coast of Scotland—a country of high unemployment.

The effect of this change of viewpoint, and the tougher laws against pollution, is to improve the whole environment. If regulations are significantly different from country to country, or region to region, however, locational change may also be expected. The cost of some anti-pollution devices is still very high and may have a significant bearing on the location of noxious industries. Also, older plants may find it difficult to modify their techniques and so be forced out of operation prematurely. Regulations apply to many other aspects of manufacturing as well. There are frequently incentive programmes encouraging the location of industry in specific areas (Lloyd and Dicken, 1972, pp. 238–267), programmes providing aid for vocational training and for other aspects of plant operation. In total, governments may offer a significant financial incentive to manufacturing. Within a country or province (state), there may also be a particular locational policy in evidence, such as the stimulation of specific growth centres, and the discouragement of industry in some other areas. Thus government policy in total may be very significant in affecting the location of industry (Cannon essay). Changes in policy are likely to be very difficult to predict.

At the municipal level also, local opinion and policy will be important. Some towns or cities may decide to limit growth, while others pursue a vigorous policy of attracting industry in order to improve their tax base. At this local level, intra-urban industrial location is significantly affected by zoning policy (see Bastié essay). The local council may set up industrial parks, try to phase out industry in some areas or follow other planning strategies. The contrast between areas dating from the late nineteenth century with their mixed land uses, and the modern separation of residential areas from industrial parks is very considerable.

Changes in Attitudes of the Labour Force. Labour costs often form a significant proportion of total production costs, and are of considerable locational importance to many industries (Segal, 1960; Economic Commission for Europe, 1967, pp. 2–5). These costs reflect general conditions of supply and demand as well as government regulations concerning minimum wages. The attitudes of the people who form the labour supply may be very important in determining future costs because they are responsible for supply conditions in the labour market. For example, if more people prefer welfare to work, or office to manual work, there could be shortages of labour for manufacturing. As education levels rise, shortages of labour for manual work are frequently noticed. Some of these features may be related to ethnic background. Another aspect of the labour situation is reflected in unionization and attitudes to bargaining. A militant labour tradition in a place may well discourage some manufacturers, while some smaller towns have been receiving plants partly because non-union shops can be operated in them.

Having considered possible modifications to production factors, it is necessary to return to demand conditions and note a further complication in the study of locational dynamics. The initial discussion of this topic was based on the premise of simple population, and market, growth. But there is no reason why the demands of people should continue to be the same, nor why new generations or immigrants, should perpetuate the demands of the past. The twentieth century has already witnessed massive growth of some new industries, such as electronics and automobile production, while the relative importance of others has declined. There is clearly a close relationship between changing tastes and inventive activity. Projecting the trend of either is complex. Nevertheless, new industries have new locational requirements and may be responsible for industrial development in new areas, or the rejuvenation of old. A general trend to date suggests that areas with large markets are likely to be favoured because the material component of the product is usually reduced, and that existing industrial areas will receive a disproportionately high level of the new activity. In some cases, areas with well developed research activities may be stimulated as has been the case in New England (Estall, 1966, pp. 79–111). On the other side of the coin, industries in absolute or relative decline will leave some areas with a reduced manufacturing base. A likely feature in this case is that problem areas will suffer even more, because the marginal plants often are in less attractive areas, especially ones which were developed under a set of locational requirements appropriate to an earlier era. Thus, for example, textile mills are frequently in somewhat remote sites originally developed to use water power.

Up to this point, little has been said about the actual decision-makers themselves but to discuss locational dynamics is really to discuss the results of the actions of a large number of manufacturers. So far it has been assumed that this behaviour will be much the same as it has been in the past. However, there is considerable scope for modification here. Just as attitudes in the general public may change, so may those of manufacturers. Thus, their goals may be modified. Suppose that secure, steady profits are desired by all manufacturers and no-one is prepared to take a risk with new products or locations, then a strong tendency to locational inertia may be expected. The opposite is likely if the business climate encourages innovation. Similarly, goals may change with respect to desirable locations as a result of the political situation in various places or to a change in evaluation of big city as opposed to small town living. If a significant increase took place in those who preferred small country towns, it is quite likely that some industry would follow because of the need for labour and executive skills.

At the present time also, a large number of decisions do not seem to be very carefully made, so that locational patterns are far from those which seem to be theoretically the best (Pred, 1967, pp. 21–63 and 81–95). Any change in the thoroughness of the locational search should lead to a more rational pattern, encouraging good new sites to be found more quickly and poor ones to be abandoned sooner. There seems to be plenty of scope for a change in this direction but this does not mean to say it will take place. Perhaps even less care will be taken in the future!

Finally there is the whole question of interpreting how manufacturers will react to uncertain situations. Location theory has been written mainly on the basis of decision-making under certainty but in fact this is unrealistic. In addition to the anticipation of future trends in cost and demand factors, manufacturers may also be concerned about the future behaviour of specific competitors. In a recent study of the effects of uncertainty on location, a very strong theme is the way in which this encourages the growth of existing urban centres, especially large ones (Webber, 1972). Webber discusses the effects on scale of plants, distance costs and agglomeration economies, as well as the role of innovation in encouraging cumulative advantages (pp. 274–279). These results are obtained because of the desire of manufacturers for long-term security of profits. As noted above, perhaps such goals will not always be pursued, but in a capitalist system the likelihood of a change does not seem to be very great.

A special note should be added about the probable effect of very large multi-plant corporations on future location patterns. The proportion of manufacturing output under the control of such companies is large and increasing so that it has been suggested that their decision-making be carefully analysed (McNee, 1960). A number of studies have now examined the behaviour of such firms in response to changing external conditions (e.g. Fleming and Krume, 1968; Steed, 1968; and Krumme and Hayter essay).

What is still not clear is the extent to which their decision-making is predictable and the extent to which it closely reflects a purely economic evaluation of location factors. The scope for research in this area is considerable.

Organization of the Volume

In Part I, the principal focus of the essays is on theory and concept. The volume is opened with an essay by Norcliffe who searches for a framework that is both relevant to today's conditions and explicitly concerned with geographical relationships. Norcliffe's theory emphasizes places rather than people and is very comparable to central place theory. The stress is on attributes of places which will be important in terms of their ability to attract various types of manufacturing activity. At a regional level, centre-periphery differences are stressed while, at the urban scale, relationships between city size and a number of plant characteristics are outlined.

Gilmour examines the processes operating in the development of a regional economy during a particularly important growth phase. His case study is Southern Ontario in the latter half of the nineteenth century. This essay represents the working out of a combination of theories concerned with regional economic growth and with the location of manufacturing. Although there are no longer many relatively empty and undeveloped areas in the world, the insights obtained from a study of export-base regions is helpful in understanding the economic growth and spatial structure of a wide variety of areas.

Somewhat more specific subjects are dealt with by Feller and Cannon. Technological change and the role of governments in affecting manufacturing location are both topics of importance and one in which anticipation of the future is very difficult. Feller notes that innovation and its diffusion have been relatively neglected in the realm of manufacturing. His essay explores relationships between technological change and manufacturing location and concentrates attention on outlining questions which need to be asked and problems which should be faced if our understanding of such relationships is to be improved. Government incentive programmes rather than the whole range of potential government influnces provide the focus for the essay by Cannon. The more general outline of the locational importance of such schemes is supplemented by a detailed analysis of the Canadian federal programme in operation for several years during the 1960's.

Part II of the volume emphasizes methods of studying locational dynamics. In the first essay in this section, Walker attempts to integrate findings obtained in studies of locational decision-making with those derived from the more typical, economically-oriented location theory. A flexible simulation model, which provides a method of exploring locational change over time under varying decision conditions, is oulined.

Koenig, Lewis and Ray's essay similarly outlines an approach and indicates a methodology to implement it. The concept of allometry is discussed, focusing on the idea of a balance between the growth of a system and that of one of its parts. A three-stage mathematical methodology is developed to examine employment growth in manufacturing over time; and this is applied to the case of Canada from 1951–1969.

Cant and Collins are more specifically concerned with statistical methods. Cant's essay using employment data provides an example of the use of three-mode factor analysis in a study of structural and locational change, the case study being New Zealand from 1951–1970. A similar problem is dealt with by means of Markov chain analysis in the work of Collins, using establishment data for Ontario from 1961 to 1965. In both of these essays, details of procedures, assumptions and difficulties are provided.

The final Part of the book is devoted to empirical studies. Naturally, this does not imply that it is devoid of conceptual or methodological material but rather that concepts and methods are not discussed to any great extent, the focus being placed on actual changes which took place in the cases examined.

Collectively Bater, Bastié and Lever look at intra-urban and urban regional change. The Bater study concerns late nineteenth-century St. Petersburg and emphasizes changing linkage patterns. From 1867 to 1913, there was some increase in the clustering of factories but inter-industry goods linkages tended to be lengthy, so that linkage did not appear a strong location factor. Bastié concentrates on post World War II developments of industrial activity in the Parisian Agglomeration but also outlines the historical evolution from the early nineteenth century. The main aim of the study is to assess the relative impact of birth/death differentials, dispersion and decentralization with respect to both employment and establishments in changing the industrial landscape of the Paris region. Lever is also concerned with manufacturing decentralization, particularly in relation to production theory. Costs of land and labour, and external economies are evaluated in relation to the requirements of various manufacturing types in Birmingham and Glasgow. In addition a Markov chain model is used to predict decentralization in terms of four concentric zones in each city.

The remaining two empirical studies concern firms rather than cities or regions. Krumme and Hayter emphasize the analysis of product developments within large corporations and the way in which the stages of their development may have important spatial repercussions. Such effects are most problematic in the case of multi-plant firms because they may have major implications for the economic development of areas in which the various plants are located. Thus relative regional growth rates will be partly dependent upon corporate policy with respect to the allocation of production to the various plants within the firm. A more directly spatial aspect of firm behaviour is considered by Watts in his study of market areas. Watts discusses measures of market areas and methods of analysing structural changes. His case studies consider the extension of market areas and their intensification by means of increased sales within existing areas.

The volume is rounded off with a short editorial review of research prospects in the realm of the locational dynamics of manufacturing activity. Several authors have made suggestions which were incorporated into these concluding comments. It is hoped that some of the research avenues indicated will be followed by other workers in the field, so that some of the gaps in knowledge may soon be filled.

References

Bater, J. H. and Walker, D. F. (1971), *The Linkage Study of Hamilton Metal Industries*. Hamilton, Ontario: Hamilton Planning Department, Hamilton Chamber of Commerce, Hamilton Economic Development Commission.

Cameron, G. C. (1972), 'Intra Urban Location and the New Plant', *Urban and Regional Studies Discussion Papers*, **5.** University of Glasgow, mimeographed.

Cant, R. G. (1971), Changes in the Location of Manufacturing in New Zealand 1957–1968. An Application of Three-mode Factor Analysis, *New Zealand Geographer*, **27**, 38–55.

Collins, L. (1972), *Industrial Migration in Ontario: forecasting aspects of industrial activity through Markov chain analysis*. Statistics Canada: Ottawa.

Conkling, E. C. (1964), The Measurement of Diversification, in Manners, G. (ed.), *South Wales in the Sixties*, London: Pergamon, 161–184.

Economic Commission for Europe (1967), *Criteria for Location of Industrial Plants (Changes and Problems)*. New York: United Nations.

Estall, R. C. (1966), New England: *A Study in Industrial Adjustment*. London: Bell.

Ferguson, A. G. and Forer, P. C. (1973), Aspects of Measuring Employment Specialization in Great Britain, *Area*, **5**, 121–128.

Fleming, D. K. and Krumme, G. (1968), The 'Royal Hoesch Union': Case Analysis of Adjustment Patterns in the European Steel Industry, *Tijdschrift voor Economische en Sociale Geografie*, **59**, 177–199.

Gilmour, J. M. (1966), The Joint Anarchy of 'Confidentiality' and Definitional Change, *Canadian Geographer*, **10**, 40–48.

Greenhut, M. L. and Colberg, M. R. (1962), *Factors in the Location of Florida Industry*. Tallahasee, Florida: Florida State University.

Haggett, P. (1965), *Locational Analysis in Human Geography*. London: Arnold.

Hall, P. G. (1962), *The Industries of London Since 1861*. London: Hutchinson.

Hirschman, A. O. (1958), *The Strategy of Economic Development*. New Haven: Yale University Press.

Hymer, S. H. (1972), The Efficiency (Contradictions) of the Multinational Corporations, in Paquet, G. (ed.), *The Multinational Firm and the Nation State*. Don Mills, Ontario: Collier-Macmillan Canada, 49–65.

Keeble, D. E. (1968), Industrial Decentralization and the Metropolis: The North West London Case, Transactions, *Institute of British Geographers*, **54**, 1–54.

Keeble, D. E. (1972), Industrial Movement in South East England: Final Report to the Nuffield Foundation, unpublished manuscript, 5 pp.

Kerr, D. P. and Spelt, J. (1958), Manufacturing in Suburban Toronto, *The Canadian Geographer*, **12**, 11–19.

Lever, W. F. (1972), The Intra-Urban Movement of Manufacturing: A Markov Approach, *Transactions, Institute of British Geographers*, **56**, 21–38.

Levitt, K. (1970), *Silent Surrender: The Multinational Corporation in Canada*. Toronto: Macmillan of Canada.

Linge, G. J. R. (1963), The Diffusion of Manufacturing in Auckland, New Zealand, *Economic Geography*, **39**, 23–39.

Lloyd, P. E. and Dicken, P. (1972), *Location in Space: A Theoretical Approach to Economic Geography*. New York: Harper and Row.

Martin, J. E. (1966), *Greater London: An Industrial Geography*. Bell's Advanced Economic Geographies.

McNee, R. B. (1960), Toward a More Humanistic Economic Geography: The Geography of Enterprise, *Tijdschrift voor Economische en Sociale Geografie*, **51**, 201–206.

Miernyk, W. H. (1965), *The Elements of Input–Output Analysis*. New York: Random House.

Morrison, J. L., Scripter, M. W. and Smith, R. H. T. (1968), Basic Measures of Manufacturing in the United States, 1958, *Economic Geography*, **44**, 296–311.

Myrdal, G. (1963), *Economic Theory and Underdeveloped Regions*. London: Methuen.

Nourse, H. O. (1968), *Regional Economics*. New York: McGraw-Hill.

Patni, R. L. (1968), A New Method for Measuring Locational Changes in a Manufacturing Industry, *Economic Geography*, **44**, 210–217.

Pred, A. R. (1965), Industrialization, Initial Advantage, and American Metropolitan Growth, *Geographical Review*, **55**, 158–185.

Pred, A. R. (1967), *Behaviour and Location, Part 1*, Lund: C. W. K. Gleerup.

Putnam, S. H. (1967), Intraurban Industrial Location Model Design and Implementation, *Papers and Proceedings, Regional Science Association*, **19**, 199–214.

Ray, D. M. (1972), The Economy, in Gentilcore, L., (ed.) *Studies in Canadian Geography. Ontario*. University of Toronto, 45–63.

Reeder, L. G. (1954), Industrial Location Trends in Chicago in Comparison to Population Growth, *Land Economics*, **30**, 177–182.

Sant, M. E. C. (1974, forthcoming), *Industrial Movement and Regional Development*, London: Pergamon.

Segal, M. (1960), *Wages in the Metropolis: Their Influence on the Location of Industries in the New York Region*. Cambridge, Mass.: Harvard University Press.

Steed, G. P. F. (1968), The Changing Milieu of a Firm: A Case Study of a Shipbuilding Concern, *Annals, Association of American Geographers*, **58**, 506–525.

Steger, W. A. (1965), "The Pittsburgh Urban Renewal Simulation Model", *Journal, American Institute of Planners*.

Webber, M. J. (1972), *Impact of Uncertainty on Location*. Cambridge, Mass: M.I.T. Press.

Weber, A. (1929), *Theory of the Location of Industries*. Trans. by C. J. Friedrich. University of Chicago.

Wise, M. J. (1949), On the Evolution of the Jewellery and Gun Quarters, *Transactions, Institute of British Geographers*, **15**, 57–72.

Part I
Theoretical and Conceptual Considerations

1　A Theory of Manufacturing Places

G. B. NORCLIFFE

The purpose of this essay is to identify a framework in which to develop a theory of manufacturing location that is explicitly concerned with geographical relationships, that is more relevant to contemporary conditions than is classical location theory, and that is flexible enough to permit certain changes in locational patterns through time. Clearly, this is a very broad brief, and the statement presented here is both preliminary and incomplete.

Classical location theory is used as a point of departure for the discussion because the argument follows a tack somewhat different from that adopted in much of the contemporary thinking on manufacturing location. In particular it differs from the behavioural approach which grew out of the seeds planted by Alchian, Boulding, Cyert, March, Simon, Tiebout and several others in the 1950's. It is not intended to downgrade the importance of these alternative approaches, indeed they have advanced our understanding of activity location a great deal. Quite simply, classical location theory provides a more convenient starting point.

Without becoming embroiled in the debate concerning the relative merits of the positive and normative viewpoints (Friedman, 1953), constraints both of time and of space dictated the adoption of a positive approach in this essay. It may be possible to articulate a parallel normative theory at a later stage, but at this juncture my conception of such a theory is still rather fuzzy.

In adopting a positive viewpoint, one very potent influence on contemporary locational patterns is omitted, this being governmental policy aimed at manipulating regional development. This is done because, over and above any academic justification, it is desirable that theoretical contributions in this field should provide pointers for policy formulation. Before one starts engineering the economic environment, it is helpful to observe locational patterns as determined by non-governmental influences.

Reflecting the prejudices of a geographer, the proposed theory takes geographical realities into account. This point deserves brief elaboration. Classical location theory has, for the most part, assumed a uniform plain or an undifferentiated space in which locational patterns develop; and, with notable

19

exceptions, much of the subsequent work by economists has adhered to this assumption. For instance, the pedigree of literature sired by Hotelling's paper on duopolistic competition in a linear market has introduced realistic assumptions about human behaviour; Lerner and Singer (1937) allow the sellers to be as wise in price fixing as in location selection; Smithies (1941) rejects two of Hotelling's assumptions—inelastic demand and outright competition between the two sellers—replacing these with consumers whose demand for a product is elastic, and some cooperation between the sellers; Stevens (1961) treats the problem as a game between two players with various strategies; and Devletoglou (1965) introduces psychological factors and the concept of a 'doubtful area'. The notable exception in this case is Ackley (1942) who rejects the notion of uniform linear demand in favour of a highly concentrated pattern of consumers. The study of point processes indicates that even under purely stochastic rules, a random clumping (and therefore a differentiated market) will emerge: and human behaviour being what it is, most activities are considerably more agglomerated than random processes permit. It is suggested that a more geographical approach to location theory would be to accept a differentiated terrestrial surface as a starting point.

As Machlup (1963) has pointed out, considerable confusion surrounds the use of the term 'dynamic', and it is frequently abused. The theory described here is not dynamic if a dynamic theory is defined strictly as one which internally prescribes change and growth. On the other hand, if the term dynamic is used loosely to include matters relating to development, then the theory has dynamic implications in at least two ways. First, it is recognized that technological and economic development alter the influence of locational factors. Second, although change is not internally predicted, externally produced changes will alter the expected patterns of location.

The argument will be developed in four stages. First, it is contended that classical location theory is relevant to a set of economic activities that are dwindling in relative importance: this diminution of explanatory power has progressed to a point where industries that do not conform with the classical theories are probably in the majority. The second step is the identification of certain factors which are considered to be important to contemporary and future locational decision-makers. The third step involves using these factors to predict certain patterns of order in the manufacturing landscape. These patterns constitute the rudiments of a theory of manufacturing places. The final step is to relate theory to reality, in so doing pinpointing certain problems.

1.1. The Diminishing Utility of Classical Location Theory

Critical examinations of classical location theory by several authors (notably Beckmann (1968), Greenhut (1956) and Isard (1956); have demonstrated the existence of a number of logical shortcomings. Aside from these theoretical considerations, the utility of classical location theory can also be questioned on empirical grounds. No doubt August Lösch (1954) would disagree with such a proposition for he has stated:

> 'The question of actual location must be distinguished from that of a rational location. The two need not coincide . . . it would be dangerous to conclude that what is must also be rational since otherwise it could not exist, and that any theoretical determination of the correct location would therefore be superfluous. Such a capitulation to reality is as useful as the advice of those who in principle contradict no one. . . . The real duty of the economist is not to explain our sorry reality, but to improve it. The question of the best location is far more dignified than the determination of the actual one.' (p. 4).

Lösch adopts a rigid normative viewpoint and spurns that of the pragmatist. This attitude is strictly correct, but it is difficult to see how one can proceed to implement the findings of a normatively based theory without also being aware of how real world locational patterns emerge. For instance, as Harvey (1972) has pointed out in his essay on social justice, the implementation of the equality norm that he espouses would almost certainly be facilitated by our empirical knowledge about the way growth poles operate. In other words, if the only measure of the utility of a normative theory is its internal logical consistency, then Lösch cannot be faulted. But if a theory has the potential to influence policy and planning decisions, then its explanatory power should also be taken into account in assessing its utility. This section is aimed at showing that changes in the real world have lessened the explanatory power of classical location theory, and hence from a pragmatic viewpoint, have lessened the utility of the theory.

Least Cost Theory

According to Weber, the primary factor influencing manufacturing location is transportation cost. Weber therefore constructed a theory of manufacturing location which begins by identifying a minimum transport cost location, and then, by using isodapanes, seeks a deviation to a better location either due to savings in labour costs, or agglomeration economies: where these savings exceeded the additional transport cost, a critical isodapane is defined and a new optimum location is identified. Transportation and labour costs are considered as the two general factors, and agglomeration economies (and diseconomies) as the only regional factor. Subsequent improvements and modifications of Weber's theory by Palander (1935), Hoover (1937, 1948), and D. M. Smith (1966, 1971) still emphasize the essential role of transportation costs, while Isard's (1956) general theory of location begins with a locational equilibrium defined by transport inputs, and then uses a substitution framework to introduce other factors.

Except in the case of those few industries using ubiquitous or semi-ubiquitous inputs (ice manufacturers, for example), all industries are bound to incur some transportation costs in assembling their inputs: likewise, all industries selling (cost–insurance–freight) incur transportation costs in delivering their products to their customers. But transportation costs are no longer of great importance to a large number of industries which, in consequence, are relatively 'footloose'. This is not to say that Weber was in error. At the turn of the century his theory had considerable relevance, but subsequent developments call for a revision of the theory. This downgrading in the importance of transportation is attributed to several developments.

First, the composition of the manufacturing sector has changed radically, as heavy industries have undergone relative decline and lighter industries have expanded: indeed, decline of the heavy industry sector has, in some instances, not only been relative, but absolute. Implicit in this compositional change is the increasing importance of high value-added industries (Pred, 1965). Not surprisingly, empirical evidence indicates a generally negative relationship between value added by an industry and transportation costs as a proportion of total production costs. It does not necessarily follow that transport costs are therefore unimportant to high value-added industries: a variable could decline in importance as a proportion of total costs, yet simultaneously increase in importance as a locational factor if the *spatial variability* of the costs associated with that variable were to become more marked. However in this case, there are no obvious grounds for supposing that this does apply. The indications are, therefore, that the expansion of light industries may be associated with a decline in the influence of transportation cost on activity location.

Second, the more efficient use of material inputs has tended to reduce the influence of raw materials on plant location. It is often pointed out that at the turn of the nineteenth century, six tons of coal were needed to smelt one ton of iron, whereas today about one and a quarter tons of coal are needed or, in the case of electric furnaces, no coal at all at the place of manufacture. This is an extreme case, but the general principle stands. Of equal importance, the by-products of basic production processes are now being put to increasingly efficient use, hence one reason for Isard's advocacy of industrial complex analysis. Another aspect involving more efficient use of inputs is the re-cycling of waste materials produced by cities: this is becoming of increasing importance as concern about resource exhaustion and environmental destruction rises. With reference to the Varignon analogue, it is easy to demonstrate that more efficient use of inputs, resulting in a reduction of the amount of raw materials per unit output, reduces the attraction of raw material locations.

Third, and related to the second, is the improvement in the quality, or purity of raw materials as a result of technological advances in recent decades. A familiar example is the beneficiation of low grade iron ores at, or near to, the minehead so as to raise the iron content from roughly 35 per cent to about 65 per cent (Earney, 1969; Madigan, 1969; Mason 1969). Technological developments are certain to promote this trend: for instance, Fleming (1971) reports on innovations in the pre-reduction of iron pellets to 90 per cent pure iron content. Refining raw materials at, or close to, their source has the effect of decreasing the influence of transportation costs on manufacturing location.

Fourth, and again related to the second point, substitution of material inputs has frequently reduced the transportation constraints on activity location. The case of electric steel furnaces has already been alluded to, and this is one of a considerable number of instances. Weberian theory was developed in the age of steam power, where today steam boiler equipment is prized by industrial archaeologists, and steam engineers are almost as rare as coopers. Electricity has become the dominant source of power in western economies, and although the construction costs of high voltage electric grids, per unit distance, are extremely high, the national grids of most countries are sufficiently well developed that only in remote districts does inadequate electric supply act as a constraint on plant location at the regional level. Coal is still frequently used as a source of energy for making electricity, but pit head thermal power generation eliminates the necessity to transport coal and similar fuels (Caesar, 1964). Oil and natural gas have also become important sources of power and for these fuels pipelines provide a convenient means of bulk transportation. It is of interest to note that whereas many coalfields became important industrial regions in the nineteenth century, few gas fields have experienced a comparable development in the twentieth century. Coal has been largely replaced by alternative fuels and energy sources that can be transported much more readily.

A fifth reason for demoting transportation from a position of dominant influence on activity location is the development of transportation technology. The catalogue of changes wrought in the twentieth century is very large indeed—containers, supertankers, pipelines, air cargo, expressways, electric transmission and radio communications are but a few. The net effect has been to make it easier to transport goods quickly, often cheaply, and with considerable reliability to any location well served with transportation facilities.

Decline in the importance of transportation is widely recognized; for instance D. M. Smith (1971), whose approach to activity location may be viewed as neo-Weberian, has stated:

'Transportation is often considered to be the most important single determinant of plant location. This is less true than it has been historically, but transportation is still a major factor in the location of many industries.' (p. 69).

It is felt that the role of transportation needs qualifying even further: for some industries, especially heavy industries characterized both by large volumes of material inputs and by high material indexes, transportation costs are indeed important. But these industries now represent a relatively small proportion of the total economy.

For the majority of lighter industries transportation costs do not vary greatly from location to location within the industrial heartland, although in peripheral regions remote from important markets, costs do begin to rise more steeply. Provided that the main cost variable is delivery to markets, this assertion can be supported on theoretical and empirical grounds. Lindberg (1953) has provided the theoretical grounds. By substituting the industrial heartland for Lindberg's 'harvest area', and by substituting delivery of manufactured goods from a plant to an areally extensive market for assembly of agricultural products at a processing plant, one obtains a pattern of distribution costs that varies relatively little within the industrial heartland, but which rises more steeply in peripheral regions.

Empirical evidence which substantiates Lindberg's theory is provided by Harris (1954) who uses an index of comparative transport costs: this index is the marketing equivalent of Lindberg's procurement cost curve. Maps of comparative transport costs in the United States show a low transportation cost index throughout the manufacturing belt, but high values in other parts of the country. Smith (1971, p. 379) also presents corroborative evidence: a map of freight costs for a firm producing electronic equipment—which is a good example of a high value-added industry—shows a region of low transport costs extending from the Manufacturing Belt through to the Middle West. Within this region covering half of the United States, freight costs do not vary more than 16 per cent above the minimum, whereas in areas remote from the centre of the national market they rise much higher.

Yet further empirical evidence is provided by Törnqvist's (1962) study of transport costs for the Swedish garment industry. Combining procurement and delivery costs for a hypothetical plant serving the whole Swedish market, it transpires that these costs are lowest in the Borås-Gothenberg area, they vary relatively little within the main market area in southern Sweden, but rise rapidly as one moves northward so that in the extreme north transport costs are 200 per cent higher than the minimum cost location. However, and this interesting evidence is in support of the preceding argument, total transport costs form only 0·7 per cent of total production costs at the minimum cost location, and 1·8 per cent at the maximum cost location. Although these figures represent an industry with very small and light material inputs, they are not dissimilar from those of many high value-added industries.

One further consideration: freight rates generally discriminate in favour of raw materials, so that the cost of transporting manufactured goods per unit distance is greater than the cost of transporting raw or partly processed inputs. Chinitz (1960) notes that between 1930 and 1960 the rates for finished products tended to rise faster than those for raw materials, although container-ization may subsequently have halted this trend. This discrimination favours market orientation.

In summary, transport costs are demoted from the sovereign position accorded to them by Weber. For manufacturing industry with voluminous material inputs and high weight loss, they remain important, but for the majority of medium-to-high value-added industries they tend to confine plant location to the industrial heartland, within which transportation costs to accessible points on the network vary relatively little.

The second general factor discussed by Weber is the cost of labour. According to Weber, a deviation from the minimum transport cost location will occur when substantial savings in labour costs are available. Development during the twentieth century and likely future developments indicate that, as in the case of transport costs, labour costs should be demoted from the position of prominence accorded to them by Weber, but not dismissed entirely as a factor influencing industrial location. The expansion of communication networks, of minimum wage legislation, of collective bargaining, of government's attempts to reduce regional income disparity, and the increase in occupational and residential mobility all point to a reduction in spatial variations in wage levels—at least at the regional scale. Demands for parity suggest that equalization of wage levels between regions is becoming an acceptable goal.

Empirical evidence points to a general reduction in regional income disparities although, at least in the case of the North-South differential in the United States, equalization is less evident at the national level. Income disparity also appears to be very persistent at the local and at the international level. However, to return to the regional scale in the United States, Scully (1971) has examined changes in the period 1869 to 1919, and has summarized much of the literature covering the more recent period.[1] He finds that although the adjusted North-South wage differential averaged about 20 per cent during the last century, for the 1869–1919 period there was a secular decline in variations in wage levels *within* the North and *within* the South. Likewise Easterlin (1958), in examining differentials amongst the States between 1880 and 1950, found a trend towards equality that was stronger in the pre-1920 period than in the post-1920 period, and which experienced periodic reversals particularly following both World Wars. This is supported by Borts (1960) who found a divergence in income levels from 1919 to 1929, and 1948 to 1953, and a convergence from 1929 to 1948. For Canada (excluding Newfoundland) during the period 1926 to 1964 Chernick (1966) has found a slow and irregular trend towards equality, with reversals in this overall trend from 1926 to 1932 and 1945 to 1950.

The evidence indicates, therefore, that since the time of Weber's writings, there has been an overall trend towards the reduction of regional wage inequalities. Although labour costs are an important absolute cost (Segal (1960) points out that in 1954 in all U.S. manufacturing, they summed to 21 times the total cost of state and local taxes), their spatial variability is tending to decline at the regional level, and a number of industrialists have predicted a further decline in regional wage differentials due to more efficacious collective bargaining.

A further qualification needs adding. Although most studies of wage differentials are concerned with the monetary cost of labour, location theorists ought to be concerned with the real cost of labour, which is to say, the cost in relation to labour productivity. *Ceteris paribus*, if labour in region Y commands wages 10 per cent less than a in region X, but is also 10 per cent less productive, then in real costs, the industrialist located in region X has nothing to gain from relocating in region Y. Little is known about spatial characteristics of the intrinsic productivity of labour—i.e., productivity attributable to the skills and motivations of labour, holding constant such factors as equipment, industrial composition, and size of plant. However, one piece of evidence fitting with the argument for downgrading the importance of labour costs is provided by Scully (1969), who has found that education levels influence productivity levels. He therefore suggests that educational levels should be incorporated into production functions. The concentration of institutions of higher education in the industrial heartland, coupled with the out-migration of skilled personnel from peripheral areas both point to higher productivity in the manufacturing heartland where wage levels are higher. In other words, there is some indication that wage levels and the intrinsic productivity of labour are positively related.

Borts (1960) provides evidence that capital investment plays a key role in explaining income growth, and also that capital is invested largely in areas where entrepreneurs make demands for capital, rather than in areas which offer the greatest investment opportunities. Given that in the present context, capital investment is expressed as the expansion and modernization of existing plant and the opening of new plants, then this implies that even where opportunities such as a region with low labour costs exist, industrialists rarely take this into account in selecting the site for new plants. Indeed, there are some indications, according to Borts, that the relationship between plant location and labour costs is the reverse of that predicted in Weber's theory: in the theory, plants are attracted to areas where savings in labour costs may be achieved; in practice, unemployed labour tends to migrate from low income areas to job opportunities created by investment in already established manufacturing regions.

In summary, the influence of labour on activity location in the latter part of the twentieth century would appear to be both weaker than that attributed to it by Weber, and also more complex. Spatial variability of wage levels is apparently declining at the regional level. Variations in actual wage levels are partly compensated by variations in productivity level, so that geographical differences in the real cost of labour are probably less than are differences in wage levels. Also, Weber's assumption that capital and industry move to areas with surplus employment and low wage levels may be a reversal of the actual migratory behaviour of labour and capital.

Market Area Theory

Weberian location theory is founded on a partial equilibrium approach which assumes, as given, demand and the location of raw materials and markets. Lösch sought a theory of partial spatial equilibrium based on distributional efficiency. The essence of Lösch's theory lies in the apportioning of demand on a uniform continuous surface to points of supply. It is suggested that the explanatory power of Lösch's theory is decreasing: the points to be made in developing this argument are those that serve as indicators for the attempt at constructing a geographic theory that follows.

Geographers find Lösch's assumption of a uniform and unbounded plane difficult to accept: although it serves as a useful starting point on which an elegant theory has been constructed, for all but a few economic activities which are of dwindling importance (these are mainly agricultural) it represents a gross distortion of reality. Final demand is spatially concentrated to a high degree, and the majority of manufactured products are sold either to intermediate producers or wholesalers who are considerably more concentrated than are the ultimate consumers. This highly uneven distribution of demand can be discerned both at the regional and the national scale: at the regional scale, towns, and metropoles in particular, dominate economic life; at the national scale, the industrial heartland has an economic structure markedly different from that of the resource-oriented periphery.

A number of people have pointed to a logical inconsistency in Lösch's theory relating to the assumption of a uniform demand surface. A network of production and distribution centres are predicted using this assumption, yet once these centres come into existence, the agglomeration of labour and other economic activities in the centres will transform the demand surface into an uneven one. Isard (1956, p. 271) considers this to be 'perhaps the most serious deficiency' in Lösch's theory. Rather than assuming away the uneven spatial distribution of demand, it is suggested that this universal phenomenon be accepted as a starting point for theory construction.

Lösch's theory is constructed on the premise that suppliers wish to maximize their profits by extending the boundaries of their market areas up to the margin where demand reaches zero: hence Lösch's demand cones, modified to hexagonal pyramids to produce a tessellated form. Specifying for industrialists the locations where their profits will be maximized requires one to fathom not only the numerous interdependencies on the supply side, but also income and substitution effects on the demand side. The increasing complexity of these interdependencies, resulting in part from the expansion and elaboration of trading systems, have almost certainly added to the intractability of this problem.

Attempts have been made to adapt Lösch's market areas to an unevenly populated landscape, notably by Isard (1956, Figure 52, p. 272), who used irregular hexagons, and by Getis (1963) who used space distortions. This appears to work satisfactorily for retail and other service activities, but it is useful only for a few market oriented activities in the manufacturing sector, and is of decreasing value even then. For instance, to take the brewing industry, which in the literature is often cited as a good example of market orientation in view of its low material index: changes in the production economies of brewing in conjunction with bulk transfer and other transportation improvements have, in recent years, led to the elimination of many small breweries and expansion of the market areas of those breweries which have survived (Gilmour, 1970). Today, the market area supplied by breweries located in London cover much of South-East and Central England; likewise those located in Toronto serve a substantial portion of Southern Ontario, so that there is some ambiguity as to whether this industry is still strictly market oriented. Not many manufacturing activities have market areas as small as those of breweries, and for a host of activities ranging from the manufacture of motor vehicles, garments and television sets to butter, books and toys, markets are truly worldwide: and this applies despite the numerous trade and tariff restrictions which inhibit international trade.

There is a further problem associated with the discrete partitioning of market areas that Lösch envisaged, namely the problem of overlap. This phenomenon has been discussed by a number of location theorists, and Isard (1956) points to the lacuna between theoretical and actual market areas.

'As is widely recognized, the sharpness of the boundary lines presented . . . in preceding figures is much exaggerated. Producers . . . do not behave according to the criteria which have been implicitly assumed. . . . They typically are able to influence price, to discriminate amongst customers, to induce consumers by advertising, price cuts, or other means to shift their allegiance from a competitor. Producers relocate at times, take cognizance of each other's reactions, form coalitions, set prices and quotas. All these types of monopolistic and oligopolistic behaviour tend to invalidate the simple, clear-cut boundary lines customarily depicted. At best boundary lines are blurred, and tend to degenerate into overlapping zones.' (p. 264).

The overlap of market areas occurs not only because of the behaviour of sellers (as Isard indicates), but also because of the behaviour of buyers whose individual tastes, product loyalties, propensities to imitate group leaders and desires to exceed their peers renders the concept of discrete market partitioning an almost complete misrepresentation of reality. It is suggested that the continuing tendency for transport costs to decline, relative to other costs, will, at least in theory, have enlarged the zones of indifference that separate market areas, and will therefore have promoted overlap.

Having questioned both the utility of demand cones when they reach continental proportions and the existence of discrete market areas, and having pointed to the agglomerating effect of an unevenly distributed demand surface, one further problem makes Lösch's theory particularly unsuitable for the study of locational dynamics: the optimal arrangement of market areas predicted by Lösch is based on static conditions. Small changes can render the whole system sub-optimal, yet there is considerable inertia built into locational decisions, so that the arrangement of centres and market areas is not likely to adjust to a new equilibrium after each small change in demand patterns. Lösch (1954, pp. 264–359) incorporates dynamic aspects as a transfer problem using price waves as a transfer mechanism. Changes in demand or supply have an immediate impact on prices at the market centre concerned, and then spread progressively to adjoining areas with diminishing impact as the area affected increases. As the price change is passed from buyer to seller repeatedly, the wave is damped until the effect becomes infinitesimally small.

The burden of the above discussion is that Market Area Theory, as formulated by Lösch, is of limited value in predicting patterns of manufacturing location in the real world: either, as Lösch might insist, the world is highly irrational or, as seems more reasonable, an alternative theoretical basis is required. Of course some industrial activities do conform to the market area arrangement fairly well, these being mainly industries that add bulk or use semi-ubiquitous raw materials, or both. The cement, brick, brewing, baking and soft drink industries all show a considerable, although diminishing, degree of order in the patterning of their market areas, while multi-plant firms with a loyal and stable market (a quasi-monopolistic situation) may locate branch plants in strategic locations so as to minimize distribution costs.

Although Canada is not a perfect example due to the late development of manufacturing and the strong representation of resource-based industries, the following data recording changes from 1910 to 1961 are indicative of the trends that have been asserted. Problems of data comparability make it pointless to present exact figures, but in 1910 approximately 40 per cent of the work force was employed in material-oriented industries, whereas in 1961 this figure had fallen to 23 per cent and today must be close to half of the percentage recorded in 1910. Industries drawn to market locations because delivery costs are an overriding locational factor accounted for nearly 11 per cent of the work force in the earlier year, but only a little over 7 per cent at the later date. Hence in rough and ready figures we may state that whereas classical location theory was useful in explaining the location of something over half of manufacturing activity at the beginning of this century, today it accounts for about 30 per cent, leaving something in the order of 70 per cent of Canadian manufacturing activity in need of better explanation. It is to this majority that the following theory is addressed.

1.2. Factors Important To Contemporary Industrial Location

In this section, three factors are identified as having an important influence on the location of new plants in those industries which are somewhat ambiguously referred to as 'footloose'. It is contended that the location of these industries is largely confined to a system of manufacturing places within which plants have varying degrees of freedom of location.

Whereas economic location theory is concerned mainly with cost factors, the range of variables permissible in a geographic location theory is much broader. Of course, most factors have cost implications but this does not imply that it is desirable to reduce the 'non-economic' factors to monetary values for two reasons. First, being able to cost a factor does not mean that it can be readily bought: thus a least cost location may not be a feasible location. Second, the incidence of costs is often quite different from those assumed in economic location theory.[2] It is therefore convenient to think in terms of locational influences rather than simply costs.

Three factors are considered to have an especially strong influence on the location of modern industry, and are also expected to have a continuing, or even an increasing influence, if contemporary locational trends away from strict material and market orientation can be extrapolated. These influences are: infrastructure availability; internal and external economies; and linkage and contact fields. These three influences, which will be discussed *seriatim*, are stressed as characteristics of a place.

Infrastructure Availability

Rawstrom (1958) has identified three restrictions on industrial location: physical, economic and technical. The availability of a site with the prerequisites for production may be viewed as an extension of Rawstrom's physical restriction.

Physical restrictions on manufacturing location are frequently overlooked in empirical studies, probably because their effect is so obvious. There may also be a residual fear of being branded as an environmental determinist. Nevertheless, it is suggested that if one were to discriminate between areas adopted and areas avoided by new manufacturing, the discriminant function would load quite heavily on physical variables.

Physical restrictions are here widened to include the infrastructure required by most plants. The argument, briefly put, is as follows: small-to-medium-sized firms will, with few exceptions, locate their plants at serviced sites, for few firms of this size can afford the capital outlay to prepare a site which lacks essential services. Commonly, the provision of services is a municipal responsibility with the costs being partly underwritten by central governments. The tendency is for small and rural municipalities to resist the intrusion of manufacturing plants and for governments to be unwilling to underwrite the cost of servicing sites in areas with a low site turnover rate: the reverse is characteristic of large communities.

In this context, there are reasons for treating a site as a commodity offered for sale. Following Curry's (1962) highly illuminating theory of service centres, a serviced site becomes a high order shopping good; there is a long good interval between purchases and the decision to purchase involves some shopping amongst alternatives. Purchasers are likely to concentrate their search for a site in large towns where a variety of sites may be available at any one time: the result is a fairly rapid site turnover rate in large towns. In places lacking manufacturing activity, few inquiries for plant sites are anticipated, and a low turnover rate of available sites would be the result. Indeed the cost of preparing a site for marketing, and then holding that site as inventory over a long period during which both maintenance costs are incurred and interest on the capital outlay has to be paid, is likely to deter both local and central governments from creating many serviced sites in small and rural municipalities. This generalization may be violated in the case of government assistance to depressed areas, but even then the 'growth pole' concept is sufficiently widely accepted that development is mainly concentrated into larger towns.

A large firm establishing a smaller branch plant may have the resources to install infrastructure, but the costs of this relative to other costs are normally quite high so that they act as a strong deterrent. The construction of a large plant by a giant corporation, in contrast, involves such a large capital outlay that service provision costs are relatively small and therefore may be acceptable. On the other hand, a plant of such a size needs to recruit a large labour force so that other factors come into play to restrict plant location to existing centres.

Up to this point, the argument has referred to the location of new plants. It should be pointed out, however, that in the developed nations, the majority of industrial expansion takes place through the extension of existing plants rather than the opening of new ones. While a variety of considerations influence the choice between opening a new plant and expanding an operational unit, the fact that an existing plant is serviced, often with spare capacity, is one of the advantages to expanding *in situ*.

The Design for Development for the Toronto Centred Region (Government of Ontario, 1970) contains several references to the importance of infrastructure availability, and the constraint that is imposed on development in the 'commutershed' (a zone inland of Toronto and south of Lake Simcoe) by the difficulty of increasing the level of service provision. Statements such as:

> The high cost of providing sewer and water services throughout this zone is an important consideration in the decision to reserve (the commutershed) for non-urban uses. (p. 20).
> ... full scale development beyond the Lake Ontario watershed will require the pumping of treated sewage effluent back into Lake Ontario to minimize the pollution dangers of Lake Simcoe. (p. 21).

In essence the plan is to direct development towards areas adjacent to the lakeshores, especially to the east of Toronto, and to curtail development inland because of the high cost of water provision and sewage disposal in areas remote from major water bodies. However, where established manufacturing places located in the commutershed have servicing problems (Kitchener-Waterloo is the most notable case) these are to be alleviated as quickly as possible by increasing the capacity of water and sewage facilities. Such a strategy builds considerable inertia into the system.

Some of the more important service requirements have already been mentioned but a brief inventory will be useful in pointing to likely future trends. Electricity is the most common source of power: there is usually spare capacity in urban places sufficient to meet modest increases in demand. Major power users, on the other hand, may require large increases in power supply and the construction of high voltage transmission lines connecting into the national grid. The high cost of constructing power lines may, as Caesar (1964) pointed out, have a centralizing effect. Other sources of heat and power—gas, oil, coal and steam—are not critical site factors for most types of manufacturing. As a site factor, the absence of roads is not likely to prove a major hindrance: road networks are so extensive that few locations cannot be provided with road access. On the other hand the demand for local access to rail, air and limited access roads is likely to make sites in or near to metropolitan centres highly attractive; metropolitan areas are linked to each other by limited access roads, and in them are located major rail freight depots and the great majority of international airports.

The site factors that here are accorded a prominent position are water availability and waste disposal. The example of the Toronto Centred Region has been quoted, and this is but one instance of a general problem which has also been remarked upon by Hoover (1968).

> 'Another relatively new location factor in recent years ... is water supply. Not so long ago it was customary in discussions of location to class water as a "ubiquitous" input.... There has been a vast increase in the industrial use of water which is not incorporated into the product but is required for cooling or flushing away wastes in the process. Together with rapidly rising levels of per capita residential use of water, this trend has brought severe problems of water shortage to a large proportion of major urban areas.... The effect, in the United States and elsewhere, has been to limit further industrial growth in many areas.' (pp. 13–14).

The availability of good local water resources at serviced sites has become a locational factor of some significance. The fact that the American Manufacturing Belt has, on the whole, a good water resource endowment provides a basis for arguing that the concentration of activity in this Belt may persist in the future. Johnson (1971) has pointed out that by renovating waste water, one can increase effective supply levels quite substantially. One might suppose that waste water renovation could lead to some dispersal of industry, but it is strongly suspected that the installation of water recycling facilities will initially be confined to major towns, so that existing concentrations of economic activity will again be reinforced.

The case of waste disposal is especially important, for it is anticipated that over the next decade pollution regulations will become so stringent that the wide range of industries producing noxious waste products will require good disposal services. Waste disposal services display many of the characteristics common to the provision of infrastructure in general. First, there are marked economies of scale. Second, and as a corollary to the first point, these services are not uniformly available, but tend to be concentrated at existing urban centres. This should be coupled with the continuing ability of larger towns to keep pace with expanding physical requirements, and the priority status attached to large towns in receiving new forms of infrastructure.

Internal and External Economies of Scale

Scale economies constitute such a large topic that it is difficult to do more than summarize the main argument. Commonly referred to as agglomeration economies, a good review is to be found in Hoover's (1937) work on the Shoe and Leather Industry where he identifies three types of agglomeration economies: (1) plant internal economies of scale; (2) localization-of-a-single industry economies; (3) urbanization economies. To these a fourth will be added, namely centralization economies; these are similar to urbanization economies but operate on a larger scale so that the former apply strictly at the urban level, while the latter applies at the regional level.[3]

Throughout the last century, there has been a slow and progressive trend towards production in larger plants as successive internal economies of scale became available. Using shop-floor employees as a measure of size, this process has slowed in recent years but still continues,[4] so that in Britain today, plants employing more than 500 employees account for little over 5 per cent of the total number of establishments but over half of the national work force in manufacturing, and this is typical of most western countries. Insofar as technical progress tends to eliminate jobs, value-added at constant prices is probably a better measure of plant concentration; this measure indicates an even greater concentration of activities through time. Growth has operated not only in the largest plants, but also in medium-sized plants, many of which are branch plants. Meanwhile small workshops and plants employing less than 20 employees have declined quite rapidly in importance.

The locational expression of this growth in average plant size is increasingly to restrict new plant openings to manufacturing places that are large enough to accommodate such an event without major disruption in the provision of essential infrastructure, work force availability, the capacity of the service sector to meet the expanded demand, housing stock and so on. Well established and sizeable manufacturing places are best able to absorb the medium and large-sized plants that are typical of most new industrial enterprises. As Gilmour (1970 and 1972) has shown for the Ontario brewing industry, the opening of plants with larger capacity is usually accompanied by the elimination of small plants many of which, at least in the brewing case, were formerly located in small towns in rural Ontario.

One trend in technological development that is deserving of mention is the more rapid progress being made in many industries in producing efficient small machines. As early as 1942, Blair pointed to this trend, while a recent examination of costs in thermal power generation provides a more detailed case study (Galatin, 1968). Such a development has implications for the plant, without affecting the scale economies of the firm: the result therefore is probably to foster a branch plant economy operated by multi-plant firms. This centralization of ownership is also connected with linkage patterns which are discussed below.

Surprisingly little is known about temporal trends and the strength of localization economies: are they increasing in importance and tending to concentrate industry or vice versa? Empirical evidence is likewise confusing. As gun, jewellery, and clothing quarters of the type examined by Wise (1950) and Hall (1962) disappear, so major complexes such as the petro-chemical and artificial fibre complexes as examined by Isard et al. (1959) emerge. Certainly there are connections between economic linkages and spatial proximity, as Richter (1969) and Streit (1969) have demonstrated, but one is inclined to think that the strength of these connections may be diminishing for at least three reasons. First, many groupings of small plants of the gun quarter type have been replaced by a few large plants: in other words localization economies have simply been internalized. Second, improved transportation has loosened the movement constraint on proximity. Third, increased labour mobility makes it possible to attract a work force with particular skills to locations which are attractive on other grounds.

The external economies which are felt to exert an increasing attraction upon industry are urbanization economies. These are economies in the costs of production gained by the presence of other industries in the same urban area. The range of urbanization economies that accrue to urban based manufacturers is very broad, the more important ones including the ability to make bulk transactions, the variety and quality of specialized goods and services (including transportation), the continuity and reliability of services, size and varied skills of the labour pool, and the presence of institutions such as universities and government organizations. Neutze (1963, 1965) and others have argued that external diseconomies should be set against these economies: but in practice, and with the obvious exception of high rents and land prices, the community tends to bear the brunt of these diseconomies. Rush hour congestion cuts into the individual's leisure time, pollution affects the community as a whole, while mental stress is most prevalent amongst housewives and the aged.

To simplify the discussion and avoid a catalogue of specific economies, two general principles will be propounded concerning the relationship between contemporary plant location and urbanization economies.

The first principle states that the level of technology and sophistication of marketing achieved by modern industry places locations that lack these specialized technological and marketing services at a disadvantage. The technological aspect applies mainly to the plant, the marketing aspect mainly to the firm. Typically the modern plant is organized as a production line with large investments in capital equipment. These capital overheads necessitate high output levels if profitability is to be achieved: for instance the break-even point in some drinking glass and light bulb production lines requires capacity operation for over 90 per cent of the time. Any hitch in the smooth operation of the process must be rectified quickly otherwise the cost penalty is large. The range of skills required in fixing technical hitches is both beyond that of the average handyman, and maybe outside that permitted by job demarcation. For a sophisticated modern plant, it has become important to locate in a large town where a wide range of specialized labour skills including experts in water and air conditioning, micro-wave engineering and the like are available. These capital intensive light industries belong to the high value-added group discussed by Pred (1965), who has argued along lines similar to the above principle.

Marketing is a head-office function, and in the multi-plant firm is commonly handled by a unit separate from production operations. This gives rise to an organizational arrangement commented upon by Törnqvist (1968). Marketing and other types of linkages to be discussed shortly confine head offices largely to metropolitan areas; technically sophisticated productive activities are also concentrated in large towns. On the other hand most straightforward production processes, for instance book printing and the manufacture of car seats and television frames, can be decentralized to branch plants in smaller towns located, quite commonly, within the orbit of the parent plant. In the latter case activity is still concentrated in the industrial heartland, but may take place in smaller manufacturing places.

The second principle states that with the economic environment changing at an accelerating rate, corporate decision-making is increasingly concerned with risk minimization, rather than simply cost minimization. Hoover (1948, pp. 120–121) points to three types of urbanization economies: by exceeding minimum size thesholds, a whole variety of specialized services become available; the pooling of reserves, both of materials and labour, make for their more efficient use; and bulk transactions are associated with favourable rates and a superior service. These urbanization economies stand in their own right, but they can also be interpreted as factors which reduce uncertainty. It is abundantly evident that decision making is facilitated by the reduction of uncertainty (Cohen, 1964), hence the economic impact of these urbanization economies should be compounded with their risk reducing effects.

To illustrate this, reference will be made to an urbanization economy noted by Lefeber (1958, p. 130) which could be tenuously classified as a type of pooling of reserves. In opening a plant, a firm cannot be certain that the plant in question will operate indefinitely: changes in market tastes, trading conditions and technology may lead to its closure. In the light of this uncertainty, some firms take into account the opportunity costs associated with closure. It is generally easier to dispose of premises and equipment located in major urban centres; as a result of these particular opportunity costs being lowered, one element of uncertainty is also reduced.

Centralization economies include access to the market as a whole, to alternate suppliers of components and sub-assemblies, to investment funds, to labour with specialized skills, and to high order industrial services (Harris, 1954; Clark, 1966). They cannot operate until an industrial heartland has developed, but once this stage is reached, these economies tend to perpetuate the macro-differentiation of the space-economy into a heartland and a hinterland. Pred (1966) has developed this argument at some length.

Linkage and Contact Patterns

In recent years, a number of authors have come to recognize the importance of contacts to industrialists. Alonso's (1968, p. 23) statement that 'The subtle but enormous importance of face-to-face relations is not sufficiently recognized in the preceding formulation of external economies' summarizes what is becoming a new orthodoxy. Alonso's argument relates to the situation in developing countries, but it is felt that linkage and contact patterns are also a very significant factor in the developed world.

The argument to be developed here is based on the important work conducted by Törnqvist's (1968, 1969, 1970) under the general title *Regional Development Trends in the Swedish Economy*. The following syllogism represents a highly condensed version of Törnqvist's basic theme:

Major premise: Face-to-face contacts are becoming increasingly important to upper level business and government administrators.
Minor premise: Personal contacts are best facilitated in a network of large urban centres.
Conclusion: Administrative units are accordingly becoming concentrated in large urban centres, which become the foci of decision-making activity.

This argument involves the separation of manufacturing into production units and administrative units: the former are concerned with the actual manufacturing process, and any decision-making that is required is of a fairly routine nature; the latter include the ever-growing body of bureaucrats and technocrats who make non-routine decisions. Törnqvist's studies indicate that in Sweden during the 1960's, employment in production units remained fairly static, and some decentralization of these units out of major towns occurred.

Employment in administrative units, on the other hand, grew quite rapidly, and was characterized by increasing concentration in large urban centres. This concentration of highly-paid administrators in large towns has a multiplier effect on tertiary and quaternary sectors of the local economy and also on market-oriented manufacturing activity.

If Törnqvist's findings can be extrapolated into the future, the resulting scenario is quite different from that envisaged by Berry (1970), who sees a freeing of locational constraints as a result of administrators using n-way T.V.-phones and the like. Berry detects an inversion process whereby the upper-income white population of America is moving into the 'inter-urban peripheries' while the minority group poor are moving into the cities. Telemobility, Berry predicts, will advance this process by eliminating the need for face-to-face contacts to take place in the Central Business District.

It is felt that remote decision-making will not supplant personal contacts in non-routine decision-making and that face-to-face communications will remain essential. Hoover (1968, p. 9) has opined along similar lines in stating his belief that cities will retain their role as the foci of business contacts. Four reasons (based largely on Törnqvist (1970, p. 28)) can be advanced in defence of this assertion. Face-to-face contacts take place in a common environment and therefore involve a meeting of minds with standardized background noise so that uncertainty is reduced and misunderstandings more quickly appreciated and corrected; they permit immediate reaction and the simultaneous discussion between several participants with complex feedback; moods and emotions (a critical form of feedback) are often subtly expressed, and can only be detected in personal contact; as a corollary to the previous point, confidence between participants is essential to decision-making, and confidence is greatly advanced both by the privacy of direct contact and by being able to judge other people's total reactions; another aspect of confidentiality that may not be trivial at upper levels of decision-making is the avoidance of industrial espionage.

Having demoted the traditional factors of labour and transportation costs from a dominant role in the determination of locational patterns, three factors have been erected in their place—infrastructure availability, internal and external economies, and contact and linkage patterns. These three factors are themselves closely interrelated, as will be briefly demonstrated.

In addition to the importance of face-to-face meetings, transportation has played a very important role in the polarization of flows and linkages between metropolitan centres. Road, rail and air transportation have all contributed to this process. Limited access highways, which typically reduce travel time by 25 per cent to 50 per cent over conventional roads, form a web linking large towns, the only major exception to this pattern being 'roads to recreation'. Rail passenger transport only survives in commuter systems and between major cities, while competition from road haulage has placed rail freight emphasis on longer hauls between large towns in which the main freight yards are located. The scheduled flight end of air transportation is also highly primate in character.

Economies of scale have contributed considerably to the concentration of both transportation facilities and several other components of industrial infrastructure in major cities, in many cases because of the indivisibility of the units involved. Finally, many of the links between modern plants and financial institutions, sales and advertising organizations, specialized technical services and the like are influenced by the primate character of these services. This represents a reversal of Törnqvist's (1970, pp. 131–133) multiplier argument: he sees the tertiary sector following the lead of manufacturing. Here locational characteristics of the service sector are considered to exert some influence on the location of modern manufacturing although, of course, there will be a feedback into consumer-oriented services. Incidentally if correct, this makes the terms 'basic or city forming' and 'non-basic or city serving' misleading.

It bears repeating that these three factors exert their greatest influence in urban centres and within the industrial heartland. Their combined effect is to attract many of the additions to the manufacturing sector to pre-existing manufacturing places. An attempt will now be made to articulate some of the relationships between manufacturing industry and manufacturing places.

1.3. Outline of a Theory of Manufacturing Places

It is assumed that a differentiated and bounded space economy exists, and that industrial development within this space economy has proceeded to a stage where a manufacturing belt or heartland is discernible: in some cases there may be more than one such manufacturing region. A mature system of cities is also assumed, with many of the larger towns located in the heartland. From this starting point, the question is then posed: given the economic, social and technical conditions prevailing in the latter part of the twentieth century, what relationships may one anticipate at the regional and urban level between the existing structure and the location of manufacturing industry?

The Regional Level

It will be apparent that at this scale, industrial location merges into regional development, and most of the important contributions on this topic are found in the literature on regional development.

Perloff and Wingo's (1961) summary of the major study of Regions, Resources and Economic Development in the United States provides a convenient starting point. They designate a heartland including the New England, Middle Atlantic and Great Lakes regions, and a hinterland to which the rest of the United States belongs. The heartland maintained a fairly high level of specialization in manufacturing from 1870 to 1950, while the hinterland was dominated quite steadily by resource-oriented activity. Although individual regions changed their position, this overall pattern was quite stable. Subsequently, there has been some decentralization of industry into the South and West (Stevens et al., 1969), but the aggregate change is still fairly small.

In elaborating this point, the trichotomy of industrial activities used by Wallace (1972) is combined with Törnqvist's dichotomy to obtain a four-fold classification as follows:

(1) Processing activities: the major input(s) to the manufacturing process are raw materials.
(2) Fabricating activities: the major inputs have already been processed, but are then transformed further. The outputs are frequently intermediate products.
(3) Integrative activities: the inputs undergo little (if any) further transformation, but several fabricated products are assembled. The outputs are normally final products.
(4) Administrative activities: except in the case of research and development activities, no physical inputs or outputs are involved.

More than one type of activity may be conducted in any given plant, and the distinction between these activities will not always be clear cut.

Processing activities frequently involve bulky inputs, weight loss, and, in the case of food industries, perishable raw materials. These are the assumptions that fit best with Weberian theory. Insofar as they are material oriented, the location of processing activities will correspond with the fortuitous location of the materials that are processed. Accordingly, processing activities are likely to be found both in the heartland and in the hinterland.

The spatial dimensions of activity systems in general and the supply areas of food processing plants in particular have tended to increase in recent years. Although, as Stevens et al. (1969, p. 8) have found for food processing in the United States, this is sometimes accompanied by a shift of plant location to established urban centres, it probably has little impact at the regional scale. However, two trends promoting the concentration of processing activities in the periphery can be discerned; the first relates to mineral extraction, the second to the processing of agricultural products.

The tendency in most industrialized societies is to exploit the most accessible raw materials (implying those closest to final markets) first, and then, as each supply area becomes exhausted, to substitute a more remote supply area and/or a different raw material. For instance, the British and American steel industries began by using local coal body ores, and then switched to more remote sources so that today Labrador, Algeria, Northern Sweden and Venezuela are major supply areas. The same substitution process has led to oil exploration in the Arctic. Although this process operates at an international scale, within a country, the tendency is to exhaust raw material supplies in the heartland first; this exhaustion process concentrates material-oriented activity in the periphery.

The second trend involves extending Sinclair's (1967) argument that urban sprawl is inverting the land-use intensity pattern predicted in the von Thunen model: Sinclair saw land speculation, recreation and other urban influences lowering the intensity of land use close to urban areas. As Found and Morley

(1971) have discovered, metropoles exert an influence on rural land use over a large area: in the Toronto case, a radius of 100 miles is a conservative estimate. The construction of expressways connecting metropoles to recreational areas can extend this influence up to a distance of 200 miles or even more, so that within the heartland, such zones of influence often coalesce. Commonly, these metropolitan influences result in land being taken out of intensive agricultural uses and into less intensive uses.

If land use theory is switched to a broader substitution basis, so that substitution takes place not only between different land uses but also, for the 'actors' involved, between different occupations, then a more pervasive explanation of the inversion of land use intensity patterns is available. Not only does one find land speculation, the sprawl of recreational activities, retirement to small holdings and the purchase of hobby farms on the urban fringe, but also farmers living within the commutersheds of towns can often increase their total income by taking a job in the city and farming on a part-time basis. This process of land use inversion is occurring quite rapidly. The implication for manufacturing location is a decline of processing industries based on agricultural produce in the heartland, and this in turn indicates a relative shift of processing activities to peripheral areas remote from the influence of metropoles.

While these two trends should promote the emphasis on processing activities in the periphery, they have little influence upon the concentration of fabricating, integrative and administrative activities at the centre. It might be assumed, therefore, that the centralization and urbanization economies mentioned earlier will lead to the massive concentration of these types of manufacturing at the centre: but this would be too simple an interpretation, for there are countervailing centrifugal forces of some consequence. In particular, consideration must be given to the influence of amenities which, since the time of Ullman's seminal paper (1954), have been given increasing attention in the literature. For instance, they are an important element in Christaller's (1964) theory of peripheral places. Alonso (1968, p. 15) considers the personal space preferences of managers and technicians to be 'in some ways the most powerful one in operation': to be located away from a big city is, for many, tantamount to exile. Although these remarks relate primarily to the less industrialized countries, Alonso notes that this factor is quite relevant to contemporary American industrialists. Gould's (1966) study of space preferences in the United States indicate that many people have a liking for the climatically attractive areas in the south and West, and Wilson (1966) presents a case study demonstrating the influence of this factor in the growth of Tucson in Arizona. Combining these preferences for both climatic and urban amenities, the following proposition emerges: that in the most advanced industrial societies where levels of affluence are such that amenity factors enter in an effective way into activity location decisions, some decentralization of industry will occur, but this will be to towns in the periphery that are able to offer the types of services and social amenities that managers expect.

The Urban Level

Within the heartland certain non-random relationships are anticipated on the basis of the preceding discussion. There remains, of course, much that is not explained, and which may possibly be attributable to the type of stochastic growth process proposed by Curry (1964) that gives rise to arc-sine frequency distributions of specialization in manufacturing. More probably the results are inexplicable not so much because behaviour is deliberately random, but because, as Pred (1967) has argued, decision-makers have varying degrees of knowledge and differing abilities to use the information that is available to them.

The present theory relates to cities defined as functional units. Quite frequently, this implies an area larger than that used for statistical purposes: for example, several of Canada's metropolitan areas (as defined by Statistics Canada) are now underbounded. Berry's Daily Urban Systems come closer to the definition that is sought, although they relate to total employment rather than manufacturing activity. The need for a comprehensive definition of an urban area is stressed because many of the industrialized nations are experiencing rapid suburbanization of industry, with new plants being opened at the fringe, or even beyond the continuously built up zone of the city.

Three types of relationships between manufacturing activity and urban places are expected: a relationship between plant size and city size; a relationship between plant function and city size; and a relationship between industrial composition and city size.

Plant Size and City Size. Although almost totally neglected in location theory, it is contended that the size of a plant is one of the most important characteristics of a manufacturing establishment. One notable exception is Czamanski's (1964) claim that

' . . . size of plant is an extremely important factor in determining whether a particular industry will be attracted to a city or not. . . . It may well be that as an element of industrial location, size of plant is second in importance only to industrial category, or to the type of goods the factory turns out or the technology it uses.' (p. 185).

Importance is attached to plant size for two quite different reasons. First, insofar as the size distribution of plants tends to be highly skewed, and usually conforms to the lognormal (Gibrat) distribution, the few largest plants account for a disproportionate amount of economic activity in a country. Even if one could not predict the location of all plants, an ability to predict the location of large plants is extremely useful. Second, in a developmental sense, large plants are important in that they probably far outweigh small plants in terms of their multiplier effects. Given the tendency for integrative activities to take place in large plants, then these plants are likely to require a series of satellite plants that supply various components to be assembled.

According to the proposed theory, certain relationships exist between the size of a plant and the size of a town in which it is located. To begin with, consider a new plant which is to be located in an established town where no plant closure has recently occurred. The opening will involve an increment in local employment, will require housing for the new employees, and will require additions to the service sector in accordance with prevailing basic-nonbasic ratios. People who are economically active may be expected to have dependents—wives, children and elderly relatives—hence we find that for each job created in the 'basic' manufacturing sector, roughly ten residents are added to the community. For the purposes of the present argument, assume that in any one year (during which a plant is to be opened and all the associated adjustments made) the maximum increase that can be accommodated in such services as policing, health, education, housing, water supply, recreation facilities and so on is ten per cent. Under these rules, the population of a town must be at least one hundred times as large as the work force of a new plant.

The argument obviously has some big loopholes: many plants grow from small beginnings, and the enlargement of existing plants is commonly a bigger component of industrial growth than is the opening of new plants; new towns and industrial estates are often created as part of a rapid growth programme; disruption of services does sometimes occur as a result of the rapid growth of industry. Nevertheless the basic truth remains that problems of adjustment in housing, infrastructure and the service sector do impose a flexible constraint on the size of town in which a plant of a given size may be located.

A second mechanism with similar effects involves thresholds and the availability of specialized services. The concept of a threshold is crucial to central place theory, and two are normally identified: a lower threshold size below which an activity is totally absent, and an upper threshold above which an activity is omnipresent. The more specialized an activity, the higher are these thresholds so that certain functions are only present in a few very large towns.

What are the relations between plant location and such thresholds? Do some manufacturing activities require services that are only present in large towns? What are these services? Has this relationship changed through time? These four questions will be considered in turn.

First, a manufacturing plant will not be located in a town unable to provide certain services critical to the working of that plant. On the other hand (and here there is a divergence from central place theory) except in the case of market-oriented industries, there will not be an upper threshold above which the presence of an activity is mandatory. This implies a one way relationship such that a plant makes certain minimum service demands of a town to operate efficiently: on the other hand, the ability of a town to satisfy these minimum service demands does not guarantee the presence of an industry in that town.

The relationship to central place theory is particularly interesting. In central place theory *demand* is given; when demand exceeds the lower threshold, a service may be present while it is always present when demand exceeds the upper threshold. in this theory, it is the *supply* of the specialized service that is given: a new manufacturing plant may be attracted to any one of a number of towns supplying this set of requisite services.

Second, it is quite clear that as manufacturing activities become more specialized, so also do the services demanded by the manufacturer. In some instances, these services can be provided within a plant through division of labour. In other cases, the level of demand is too low to justify their provision within a plant, in which case a group of plants may generate a demand sufficient to sustain that service—and this immediately suggests that a centre will be fairly large for such an agglomeration of manufacturing to be present.

An indication of the range of 'non-goods linkages', that is, services, required by modern manufacturing is given by Bater and Walker (1971) in their study of Hamilton's metal industries. The nine services most commonly used on a daily basis are (in rank order): transport services, banks, security, investment dealers, data processing, sub-contract work, waste disposal, repair shops and advertising, printing and photography. Most of these are also used on a weekly and monthly basis, but at these longer time intervals, insurance, accounting, legal and management consultants, engineering and scientific services, plumbing, electrical and moving services should be added as other important non-goods linkages. It is also important to note that over 80 per cent of these services are obtained in the Hamilton area: the only other important centre providing these services for the metal industries is Toronto (which is located 43 miles from Hamilton). Hence in this example, which would appear to be typical, most of these non-goods linkages need to be available in fairly close proximity to the plant.

The fourth question concerns temporal changes in the relationship between plant size and city size. The indications are that new large plants may be increasingly attracted to large towns or their environs for two reasons. First, as was pointed out in discussing internal economies in scale, average plant size continues to grow. Second, the trend appears to be towards increasingly specialized services which are highly primate, as technology, marketing, purchasing and transportation become more and more sophisticated.

It has been argued that large plants are, for the most part, located in large towns, partly because only large towns can absorb new plants of this size without undergoing major disruption and partly because of the hierarchical arrangement of many specialized services which are vital to the operation of new large industrial establishments. A third reason for advancing this argument is because the superior infrastructure available in large towns (as discussed in section 1.2).

The anticipated relationship between plant size and size of town is summarized thus: a minimum threshold size of town exists for plants of any given size, and towns below the threshold size are not likely to be selected as locations, so that large plants tend to be confined to large towns. This does not imply that the plants located in large towns are exclusively large ones: small plants may be located in towns both large and small because their minimum threshold is commensurately small. This relationship will be violated in cases where plants have grown over a long period and have come to dominate a town.

In Figure 1.1, five sizes of plants are portrayed. The largest circle represents large establishments, the second and third circle medium-sized plants, and the two remaining circles small plants. Two thresholds are indicated, one below which large plants are absent and a second below which medium-sized establishments are absent. It can be seen that plants representing size groups both large and small are found in large towns, while in small towns one only finds establishments belonging to the smaller size groups.

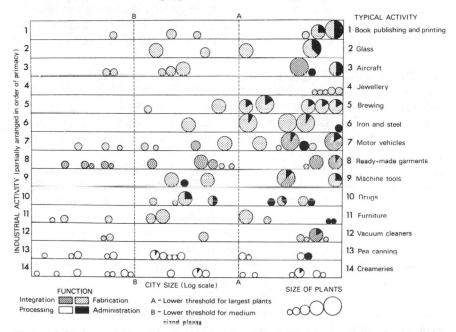

Figure 1.1. A summary of the proposed relationship between city size and the function, size and activity of a plant

Plant Function and City Size. The discussion in this section makes use of the classification of manufacturing into processing, fabricating, integrative, and administrative activities. Processing activities, it has been suggested, will be especially prominent in peripheral regions and under-represented at the centre of the space economy. It is now suggested that administrative activities will be concentrated, but not exclusively located, in metropoles, and integrative activities in large towns.

A two-tier structure of manufacturing places is predicted on the basis of contact patterns. First, Törnqvist (1968) has provided the grounds for suggesting that administrative activities will be highly primate; the earlier discussion on linkages and contact fields forms the basis for this part of the theory. Administrative activities are being progressively polarized in metropoles which enjoy linkages that are vastly superior to those of non-metropolitan centres. Second, external diseconomies resulting from congestion, space limitations, and high rents and land prices are causing the decentralization of some fabricating activities out of the largest towns (where these diseconomies are most marked) and into medium-sized and smaller towns within the industrial heartland. At a high level of economic development, for instance the stage the United States appears to be entering, decentralization may even occur to towns in the periphery, particularly to those with attractive climatic and environmental resources. The fabricating activities most likely to be decentralized are those of a routine nature, ones that can operate efficiently without good access to information channels. Fabricating activities often take place in branch plants, and an administrative unit in a metropolis may control the activities of several branches located in surrounding areas.

Integrative activities, the assembling of various components to form final products, is typically an activity that takes place in a large plant organized on a production line basis. Plants engaged in integrative activities are expected to be found in, or close to, large towns in the heartland, partly as a function of their size, and partly because of the advantages of being accessible to suppliers of components and sub-assemblies.

Theoretical support for this argument involving distinctive patterns of location for administrative, fabricating and other functions can be found in a paper by Guthrie (1954) whose ideas relate to, but precede those of Törnqvist by a decade. Guthrie notes that the optimal size of a plant can be defined with respect to technical, managerial and marketing economies, which are commonly combined to create an aggregate optimal size. However, these economies will coincide only rarely; for example, if managerial economies are greater than technical (production) economies, then a single administrative unit may be created to coordinate the activities of several branch plants. Hence there are sound economic reasons for arguing that the locational patterns of the various functions will differ.

In Figure 1.1 it can be seen that, although some administrative and integrative activities are present in medium-sized towns, they are found mainly in large towns. Conversely, processing activities are most strongly represented in small towns. Almost by default, this leaves fabricating activities concentrated in medium and medium-to-large-sized towns.

Industrial Composition and City Size. The relationship between composition and the size of a city has been relatively neglected in the literature, and the research that has been reported is concerned mostly with identifying empirical relationships rather than offering theoretical explanations. The theoretical explanation offered here relates both to the supply side of production and to the demand side.

Each production process is characterized by a unique production function: some functions demonstrate marked economies of scale favouring large plants, others permit production in small plants with little cost penalty. The former, such activities as iron and steel smelting, shipbuilding, the manufacture of artificial fibres and motor vehicle assembly, are characterized by considerable economies of scale, and therefore almost invariably take place in large plants. In some cases, such plants have grown from small beginnings over long periods, and towns have grown around the plants: but the majority of large plants of this type opened in recent years are located in, or close to, large towns for reasons already discussed.

The other aspect of supply which relates industrial composition to city size is the differing needs of industries for specialized services. The case of large plants has already been dealt with, but there are certain activities conducted in medium-sized plants which could be located in smaller towns, except for their specialized service requirements available only in large towns. Industries clustering around airports are an example, the specialized service in this case being good air transportation facilities. Keeble (1968) has found evidence suggesting that a third London airport will attract to it a variety of light, high value-added industries (he cites capacitators, hearing aids, stainless steel pumps and wigs as typical of such industries attracted to London's Heathrow Airport).

On the demand side, it has already been suggested that there remains a variety of market-oriented activities which conform to the Löschian schema, although many smaller plants of this type located in towns generating only a small demand for the product have been eliminated by changes in the economies of production. The other aspect of demand (this may be viewed as a specialized case) is where an industry is market oriented not because of transportation costs, but because demand for the product is highly primate, and is very sensitive to changing tastes. Three obvious examples of this, well exemplified in New York, are jewellery, furs and customized tailoring (Hoover and Vernon, 1959).

An attempt to represent this relationship using a small sample of industries is to be found in Figure 1. For example, the jewellery industry (4) is highly primate, whereas the two food processing industries at the bottom of the diagram (13 and 14) show no primacy whatsoever, and the assembly and administrative sections of the aircraft industry (3) are found in large towns but the manufacture of parts takes place in towns of all sizes.

1.4. Empirical Evidence

Empirical evidence will not be presented *in extenso*: where sources providing useful evidence are available, they will in most cases simply be cited. There is little to be gained from reproducing all the evidence here.

Countries such as Canada, the United States and Australia are considered to be the most useful sources of evidence for two reasons. First, settlement and industrial development has taken place quite recently so that the effect of locational decisions made prior to the present era are minimized. In Canada and Australia in particular, industrial development largely postdates the era when coalfields were the foci of complexes of heavy industries, hence the coalfield legacy, which so dominates locational patterns in Britain, Belgium and Germany, is largely absent. Second, the governments of these countries have not exerted a strong influence on plant location, at least as compared to countries such as the United Kingdom, the Netherlands and those in Eastern Europe.

Berry's (1961) analysis of city size distributions in a number of countries provides some indication of the effect of this historical legacy. The urban size distribution of the United States is lognormal, while in Canada and Australia a concentration of population in the few largest towns is evident. Concentration in a few large metropoles is considered to be typical of countries that industrialized in the twentieth century. Britain and, to a smaller extent, Belgium have an 'excess' of middle-sized towns (over the number expected in a lognormal pattern), and this is considered to reflect nineteenth century conditions passed on to the twentieth century.

At the regional level, the heartland-periphery dichotomy has been examined in the context of the United States by Ullman (1958), Perloff, Dunn, Lampard and Muth (1960), Fuchs (1962), Zelinsky (1962), and Pred (1965), among others. Variations in the boundary of the heartland (manufacturing belt) account for some discrepancies in the findings of these authors, but up until recently the concentration of manufacturing in the heartland and the special-ization of the periphery in processing activities appears to have been fairly stable. Very recently, some changes have been detected with certain types of manufacturing shifting out of the North-East. Electrical machinery, for instance, is an industry experiencing some shifts into the periphery and particularly to the South (Stevens et al., 1969). Whether or not this recent development involves all types of activities in the electrical machinery industry, it is not yet clear, but if the previous argument is correct then one would anticipate that administrative activities are less involved in the shift from the North-East than are fabricating and integrative activities, and that routine fabricating activities are the most likely to be involved in decentralization.

In Canada in 1961, a fraction over 50 per cent of total manufacturing employment was located in the eight largest metropolitan areas, namely Montreal, Toronto, Vancouver, Winnipeg, Ottawa, Hamilton, Quebec and Edmonton. Five of these metropoles lie in the Canadian heartland which extends through Southern Ontario and up the St. Lawrence Valley. Using the same definition of the heartland, Maxwell (1965) has found cities located therein to show a marked specialization in manufacturing. Nearly all cities in the periphery specialize in service functions, the exceptions being a few resource-oriented manufacturing centres such as Arvida and Shawinigan Falls (aluminium smelting) and Sault Ste. Marie (steel).

The Australian heartland is less clearly developed, and it is probably easier to define two, one around Sydney–Newcastle, the other around Melbourne. These three Statistical Divisions in themselves accounted for 44 per cent of the Australian population and two-thirds of Australian manufacturing employ-ment in 1966. The same pattern is recognizable in most developed countries (Robertson, 1953) and, as Friedmann's study of Venezuela (1966) shows, economic development in underdeveloped countries is also quite polarized, with fabricating, integrative and administrative manufacturing functions concentrated in the centre, leaving primary industries and resource-oriented manufacturing to dominate the periphery.

In the absence of published empirical studies on the relations between plant size and city size, use will be made of data that this author has collected for the South West Economic Planning Region in England (Norcliffe, 1970). The theory predicts that although small plants may be found in towns of any size, large plants are located mainly in large towns. This relationship was examined in two ways.

First, the largest plant in each of 69 functional urban areas was identified and regressed against the population of the largest town within that functional urban area. Not surprisingly, the relationship was strongly positive, and the t-statistic highly significant (Figure 1.2). Although this evidence is in accordance with the postulated relationships, most of the large plants have grown over several decades to attain their present size; the largest plant opened in each functional urban area between 1956 and 1964 proved to be considerably smaller than the largest plant operating in 1964 in virtually every case.

The second approach involved extracting from the data files every plant opening between 1956 and 1964 involving more than 99 employees. A few cases were omitted when an opening followed upon an immediately preceding closure, particularly when the same building was involved. The remainder were tabulated by size of plant and town (Table 1.1); the results show a reasonable correspondence with predictions. Functional urban areas in which the largest town had a population under 50,000 accounted for 37 per cent of the total work force in manufacturing, yet received only 16 per cent of the work force employed in large new plants. The functional urban areas surrounding the eight largest towns (Bristol, Plymouth, Swindon, Bath, Exeter, Cheltenham, Gloucester, and Torquay) accounted for a disproportionately large share of the employment in new large plants and, with one exception, all the new plants with a work force exceeding 199 persons.

The main source of evidence on the relationship between plant function and city size is Törnqvist's (1970) study of recent trends in Swedish activity location. He found that the three major urban areas (Stockholm, Göteborg, and Malmo) have about 30 per cent of Sweden's population, 32 per cent of the total number of workers employed in manufacturing, construction and wholesale, over 40 per cent of administrative personnel and nearly 50 per cent of the most contact intensive personnel who form the upper echelon decision-makers. The concentration of top level employees in state business enterprises is even more marked, with about 65 per cent of these people in the Stockholm area alone. Furthermore, changes during the 1960–1965/66 period reinforced this pattern of concentration. The total manufacturing labour force in Stockholm declined substantially, but the number of salaried employees grew slightly, and the work force of contact intensive employees grew quite substantially. Some of the evidence presented by Ullman (1958) indicates a

TABLE 1.1. Large plants opened 1956–1964 in south-west England, classified by location

Shop-floor labour force of new plant	Size of largest town in functional urban area, 1961						
	(Bristol) 437,048	(Plymouth) 204,409	(Swindon) 91,739	50,000–80,901	25,000–49,999	10,000–24,999	10,000
100–199	13	5	4	9	4	5	5
200–299	2	4	3	2	—	—	—
300–499	1	—	—	2	1	—	—
>500	2	2	—	2	—	—	—
Manufacturing work force in functional urban areas	83,614	30,918	25,081	38,248	19,314	31,886	53,297
% of regional total	29·61	10·95	8·88	13·55	6·84	11·29	18·88
Total employment in large new plants	3,491	2,872	1,280	3,294	815	600	650
% of regional total	26·85	22·09	9·84	25·33	6·27	4·61	5·00

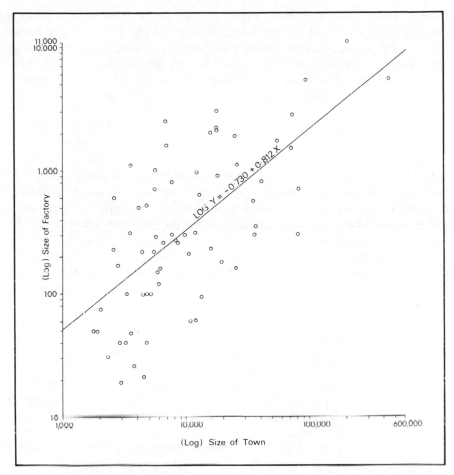

Figure 1.2. The relationship between the population of the largest town and the employment in the largest plant for 69 functional urban areas in South-West England in 1964

similar pattern in the United States: the headquarters of the 100 largest companies, membership of the National Academy of Sciences, the origin of patents and several other indices all testify to the dominance of metropolitan places over administrative activities. Winsborough's (1959) finding that processing activities in the United States are less urbanized than are fabricating activities also conforms with the theory. Winsborough (1960) found primacy to be present in most administrative activities, even in farm administration:

'... when the tendency for agriculture to be located in smaller towns and rural areas has been held constant, farmers and farm managers show a positive gradient with size.... This finding suggests that the administration of farming is done in larger places, on the average, than the actual production.' (p. 896).

Evidence providing circumstantial support for the argument in Canada is provided by Ambrose (1970). Between 1951 and 1961, employment in the primary sector declined rapidly, the secondary sector grew slightly and the tertiary sector grew rapidly. Growth was especially marked both in large towns, and in such service sectors as miscellaneous services, business services, education, government administration (at all levels) health and communications. These services are precisely the ones that are important to administrative and 'contact-intensive' functions within the manufacturing sector.

The third relationship that was proposed at the urban level was between city size and industrial composition. Some clues, although for present purposes not very strong evidence, are to be found in Czamanski's (1964) study of industry in the United States. He develops a model of urban growth using a three-fold classification of manufacturing into geographically (mainly resource) oriented, complementary, and urban-oriented industries: the last type is composed of 'industries for which the existence of the city is the main locational factor'. By classifying a sample of 232 cities into four groups and within each group correlating employment in an industry with population, he found over half of the 74 industrial activities to be urban-oriented in all four size groups. However, nearly all of these 74 activities were tertiary industries and only three manufacturing activities, construction, baking, and printing and publishing fell in this category: these three activities are well known to be market-oriented. More interesting are the 15 activities that were urban-oriented for the larger city size groups, but not urban-oriented for the smaller size groups, because primacy is one possible explanation of the arrangement. Unfortunately only one manufacturing activity, namely the apparel industry, fits in this mould, and an alternative explanation—that these activities are complementary or resource-oriented industries concentrated in smaller towns—appears to account for most of these cases.

A more useful methodology was used by Winsborough (1960) in his search for primacy in activity location patterns. Standardizing his data so as to allow for variations in industrial composition between different size bands of town, Winsborough found that those industrial activities which do not require much administration do not display primacy in their locational patterns.

Hoover (1971, pp. 156–158) has tackled this problem by relating location quotients for a variety of industries to six city-size categories. Quite a few industries are not concentrated by city size, but the location quotients for many other industries are sufficiently large that concentration in a given size band has probably not come about by chance. In cities with more than half a million inhabitants, furs, millinery, bookbinding, typesetting, dolls and other industries with marked external economies are concentrated: at the other end of the scale (places with fewer than 2,500 inhabitants) one finds a concentration of clay products, beet sugar, lime and other industries closely linked to their raw material supplies. Hoover's data relate to 1954, but it is probable that the general trends indicated still prevail today, although individual industries such as the manufacture of motor vehicles may well have changed their concentration, by city size class, in the meantime.

Stafford's (1966) study of population as a determinate of industrial type comes closest to examining the relationship proposed here. For the 102 counties of Illinois, using 138 industrial categories, he computed point biserial correlations between the presence-absence of an industry and the population of a county. In only 23 counties did r_{pb} exceed 0·5, and in a mere six counties was r_{pb} greater than 0·9: in other words, for the majority of industries, population was not a good predictor of the presence of an industry in a country. The industries that were predicted fairly well are certain high value-added and consumer-oriented specialist industries, including sugar, tobacco, fabrics, furs, leather tanning, bicycles, optical instruments and jewellery: these were found only in the largest counties. A few industries were concentrated in smaller counties, and in this case were mostly resource oriented or market-oriented because of the bulk or perishability of the product. Included in this group were food industries, lumber, newspapers, commercial printing, concrete and gypsum products. However, for approximately four-fifths of the industrial categories, population was not a good discriminator of industrial type.

Conclusion

In the preceding discussion, an attempt has been made to construct a theory of manufacturing places. This theory provides a framework in which the dynamics of contemporary manufacturing location may be viewed. Constraints both of time and space have prevented detailed infilling, but this is relatively unimportant at this stage because the validity, or otherwise, of the general framework has yet to be established. The theory is cast in a partial equilibrium framework, although this is implicit rather than explicit. No attempt has been made rigorously to specify the nature of that equilibrium, although the emphasis put upon infrastructure availability, internal and external economies, and contact fields clearly makes this partial equilibrium a function of the prevailing technology.

The argument is developed at a fairly general level on the grounds that there is still a need for contributions to manufacturing location theory of this type. The theory relates to Western economies not because the author is disinterested in the Third World, but because of his limited knowledge of developing countries, and because of his belief that the rest of the world will probably not follow patterns of locational development exhibited in economically advanced countries.

The very title that is proposed for the theory indicates the close relationship that it has to central place theory. The two theories have obvious differences, but they are similar in at least two ways. First, space is explicitly built into both theories. Central place theory incorporates market areas of specified dimensions, while in manufacturing place theory, space is partitioned into a centre and a periphery at the regional level, and at the urban level a system of cities is superimposed on this arrangement. Second, different patterns are expected at different spatial scales. Central place theory postulates a neat hierarchical arrangement of centres and market areas, whereas manufacturing place theory jumps from the regional to the urban scale: it could possibly be extended to the intra-urban scale to relate to manufacturing places within cities, and to the global scale, but this has not been attempted here.

A major difference between central place and manufacturing place theory lies in the emphasis on demand considerations in the former and supply considerations in the latter. Three factors were deemed to be of especial importance to the theory, these being infrastructure availability, internal and external economies and communication and linkage patterns. All three are essentially supply factors. It is acknowledged that demand factors are of some importance to manufacturing: specifically, industries oriented to markets because of delivery costs were considered to be of moderate (but declining) significance, while access to the market at the national scale was included as a centralization economy. Overall, however, the argument underlying the proposed theory of manufacturing places relates to the supply side of production.

At the regional scale, a centre-periphery arrangement was used to summarize the location of economic activity. Processing activities and certain routine fabricating activities are expected to be concentrated in the periphery, administrative, integrative and the majority of fabricating activities at the centre. At the urban scale, associations between city size and the size, function and industrial composition of a plant were posited. Specifically, the following relations are anticipated: a positive relationship between plant size and city size; a concentration of administrative activities in metropoles, integrative activities in large towns and fabricating activities in medium-sized and smaller towns; and particular types of industries to be well represented in towns of a given size group.

The content of the proposed theory is highly derivative, indeed its main novelty lies in the framework in which the various observations and ideas have been set. It clearly falls short of what has been suggested as the ultimate goal of geographic theory—one that simultaneously incorporates time and space dimensions—but it is a theory that can accommodate, although not predict, changes through time. The hallmark of the present theory is its empirical foundation. The argument is factually based, and in particular it draws upon work that recognizes the essential symbiosis between manufacturing systems and urban and regional systems. Supporting evidence has been cited, but data non-availability and definitional problems place beyond the present time horizon that elusive goal of finding conclusive evidence. One hopes, however, that as fragmentary evidence becomes available it will substantiate the proposed theory.

Notes

1. There is quite a large literature on this topic: Scully (1971) and Borts (1960) list most of the important items.

2. For instance, least cost theory sets external diseconomies against external economies, yet while entrepreneurs often benefit from the latter, those related to the former are usually borne by the community at large, and tend to be discounted in the industrialist's decision-making procedure. Again, Pullen (1964) suggests that some firms absorb delivery costs in a deliberate attempt to expand their market areas and thereby shift to a more favourable production function.
3. Törnqvist (1970, p. 22) reports that Thorngren (1967) has also identified external economies operating at a scale larger than the urban scale: these he refers to as 'regional external economies'.
4. Rosenbluth (1957), Dunning and Thomas (1961), P. S. Florence (1962), Armstrong and Silbertson (1965), and Regional Planning Council, Baltimore (1967) discuss plant concentration in Britain, Canada and the United States.

Acknowledgement

The thoughtful comments made by Dr. Morgan Thomas on an earlier draft of this paper are gratefully acknowledged.

References

Ackley, G. (1942), Spatial Competition in a Discontinuous Market, *Quarterly Journal of Economics*, **56**, 212–230.
Alonso, W. (1968), Industrial Location and Regional Policy in Economic Development, *University of California, Berkeley, Institute of Urban and Regional Development*, Working Paper 74.
Ambrose, P. J. (1970), Patterns of Growth in the Canadian Labour Force 1951–1961. *Canadian Geographer*, **14**, 139–157.
Armstrong, A. and Silbertson A. (1965), Size of Plant, Size of Enterprise and Concentration in British Manufacturing Industry 1935–58, *Journal of the Royal Statistical Society*, **128 A.**, 395–420.
Baltimore Regional Planning Council (1967), *Manufacturing Industries; Projections of Locational Decisions*. Baltimore: The Regional Planning Council.
Bater, J. H. and Walker, D. F. (1971), *The Linkage Study of Hamilton Metal Industries*. Hamilton: Hamilton Economic Development Commission.
Beckmann, M (1955), The Economics of Location, *Kyklos*, **8**, 416–421.
Beckmann, M. (1968), *Location Theory*. New York: Random House.
Berry, B. J. L. (1961), City Size Distributions and Economic Development, *Economic Development and Cultural Change*, **9**, 573–587.
Berry, B. J. L. (1970), The Geography of the United States in the Year 2000, *Transactions, Institute of British Geographers*, **51**, 21–53.
Blair, J. M. (1942), The Relation between Size and Efficiency of Business, *Review of Economics and Statistics*, **24**, 125–135.
Borts, G. H. (1960), The Equalization of Returns and Regional Economic Growth, *American Economic Review*, **50**, 319–347.
Caesar, A. A. L. (1964), Planning and the Geography of Great Britain, *Advancement of Science*, **21**, 230–240.
Chernick, S. E. (1966), *Interregional Disparities in Income*. Economic Council of Canada: Staff Studies No. 14. Ottawa: Queen's Printer.
Chinitz, B. (1960), The Effect of Transportation Forms on Regional Economic Growth, *Traffic Quarterly*, **14**, 129–142.
Christaller, W. (1964), Some Considerations of Tourism in Europe: The Peripheral Regions—Underdeveloped Countries—Recreation Areas, *Papers and Proceedings, Regional Science Association*, **12**, 95–105.

54

Clark, C. (1966), Industrial Location and Economic Potential, *Lloyds Bank Review*, **82**, 1–17.

Cohen, J. (1964), *Behaviour in Uncertainty and its Social Implications*. London: Allen and Unwin.

Curry, L. (1962), The Geography of Service Centres Within Towns: the Elements of an Operational Approach, *Lund Studies in Geography, Series B, Human Geography*, No. 24, 31–54.

Curry, L. (1964), The Random Spatial Economy: an Exploration in Settlement Theory, *Annals, Association of American Geographers*, **54**, 138–146.

Czamanski, S. (1964), A Model of Urban Growth, *Papers, Regional Science Association*, **13**, 177–200.

Devletoglou, N. F. (1965), A Dissenting View of Duopoly and Spatial Competition, *Economica* (New Series), **22**, 140–160.

Dunning, J. H. and Thomas, C. J. (1961), *British Industry: Change and Development in the Twentieth Century*. London: Hutchinson.

Earney, F. C. F. (1969), New Ores for Old Furnaces: Pelletized Iron. *Annals, Association of American Geographers*, **59**, 512–534.

Easterlin, R. A. (1958), Income Differentials among States 1880–1950, *Papers and Proceedings, Regional Science Association*, **4**, 22–59.

Fleming, D. K. (1971), Iron Ore Pelletization, *Geographical Review*, **61**, 143–145.

Florence, P. S. (1962), *Post-war Investment, Location and Size of Plant*. National Institute of Economic and Social Research, Occasional Paper XIX; Cambridge University Press.

Found, W. C. and Morley, C. D. (1971), A Land-Use Transportation Model for the Rural Toronto Area, York University, Ontario: Mimeo.

Friedman, M. (1953), *Essays in Positive Economics*. Chicago: University of Chicago Press.

Friedmann, J. (1966), *Regional Development Policy. A Cast Study of Venezuela*. Cambridge, Mass.: M.I.T. Press.

Fuchs, V. R. (1962), *Changes in the Location of Manufacturing in the United States since 1929*. New Haven: Yale University Press.

Galatin, M. (1968), *Economies of Scale and Technological Change in Thermal Power Generation*. Amsterdam: North-Holland Publishing Co. (Contributions to Economic Analysis No. 53).

Getis, A. (1963), The Determination of the Location of Retail Activities with the Use of a Map Transformation, *Economic Geography*, **39**, 14–22.

Gilmour, J. M. (1970), Economies of Scale and Plant Elimination in Brewing, *Proceedings, Canadian Association of Geographers*, University of Manitoba.

Gilmour, J. M. (1972), *Spatial Evolution of Manufacturing: Southern Ontario. 1851–1891*. University of Toronto, Department of Geography, Research Publication, No. 10.

Gould, P. R. (1966), on Mental Maps, *Michigan Inter-University Community of Mathematical Geographers*, Discussion paper 9.

Government of Ontario (1970), *Design for Development: The Toronto-Centred Region* Toronto: Queen's Printer.

Greenhut, M. L. (1956), *Plant Location in Theory and Practise*. Chapel Hill: University of North Carolina Press.

Guthrie, J. A. (1954), Economies of Scale and Regional Development, *Papers and Proceedings, Regional Science Association*, **1**, 121–131.

Hall, P. G. (1962), *The Industries of London Since 1861*. London: Hutchinson University Library.

Harris, C. D. (1954), The Market as a Factor in the Localization of Industry in the U.S., *Annals, Association of American Geographers*, **64**, 315–348.

Harvey, D. W. (1972), Social Justice and Spatial Systems, *Antipode*, **4**, No. 2, July 1972, pp. 1–13.

Hoover, E. M. (1937), *Location Theory and the Shoe and Leather Industries*. Cambridge, Mass.: Harvard University Press.

Hoover, E. M. (1948), *The Location of Economic Activity*. New York: McGraw-Hill.

Hoover, E. M. (1968), Trends in Location and Location Theory, *Centre for Regional Economic Studies, University of Pittsburg* Occasional Paper No. 6.

Hoover, E. M. (1971), *An Introduction to Regional Economics*. New York: Alfred A. Knopf.

Hoover, E. M. and Vernon, R. (1959), *Anatomy of a Metropolis*. Cambridge, Mass.: Harvard University Press.

Hotelling, H. (1929), Stability in Competition, *The Economic Journal*, **39**, 41–57.

Isard, W. (1956), *Location and Space-Economy*. Cambridge, Mass.: M.I.T. Press.

Isard, W. and Schooler, E. W. (1959), Industrial Complex Analysis, Agglomeration Economies and Regional Development, *Journal of Regional Science*, **1**, 19–33.

Isard, W., Schooler, E. W. and Vietorisz, T. (1959), *Industrial Complex Analysis and Regional Development*. Cambridge, Mass.: M.I.T. Press.

Johnson, J. F. (1971), *Renovated Waste Water*. University of Chicago, Department of Geography, Research paper No. 135.

Keeble, D. E. (1968), Airport Location, Exporting and Industrial Growth, *Town and County Planning*, **36**, 209–214.

Lefeber, L. (1958), *Location in Space*. Amsterdam: North-Holland Publishing Company.

Lerner, A. P. and Singer, H. W. (1937), Some Notes on Duopoly and Spatial Competition, *Journal of Political Economy*, **4**, 145–186.

Lindberg, O. (1953), An Economic Geographical Study of the Localization of the Swedish Paper Industry, *Geografiska Annaler*, **35**, 28–40.

Lösch, A. (1954), *The Economics of Location*. (Translated by W. H. Woglom and W. F. Stolper.) New York: Wiley.

Machlup, F. (1963), Statics and Dynamics: Kaleidoscopic Words, in Machlup, F., *Essays on Economic Semantics*. Englewood Cliffs, N.J.: Prentice-Hall.

Madigan, R. T. (1969), Iron Ore Marketing Trends—with Special Comment on Metallizing, *Engineering and Mining Journal*, **170**(5), 94–96.

Mason, P. F. (1969), Some Changes in Domestic Iron Mining as a Result of Pelletization, *Annals, Association of American Geographers*, **59**, 535–551.

Maxwell, J. W. (1965), The Functional Structure of Canadian Cities, *Geographical Bulletin*, **7**, 79–104.

Neutze, G. M. (1963), The External Diseconomies of Growth in Traffic, *Economic Record*, **39**, 332–345.

Neutze, G. M. (1965), *Economic Policy and the Size of Cities*. Canberra: A.N.U. Press.

Norcliffe, G. B. (1970), Industrial Location Dynamics, Unpublished Ph.D. Dissertation, Department of Geography, University of Bristol.

Palander, T. (1935), *Beitrage zur Standortstheorie*. Uppsala: Almgrist and Wiksells.

Perloff, H. S., Dunn, E. S., Lampard, E. E. and Muth, R. F. (1960), *Regions, Resources and Economic Growth*. Baltimore: The Johns Hopkins Press.

Perloff, H. S. and Wingo, L. (1961), Natural Resource Endowment and Regional Economic Growth, in Spengler, J. J. (ed.), *Natural Resources and Economic Growth*, Washington, D.C.: Resources for the Future Inc. 191–212.

Pred, A. R. (1965), The Concentration of High Value Added Manufacturing, *Economic Geography*, **41**, 108–132.

Pred, A. R. (1966), *The Spatial Dynamics of U.S. Urban-Industrial Growth 1800–1914*. Cambridge: M.I.T. Press.

56

Pred, A. R. (1967), *Behaviour and Location: Part 1*. Lund Studies in Geography, Series B, Human Geography, 27. Lund: C. W. K. Gleerup.

Pullen, M. J. (1964), Transportation Costs and the Disappearance of Space in the Theory of the Firm, *Yorkshire Bulletin*, **16,** 3–14.

Rawstrom, E. M. (1958), Three Principles of Industrial Location, *Transactions and Papers, Institute of British Geographers*, **27,** 135–142.

Richter, C. E. (1969), The Impact of Industrial Linkages on Geographic Association, *Journal of Regional Science*, **9,** 19–28.

Robertson, C. J. (1953), Scotland: a Peripheral Region, *Tijdschrift Voor Economishe en Sociale Geografie*, **44,** 249–256.

Rosenbluth, G. (1957), *Concentration in Canadian Manufacturing Industries*. Princeton: National Bureau of Economic Research, General Series, no. 61.

Scully, G. W. (1969), Human Capital and Productivity in U.S. Manufacturing, *Western Economic Journal*, **8,** 334–340.

Scully, G. W. (1971), The North-South Manufacturing Wage Differential, *Journal of Regional Science*, **11,** 235–252.

Segal, M. (1960) *Wages and the Metropolis*. Harvard University Press, Cambridge, Mass.

Sinclair, R. (1967), Von Thunen and Urban Sprawl, *Annals, Association of American Geographers*, **57,** 72–87.

Smith, D. M. (1966), A Theoretical Framework for Geographical Studies of Industrial Location, *Economic Geography*, **42,** 95–113.

Smith, D. M. (1971), *Industrial Location: An Economic Geographical Analysis*. New York: Wiley.

Smithies, A. (1941), Optimum Location in Spatial Competition, *Journal of Political Economy*, **49,** 423–439.

Stafford, H. A. (1966), Population as a Determinate of Industrial Type, *East Lakes Geographer*, **2,** 71–79.

Stevens, B. H. (1961), An Application of Game Theory to a Problem in Location Strategy, *Papers, Regional Science Association*, **7,** 143–157.

Stevens, B. H., Douglas, R. C. and Neighbor, C. B. (1969), Trends in Industrial Location and their Impact on Regional Economic Development, *Regional Science Research Institute*, Discussion Paper 31.

Streit, M. E. (1969), Spatial Associations and Economic Linkages between Industries, *Journal of Regional Science*, **9,** 177–188.

Thorngren, B. (1967), Regionala External Economies, Ekonomiska Forskningsinstitutet vid Handelshogskolan i Stockholm: Mimeographed.

Törnqvist, G. (1962), *Transport Costs as a Location Factor for Manufacturing Industry*. Lund Studies in Geography, Series C., General and Mathematical Geography 2.

Törnqvist, G. (1968), Flows of Information and the Location of Economic Activity, *Geografiska Annaler*, **50B,** 99–107.

Törnqvist, G. (1969), *Flows of Information and the Location of Economic Activities*. Lund Studies in Geography, Series B, Human Geography, 30.

Törnqvist, G. (1970), *Contact Systems and Regional Development*. Lund Studies in Geography, Series B, Human Geography, 35.

Ullman, E. L. (1954), Amenities as a Factor in Regional Growth, *Geographical Review*, **44,** 119–132.

Ullman, E. L. (1958), Regional Development and the Geography of Concentration, *Papers and Proceedings, Regional Science Association*, **4,** 179–198.

Wallace, I. (1972), Towards the Integration of Industrial Location and Commodity Flow Studies, *International Geography*, **2,** 1209–1211.

Weber, A. (1929), *Theory of the Location of Industries* (Translated by C. J. Friedrich), University of Chicago Press.

Wilson, A. (1966), The Impact of Climate on Industrial Growth—Tucson, Arizona, in Sewell, W. R. D. (ed.), *Human Dimensions of Weather Modification*. University of Chicago, Department of Geography, Research Paper No. 105.

Winsborough, H. H. (1959), Variations in Industrial Composition with City Size, *Papers and Proceedings, Regional Science Association*, **5**, 121–131.

Winsborough, H. H. (1960), Occupational Composition and the Urban Hierarchy, *American Sociological Review*, **25**, 894–897.

Wise, M. J. (1950), On the Jewellery and Gun Quarters of Birmingham, *Transactions and Papers, Institute of British Geographers*, **15**, 59–72.

Zelinsky, W. (1962), Has American Industry been Decentralizing? The Evidence for the 1939–54 Period, *Economic Geography*, **38**, 251–269.

2 The Dynamics of Spatial Change in the Export Region

JAMES M. GILMOUR

During a period of less than two hundred years Southern Ontario has changed from being an almost unpopulated and economically unused region to one characterized by urban areas and manufacturing. In the achievement of such a precipitous transformation Southern Ontario can make no claim to uniqueness. Many parallels are found in the 'new countries'—the 'empty' areas of the world settled by Europeans in the past four centuries. Southern Ontario has followed a fairly well trodden path and is today the product of a sequence of events, which in broad outline, have unfolded in several other areas. In seeking for generalized explanation of the growth mechanisms of the type experienced in Southern Ontario, economists and economic historians have evolved the export-base model of regional economic growth, or, as it is sometimes called, the staple theory of economic growth. This is a very specialized theory of economic growth. It does not, for example, apply to export oriented economies in general. The case of the 'third world' country currently trying to promote growth *via* export earnings, lies outside its ambit. It applies specifically to the atypical and never to be repeated case of the 'new country'.

The staple economy, the growth of which economists have tried to explain in general theoretical terms, is the aggregate of phenomena that are spatially distributed. However, few attempts have been made so far to formulate general statements about the spatial evolution of economic activities in export-based regions. It is the purpose of this essay to improve upon such generalizations. As befitting the aims of this book, manufacturing is considered almost to the exclusion of other activities.

2.1 The Export-based Model

It is hardly surprising that the staple approach to economic growth is chiefly a Canadian innovation because Canadian history has been intricately interwoven with and moulded by a succession of export staples derived from the primary resource base. The history of Canada has been the history of fur, fish, lumber, wheat and many other individually less important commodities. It is in the work of pioneer Canadian historians such as Innis (1930, 1940), Mackintosh (1923, 1936), and Lower (1933, 1938), who studied the growth and structure of the great staple industries and their effects on Canadian economy and society, that the export-base model finds its origins. These scholars were in no way concerned with the creation and testing of economic growth models, rather they craved an understanding of their country's history using the crucially important staples as a unifying theme. Nevertheless they laid the foundation for a framework of analysis which was eventually shaped and explicitly stated as the export-base model by scholars in Canada and the United States who had interests in the growth process rather than in history.

Applying as it does to only 'empty' lands, the model is structured in response to two conditions which are likely to characterize settlement in the early phases of growth. These are, the absence of population pressure problems, and the absence of inhibiting traditions (Watkins, 1963). In response to the politico/economic tradition in which the empty regions developed, the model applies only to regions that grew up within a framework of capitalist institutions which were capable of responding to profit maximizing opportunities in which factors of production were relatively mobile (North, 1955).

Export-base theory explains growth as a diversification process around the export sector; the only sector in a newly settled land that is likely to be a source of profitable opportunity. With its impact expressed through a disaggregated multiplier mechanism, the export sector leads the economy along, promoting growth in other sectors. Development depends very heavily on two related sets of factors: the production function of the export industry (or industries) and the distribution of income from the export sector. These, in particular the former, are the main determinants of the strength of the inducements to invest in the domestic economy. The more 'favourable' the production function, and the more equitably distributed the income deriving from the export sector, the greater are the opportunities for investment in non-export activities. The needs of a flexible and successfully growing export sector may stimulate investment in infrastructure, for example, in a transportation system that can handle the region's inflows and outflows, and this in turn may become associated with investment in exchange activities located at nodal points on the evolving transportation system. Depending on the production functions the possibilities may exist for the investment in the production of equipment and goods required by the export sector in its production processes. With time, the basic export commodities which in almost every case derive from agricultural and other extractive sources, may be subjected to further processing before export. A typical sequence may be, first the export of logs, then milled lumber, followed by the production of plywoods and veneers, and finally the production of wood and paper products, such as furniture and newsprint. Each forwardly linked step in the sequence raises the number of domestic investment opportunities and increases regional income. As opportunity and income grow, so does population both from natural increase and from immigration, thus further enchancing the attractiveness of the region for investment from foreign and domestic sources.

The mechanisms which connect the export sector to investment in infrastructure and directly productive activities have been categorized by Watkins partly in terms borrowed from Hirschman (1958, pp. 98–119), as backward, forward and final demand linkage (Watkins, 1963, p. 145). The first relates to inducements to invest in the production of goods required by the export sector. Here, the production functions of the staple industries are important for they condition the nature and strength of backward linkage effects. The second relates to opportunities for investment in industries using the output of the export industry as an input, while the third describes the inducement to invest in consumer goods industries producing for factors in the export sector. In this case the distribution of income stemming from the export sector is of great significance. For example, an equitable distribution of income creates opportunities for the mass production of goods; permits achievement of scale economies and increases regional productivity. On the other hand, a skewed distribution of income may lead to low levels of consumption in the mass of the population; and in the small wealthy minority—luxury consumption, associated with imports. This condition would retard development of secondary manufacturing (Baldwin, 1956).

In the initial phases of development the greatest impact of the linkages will be felt outside the region, most likely in the markets of the metropolitan power to which the region is economically and even politically tied. However, should income and population growth continue as a result of growth in exports, the linkage relationships may begin to change. Thresholds for the production of goods and the provision of services may be reached within the region itself, enabling it to substitute domestic production for imports. Provided that the export sector does not falter (and there are many reasons why this is a real possibility) the economy may grow and diversify until it ceases to have the characteristics of an export-based region, and the export sector relinquishes its dominant role.

The pattern of development so briefly outlined above describes the path likely to be followed by a region if it is to experience the structural transformation from a zone of primary exploitation to an economically mature urban/industrial region. These are the ideal circumstances. However, throughout the growth process, unfavourable conditions may be encountered, and these may have the effect of slowing down growth, or indeed causing a permanent low income economy dominated by primary extractive activities. From the very beginning, the production functions may have the wrong kind of characteristics; unpromising in the promotion of desirable linkage effects. Income distribution may be lopsided as it was for so long in the southern part of the United States, thereby inhibiting investment in consumer goods industries and limiting the domestic demand for services and thus restricting the development of service centres. Normally, staple exports can only be drawn from the primary resource base which may be bountiful or niggardly in what it offers for exploitation and export. Staple industries may only be founded on commodities in demand in international markets, and in which a region has a competitive advantage. It follows that regions may have no choice but put their eggs in the wrong baskets; forced by circumstances to work with exports having undesirable characteristics as far as long-term development is concerned. New France, for example, could find profit only in the fur trade, an industry which had minimal spread effects. The export sector must grow and maintain flexibility, shifting commodities, markets and production techniques when needs must or when benefits would accrue. Lacking flexibility, regions may be forced into the staple trap, eking out a marginal existence by means of uncertain returns from the same old staples. The cases of Newfoundland and the Gaspé Peninsula with their very narrow resource bases, come readily to mind. In brief, there are many reasons why a region may falter and fail to match the idealized economic transformation described by staple theory which sets down only the likely conditions for successful economic growth.

It must be observed that staple theory has not been without its critics. The strongest of them was Tiebout (1956), who directed his words against the work of Douglas North (1955, 1956). Amongst other things he voiced the suspicion that the model overemphasizes the role of exports, and under-stresses or ignores those of business investment, government expenditures and the volume of residential construction in determining regional income. However, with knowledge of these and other criticisms a number of Canadian and American economists, including Caves and Holton (1961), Bertram (1963), Watkins (1963), and Lithwick and Paquet (1968), have reappraised the model, and consider it, at least as far as the Canadian growth experience is concerned, the most applicable of all available growth theories.

2.2 Structural Change

In view of the initial emptiness of export-based regions primary resources represent the sole source of exports, unless one considers trading as an export activity. It is conceptually useful to think of output or occupational structure in the export region commencing with the primary sector totally dominant. The growth unavoidably engendered by primary activity such as forestry or farming is reflected in some diversification of the economy. Service industries, construction and manufacturing appear. Should no major obstacles be set up against the ideal sequence of development, the economy will gradually experience a complete structural transformation. The dynamics of growth will shift to the secondary and tertiary sectors, while the primary sector with its comparatively fewer profitable opportunities and its greater economic uncertainties will assume a subsidiary role. In the normal case, primary activities will continue to grow in absolute terms, but will decline in a relative sense as the secondary and tertiary sectors move toward dominance.

The spread effects of the export sector create opportunities for investment in manufacturing, and if the export sector maintains its growth, there will be a growing effective demand for manufactured goods associated with greater scope for specialization of labour. Of the several writers who have considered staple theory, only Douglas North has suggested a classification of the manufacturing that develops in response to the success of the export sector (1955, p. 250). He defines four kinds of manufacturing. The first group is composed of materials—oriented industries; weight-loss activities more economically located at the source of raw materials than close to the market for the processed raw material. Service industries to the export sector, for example, agricultural implement manufacturing, make up the second group. Third, he identifies residentiary industries producing for local consumption, and his fourth group contains footloose industries for which transfer costs are of little significance in location. North says nothing about the sequence in which these industries will appear, their changing relative importance, or their spatial distribution except what is implicit in his definitions of them.

The examination of distributional change in this paper employs an alternative classification adopted from Dales (1962 and 1963). While not new, it has not been used in the context that is now suggested. It is a reasonable proposition that the structure of manufacturing in the export region represents the product of the particular growth processes by means of which such regions are identified. It is equally reasonable to propose that the spatial evolution of manufacturing is related to its structure. If progressive structural change occurs as the region develops, it seems likely that there will occur related progressive changes in spatial pattern because different types of manufacturing have different locational requirements, and the relative importance of types is altered as the region matures.

If manufacturing can be disaggregated in such a way that the parts describe different linkage effects it becomes possible to relate structure and growth meaningfully to spatial pattern. A classification which meets these requirements is as follows:

SECONDARY MANUFACTURING

Consumer Goods	food, drink, tobacco
	consumer sundries
	clothing and footwear
	household goods (semi-durable)
	consumer durables
Producer Goods	construction materials
	supplies to primary and tertiary sectors
	investment goods

Unfinished Producer Goods

PRIMARY MANUFACTURING

food
construction
unfinished producer

It is unnecessary here to explain how industries are allocated to this classification or to discuss its advantages or disadvantages in relation to alternative schemes (see Gilmour, 1972, pp. 21–25). However, it should be noted that it deals with commodity industries defined by markets for material outputs, and not with establishment industries as is the normal case with classifications employed by geographers.

The single most important division is that between primary and secondary manufacturing. The rationale for its use lies in the fact that certain industries are so closely tied to the primary sector industries from which their raw materials are derived that they are really extensions of the primary sector and conceptually different from the rest of manufacturing industry as it is normally understood in highly industrialized countries. Furthermore, it is important to isolate a primary manufacturing category for areas in which the primary sector and related manufacturing industries have been of paramount importance in promoting economic development. The definition of primary manufacturing employed in this paper was put forward by Dales (1962 and 1963):

'Primary manufacturing industries are industries engaged in the processing of domestic natural products (including hydroelectricity as a natural product) up to the point where the output of the industry is economically transportable over long distances. A corollary of this definition is that no primary manufacturing industry processes a natural product that enters into inter-regional or international trade in any significant volume (pp. 77).'

It follows from this definition that secondary manufacturing industries are not necessarily locationally related to their material supplies.

There is a strong correspondence between the major components of this scheme and the linkage mechanisms of export-base growth, although the correlations are not perfect. The consumer goods group corresponds to the final demand linkage effects, while primary manufacturing industries are indicative of forward linkage effects. Producer goods are the product of backward linkage effects. The relationships between activities are certainly more complex and more indirect than assumed in this simple model. As any input-output table demonstrates, the impact of one activity upon another occurs both in a direct way and in many indirect ways. However, the data which would enable the researcher to trace all the linkage relationships between all activities were never collected, and we must rest content with our rather simplistic model which deals with only a few direct relationships. Simplified as it is, the classification is quite suitable for describing the structural development of the manufacturing sector.

After the inception of the growth process it is not long before some manufacturing activity is established within the region. (See Tables 2.1 and 2.2). If population, income and economic activity in general grow, there is almost certain to be growth in manufacturing and constant change in its structure. Table 2.3 provides evidence of the structural change in Southern Ontario between 1851 and 1891. It should be noted that by 1851 the region had been receiving agricultural settlers for approximately 75 years. The most noticeable feature of manufacturing at this time was the importance of consumer goods, but also significant was their decline relative to producer goods between 1851 and 1891. It is in the relationship of these two groups to one another that the basis of a general explanation of structural and distributional change is to be found, but before considering this in detail some remarks on primary manufacturing are in order.

Table 2.1. Structure of final demand in Canada in 1870–1965

	Share of output		
Year	Primary %	Secondary %	Tertiary %
1870	51	25	24
1920	29	32	39
1965	14	32	54

Source: N. H. Lithwick and Gilles Paquet, eds., *Urban Studies: A Canadian Perspective*, Toronto, Methuen, 1968. Table 2-3, p. 29. With permission.

Table 2.2. Structure of Southern Ontario's labour force 1851–1891

	Primary		Secondary		Tertiary	
Year	Employment	%	Employment	%	Employment	%
1851	87,598	57	31,121	20	35,264	23
1871	228,708	49	98,871	20	140,845	30
1891	344,791	47	158,833	22	226,603	31

Sources: Census of Upper and Lower Canada, 1851. Censuses of Canada 1871 and 1891. Data transformed by author.

Table 2.3. Structure of manufacturing employment by major groups: Southern Ontario—1851–1891

Group	1851 d%	1861 %	1871 %	1881 %	1891 %
Consumer goods	59·7	52·1	46·1	45·5	47·2
Producer goods	25·2	25·7	26·5	28·4	28·2
Primary manufacturing	15·2	22·1	27·4	25·7	24·6

Sources: Censuses of Upper and Lower Canada, 1851 and 1861. Censuses of Canada, 1871, 1881 and 1891. Data transformed by author. Source for all other tables is the same, except when another source is specified.

The relative importance of primary manufacturing within the manufacturing sector is completely random. Through time there may be a good deal of primary manufacturing, or there may be little, and there is no reason to expect a similarity in the experience of export regions as far as this type of manufacturing is concerned. The most obvious reason for this is the dependency of primary manufacturing upon the regional resource base; a factor which is distinctive to each region and which varies through time according to perception and technology. The known resource base at any time is utilized for the production of particular commodities which may or may not provide the basic input to primary manufacturing, dependent upon many factors, the most important of which are, the transportability of unprocessed materials *versus* that of processed material, transfer costs within and without the region compared to those of competing regions, extraction and processing costs, the external demand for the products of potential primary manufacturing industries, the state of production and transportation technology, the availability of funds for investment in primary manufacturing, and last but not least, the potential profitability of any activity. There is therefore, no inevitability in the appearance of export-oriented primary manufacturing industries, although it is likely that some domestically oriented ones, such as sawmills and food processing plants will appear sooner or later in all regions. The result is that the structure of the manufacturing sector, in terms of the relative strengths of secondary and primary manufacturing, need not demonstrate any discernible trend during the development process. Also, there is not likely to be any homogeneity of experience among export regions.

Within secondary manufacturing there is reason for much greater certainty about structural trends. In terms of the division between the production of consumer goods and producer goods, the same definite trend will manifest itself in all export-based regions. Initially, secondary manufacturing is very strongly dominated by the consumer goods industries, followed by a gradual

Table 2.4. Structure of secondary manufacturing employment: Southern Ontario, 1851–1891

	1851 %	1861 %	1871 %	1881 %	1891 %
Consumer goods	70·3	66·9	63·5	61·2	62·6
Producer goods	29·7	33·1	36·5	38·8	37·4
All secondary	100·0	100·0	100·0	100·0	100·0

Table 2.5. Value of output of consumer and producer goods industries as a percentage of total manufacturing output in Canada: 1870–1949

	1870 %	1880 %	1890 %	1900 %	1910 %	1949 %
Consumer goods	55·0	51·0	47·5	43·0	39·0	34·5
Producer goods	25·0	29·0	31·5	33·5	42·5	48·5

Source: J. H. Dales, Estimates of Canadian Manufacturing Output by Markets, 1870–1915, *Papers*, Canadian Political Science Association Conference on Statistics, 1962 and 1963, p. 75.

relinquishment of dominance both relatively and absolutely to producer goods industries. Should this latter group become more important, it is an indication that a mature industrial economy has been created. However, in view of all the difficulties that may beset the growth process in the export region, there is no inevitability that this state of maturity will be reached. The producer good component of many export-based regions has remained small and relatively unimportant. Tables 2.4 and 2.5 show the typical sequence of change that all regions can be expected to reveal to a greater or lesser degree.

The early dominance of consumer goods industries is a response to several related factors. In the first place, no region, except under very special circumstances, can function normally without the domestic production of certain consumer goods such as newspapers, bread and other perishable commodities. Second, export-based regions have modest origins, and for quite some time, population and regional and *per capita* incomes are likely to be low, with the consequence that effective demands will be limited to a few basic needs such as food, clothing, shelter, fuels and tools. Industrial structure will reflect these needs. Of course, the primary sector upon which the region's livelihood depends will generate a demand for at least some producer goods, but production functions in the primary sector will tend toward labour intensiveness, thus limiting the possibilities for the production of investment goods. Nevertheless the fisherman must have a boat and nets, and the farmer cannot function without some tools, however rudimentary. These backward linkage effects may promote domestic manufacturing. There is also likely to be a need for more sophisticated, larger investment goods, but the domestic attainment of thresholds for the production of complex machinery required by the primary sector and by associated manufacturing, as well as by service industries, will take longer than is the case with simple consumer goods required by all members of the population. In any case, the more complex producer goods are likely to require skills, experience, and specialized support industries which develop slowly, if at all.

The emergence of demand for unfinished producer goods takes even longer than is the case with investment goods. Unfinished producer goods are goods that are yet to be incorporated into final consumer or producer goods, so that their appearance is dependent upon the division of labour between industries that create a demand for intermediate goods. Industrialization in the export region can start only with industries that deliver to final demand. Assuming extension of their market, final demand industries may subdivide their production processes causing the creation of industries catering to intermediate demand. Unfinished producer goods industries have to wait longer for threshold attainment; an important factor in keeping down the relative importance of producer goods and supporting the supremacy of consumer goods during the early phases of development. Naturally, should the export region face obstacles to expansion, a relatively large consumer goods sector may become a long lasting condition as would appear to be the case with most 'developing' countries in the 'third world' at the present time.

2.3 Distributional Change

Up to this point discussion has been confined to aggregate change within the export-based region, with all remarks directed toward a spaceless economy. As we are often painfully aware, economies have spatial dimensions and are economically varied through space because economic phenomena are inequitably distributed and distributions change through time. Manufacturing is very striking in this regard, in general having moved from being widely distributed to being highly concentrated in space. Geographers and economists have devoted much thought and analysis to understanding location, and to a lesser extent, the distribution process, but despite the exhortations of a number of researchers, they have done little to relate the dynamics of economic growth to those of distributional change. This is surprising because economic growth produces structural change which in turn implies distributional change; there being a response to the fact that new economic elements with their own specific locational requirements are constantly being added to the economy, and the amounts and proportions of existing activities are also in a state of change.

It has already been shown that primary extraction is at first the dominant element in the export region, possibly to be gradually eclipsed by other sectors. Therefore, there is every reason to expect such a major structural change to be matched by far reaching distributional changes in economic activity as a whole. Likewise, we would expect the manufacturing sector to experience redistribution if there were a structural change that led from a consumer goods industries' to a producer goods industries' dominance. However, in recognizing this, it is easy to forget that structural change has its own spatial dimensions which impinge upon distribution.

In a longer study the writer attempted to show in detail the relationships between spatial variation in economic structure and the distribution of economic activity (Gilmour, 1972). The idea was developed that the distribution of economic activities was a function of the operation of the growth mechanisms through time and space. For most growth situations there would be no reason to expect any predictable spatial patterns to be manifested by the growth mechanisms but in this regard the export-base region is a very special case. The unique feature of growth in the export-base economy is that for some time it takes place under conditions of spatial economic expansion. It is the unavoidable consequence of settling an 'empty' region that growth is accompanied by expansion of the space economy until such time as the ultimate borders of the region are reached. Empty regions can scarcely be settled in a matter of days or months; settlement proceeds slowly, expanding outwards from a point or an area, until all economically usable areas are occupied, which means that the structure of the economy, and more specifically, of the manufacturing sector, is at various stages of advancement in different parts of the region.

If there is a spatially expressed time-lag in settlement there should be a complementary variation in time and space of all facets of growth. Viewing growth and resultant structural change as a continuum, and ignoring possible obstacles to growth that may occur in different parts of the region, we may regard the distribution of activities as controlled by the growth processes, with the stage of growth reached by any part of the region represented by its economic structure, and by the structure of its manufacturing industry. Some parts of the region for example, may be overwhelmingly primary in character, while other areas of older settlement, have enjoyed beneficial spread effects from the export sector, and seen a reduction in primary activities in favour of secondary and tertiary activities. Similarly with manufacturing industry, some areas occupied early in the settlement process will have seen producer goods reduce the importance of consumer goods, while other areas at the outer edges of the region have little manufacturing and it is mainly consumer. In brief, the spatial operation of the growth mechanisms which is a response to time, controls the distribution of activity, and this is reflected in spatial variation in structure.

Admittedly this is rather simplistic, but empirical examination of Southern Ontario shows that it nevertheless has considerable validity. Most parts of this region were settled to a greater or lesser degree between 1775 and 1851—a span of 75 years between the earliest and the latest settlement. At first, there was a lateral development of settlement along the St. Lawrence River and Lake Ontario, followed by a movement inland along a rather broad front, although this advance was characteristically spear-headed along lines of natural accessibility (Figure 2.1). Clearly, if the same patterns of growth are repeated from one part of the region to another, and there has been a progressive diminution through space in the time that the growth processes have been able to operate, one would expect the spatial variations in economic structure to correspond to the diffusion of settlement.

To test this notion, the structure of the economy and the structure of secondary manufacturing were examined in contiguous counties that were settled at progressively later dates. Figure 2.2 depicts the counties and shows two lines: A–B which runs through counties settled at the same time and line C–D which runs through counties settled at progressively later dates. These are only two out of many lines that could be drawn, but they were quite adequate to demonstrate the main findings. In Figures 2.3 and 2.4, counties have been arranged according to their position on lines A–B and C–D respectively. Shown on Figure 2.4 are the counties along line C–D extending from Wentworth to Bruce, that is from one of the first areas to be settled to one of the last areas to be settled. For each county for each decade between 1851 and 1881, the relative importance of the primary, secondary and tertiary sectors (percentage share of total labour force) were plotted on the vertical axis. These graphs clearly show the fall in the relative importance of the primary sector through time in all counties and the rising importance of the other two sectors. They also show that the relative importance of the primary sector at all times increased from the oldest to the youngest areas, and the relative importance of the secondary and tertiary sectors increased in the opposite direction, so that

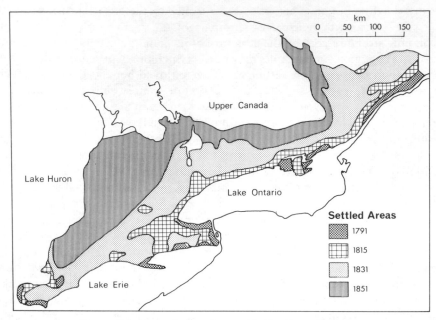

Figure 2.1. Spread of settlement in Southern Ontario

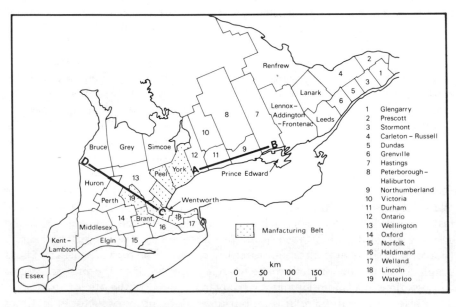

Figure 2.2. Areal subdivisions of the study area

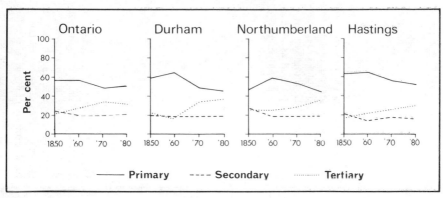

Figure 2.3. Relative importance of the primary, secondary and tertiary sectors in the areal units along line A–B (employment in each sector expressed as percentage of total employment)

the relative positions of the counties remained unchanged between 1851 and 1881. No such pattern of change through space is found in the counties settled at the same time (line A–B). The relative importance of the three sectors was approximately the same in all counties. In all of them there was a relative decline in the primary sector and a rise in the other two sectors, but clearly, no county was structurally more mature than any other. If the secondary sector is regarded as synonymous with manufacturing industry, there is strong evidence to suggest that the relative importance of manufacturing varied through space in approximate reflection of the varying time that had been available for the growth mechanisms to operate.

Structural variation within secondary manufacturing was examined in exactly the same way. (Primary manufacturing is not considered here because its locations are quite random.) It was expected that all areas would manifest a consumer goods dominance at an early stage of their development and subsequently experience a growth in the relative importance of producer goods industries. It was also anticipated that the longer an area had been settled and developed, the greater would be the importance of producer goods. As is evident from Figures 2.5 and 2.6 these expectations were only partially realized. Between 1851 and 1891 most counties experienced a relative increase in the producer goods group and a corresponding decline in the relative importance of the consumer goods industries. In short, in most of the region manufacturing was maturing. However, with values rising and falling haphazardly in each county there was not, except in 1851, a progressive decline of consumer goods from the longest settled to the most recently settled areas. In 1851 the relative importance of the consumer goods group varied spatially in a way which does not seem accidental. All the areas where consumer goods were of least relative importance were the early settled areas along Lake Ontario, while the peripheral parts of the region—the last areas to be settled and exploited—had the greatest reliance on the consumer goods group of

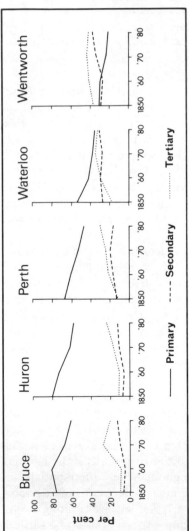

Figure 2.4. Relative importance of the primary, secondary and tertiary sectors in the areal units along line C–D (employment in each sector expressed as percentage of total employment)

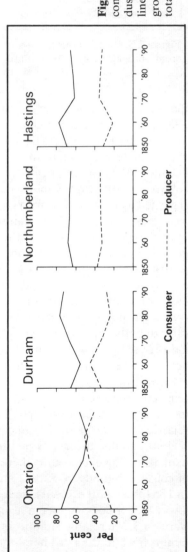

Figure 2.5. Relative importance of consumer and producer goods industries in the areal units along line A–B (employment in each group expressed as percentage of total employment in secondary manufacturing)

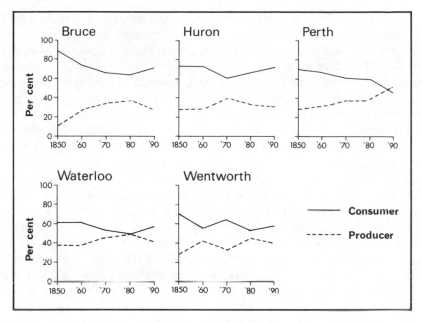

Figure 2.6. Relative importance of consumer and producer goods industries in the areal units along line C–D (employment in each group expressed as percentage of total employment in secondary manufacturing)

industries. To achieve understanding of the spatial variation in the structure of manufacturing it is necessary to take a close look at the distributional processes of secondary manufacturing industries.

Secondary manufacturing is at first dominated by consumer goods industries. During the period of their supremacy, their small production units distribute themselves widely throughout the region; more or less following in the wake of the pioneer settlements and catering to the immediate and most basic needs of the primary producers. Their wide dispersal is explained in terms of the following factors. First, during the early phases of growth, regional population and income are low, as are per capita incomes, with the result that the effective demand for manufactured goods is weak. This condition favours dispersal, for when the market is small the obstacles to spatial concentration are considerable and the advantages are slight. Low demand prevents the achievement of internal and external economies of scale. Such economies are realized at higher levels of output which exceed domestic needs. The primary character of the region is also an important factor. For the most part, extractive activities are spatially widespread, thus dispersing the population which is the market for consumer goods and causing high transfer costs on the demand side. In consequence, scale economies are inhibited and the industrial response is many small and widely distributed production units. It is also significant that it may take a long time before the export region develops an efficient transportation

74

system. This reinforces the barriers to spatial concentration stemming from the dispersal of the market. In any case, the particular characteristics of these early industries are conducive to dispersal. Some of them use nearly ubiquitous materials, like wheat, wood and clay. Many products are bulky but of low value, others are fragile and some are perishable; commodities such as furniture, beer mineral waters, bricks, tiles, planks, newspapers, and rudimentary metal products have one or more of these qualities. Some industries require close contact with their customers for they work on a made-to-order basis. Boot and shoe makers, tailors, dressmakers, printers, and founders cannot operate on a mass-production basis, and so concentrate on small-scale production supplying small, easily reached local markets.

Needless to say, perfect equality in distribution is never achieved. Affected by intra-regional variation in resource endowment, accessibility to ports and external markets, and by entrepreneurship, the potential for the development of manufacturing varies within the region. But a more important source of distributional inequality is the spatially expressed time-lag in settlement and development. Because of it early settled areas are likely to have a larger and more diversified manufacturing sector. Their population and per capita incomes are greater. Urban growth has proceeded further, the primary sector is of less relative importance, while the market is more compact. In other words, some degree of spatial concentration in manufacturing is built into the spatial economic structure of the export-based region from the very outset of its development (Figure 2.7) and the effects tend to be cumulative through time (Figure 2.8).

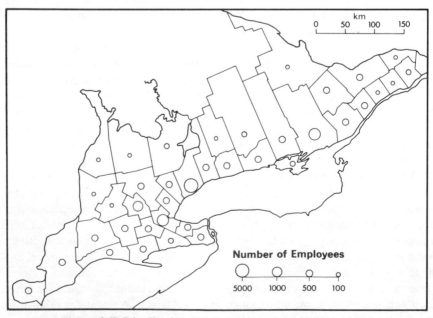

Figure 2.7. Distribution of secondary manufacturing 1851

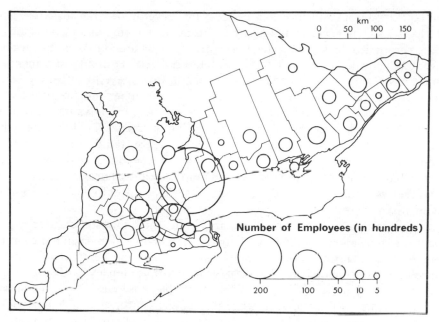

Figure 2.8. Distribution of secondary manufacturing 1891

At first, the initial advantage of early settled areas for growth in manufacturing is considerably offset by the general impediments to spatial concentration discussed above, so that although there is some concentration in the older areas, a relatively wide dispersion of secondary manufacturing (mainly consumer goods industries) is achieved. But, if the region maintains its economic momentum on the basis of its exports, population and incomes will grow, the transportation system will be improved, transfer costs will fall, the market will become more compact as the urban centres develop, and the relative importance of the primary sector will decline. All these related trends mean that in the successful export-based region the barriers to the spatial concentration of manufacturing industries are gradually lowered and sooner or later the following spatial trends will manifest themselves in the widespread consumer goods industries.

(1) Spatial contraction occurs.

(2) The number of production units relative to population decreases.

(3) The number of production sites (urban centres) at which production units are located, diminishes.

The most likely, if not entirely inevitable effect of these trends will be gradual spatial concentration of manufacturing in the areas where exploitation of the region was started.

The spatial concentration of consumer goods industries and for that matter, of any producer goods industries that become widely distributed occurs through the operation of a dilution or elimination process. The growth of the market in general and of urban centres, the lowering of transfer costs, and perhaps also, changing technology both in manufacturing and in transportation, permit firms at some production centres to achieve economies of scale and eventually to eliminate smaller firms with lower levels of output and higher per unit costs. Consumer demand in any region is always unevenly distributed due to spatial variation in population density and consumer purchasing power, therefore some production sites will turn out to be more advantageous than others for entrepreneurs desirous of increasing their sales and lowering costs through scale increases. In particular, it may be asserted that the larger the population of the centre at which a plant is located, the fewer are the difficulties in reaching economies of large scale production, because there is less likelihood that the economies related to scale increases will be offset by total transportation cost increases.

Once a size differential between plants in the same industry exists, the gap between small and large plants is likely to continue to widen, even if the larger plants have exhausted available scale economies. Beyond a certain point in the development of an industry, the cost of growth to optimum levels of production becomes too great for the smaller firms, with the consequence that the larger plants and firms will get bigger, while the smaller concerns, unable to achieve greater levels of output at lower per unit costs, will gradually go out of business or enter other lines of production. Whichever event occurs, the outcome may still be regarded as elimination.

The relationship between economies of scale and the spatial development patterns of an export-based region is quite an obvious one. Population density, the size of urban centres, and the volume and spatial intensity of demand are likely to be greater the longer an area has been settled and developed, so that obstacles to greater output levels will probably increase with distance away from the areas that were settled first. Therefore, the larger production centres and the larger producers of the first settled areas have a better chance of survival than other producers. Of course, in some industries, as for example brewing, distribution costs may restrict spatial concentration. The likelihood in such cases is that elimination will occur with production remaining dispersed as it concentrates in larger centres throughout the region.

The soap and candle making industry serves to provide exemplification of the spatial and economic trends discussed above. Both commodities were initially produced in the home by pioneer farmers. Then production gradually shifted to small workshops and finally to factories. In 1871, nearly one hundred years after Southern Ontario had received its first empire loyalist settlers, the industry was still very small, with only 154 workers in 38 widely distributed establishments. Twenty years later, in 1891, the number of establishments had fallen to 32, employment had increased to 236, and the value of output was considerably greater.

With output growth and plant elimination, the average size of production units could be expected to rise. This indeed was so. The average employment per establishment increased from 4·05 workers in 1871 to 7·4 in 1891.

However, these figures mask the substantially greater scale increases achieved by a few producers. The first 50 per cent of output by volume came from counties which had seven establishments, the average size of which was approximately seven times greater than that of the 23 establishments in the areal units producing the last 25 per cent of output. At the same time, a major localization appeared in York county, and lesser concentrations in other early settled counties. Most of the growth had occurred in York however, and other growth areas showed but slight progress in comparison. Over half the counties in which the industry was found in 1871, showed no growth at all between 1871 and 1891. The result was that three counties accounted for 75 per cent of total production in 1891.

Table 2.6. Soap and candle making: industry characteristics by output share: 1891

	Number of establish- ments	Average employment per establishment	Output: capital share
First 50% of output	7	25·4	1·22
Third 25% of output	2	13·5	1·27
Last 25% of output	23	3·7	0·66

It appears that during this period, the industry had become a factory industry, and that the few counties which had acquired factories were reducing the areas with the small workshops to insignificance. Although available data are not sufficient to conclusively prove that factories were more efficient and therefore, theoretically at least, in a position to encroach on the markets of small producers, they strongly suggest that greater size was associated with a higher return on each unit of labour and capital input. Table 2.6 shows the output: capital share ratio which was calculated as follows. Each county's shares of the total regional output by value and total capital value of the industry were calculated. When an area's share of both was the same, a ratio of unity was recorded. This was regarded as normality. A ratio of less than one indicated that a unit was getting an output less than proportional to its share of the industry's capital value, while a ratio greater than one indicated the contrary, and was taken as indicative of greater efficiency. It seems that the small factories in York and one or two other counties were making considerably better use of their resources than most other plants. They were getting an average of 85 per cent more output per unit of capital in plant and machinery, than the small workshops in other areas.

At the same time as consumer goods industries, characterized by small establishments, are moving into the outer reaches of the region and experiencing elimination in longer settled areas, major associated structural changes are likely to be occurring in the manufacturing sector of the region as a whole. These will reflect the totality of change within the region but not necessarily the change within any particular part of it.

If the region continues to grow, new industries are introduced. For example, between 1851 and 1891, Southern Ontario acquired amongst many others, factories for the production of baking powder, underwear, umbrellas, glassware, ink, mirrors, nuts and bolts, elevators, hubs, spokes, and emery wheels, all of which had previously been acquired solely from abroad. Both producer and consumer goods industries were represented. Unlike the early consumer goods industries these new industries exhibited much weaker tendencies toward spatial dispersal. The first establishments preferred the more populous, early settled zones, as also did the succeeding new establishments which were founded year after year. Part of the explanation for this is rather axiomatic; if existing industries are going through a process of spatial contraction accompanied by elimination of plants, it would appear that the conditions which favoured dispersal have been reduced in force, if not entirely obviated, so that new industries entering the region can short-circuit the dispersal-elimination process. Second, it has already been noted that the growth of manufacturing in the successful export-based region leads to a gradual increase in the absolute and relative importance of producer goods, which because of their proclivity toward spatial concentration strengthen the general forces leading to spatial concentration of manufacturing as a whole.

In view of the spatially expressed time-lag in development, the areas which are settled first have a set of initial advantages which find expression in greater economic maturity, and in a more mature manufacturing structure; characteristics which are in cause and effect relationship with such factors as a greater population, more purchasing power, lower transfer costs, etc. It is probable therefore that new industries will be attracted to these more developed areas, with their greater economic advantages and opportunites; and it is also likely that existing industries will increasingly prefer to expand in these areas. These trends indicate that the growth processes in manufacturing begin to operate in such a way as to diminish the force of the 'space-time' continuum in development. Whilst the pioneering consumer goods industries diffused through the region in the wake of agricultural settlement, producer goods industries in their drive to dominance, as well as new consumer goods industries involved in the manufacture of more sophisticated products than their early predecessors, manifest a diminishing proclivity to do the same. The role of intermediate goods production is central to this tendency.

Maturation of the structure of manufacturing is strongly related to division of labour which is influenced by the size of the market (Stigler, 1951). When the market is small and spatially widespread, domestically oriented establishments are small and widely distributed; qualities militating against division of function between establishments. Growth of the market may enable producers to relinquish the manufacture of certain articles or parts, or the performance of certain processes to other establishments which can produce at higher levels of output with lower per unit costs. It is in this way that the production of unfinished producer goods becomes established within the region and the structure of manufacturing matures. But, division of labour, particularly as

evidenced by the emergence of unfinished producer goods is as dependent
upon spatial concentration of the market, and indeed upon the concentration
of manufacturing itself, as it is sheer market size. It partially depends upon
spatial concentration for its existence then further strengthens the forces
making for spatial concentration. In the case of the export region it is the
spatially expressed time-lag in development which is responsible for creating
the initial small concentration of manufacturing (Figure 2.7) in which the
division of labour can gain a foothold.

The concentration of manufacturing in a restricted area improves on the
opportunities for the division of labour created by the growing market. It is in
the urban centres of the first settled areas with their more numerous and
experienced manufacturing industries that the opportunities for division of
labour and the economic opportunities relating to it are more likely to be first
perceived. As unfinished producer goods industries emerge from the subdivision of existing industries one expects the growth of the close inter-industrial
linkages which underlie all industrial agglomerations. Such ties require, or at
least, derive great benefit from the spatial propinquity of firms and the
concomitant facility of contact between them. The processes which create
industrial agglomerations tend to be cumulative thus causing disproportionate
growth in a few urban centres which possessed some initial advantages (Pred,
1965, 1966a, 1966b, 1966c) and widening the intra-regional disparities
created by the spatial time-lag in development. While manufacturing as a
whole concentrates in a few rapidly growing cities, unfinished producer goods
production, which partially depends on this overall concentration for its
emergence and growth, can be expected to develop an unusually high spatial
concentration in its own distributional patterns. An examination of the
allocation of manufacturing between the area which later came to be recognized as Ontario's manufacturing belt and the rest of Ontario shows this
expectation to be realized. Between 1851 and 1891 manufacturing concentrated into this band of early settled counties (Figure 2.2), showing greater

Table 2.7. Share of employment and population in the 'manufacturing belt' and the*
rest of Southern Ontario, 1851 and 1891

| | Manufacturing belt | | The rest | |
	1851 %	1891 %	1851 %	1891 %
All secondary	34·9	44·8	65·1	55·2
All consumer	33·1	42·9	66·9	57·1
All producer	38·4	47·1	61·6	52·9
Unfinished producer	36·6	51·7	63·4	48·3
Population	25·0	24·0	75·0	76·0

* An area of high absolute and relative concentration of manufacturing, containing 57·5% of all
manufacturing (measured by selling value of factory shipments) in Southern Ontario in 1961.
Calculation based on data obtained from Canada, DBS. *The Manufacturing Industries of Canada,
1961, Section G Geographical Distribution* (Ottawa: Queen's Printer, 1964).

concentration than population. In the latter year unfinished producer goods production was the only manufacturing group to have more than 50 per cent of its employment in the manufacturing belt and was the most concentrated in space of all industrial groups.

Once consumer and producer goods industries begin to enjoy the economic benefits of spatial concentration the economic disadvantages of a location beyond the borders of the larger industrial complexes tend to increase, and this will be reflected in the locational decisions of new industries and their establishments. Maturation of the structure of manufacturing becomes strongly associated with a relatively small part of the region, which acquires to itself an increasing proportion of the region's manufacturing, and in particular, as already noted, a disproportionately large share of the unfinished producer goods industries. Most of the region experiences relative decline and structural stagnation and the consumer good element acquires an above average importance.

It is the spatial concentration of manufacturing in a small area which leads to the haphazard spatial variation in the structure of manufacturing referred to earlier. Spatial concentration means that a small areal segment of a region contains a high proportion of the manufacturing while the rest and greater part of the region has a small proportion. As the number of firms and establishments becomes smaller, the greater becomes the probability that one decision or one new factory can greatly alter the structure of manufacturing. We may confidently assert that manufacturing as a whole and its major subdivisions will cluster in a small part of the region but we can never be certain about what an individual will do or where he will locate his business. The individual economic actor need not obey our abstract spatial-economic theories. He is neither perfectly rational nor completely informed about the present. His ability to predict the future is exceedingly limited and he is driven and influenced by a variety of forces amongst which the desire to maximize profits may be of little or no importance. Hence, at the same time as manufacturing as a whole displays characteristic concentrative tendencies some individual entrepreneurs will make decisions to locate or expand in areas with little or no manufacturing industry. In so doing they may alter drastically the structure of the small local manufacturing sector. On the other hand, decisions taken to locate in the growing major industrial areas are much less likely to individually alter the structure of the industrial complex. Only the sum of many decision will do that.

2.5. The Export Region in a Wider Setting

It must be emphasized that the processes described in this essay belong to the past. The likelihood of their repetition in entirety elsewhere is slim indeed. The world still has a few relatively empty regions that are quite promising in terms of economic prospects. The Brazilians, for example, eagerly anticipate the production of great wealth in their Amazonian lowlands, and are presently taking some steps to turn their dreams and national aspirations into realities.

Additionally, one should not preclude the possibility of catastrophe or long-term forces creating empty, but economically useful, regions in the future. But the patterns of development experienced by Southern Ontario are not likely to be repeated. Technology does not stand still, and neither, for that matter, does the morality of society. New forces, drives, goals and aspirations would most certainly endow the development of contemporary or future empty regions with characteristics presently unforeseeable.

Some recognition should be given to extant export-base regions; those settled late in the spatial economic expansion of Western industrial society. Some of them, so to speak, are still in the first healthy flush of export-base development. British Columbia is an excellent example of a prosperous region that largely owes its economic well-being to primary exports and the output of primary manufacturing industries. But should this and other regions be transformed into mature industrial areas, it is likely that the development processes will reflect the technological, political and economic changes which have occurred since Southern Ontario consolidated its position as an important industrial region. At the same time, however, there should be many strong parallels with the older export-based regions which made the same transformation in earlier times.

While it should be axiomatic, it is as well to point out that it is only in the totality of its development that the export-region is unique. The human responses, growth mechanisms, distributional trends, and resulting spatial economic structures echo those of regions which experienced the transition from rural-peasant to urban-industrial economies. Likewise there are many characteristics shared by the older successful export-based regions like Southern Ontario and contemporary 'Third World' countries with some dependence upon primary exports. In each case, for example, there has been to a greater or lesser degree spatial agglomeration in secondary manufacturing, and there is no doubt that the causes of it are fundamentally the same. But, the general social, economic and technical conditions, and the pre-existing spatial economic structures within which manufacturing has evolved, or is evolving, are quite different.

References

Baldwin, R. E. (1956), Patterns of Development in Newly Settled Regions, *Manchester School of Economic and Social Studies*, **24,** 161–179.

Bertram, G. W. (1963), Economic Growth in Canadian Industry 1870–1915; The Staple Model and the Take-off Hypothesis, *Canadian Journal of Economics and Political Science*, **29,** 159–184.

Caves, R. E. and Holton, R. H. (1961), *The Canadian Economy: Prospect and Retrospect*. Cambridge, Mass: Harvard University Press.

Dales, J. H. (1962 and 1963), Estimates of Canadian Manufacturing Output by Markets, 1870–1915, *Papers, Canadian Politician Science Association Conference on Statistics 1962 and 1963*.

Gilmour, J. M. (1972), *Spatial Evolution of Manufacturing*. University of Toronto, Department of Geography Research Publications. Toronto: University of Toronto Press.

Hirschman, Albert, O. (1958), *The Strategy of Economic Development*. New Haven: Yale University Press.

Innis, Harold (1930), *The Fur Trade in Canada: An Introduction to Canadian Economic History*. New Haven: Yale University Press.

Innis, Harold (1940), *The Cod Fishery: The History of an International Economy*. New Haven: Yale University Press.

Lithwick, N. H. and Paquet, G. (1968), Urban Growth and Regional Contagion, in Lithwick, N. H. and Paquet, G. (eds.), *Urban Studies: a Canadian Perspective*. Toronto: Methuen, 18–39.

Lower, A. R. M. (1936), *Settlement and the Forest Frontier of Eastern Canada*. Toronto: Macmillan.

Lower, A. R. M. (1933), *The Trade in Square Timber*. University of Toronto Studies, History and Economics, Vol. 6, Toronto: University of Toronto Press.

Lower, A. R. M. (1938), *The North American Assault on the Canadian Forest*. Toronto: Ryerson Press.

Mackintosh, W. A. (1923), Economic Factors in Canadian History, *Canadian Historical Review*, IV, 12–25.

Mackintosh, W. A. (1936), Some Aspects of a Pioneer Economy, *Canadian Journal of Economics and Political Science*, **II**, 457–463.

North, D. C. (1955), Location Theory and Regional Economic Growth, *Journal of Political Economy*, **63**, 243–258.

North, D. C. (1956), A Reply, *Journal of Political Economy*, **64**, 165–168.

Pred, Allan R. (1965), Industrialization, Initial Advantage and American Metropolitan Growth, *Geographical Review*, **55**, 158–185.

Pred, Allan R. (1966a), Manufacturing in the American Mercantile City: 1800–1840, *Annals, Association of American Geographers*, **56**, 307–338.

Pred, Allan R. (1966b), Some Locational Relationships Between Industrial Inventions, Industrial Innovations and Urban Growth, *The East Lakes Geographer*, **2**, 45–70.

Pred, Allan R. (1966c), *The Spatial Dynamics of U.S. Urban-Industrial Growth, 1890–1914: Interpretive and Theoretical Essays*. Cambridge, Mass: M.I.T. Press.

Stigler, G. T. (1951), The Division of Labour is Limited by the Extent of the Market, *Journal of Political Economy*, **59**, 185–193.

Tiebout, C. M. (1956), Exports and Regional Economic Growth, *Journal of Political Economy*, **64**, 160–164.

Watkins, M. (1963), A Staple Theory of Economic Growth, *Canadian Journal of Economics and Political Science*, **29**, 141–158.

3 Invention, Diffusion and Industrial Location

IRWIN FELLER

This essay specifies the elements of an analytical framework within which major components of technological change, i.e., invention and diffusion, can be related to the changing location of manufacturing activity. Technological change affects not only the secular growth of economies, but also the spatial distribution of economic activity. The essay seeks to highlight in a conceptually dynamic framework those aspects of inventive activity and the spatial diffusion of innovations which affect the location of manufacturing activity. The essay is frankly exploratory. It attempts to link together theories and findings on invention, diffusion, and industrial location while a search continues in each case for more adequate theories. Moreover, while it seeks to develop a generally applicable conceptual framework, the analysis rests upon observations drawn from the American experience between 1860 and 1970. During this 110-year time period, structural changes occurred in the underlying determinants of technological change. The relationship between technological change and industrial location therefore changed over time, making it necessary to specify a time period during which a particular form of the relationship held.

Technological change refers to the development of new production processes and products and to the spread of their use in the economy (Mansfield, 1968; Schmookler, 1968). For purposes of brevity, the first phase will be referred to as the inventive, or research and development (R & D) phase (Kuznets, 1962; Machlup, 1962; Nelson, Peck, Kalachek, 1967). This usage reflects both the changing institutional framework within which the bulk of inventive activity is performed, from that of the individual inventor to that of the corporate scientist or technician, and the changing data base by which inventive activity is measured, from patent statistics to R & D expenditures or employment. The second phase is that of diffusion, the adoption of the new technique or product by other firms or households. The latter usage compresses the far more elaborate taxonomical chain often used to link an invention to its later use, but is sufficient for present purposes. (For a more extensive discussion, see Rogers, 1962; Katz, Hamilton and Levin, 1963; Lynn, 1966; Feller, 1967; Brown, 1968; Mansfield, 1968a; Toulmin, 1969).

Another nuance compressed here is the specification of the regional unit. The relationship between technological change and the location of economic activity has sometimes focused on urban growth and other times on regional growth. Likewise, the data used to demonstrate such relationships have, at times, used the city as the basic unit of measurement, while at other times state or regional data are used. This difference is by-passed for most of the following analysis; reference is made to the general relationship between technological change and regional growth, and both urban-based and regionally-based data are used.

Analysis of technological change by economists has usually focused on the chain of influences shaping inventive behaviour (its timing, magnitude, industrial end-use, and factor bias), lags between invention and innovation, the process of diffusion (its time-path characteristics and the characteristics of the adopters), and the subsequent impact of the technology itself (output, employment and price effects), [Mansfield, 1968a]. Location theory has been directed at determining those factors which influence the spatial distribution of economic activity, usually between regions or between cities and their environs and, in the American case, at explaining the shifts in the location of manufacturing activity that have occurred during the twentieth century. With rare exception, neither body of literature has directly focused on the relationships between the location of inventive activity, the spatial diffusion of these inventions, and the influence that locational differences in inventive and innovative behaviour may have had on the location of manufacturing activity.

Location theory, both that written by geographers and by economists, does, of course, discuss technological change, especially as it relates to transport costs. In general, this analysis employs a partial equilibrium, comparative static framework in which technological change appears as an exogenous variable. This treatment ignores the interplay between locational variables and the site, magnitude, and characteristics of the processes of invention and innovation and the differential impact that patterns of invention and innovation may have on the location of manufacturing activities. There is also an extensive body of literature within geography on the spatial diffusion of innovations, particularly with respect to whether diffusion occurs as a contagious spread or as a filtering down process through a central hierarchy. The empirical base of this literature rests mainly upon the diffusion of collective goods, e.g. hospitals, waterworks, radio stations. (Commission on College Geography, 1964; Crain, 1966; Hägerstrand, 1967; Pyle, 1969; Walker, 1969; Pedersen, 1970). It has rarely involved technological innovations, i.e. new production processes or products, whose diffusion could be expected to be heavily dependent upon 'Information' generated by a market, namely relative prices, and which could be expected directly to influence the location of manufacturing. Thus, within geography, there is a topical (and analytical) split between theories of location and of diffusion. In part, this dichotomy mirrors the broader methodological debate on approaches to the diffusion of production techniques. One set of explanations centres around the characteristics of the technique in question, especially its 'profitability'; another centres around the characteristics of the adopters, the processes by which they acquire information about the new technique, and their interaction with one another. The literature in economics on diffusion does share some important common traits with that in geography, especially in its emphasis on the occurrence of S-shaped paths of diffusion. This literature, however, typically omits the spatial aspects of the diffusion process. A few historical case studies and Griliches' (1957) pioneer study of the diffusion of hybrid corn are exceptions. The diffusion literature in economics does at times place considerable emphasis on the interaction between adopters and potential adopters, producing, in Edwin Mansfield's (1961) analysis, a 'bandwagon' effect. No spatial contours, however, define 'knowers' and 'non-knowers'; no mechanism other than the ubiquitous 'market' is introduced to generate information.

The essay is presented in four parts: (1) an overview of the treatment of technological change in location theory; (2) a summary of recent theories and findings on the location of inventive activity; (3) a discussion of locational influences in the diffusion of technology; (4) a summary.

3.1. Technology and Location Theory

The influence of technology on the spatial distribution of a manufacturing activity is expressed in two central analytical themes in location theory and is often touched upon, if rarely formalized or tested, elsewhere in the literature. Both of the major themes relate to the cost-minimization approach in location theory. Technological change enters less discernibly into those approaches which emphasize demand or market area considerations, although as noted below, recent theories and data on the location of inventive activity do emphasize the tendencies for industrial and inventive activity to respond in a mutually reinforcing manner to demand factors.

In the first of the two central themes, i.e., the role of transport costs as a locational factor, technological changes play a major role (Hoover, 1948; Estall and Buchanan, 1967). Developments in nineteenth century technology, initially the canal network and inland steamboats and the spread of a national railroad network, reduced transport costs sufficiently to permit an interregional division of labour between agriculture and manufacturing activities in the North-east, South, and West. Within the manufacturing sector the development of a national market permitted firms to exploit the economies of scale contained within the existing technologies, thus increasing tendencies for a regional concentration of manufacturing activities. Within the West (North Central region) the development of food processing industries, the primary manufacturing activity of that region in the ante-bellum period, was enchanced by transport cost differentials per unit of value-added between raw and processed agricultural products. The development of manufacturing in the industrializing cities was then further stimulated by 'agglomeration economies', relating to the growth at those sites of labour supplies, capital markets, and other ancillary services (North, 1963; Burloch, 1965; Davis, Easterlin and Parker, 1972). The growth of population at these sites provided a further inducement to the location of those industries for which demand factors were important locational factors (Greenhut, 1956). This concentration of manufacturing activity (and of population) was also enhanced by changes in transportation, communications, and building technologies which preserved 'the centralized communications on a vastly enlarged scale' (Warner, 1963) and made the gathering of large numbers of people within concentrated geographic areas economically and physically feasible. Twentieth-century development in transportation technology, primarily the introduction of the truck and car, then reduced the cost advantage of centralized manufacturing activities and made possible the dispersion of economic activity to the suburbs.

In the second, more general approach, attention is paid to the minimization of total production costs, rather than the minimization of aggregate transport costs. The treatment of technology here parallels its treatment in most conventional microeconomic theories of the firm: an exogenously determined parameter which, if altered, shifts the relevant cost curves and thus the equilibrium position (Karaska and Bramhall, 1969). For example, standard presentations of the elements which enter into locational decisions focus, in one form or another, on the following variables: availability of raw materials, fuel and power sources, market proximity, labour costs, availability of capital, and transport arteries. Given the relevant technologies at the various stages of the production process—procurement of materials, production, distribution—firms locate at the site which total costs are minimized. Changes in technology at any state of production will alter the least costs point and presumably induce a locational shift. To cite one example of this theoretical approach: 'Changes in the cost of individual factors of production, in techniques, and in the combination of factors influence industrial location through their effect on cost structure and on the spatial/price structure' (Smith, 1966). An example of this framework in operation is the standard analysis of locational shifts in the steel industry. Technological changes in the manufacture of steel reduced the total weight of materials assembled per ton of steel. These changes in the absence of basing-point pricing systems which prevented market pressures from becoming fully operational would have made locations that were closer to final markets more important than proximity to sources of raw materials. This pull towards location near markets was heightened by the increased use of scrap steel, which is generated in existing markets, as input in production (Isard, 1948; Craig, 1957). In general, the tendency in many industries for technological change to reduce the raw material input per unit of output has reduced the necessity to locate plants near raw materials sites and is one factor in the overall pattern of industrial decentralization in the United States in the twentieth century (Rosenberg, 1972b).

Essentially the same analytical framework has been used to study other aspects of technological change. For example, one standard question is, 'What are the effects of changes in industries which are inputs to many other industries on the locational patterns of these industries? Will the introduction of atomic power, for example, cause industry to relocate?' (Isard and Whitney, 1952). Another variant of this framework is to inquire into the likely sites of industries based upon new technologies, e.g., aluminium, given their particular input mix (raw materials, power costs, labour costs, and sensitivity to transport costs) (Krutilla, 1955). Phrased somewhat differently, the growth in the relative importance of 'knowledge' as an input has led to the belief that the high-technology industries of the recent past have tended to be 'footloose'. Derived from this is the view that 'knowledge' or knowledge-generating capabilities, e.g., institutions of higher education, are now a regional resource in the same sense as transportation facilities or raw materials.

While adequate to handle many aspects of the impact of technological change on industrial location, this framework does not differentiate sharply enough between four broad types of technological change. Such a separation is necessary if one is to assess the independent importance of the diffusion process on industrial relocation. The four types of technological change are as follows:

(1) Technological change which is site specific and which enchances the competitiveness of a region's resources. This is the standard case where new technology provides a more efficient means of extracting a region's raw materials or provides a new end use for the raw material and, by so doing, changes the regional distribution of output, e.g., Frasch process for refining high sulphur crude petroleum, pelletization of taconite.

(2) Technological change, which, by reducing production costs ('process' invention) initially shifts downward the industry's supply schedule, increasing the market for the product, and thus permitting the exploitation of economies of scale. This expansion in output and increase in minimum efficient scale of plant will lead to an initial redistribution of output among firms in an industry and, based upon this initial effect, a redistribution of the geographical distribution of output.

(3) Technological change which provides the basis for a new, 'footloose' industry ('product' invention).

(4) Technological change which is equally applicable to all firms within a regionally dispersed industry, where the subsequent location of that industry's output will depend upon the rate of adoption of the new technology by firms within each region.

These changes are not mutually exclusive. Any and all of them can concurrently affect a given industry either directly through technological change within that industry or through technological change in another industry which provides a close substitute to that industry, and thereby its regional distribution of output. In the steel industry, for example, development of improved means for pelletizing taconite not only led to a renewed expansion in the Mesabi range, as in (1), but also enchanced the competitive position of those steel-producing regions dependent upon ore from that region. The development of a plastics industry introduced a substitute product for steel. The newer industry was less tied to raw materials or characterized by appreciable returns to scale in production. Competition between products in such a case produces a changing locational pattern of output in the 'materials' industry and, in general, leads to a relatively slower growth (or possible absolute decline) of output in those regions dependent on steel production. The introduction of the basic oxygen furnace, given its different input requirements from earlier technologies, is now also held likely to produce a regional shift in the distribution of output to the southern and western producing regions (Nelson, 1971).

It should be noted that accounting for the possible means by which technological change can affect the location of manufacturing activity does not provide evidence on the historical importance of technological change as a factor in such locational changes. The above analysis has treated technological change primarily in terms of its effect on the cost schedule. Changes in industrial location have been caused by shifts in market areas as well as by changes in least-cost sites. Moreover, even when focusing only on least-cost considerations, it is still necessary to differentiate (and estimate) the relative importance of shifts in cost schedules attributable to new input requirements from regional differences in input costs, given initial input mixes. For example, how much of the now predicted regional shift in steel production is attributable to changes in technology (input mix requirements) and how much to the growth of population and output in the southern and western regions? Or, what was the role of technological change relative to differentials in labour costs, climate, or availability of raw materials in the relocation of those industries (aircraft, textiles, apparel, and chemicals) which experienced the greatest relocation, in terms of number of jobs involved, between 1929–1954? (Cunningham, 1951; Fuchs, 1962; Creamer, 1969).

These questions point out that the limited conceptual framework for treating technological change in location theory still exceeds the attention paid to it in empirical tests of the determinants of the changing location of manufacturing activity. The empirical work on this relationship has tended to focus on (1) the 'production' of technological change, e.g., inventive activity, as measured by patent statistics, for the late nineteenth century; and (2) research and development activities, as measured by expenditures or employment, in the post-World War II period, with little work done at all on the intervening years. Econometric models of state production functions can be formulated to include a technological change parameter. (Hildebrand and Liu, 1965; Leven, Legler and Shapiro, 1970). In addition, Wesley Long has recently developed a model for estimating the relationship between Research and Development (R & D) expenditures and the growth of output per worker, presumably one of the influences upon the location of manufacturing (Feller, Long and Nelson, 1972). Long's model, moreover, provides for the diffusion of R & D across states. The fact remains that although we are concerned with the interrelationships between invention, diffusion, and industrial location, it is easier to conceptualize and demonstrate locational influences on invention and diffusion than it is to demonstrate empirically the influence of all types of technological change on industrial location.

3.2. The Location of Inventive Activity

Three aspects of the location of inventive activity are intertwined with the location of economic activity. First, is there a tendency for inventive activity to be located in regions (or cities) undergoing processes of industrialization? Second, is there any relationship between the 'type' or composition of inventive activity occurring in a region and the composition of economic activity in that region? Third, is there any relationship between inventive activity in a region and the subsequent growth of that region?

(1) Early interest by geographers in the location of inventive activity centred around demonstrations that spatial patterns of concentration did, in fact, exist (Jefferson, 1929; Gilfillan, 1930). Such patterns were initially interpreted as inherent or culturally determined differences in creative abilities of the relevant populations. The existence of such a pattern was also used as part of Edward Ullman's argument that existing regional patterns of industrial concentration would be perpetuated because of a tendency for invention and innovation, generators of subsequent industrial growth, to be concentrated in the already 'industrialized' regions (Ullman, 1958). More recently, Allan Pred has postulated a more formal model for the spatial concentration of inventive activity, providing both a series of explanations for this clustering pattern and hypotheses concerning the dynamic implications of the pattern for subsequent growth. Pred's (1966) analysis applies to the interaction between urbanization and inventive activity in the United States between 1860–1910. His basic hypothesis is that:

'Inventive activity is, to a considerable degree, a function of unique supply-and-demand conditions that prevail in the cities of an industrializing economy such as that of the United States between 1860 and the early twentieth century. More precisely, many technological advances in the late nineteenth century were reliant upon a demand for inventions. This demand was most likely to occur in the burgeoning cities where manufacturing was agglomerating, where there already was an adequate supply of both potential inventors (including skilled labourers) and investment capital.' (p. 90).

Pred stresses two additional points. First, inventive activity is often undertaken to resolve specific technical problems experienced in producing a good. These '... advances in production technology usually occur as a response to particular problems that in themselves are most apt to arise in existing centres of industrial concentration' (Pred, 1966, p. 91). Second, inventive activity often involves 'technological convergence', (Rosenberg, 1963) the solution of technical problems common to many industries or the extension of a technical solution found for one industry to other industries which share a common technology:

'... if technological convergence is dependent upon the potential inventor's exposure to solutions to related problems outside his own industry, or more accurately, to multiple exposure to such solutions, ... then in a pre-mass-communications context, such as the relatively compact cities of the later nineteenth century, where diffusion of technical knowledge is highly reliant on personal interaction, the possibilities ought to be enchanced by the growing network of interpersonal communications and confrontations.' (Pred, 1966, p. 96).

Pred's hypothesis concerning the urban concentration of late nineteenth-century inventive activity has been supported, in the main, by subsequent empirical work. Irwin Feller's data for the thirty-five largest and/or most industrialized cities for census years between 1860–1910 indicate that the percentage share of patents received by residents of these cities always exceeded their relative share of the population, although there was a tendency for this pattern of concentration to decline over the period (Feller, 1971). On a state basis, Robert Higgs (1971) has shown that for the period 1870–1920 the number of patents received by residents of a state was significantly related to that state's degree of urbanization.

Although the pattern of concentration is agreed upon, the basis for it is not. Pred, in addition to the factors noted above, contended that it was not only the population size of cities that led them to have more inventions than non-urban areas but also the magnitude and relative importance of manufacturing in the urban economy. Feller's work also indicated a significant relationship between inventive activity in a city and the size of its population or manufacturing labour force. Since population and the size of a city's manufacturing labour force are highly correlated, a separate variable must be introduced to gauge the independent influence of the relative importance of manufacturing activity in a city on the level in inventive activity. When adjustments of this type are made (e.g. manufacturing employment/population as a dependent variable), no significant relationship is found.

Finally, Pred's set of demand factors in accounting for the spatial concentration of inventive activity, can be extended. In another study, for example, it has been shown by using a more detailed, if still highly aggregate picture of the content of late nineteenth-century patents, that

' ... the observed association between inventive activity and urbanization, and between population size and inventive activity, occurred because the process of urbanization generated a new set of demands which were themselves a response to the new conditions of urban life. Technology played a role in generating the conditions which fostered the concentrations of population, but once this process began, the new patterns of life in urban settings demanded adjustments in daily living patterns which could be overcome through technological change. The very same pattern of perceived economic opportunity—the profitability of inventive activity along specific lines—which has been held to have influenced the determination of inventive activity for inventions in producer durables inventions existed for consumer oriented inventive activity.' (Feller, 1973, p. 56).

(2) The existence of a link between the composition of inventive activity and the composition of manufacturing activity within a region or city has both historical and quantitative support, although, again, the extent and the basis for this relationship are still unresolved. The simplest locational influence can clearly be seen in efforts to utilize a region's raw materials (Perloff, Dunn, Lampard and Muth, 1960). The petroleum industry, for example, offers two classic examples of this pattern: the Frasch process, which removed sulphur from crude petroleum, and thus enchanced the utility of the Ohio–Indiana oil

fields; and the Dubbs process, which began as an effort to remove salt water from California crude. (Williamson and Daum, 1959; Enos, 1962). The tie between locational influences and inventive activity, even when directed at raw material utilization, may, however, be even more complex than suggested by these examples. The Burton process, developed in 1913, for example, is considered to be the first commercially successful process for cracking heavy petroleum fractions. By the first decade of the twentieth century petroleum refiners in the Midwest were already finding it necessary to import crude oil from distant fields, since crude output from the initial Appalachian and Ohio–Indiana fields did not grow as rapidly as the demand for petroleum products. Unlike the industry as a whole, which could attempt to meet this demand by discovering new fields, Midwestern refiners focused on reducing their crude oil requirements. 'The only way to do this without cutting into their sales of the profitable light products, such as kerosene, gasoline, and solvents was to increase the yield of those products from each barrel of crude oil' (Enos, 1962, p. 3). Burton's experiments between 1909–1912 were only partially successful. At the critical point of moving to the demonstration phase of the process, Burton's request to his employer, Standard Oil of New Jersey, for $1,000,000 was rejected. Following this decision, however, came the Supreme Court decision compelling the dissolution of Standard Oil, and Burton then became a director of the newly formed Standard Oil Company of Indiana:

'Whereas in New York the risk had seemed to outweigh the possible gain, in Chicago the balance was in the opposite direction. After the divorcement Indiana Standard was left with adequate refining and marketing facilities but was dependent upon outside suppliers for its crude oil. Without a sure source of its chief raw material, the company was eager to reduce the amount of crude oil that it had to purchase in order to meet its rising sales commitments. By requiring less crude oil per gallon of gasoline, the Burton process would make this reduction possible.' (Enos, 1962, p. 22).

The process was an immediate success and was soon being licensed to petroleum refiners across the country.

These examples drawn from the history of the processes used in the petroleum industry clearly indicate the conceptual difficulties encountered in subsequent parts of this analysis, namely whether there is any relationship between inventive activity in a region and the subsequent locational pattern of output in the industry. Although designed for technical or economic problems peculiar to firms within a given region, the solutions to these problems were of general applicability throughout the industry. Abstracting from any locational influence of patent licensing policies (which probably have greater influence on the profitability of the holder of the basic patent than on the regional distribution of output), the new technologies represented shifts in the cost schedules of the entire industry.

It is considerably more difficult to determine locational influences on the composition by region of industrial inventions. The existence of such a relationship has, indeed, been often asserted. As noted by Wilbur Thompson (1962):

'. . . new products and techniques are largely spawned by persons who work for or are otherwise closely associated with the industry most closely linked with the particular idea or device. To the extent that this is so, a substantial, persistent, and even cumulative advantage would accrue to any region which gained a head start in a particular industry; perhaps technological differentials tend to widen—the rich grow richer.' (p. 260). From Thompson, Locational Differences in Inventive Activity and their Determinants, in *The Rate and Direction of Inventive Activity* (ed. Richard R. Nelson), Princeton University Press. Copyright © 1962 by National Bureau of Economic Research.

Pred's model of urban growth also rests heavily on the stimulus of industrialization within a city to further inventive and innovative behaviour, and in turn, the expansionary effects of these activities upon the future growth of that city.

Limited evidence suggests that the first part of the relationship (i.e., the composition of inventive activity within a city is related to the composition of manufacturing activity in that city) does exist. In a study by Feller, a sample of patents received by the residents of the thirty-five most populous and industrialized cities in 1910 was organized into groupings that correspond, albeit somewhat arbitrarily, with industrial groupings derived from the Census of Manufactures [Feller, 1973]. Thirty-seven composite patent-industry groupings which contained just over half the total number of patents issued in the thirty-five cities were employed in a regression model where the number of patents in the ith industry grouping in the jth city was expressed as a function of manufacturing employment value-added per employee and the rate of growth of output between 1900–1910. The employment variable was significant in twenty-one of the thirty-seven industry groupings, with these groupings accounting for 82 per cent of the patents in the sample. The other two variables were significant in a limited number of cases but referred to different industries.

Thompson's earlier results also give general if not unqualified support to this relationship. His tests are based upon the composition of inventions and employment and population variables in standard metropolitan areas in 1947 for eight broad industrial groupings. Thompson found, for example, a higher correlation between patents received in an SMSA for internal-combustion engines and employment in transportation equipment than for either total manufacturing or for total population. In other industry groupings, however, correlation coefficients were as high or higher between patents and total employment or total population as they were between patents and employment in the related industry.

As noted, the results for 1910 likewise showed the existence of a relationship for some industries but not for all. Some plausible explanations have been advanced for the dissimilar industry pattern. Skill levels may be more specialized in some industries than in others. In some industries technological change may occur primarily in the plants or homes of the users rather than through the equipment producers. The match-ups between patent classes and industrial groupings may be biased in an unknown direction. Unfortunately, little detailed work has yet been done on the accuracy or importance of these issues as a complement to the strictly quantitative work.

The finding that inventive activity within a city tended to be related to employment in that city must also be incorporated into the more general framework of 'demand-pull' influences upon the direction of inventive activity. Here one must distinguish between the influence of employment as, in Nathan Rosenberg's (1969) framework, a 'focusing' device which provides information and expertise concerning technical bottlenecks in production and the profitability of allocating inventive effort to a particular industry. Patents can be viewed as a normal distribution of technical advances, ranging . . . from those which are marginal improvements in existing techniques, to those which are major, in some technical or economic sense' (Feller, 1973, p. 56). On a cross-sectional basis there may be a strong relationship between employment and inventions in a city or region. This finding, however, is of limited value in the formulation of dynamic theories of industrial or regional growth unless one has independent information on the 'average' importance of inventions in each city. Some threshold level of manufacturing activity in a city is probably necessary to induce some inventive activity toward that particular industry. Also, it is possible that cities with a substantial share of an industry's output are more likely to be the site of major inventions in that industry simply because they have more total inventions in that industry. Beyond these reasons, however, evidence does not exist, either in the form of the quantitative evidence cited above or in historical case studies, to adequately assess the proposition that:

'. . . invention in each line centres in a few regions which most abundantly produce that line, these being responsible for about all the progress in it, and the rest looking to the *fountain lands*, and rarely doing more than borrowing and adapting their inventions to local needs.' (Gilfillan, 1935, p. 8).

3.3. Locational Influences on the Diffusion of Innovations

Given that the location and composition of late nineteenth-century inventive activity were heavily influenced by the process of urbanization, what effects did the spatial distribution of inventive activity have on the subsequent industrial growth of these cities? This, of course, is a critical link in the technological change-industrial location process: do locational differences in inventive activity lead to similar locational differences in economic activity? Here, unfortunately, is where the major deficiencies exist in data, consistency of hypothesis with existing tests, and recognition within hypotheses of the historical and institutional complexities of the invention-innovation progression.

Patents are a defensible, if imperfect, measure of inventive activity. They are a poor measure of the impact or location of technological change. Economic impact occurs (1) when an invention is used, not when it is patented, and (2) where the invention is manufactured and marketed, not where it is conceived.

Inventors, like prophets, may be without honour, markets, or capital in their home regions. Thus, in 1846, Cyrus McCormick found it necessary to move production from his family farm in Virginia to Chicago before he found a region where the scale and cost conditions of agricultural activity made adoption of the reaper economically attractive (David, 1966). Eugene Houdry, a French national and inventor of a basic petroleum catalytic cracking process in 1936, experienced a cutoff of the funds, both governmental and private, which had supported his research in France during the 1920's and thus moved to America where he continued his research with corporate support (Enos, 1962).

Obviously, then, we are in the realm of the spatial diffusion of inventions. But again, there is very little in either the economic or geographic literature on the spatial diffusion of production techniques, and what little there is does not always provide information which can be related to changes in the location of economic activity. Griliches' study of hybrid corn, which remains one of the only spatially oriented diffusion studies in economics, is a case in point. Griliches' paper analyses cross-sectional differences (by state) of the date, rate, and level of adoption of the new seed (Griliches, 1957). The diffusion path within each state was expressed as a logistic function. Differences among states in the rate of adoption, the slope of the logistic curve, were attributed '. . . at least in part to differences in the profitability of the changeover from open pollinated to hybrid seed' (Griliches, 1957, p. 516). Griliches' findings generated considerable controversy, primarily among rural sociologists, who, espousing a diffusion tradition similar to that of geographers, argued that the primary determinants of the patterns of adoption were the characteristics of the adopters and the degree of interaction between adopters and non-adopters ('Tellings') (Brandner and Strauss, 1961; Griliches, 1960, 1962).

For present purposes, much of this type of debate is irrelevant. Regardless of the credence given to any of the alternative explanations, the fact remains that such a study by itself does not provide information which relates to the location of economic activity. What would be required in this specific example is how the initial technology and geographic pattern of diffusion led, over time, to changes in the location of corn cultivation. Some such redistribution is implicit in Griliches' analysis, since the earlier date of availability of hybrid corn in some states and the more rapid diffusion of the seed in these states are attributed to locational differences in profitability. It follows that farms in those regions should have experienced an increase in output, shifting the industry supply curve to the right, lowering market prices, forcing marginal producers out of the industry, and thus altering the regional distribution of cultivation.

The locational aspects of the diffusion process, moreover, are even more complex than suggested by either the historical or econometric examples cited above. Explanations in terms of entrepreneurial or labour receptivity to new techniques are not uncommon elements in almost all accounts of regional (or national) differences in acceptance of new ideas. Such differences are undoubtedly present and important to some extent in most cases, but explanations which are cast in these terms implicitly assume some 'norm' for pace of diffusion. Differences in rates of adoption of new techniques by firms and thus be region may be consistent with rational, profit-maximizing behaviour, particularly if allowance is made for regional differences in capital vintages, product mixes, and complementary technologies. A microeconomic approach to diffusion is not only necessary corrective to the above 'entrepreneurial' explanation of diffusion, but it also redresses two of the limitations contained within the econometric studies. First, in most of these studies adoption is measured in terms of either the first use of a technique by a firm or the date on which the technique accounts for a specified minimum amount of capacity. Analysis of the relationship between diffusion and the location of manufacturing activity would seem to require measurement of diffusion in terms of the percentage of total output produced by the new technique (Mansfield, 1968a; Gold, Pierce and Rosegger, 1970). Second, although the primary explanatory variable in most econometric studies is profitability (i.e., the larger the profitability, the more rapid the pace of diffusion for a new technique), the measure of profitability is an approximate one. Thus the '. . . average pay-out period required by the firms (during the relevant period) to justify investments divided by the average pay-out period for the innovation . . .' (Mansfield, 1968b, p. 143) does not indicate the full range of decisions a firm must make when confronted with technological change. This more micro-oriented approach to regional influences on the diffusion process is divided into three headings—(1) Microeconomic and Technical Aspects of Diffusion; (2) Qualitative Aspects; (3) Industry Structure.

Microeconomic and Technical Aspects of Diffusion

This interplay between the technical properties of an innovation, the microeconomic aspects of its adoption, and regional shifts in manufacturing activity involves several considerations (Feller, 1960; Rosenberg, 1972a). In assessing locational influences on the diffusion of innovations, any or all of the following microeconomic and technical factors may come into play. These influences are best perceived in terms of a competitive, multi-region industry.

Replacement Criteria. Firms in all regions may have installed capacity of an earlier type, albeit of different vintages. The appearance of a new technique does not automatically warrant the scrapping of existing equipment. Put differently, in W. E. G. Salter's (1969) phrase, a 'delay in the use of new techniques' may be consistent with profit-maximizing behaviour. At the microeconomic level, the adoption of a new technique depends upon whether its costs of production are below the average variable costs of production of installed pieces of equipment and below average costs of production with new units of the earlier, rival technique. Costs with the new technique may be above the former but below the latter. In such a case, firms with existing equipment would not have an incentive to scrap this equipment and replace it with the new technique, but they would purchase the new technique if they were adding to capacity. If for any of a number of reasons, e.g., lower wage costs, the industry is expanding rapidly in one region, firms in that region, assuming they are producing near capacity, will now purchase the new technique. Thus, expanding regions will have more up-to-date equipment than less rapidly growing regions. Their technical modernity (based upon a higher rate of adaption), however, is attributable to their higher growth rate, rather than its prime cause. As more firms in the industry adopt the new technique, putting downward pressure on price, and as maintenance costs with existing equipment rise, firms have an incentive to replace existing equipment with the new technique. Regional differences in adoption may thus reflect exogenously determined growth rate differentials, the initial distribution of capital goods within the regions, and the relative superiority of the new technique over installed techniques. Continued production with "obsolete" techniques may for a while still be consistent with profit-maximizing behaviour on the part of all firms within regions.

Technical Complementarities. For the new technique to be used efficiently, modifications in other aspects of the production process to the process of diffusion in general (Frankel, 1955). The importance of interconnections is that they raise the level of investment required to adopt the new technique and that they change the profitability question from (1) is adopting technique A profitable? (in lieu of purchasing B or of replacing existing units of B), to (2) is the technological system containing A profitable? (in lieu of purchasing B or of replacing B and its complementary components). Further, institutional problems can arise when the adoption decision involves a technological system rather than a single piece of equipment. If the complements necessary for profitable operation of a new technique are traditionally provided by other firms or industries, then the firm considering a new technology must also convince these other firms (who may be either suppliers or customers) to make the necessary investments (Kindleberger, 1964). What we are concerned with here is that there may be regional differences in the prevalence of non-compatible technologies, which, in turn, affect the regional diffusion of the innovation in question.

Output Mix Changes. The new technique may not be suited to the (changing) output mix of the industry in a region. Here we are interested in the regional phasing of two dynamic processes. Within a multi-product industry, the composition of output in different regions may be changing in accord with least-cost and demand considerations. Production techniques can fulfil a number of functions, that is, generate a stream of services or commodities, each of which competes with existing techniques. The steam vessel, for example, when it first became technically capable of trans-Atlantic crossings, quickly supplanted sailing vessels as a carrier of freight. Technological change is, in many ways, a process of 'functional displacement', during which a new technique is systematically improved so that it becomes an increasingly more attractive alternative to a process already in use. Again, this is a process which occurs over time, with the new technique being improved upon either in terms of its technical capabilities (reliability, speed, end-use) or economic capabilities. A new technique may appear which, at the time of its introduction, can be used on those products which, even if all firms in the industry were equipped with identical equipment, can competitively be produced in some, but not all, regions. As the technique is improved upon to handle a wider range of output, it may then become an attractive investment by firms in a region which had refrained from purchasing it until that date.

Short-run Maximization with Long-run Decline. A slow rate of adoption may reflect, rather then cause, economic decline. Simply put, regional differences in factory costs, proximity to markets, etc., may be so substantial that even if firms in all regions were equipped with identical technologies, some regions would not be competitive. Firms in such regions, recognizing their basic lack of competitiveness, may continue in operation, exacting whatever quasi-rents exist with installed capacity, and then leave the industry. They will be considered technological laggards, but this fact, rather than denoting entrepreneurial conservatism, represents a rational response to an adverse situation.

Learning Experiences. Technologies tend to go through a shake-down process. This is the period of greatest uncertainty concerning the technical and economic performance of the new technique (Feller, 1960). It is the reduction in uncertainty following use by the risk-taking early users that is held to produce the band-wagon effect noted in econometric studies of diffusion (Mansfield, 1961). This effect is usually put in the context of an eventually successful innovation. Early users, however, may be disappointed as they encounter unexpected performance problems with the new technique or as it fails to produce the cost-savings promised for it. Again, fortuitous regional differences may occur here. Early adopters may be located in one region, possibly near the site of the firm responsible for the new technique. Information concerning their unfavourable experience with the new technique may be rapidly diffused throughout the industry in the region, thus operating as a subsequent barrier to its diffusion. Firms in other regions may adopt the technique somewhat later and with more favourable results. Acceptance by other firms in that region will be faster than in the other region because there is no regional legacy of an adverse experience with the new technique.

Qualitative Aspects of Regional Influences on Diffusion

The above set of factors has been derived by asking, 'What are the possible regional aspects of technical and economic variables which are held to influence the diffusion of innovations?' Beyond this set there exists another group of more qualitative variables which have been used to account for differences in regional economic activity, although they apply only indirectly to the diffusion of innovation. Among these variables are market structure, entrepreneurship, capital markets, and labour supply.

Market Structure and Entrepreneurship. The relationship between technological market structure and regional growth takes at least two forms. In the simplest case, if a firm dominates the economic activity of a region and, either because of its size relative to other firms in the industry or because of the competitive structure of that industry, is relatively fast or slow in adopting a (major) new technique, that region will grow relatively rapidly or slowly as a result of the firm size/market structure influence on diffusion. The more complex case, which ties market structure to entrepreneurship, rests on Chinitz's hypothesis that competitive industries produce more entrepreneurs per dollar of output than do oligopolistic industries. Entrepreneurship is interpreted in this argument in terms of 'risk-taking', it follows that regions containing firms that belong to 'competitive' industries will tend to produce more inventions or will experience a faster rate of adoption of new technologies (both those employed within existing industries and those which serve as the basis for new industries) than regions where firms belong to less competitive industries (Chinitz, 1961, Thompson, 1965). There are obvious difficulties in testing this hypothesis, among them being measures of entrepreneurship and the competitiveness of industry mix within a region (Booms, 1973).

Capital. The diffusion process entails both a supply and demand side. The firm seeking to market the new technique must have access to capital in order to initiate production. It must also find a market for its products. Its locational decision, beyond the standard set of variables, may depend upon regional differences in access to capital and in the willingness of firms within that region which are part of a multi-regional industry to adopt the new technique. The supply of 'high-risk' capital in a region also appears to be related to the characteristics of entrepreneurship of the dominant firms within that region. Her again, we are dealing with a variant of Chinitz's hypothesis:

> 'Are banks in one area more receptive than banks in another area to the demand of new business and, if so, are these differences in attitude shaped by the industrial traditions of the area? I say yes, on both counts. ... When banks cater to a competitively organized industry, they are more likely to accept the insurance principal of making money, not on each customer, but on the average customer. If you have U.S. Steel and Westinghouse on your rolls, you do not have to learn to make money on the insurance principle.' (Chinitz, 1961, p. 286, Technological Innovation, 1967).

There is also some limited empirical evidence to suggest that access to capital is an important factor in the location of new technologically-based industries. A study by the Federal Reserve Bank of Philadelphia in 1966, for example, suggested that Boston banks were far more willing to lend to small, science-based firms than were Philadelphia banks (Deuterman, 1966).

Labour Supply. The 'quality' of a region's labour supply has often been recognized as a variable affecting the location of manufacturing activity. Attention to this fact of the regional labour force has been given added stimulus by (1) the tendency in recent empirical studies of the long-term 'sources' of economic growth to parcel out that portion attributable to 'investment in human resources', and (2) the market concentration of post World War II federal research and development expenditures in areas richly endowed in education facilities and scientific manpower. The focus here is somewhat more specific. What influence does the skill level of a region's labour force have on the regional diffusion of technology? To what extent can these differences be attributed to the regional differences in entrepreneurship noted above?

Two somewhat different hypotheses have been advanced on these questions. The most direct one is Hoover's (1948) contention that the locational histories of individual industries 'typically' involve an:

'. . . early stage of increasing concentration followed by a later stage of redispersion. This sequence can be explained largely on the basis of the supply of labour and management personnel. When an industry is young and its problems unfamiliar, it prospers best in those few places which provide the combination of appropriate basic skills [often developed in preexistent technologically 'similar' industries], together with experienced managers and some venturesome enterprisers and financial backers. . . .. When the technical uncertainties of production and the commercial uncertainties of market development are reduced to a point where other locations may successfully cope with them, independent outside competition may arise.' (pp. 173–174).

Aspects of Hoover's hypothesis seem valid—particularly the importance of the transferability of skills from one industry to another. In general, however, the hypothesis begs the questions of what specific skills are needed for an emerging industry or innovation and of why particular regions were endowed with a critical skill, if one is the fact needed. Put differently, the relevant question, beyond the existence of formal education systems, concerns the extent to which the spread of manufacturing and of particular technologies has developed regional differences in skill levels necessary to adopt subsequent technologies. Indeed, one aspect of technological innovation then becomes the spread of general technical knowledge. Albert Fishlow (1965) for example, in his analysis of the backward linkages of the effects of the development of the American railroad network in the ante-bellum period has argued that the contribution of locomotive construction to subsequent industrialization was not, as has often been held, its stimulus to the evolution of specialized machine shops, but '. . . the development of elaborate repair facilities on the railroads themselves. Here *was* a powerful force for the geographic dissemination of skills necessary to an industrial society.' (Fishlow, 1965, pp. 154–155). Fishlow contrasts this geographic dissemination with that of the steamboat, cotton and textile industries. Although the first employed more horsepower, and the latter had a higher total output (1896) than the railroad industry, neither served to diffuse skill levels as did the railroad industry.

It can, of course, be argued that changes in knowledge based (generally away from mechanical and toward electrical and chemical) upon which technologies have been derived support Hoover's hypothesis; technologies have become more particularistic and the skill levels needed to use or modify them have become more occupationally and regionally concentrated. Recalling, however, that the hypothesis relates to manufacturing activities, not to the R & D segment of the innovation process, there still remains serious doubt as to its validity—in part because it is couched in terms of technology without any tie to the particular skill requirements of new techniques or to data on the regional distribution of these particular skills. The industry and city that Hoover cites—automobiles and Detroit at the timing of the shift in production to that site—are not examples of an industry requiring unique skills possessed to a rare degree only be workmen in that area.

A second approach to the role of the labour force in the diffusion of technology is suggested by Thompson's use of the concepts of 'challenge and response' in a regional context. Economic growth, in many respects, is a process not simply of increases in factor supplies or factor augmentation through technological change, but of resource reallocation. A region can achieve sustained economic development only if it continually adjusts to changes in market demand, resource availability, and technology. Output in many industries does describe, over time, a logistic function, although the reasons for this time-path are in dispute. This reallocation requirement applies to all inputs. For the labour input, it requires a general level of literacy and technical training that permits workers to shift from industry to industry, and therefore from technology to technology.

The extent and basis of this adaptability within a given region's labour force and the significance of this potential pool of manpower on the locational decisions of firms producing new techniques, with their attendant new 'skill' requirements, all fall within the category of variables which are often referred to but upon which little historical or empirical work has been done. Certain historical regional transformations do seem to reflect the importance of the presence or absence of this adjustment quality of the labour force. The development of the electronics industry in New England not only took up the slack left by the migration of the textile and shoe industries but, granted the presence of M.I.T., also rested upon the availability of a labour pool which met the skill levels of the emerging industry (Estall, 1963). Indeed, one of the more interesting questions here is how the historical course of industrialization in particular regions has led to the accumulation of the skills needed for succeeding 'growth' industries.

A somewhat contrary example of the adaptability of a region's labour force can be derived from the continuing debate over the effects of slavery on the economic development of the South. Both in terms of microeconomic criteria (rate of return on investment) and regional growth rates, slavery in the ante-bellum period was profitable and consistent with economic growth. Abstracting from the devastation of the Civil War, it appears, however, that the post-1865 South could not have continued to grow through extension of cotton cultivation because, given the introduction of new sources of supply and the elasticity of demand for cotton, total revenue to the region from that crop was approaching a maximum. Continued growth required a redirection of resources. A legacy of meagre social investment in human resources, however, greatly restricted the range of industries in which the available labour force could be employed (Fischbaum and Rubin, 1968).

More generally, it appears that the coupling of economic and political power in a dominant single industry or firm in a region may produce a level or pattern of public investment in the labour force which may be efficient in the short-run for that industry (and region), but which, over time, limits the ability of that region to compete for new technologies (and industries). This, clearly, is the labour force variant of the access to capital argument noted above, both of which are dependent in turn on the competitive structure of the industries in a region and the degree of innovativeness and risk-taking of the entrepreneurs associated with these firms. The analysis of regional aspects of the diffusion of innovations has also clearly moved from a largely microscopic focus on cost schedules and technical properties of new techniques to more macroscopic considerations of the political and cultural influences of competitive and non-competitive industries within and among regions.

Industry Structure and Diffusion

Technologies, however, are diffused not only through space, but through industrial structures as well. The econometric literature on innovations has largely focused on testing relationships between firm size and market structure and the rate and magnitude of the diffusion process.

No conceptual or methodological integration exists between economics and geography on how the spatial and industrial structure aspects of the diffusion process are related to one another and how these components of the diffusion process, in combination, affect the location of manufacturing activity.

Studies of the diffusion of production techniques have inquired into industry or firm variables, not locational variables. What little evidence exists on the spatial-industry aspect of the diffusion process suggests that innovative behaviour in a city may differ between the industries in that city and that within an industry the behaviour of firms may differ between innovations. Philadelphia, for example, in the 1850's was the site of an emerging machine-tool and locomotive industry whose plants were held to be among the most technologically advanced of that era. The city's longer-standing cotton textile industry, however, was becoming technologically obsolete as firms lagged behind other regions in the adoption of a series of innovations (Warner, 1963).

For the twentieth century, no discernible leader follower, early-late pattern of adoption by firms has been found in four industries for which econometric diffusion studies of a number of innovations have been performed (Mansfield, 1968b). A finding, therefore, that firms within a particular region were fast or slow in adopting a particular innovation does not by itself provide much information about the general technological progressivity or laggardness of that firm, or perhaps more importantly, of the general receptivity to innovation of all firms within all industries in that region. Clearly, what would be needed here is a systematic study of whether a set of industries within a particular region have been particularly progressive or laggard in adopting a set of innovations.

The issue is not simply when and to what extent the process of invention and innovation changed from one of an individual inventor seeking to promote use of his new technique in largely competitive product markets to a Galbraithian world in which salaried inventors produce new products which their corporate employers then market to satisfy demands which they have created, and, finally, what effect this has on the changing location of manufacturing activity, although these are all obviously important questions. What this historical process has also done is to make it more difficult to secure suitable data which can be used to test for the hypothesized existence of a dynamic feedback relationship in the regional growth–invention–innovation–regional growth process. The existence of such a mechanism is an important part of most urban and regional growth models. The advent of oligopolistic industries in the late nineteenth century further reduces the utility of patent data as a measure of technological activity; it begins the process that has continued to this date of the geographic separation of inventive and manufacturing activities. This is particularly so since the emerging oligopolies often followed an aggressive strategy of patent acquisition and cross-licensing at the same time that they concentrated production in a few centres. For example, in the electric light industry there was approximately a twenty-year period of fluid and experimental technology between the late 1870's and the formation of Westinghouse Electric in 1889 and General Electric in 1882. After G.E. acquired the Thomas Houston Company, one of the technological leaders in the industry, 1893, it closed that firm's plant in Lynn, Massachusetts, and concentrated its production of lamps in Harrison, New Jersey. G.E. was likewise active in purchasing the patents of others near the beginning of the twentieth century when the activities of its own newly organized research laboratory were still very narrow and when private inventors were especially active (Passer, 1953; Bright, 1969; Vaughn, 1956). A somewhat similar pattern occurred when the Eastman Kodak Company was organized in 1901. Within the next fifteen years, the company acquired the patents in Rochester, New York. These developments eroded the basis for any meaningful relationship between the location of inventive activity, as measured by patent statistics, and the location of output and, in turn, make it impossible to go directly to the effects of inventive activity upon the locational distribution of manufacturing activity.

Little improvement is gained in the analysis by employing measures of research and development activities as an index of inventive activity. In some industries, patent statistics and R & D measures are highly correlated and predict other variables equally well (Mueller, 1960). In addition, there is a clear locational separation within industry of manufacturing and R & D activities. Daniel Creamer's (1969) data, for example, show that the states comprising the 'old manufacturing belt' held 66 per cent of total manufacturing employment in 1966, but 86·5 per cent of employment in industrial research and testing auxiliaries of manufacturing firms. Finally, use of either patent or R & D data indicates the 'corporate' form in which the larger portion of contemporary inventive activity is situated. This data provides no information on the institutional 'source' of 'important' inventions and therefore is of little value in predicting the locational patterns of future industries (Jewkes, Sawers and Stillerman, 1958; Hamburg, 1966; Long and Feller, 1972).

Stochastic Approaches to Diffusion and Location

The above three subsections, based heavily upon the work of economists, have analyzed the 'factors' which affect the spatial diffusion pattern on the location of manufacturing activity. A significantly different approach to these questions is emerging in the geographic literature, most notably in the work of Pred, already cited, and of Michael J. Webber (1972). Their approach shares a common analytical framework, although the basic model is more formally developed in Webber's work. In both, a region given some initial advantage in attracting industrial activity will be the site at which the next round of technological advances occur. These innovations will then be adopted earlier and more extensively at the point of their origin, thus giving that region the initial advantage in the next round of industrial growth. Pred refers to this as the circular and cumulative process of industrialization and urbanization.

Webber's model of diffusion and location is based upon the following: sites further from the origin of an innovation tend to receive the innovation later than towns close to origin; the concentration of population e.g., a system of unequally sized cities, is conducive to the production of innovations, with larger cities relative to their population generating more innovations than smaller size towns. Webber's first point is supported by the body of literature on the spatial diffusion of innovations in geography. His second point is supported both by Pred's and Feller's work, and by the recent findings of Allen Kelley of increasing returns to scale, albeit limited, between city size and inventions (patents) for a sample of cities for census years between 1860 and 1910 (Kelley, 1972).

For present purposes, the key part of Webber's analysis is in his integration of the above two points. Cities which are the site of inventions benefit from their earlier use of the new technique. This advantage is reduced however as the technique diffuses to other cities along predictable space-time paths. Put in a dynamic system in which new techniques are constantly being produced, the larger region 'maintains advantages over less populated areas because of its relatively greater production of innovations.' As smaller, distant, regions begin to catch up with the leader in their use of the first technique, the leader region has begun to introduce the second technique: 'In such a dynamic system, a spatial cross-section at any one point in time indicates that the rate of adoption of innovations is most advanced in the areas where most innovations are produced' (Webber, 1972, p. 253). Further, '. . . the concentration of population is created and maintained by the comparative advantages of that concentration which accrue from differences in the rates of innovation adoption.'

Webber, however, notes that this analysis is essentially confined to the short run: 'Eventually the innovation is diffused and in the long run firms located at the optimum sites; the large city, favoured by the innovation production process, may not be the long run optimum location.' This, of course, refers back to the dichotomy noted at the beginning of this essay between analysis of diffusion and of industrial location. Webber's extension of the analysis of diffusion to yield long-term equilibrium is of limited applicability for present purposes because it is couched in terms of agricultural innovations.

3.4. Summary

Impressive as is Webber's work, it still reflects the geographer's preoccupation with the innovation of agricultural practices and collective goods. If diffusion, however, is to be related to the location of manufacturing activity, attention obviously must be paid to industrial innovations. The characteristics of the diffusion of this set of innovations are little understood as neither economists or geographers have devoted much research to the question. For example, do they diffuse through an urban hierarchy, or indeed is there meaning to such a standard concept for techniques used in a regionally dispersed industry producing for a national market?

Also, although there is empirical support for associations between population and inventions, this relationship has been attenuated over time. No adequate models on the relationship between innovation and industrial location exist which can accommodate the development of corporate-centred R & D, and the visible locational separation of R & D and production facilities.

Nor, indeed, is there yet any clear understanding of the impact that technological change has had on the location of manufacturing activities. In part, this is attributable to the difficulties of isolating 'technology', other than R & D expenditures, from its impact on the standard determinants of industrial location.

What has hopefully been accomplished in this essay is an outline of the types of questions which should be asked if an understanding is to be reached of the relationship between technological change and industrial location along with a map of the specific terrain, including pitfalls around which this research must travel.

References

Booms, B. (1973), The Impact of Urban Market Structure on the Level of Inventive Activity in Cities in the Early 1900's, *Land Economics*, pp. 318–325.

Brandner, L. and Strauss, M. (1961), Congruence versus Profitability in the Diffusion of Hybrid Sorghum, *Rural Sociology*, **26**, 409–414.

Bright, A. A., Jr. (1969), *The Electric Lamp Industry*. New York: MacMillan.

Brown, L. A. (1968), *Diffusion Processes and Location*. Philadelphia, Pennsylvania: Regional Science Research Institute.

Burloch, M. J. (1965), The Interrelationship of the Changing Structure of American Transportation and Changes in Industrial Location, *Land Economics*, **41**, 169–179.

Chinitz, B. (1961), Contrasts in Agglomeration: New York and Pittsburgh, *American Economic Review, Papers and Proceedings*, **51**, 279–289.

Commission on College Geography (1964), *Spatial Diffusion*. Resource Paper No. 4, Washington, D.C.: Association of American Geographers.

Craig, P. (1957), Location Factors in the Development of Steel Centres, *Papers and Proceedings, Regional Science Association*, **3**, 249–265.

Crain, R. L. (1966), Fluoridation: The Diffusion of an Innovation Among Cities, *Social Forces*, **44**, 467–476.

Creamer, D. (1969), *Manufacturing Employment by Type of Location*. New York: National Industrial Conference Board, Table 3, p. 15; Table 16, p. 55; Table 23, pp. 70–71.

Cunningham, W. G. (1951), *The Aircraft Industry*. Los Angeles: Lorrin L. Morrison.

David, P. A. (1966), The Mechanization of Reaping in the Ante-bellum Midwest, in Rosousky, H. (ed.), *Industrialization in Market Economics*. New York: Wiley, 3–39.

Davis, L. E., Easterlin, R. A. and Parker, W. N. (eds.) (1972), *American Economic Growth*. New York: Harper & Row.

Deuterman, E. (1966), Seeding Science Based Industry, *Business Review*, Federal Reserve Bank of Philadelphia.

Enos, J. (1962), *Petroleum Progress and Profits*. Cambridge, Massachusetts: M.I.T. Press.

Estall, R. C. (1963), The Electronic Products Industry of New England, *Economic Geography*, **38**, 189–216.

Estall and Buchanan, R. O. (1967), *Industrial Activity and Economic Geography*, New York: Wiley.

Feller, I. (1960), The Draper Loom in New England Textiles, 1894–1914: A Study of Diffusion of an Innovation, *Journal of Economic History*, **26**, 320–342.

Feller I. (1967), Approaches to the Diffusion of Innovations, *Explorations in Entrepreneurial History*, **43**, 232–244.

Feller I. (1971), The Urban Location of United States Inventions, 1860–1910, *Explorations in Economic History*, **8**, 285–303.

Feller, I., Long, W. H. and Nelson, J. P. (1972), *Economic Aspects of the Relationship Between Research and Development Activities and State Economic Growth*. University Park, Pennsylvania: Centre for the Study of Science Policy.

Feller, I. (1973), Determinants of the Composition of Urban Inventions, *Economic Geography*, **49**, 47–57.

Fischbaum, M. and Rubin, J. (1968), Slavery and the Economic Development of the South, *Explorations in Economic History*, **6**, 116–127.

Fishlow, A. (1965), *American Railroads and the Transformation of the Ante-bellum Economy*. Cambridge, Mass.: Harvard Economic Studies Vol. 127.

Frankel, M. (1955), Obsolescence and Technological Change in a Maturing Economy, *American Economic Review*, **45**, 296–319.

Fuchs, V. R. (1962), *Changes in the Location of Manufacturing in the United States Since 1929*. New Haven, Connecticut: Yale University Press.

Gilfillan, S. C. (1930), Inventiveness by Nation: A Note on Statistical Treatment, *Geographical Review*, **20**, 301–304.

Gilfillan, S. C. (1935), *The Sociology of Invention*. Chicago: Follett.

Gold, B., Pierce, W. and Rosegger, G. (1970), Diffusion of Major Technological Innovations in U.S. Iron and Steel Manufacturing, *Journal of Industrial Economics*, **18**, 218–241.

Greenhut, M. L. (1956), *Plant Location*. Chapel Hill: University of North Carolina Press.

Greenhut, M. L. (1957), Hybrid Corn: An Exploration in the Economics of Technological Change, *Econometrica*, **25**, 502–522.

Greenhut, M. L. (1960), Congruence versus Profitability: A False Dichotomy, *Rural Sociology*, **25**, 354–356.

106

Griliches, Z. (1962), Profitability versus Interaction: Another False Dichotomy, *Rural Sociology*, **26**, 327–330.

Hägerstrand, T. (1967), *Innovation Diffusion as a Spatial Process*. University of Chicago Press.

Hamburg, D. (1966), *R & D: Essays on the Economics of Research and Development*. New York: State University of New York at Buffalo.

Hammer, M. F. (1940), *History of the Kodak*. New York: The House of Little Books.

Higgs, R. (1971), American Inventiveness, 1870–1920, *Journal of Political Economy*, **79**, 661–667.

Hildebrand, G. H. and Ta-Chung Liu. (1965), *Manufacturing Production Functions in the United States, 1957*. New York: Cornell University Press.

Hoover, E. M. (1948), *The Location of Economic Activity*. New York: McGraw-Hill.

Isard, W. (1948), Some Locational Factors in the Iron and Steel Industry Since the Early Nineteenth Century, *Journal of Political Economy*, **56**, 203–217.

Isard, W. and Whitney, V. (1952), *Atomic Power*. New York: Blakiston Co.

Jefferson, M. (1929), The Geographical Distribution of Inventiveness, *Geographical Review*, **19**, 649–661.

Jewkes, J., Sawers, D. and Stillerman, R. (1958), *The Source of Invention*. London: MacMillan.

Karaska, G. J. and Bramhall, D. (eds.) (1969), *Locational Analysis for Manufacturing*. Cambridge, Massachusetts: M.I.T. Press.

Katz, E., Hamilton, M. and Levin, M. (1963), Traditions of Research on the Diffusion of Innovations, *American Sociological Review*, **28**, 237–252.

Kelley, A. C. (1972), Scale Economies, Inventive Activity and the Economics of American Population Growth, *Explorations in Economic History*, **10**, 35–52.

Kindleberger, C. (1964), *Economic Growth in France and Britain: 1851–1950*. Cambridge, Massachusetts: Harvard University Press.

Krutilla, J. (1955), Locational Factors Influencing Recent Aluminum Expansion, *Southern Economic Journal*, **21**, 273–288.

Kuznets, S. (1962), Inventive Activity: Problems of Definition and Measurement, *The Rate and Direction of Inventive Activity*. Princeton, New Jersey: Princeton University Press, for the National Bureau of Economic Research, pp. 19–42.

Leven, C., Legler, J. and Shapiro, P. (1970), *An Analytical Framework for Regional Development Policy*. Cambridge, Massachusetts: M.I.T. Press.

Long, W. H. and Feller, I. (1972), State Support of Research and Development: An Uncertain Path to Economic Growth, *Land Economics*, **48**, 220–227.

Lynn, F. (1966), An Investigation of the Rate of Development and Diffusion in Technology in Our Modern Industrial Society, *Technology and the American Economy*, Vol. III. Studies prepared for the National Commission on Technology, Automation, and Economic Progress, Washington, D.C.: Government Printing Office.

Machlup, F. (1962), *The Production and Distribution of Knowledge in the United States*. Princeton University Press.

Mansfield, E. (1961), Technical Change and the Rate of Imitation, *Econometrica*, **29**, 741–766.

Mansfield, E. (1968a), *The Economics of Technological Change*, New York: Norton.

Mansfield, E. (1968b), *Industrial Research and Technological Innovation*, New York: Norton.

Mueller, D. (1960), Patents, Research and Development, and the Measurement of Inventive Activity, *Journal of Industrial Economics*, **15**, 26–37.

Nelson, J. P. (1971), An Interregional Recursive Programs Model of Production, Investment, and Technological Change, *Journal of Regional Science*, **11**, 33–47.

Nelson, R., Peck, M. and Kalachek, E. (1967), *Technology, Economic Growth and Public Policy*. Washington, D.C.: Brookings Institution.

North, D. C. (1963), *The Economic Growth of the United States*. Englewood Cliffs, New Jersey: Rutgers University Press.

Passer, H. (1953), *The Electrical Manufacturers, 1875–1900*. Cambridge: Massachusetts: Harvard University Press.

Pedersen, P. O. (1970), Innovation Diffusion Within and Between National Urban Systems, *Geographical Analysis*, **2**, 203–254.

Perloff, H. S., Dunn, E. S., Lampard, E. E. and Muth, R. F. (1960), *Regions, Resources, and Economic Growth*. University of Nebraska Press.

Pred, A. R. (1966), *The Spatial Dynamics of U.S. Urban-Industrial Growth, 1800–1914*. Cambridge, Massachusetts: M.I.T. Press.

Pyle, G. F. (1969), The Diffusion of Cholera in the United States in the Nineteenth Century, *Geographical Analysis*, **1**, 59–64.

Rogers, E. M. (1962), *Diffusion of Innovations*. New York: The Free Press of Glencoe.

Rosenberg, N. (1963), Technical Change in the Machine Tool Industry, 1840–1910, *Journal of Economic History*, **23**, 414–443.

Rosenberg, N. (1969), The Direction of Technological Change: Inducement Mechanisms and Focusing Devices, *Economic Development and Cultural Change*, **18**, 1–24.

Rosenberg, N. (1972a), *Technology and American Economic Growth*, New York: Harper & Row.

Rosenberg, N. (1972b), Factors Affecting the DiffusionTechnology, *Explorations in Economic History*, **10**, 3–34.

Salter, W. E. C. (1969), *Productivity and Technical Change*. Second Edition, Cambridge, Massachusetts: Harvard University Press.

Schmockler, J. (1968), *Invention and Economic Growth*. Cambridge, Massachusetts: Harvard University Press.

Smith, D. M. (1966), A Theoretical Framework for Geographical Studies of Industrial Location, *Economic Geography*, **42**, 95–113.

Technological Innovation: Its Environment and Management (1967), Report to the Secretary of Commerce. Washington, D.C.: U.S. Government Printing Office.

Thompson, Wilbur R. (1965), *A Preface to Urban Economics*. Baltimore, Maryland: Johns Hopkins Press.

Thompson, Wilbur R. (1962), Locational Differences in Inventive Activity and Their Determinants, *The Rate and Direction of Inventive Activity*. Princeton, New Jersey: Princeton University Press, For the National Bureau of Economic Research. 253–271.

Toulmin, S. (1969), Innovation and the Problems of Utilization, in Gruber, W. H. and Marquis, Donald G. (eds.), *Factors in the Transfer of Technology*. Cambridge, Massachusetts: M.I.T. Press.

Ullman, E. L. (1958), Regional Development and the Geography of Concentration. *Papers and Proceedings, Regional Science Association*, **4**, 179–198.

Vaughn, Floyd L. (1956), *The United States Patent System*. Norman, Oklahoma: University of Oklahoma Press.

Walker, Jack L. (1969), The Diffusion of Innovations Among the American States, *American Political Science Review*, **63**, 111–126.

Warner, Sam B., Jr. (1963), Innovation and the Industrialization of Philadelphia, 1800–1850, in Handlin, O. and Burchard, John (eds.), *The Historian and the City*. Cambridge, Massachusetts: Harvard University Press. 63–69.

Warner, Sam B., Jr. (1962), *Streetcar Suburbs*. Cambridge, Massachusetts: Harvard University Press.

Webber, Michael, J. (1972), *Impact of Uncertainty on Location*. Canberra: Australian National University Press.

Williamson, Harold F. and Daum, Arnold R. (1959), *The Petroleum Industry, 1859–1899*. Evanston, Illinois: Northwestern University Press.

4 Government Impact on Industrial Location

JAMES B. CANNON

The interaction between public policy and private investment decisions in the manufacturing sector is complex. Manufacturers have always had to regard government policies as one factor to be considered in making investment decisions. However no general agreement has ever been reached concerning the actual impact of government policy on manufacturing location. The inability to construct a clear picture of the effects of public policy on manufacturing performance is in part related to the failure to specify precise analytical frameworks within which programmes may be comparatively evaluated. Manufacturing incentives have been treated as a rather blunt instrument of policy. However when incentives are considered in relation to particular investment situations, a need for considerable precision in articulating policy becomes apparent.

Following a brief discussion of the evolutionary nature of public policy toward industrial location, this essay will turn to its major task of outlining the elements of a conceptual framework essential to formulating, applying and evaluating programmes of direct incentives to manufacturers. This framework will then be employed in examining some empirical evidence relating to incentive programmes, focusing particularly on the Area Development Agency (ADA) experience in Canada.

4.1. Evolution of Location of Industry Policy

The nature of government policies, which attempt to influence patterns of manufacturing investment, has varied with the level of economic development attained in a nation. Historically three phases of policy involvement might be identified. During periods of nation building, public policies were intended to encourage the establishment of a manufacturing sector (Eckhaws, 1961; Dales, 1970). The concern was with growth of manufacturing activity in aggregate. Manufacturers affected by these policies normally found that public policy reinforced natural market forces. Thus the spatial impact of early policies was to encourage the location of industry in emerging core regions which already possessed a comparative advantage.

109

As industrialization proceeded, the spatial pattern of manufacturing development became increasingly differentiated. This led to the formulation of *ad hoc* policies at the sub-national scale which were explicitly intended to attract manufacturing to particular areas. However much of the literature on manufacturing location relating to this phase traditionally considered government policy to be a minor factor in the location decision (Bridges, 1965). This view can probably be sustained when considering patterns of manufacturing location at a broad regional scale. But recognition of the manufacturing location decision as the outcome of a lengthy narrowing-down process—a process which often results in a final decision being made in terms of marginal factors—suggests that a government policy which may only marginally affect the attractiveness of alternative locations, can become a decisive factor at the final decision stage. Thus from the point of view of particular local areas or communities desirous of increasing their manufacturing base, government policy may well be an important factor in determining the local detail of manufacturing location patterns.

During the most recent phase, government attempts to influence choice of location have become more comprehensive and all-pervasive in the private investment decision. Manufacturers have been faced with an increasing assortment of policies intended to influence the distribution of manufacturing activities. The nature of these policies has varied considerably, ranging from attempts to modify an area's investment environment through infrastructural improvement to establishing special public corporations which enter directly into the production of goods in particular disadvantage areas (La Marca, 1970; Konings, 1971; Novacco, 1971). Manufacturers have been most directly affected by investment incentives which are offered in a variety of forms to individual private corporations to encourage them to invest in selected regions.

Recent increased efforts by government to influence the location of investment decisions are related to the general concern with regional disparities common to all developed western nations. Dramatic structural dislocations associated with twentieth century industrial change have contributed to the need to deal with the regional problem in the older industrialized nations. In addition, as the general level of national economic welfare has increased, it has become possible to devote increasing attention to issues of equity and regional balance. However, the circumstances under which government policy is attempting to influence manufacturing investment decisions contain implications for growth and change in the manufacturing sector which cannot be ignored. These implications result from the potential goal conflicts which arise from attempting to use locational incentives to achieve objectives pertinent to both private manufacturers and government social policy.

Much of the initial interest in modifying the basic distribution of manufacturing activity was rooted in policy objectives dealing with social welfare considerations of residents of depressed regions. Although a vital concern, this social orientation tends to ignore the potential effect which government policies can have in altering the location, structure and performance of

manufacturing industries. With an increase in the scale of incentive programmes industrialists, attempting to maintain their competitive positions,
have been forced to give serious attention to these programmes in developing
their investment strategies. In order to determine the way that these policies
are affecting manufacturing change, it is necessary to develop a conceptual
framework for viewing the relation of incentives to the private investment
decision.

4.2. Elements of a Location of Industry Policy

To develop a management perspective on the impact of direct incentives on
manufacturing location, it is helpful to put oneself in the position of an
industrialist faced with a strategic investment decision. Analysis of strategic
decisions, which are differentiated from the routine day to day management
decisions involved in operating a manufacturing enterprise, is of particular
interest in studying the long-run performance of manufacturers. Formulation
of an investment strategy encompasses a whole set of decisions, one of which
involves choice of location. The availability of locational incentives suggests
that the rational investment decision-maker should compare the advantages of
tying his investment plans to the government programme against the prospects
for the success of the investment in the most preferred location which lies
beyond the reach of the programme. In evaluating the merits of an inducement
for a particular investment an entrepreneur will have to consider three
elements:

(1) the specific nature of the manufacturing activity;
(2) the attributes of the areas in which incentives are available;
(3) the particular form of the inducement.

Nature of the Manufacturing Activity

Manufacturing enterprises which are the instrument of programmes of
government inducements must be recognized as fundamentally economic
institutions. Although non-economic objectives may enter into the operation
of such activities, the market test of sufficient profits must be met if a particular
enterprise is to succeed. Given this initial premise the principal issue appears to
be that of examining the relationship of choice of location to the investment
decision.

Attempts have been made to assess the effect which location can have on the
viability of manufacturing industries (Luttrell, 1962; Law, 1964; Wonnacott
and Wonnacott, 1967; George, 1970). Surveys of businessmen and analysis of
manufacturing performance data have established that perceptual and actual
cost and revenue barriers can represent significant impediments to the mobility
of industry. Although such studies of potential industry mobility have made it
possible to render some gross generalizations concerning the locational limits
of certain broadly defined industry groups, these same studies have recognized

that particular branches of industries, presumably at a disadvantage because of location, do operate successfully at 'inferior' locations. These findings emphasize that choice of location cannot be identified as an independent characteristic of a strategic investment decision. Mobility potential even within narrowly defined industry groups may be strongly influenced by such factors as the range of productive technology available to produce an output or the particular conditions of the regional economic milieu. Thus the impact of locational incentives must be seen in the broader context of the total investment decision.

Incentives are primarily intended to reorder locational preferences. Since many manufacturers apparently consider only a limited number of possible locations, an important purpose served by incentives may be to encourage a broader geographical search for a suitable location. However the information needed by manufacturers to evaluate comparatively investment potential at alternative locations is demanding and is likely to contain unique characteristics for individual manufacturers. Thus the investment decisions of particular manufacturers will be differentially affected by a given incentive.

Differences in circumstances surrounding particular investment decisions suggest that an ideal incentives policy may have to be highly discretionary. Inducements offered must be substantial enough to divert the investment toward the target area but not so generous as to introduce gross inefficiences into the manufacturing sector. In addition, because location represents only one dimension of the investment decision, it is possible that manufacturers could incorporate public incentives into their investment plans for reasons which are quite independent of the choice of location. In such circumstances it is conceivable that public inducements could permit a project to proceed that would not have been selected without the aid of an incentive or could result in a larger scale project than would otherwise have been the case. Thus the real impact of inducements may not involve locational adjustment on the part of manufacturers but may result in significant structural change in the manufacturing sector. In order to evaluate adequately the impact of incentive programmes on manufacturing, it is essential to identify the precise relation of the inducement to the investment decision-making process (Helliwell, 1968).

Attributes of Target Regions

Businessmen have their mental maps which portray the merits of particular areas for productive enterprise. Their assessment revolves around the perceived potential of an area to provide the necessary supply of inputs and the market outlets needed to assure the success of a business venture. The potential of a location depends not only upon transport distances associated with a location but upon a region's economic and social structure.

Unfortunately, properties reflecting the manufacturing potential of an area are rarely considered in delimiting policy regions (Brewis, 1969; Prescott and Lewis, 1969). Identification of areas eligible for locational inducements in terms of indicators of regional economic malaise such as high unemployment, low incomes or high out-migration may be politically expedient but offers no logic in relation to the manufacturing investment decision. Such a policy often results in the designation of large areas which have little potential for industrial development. The practice points up a difficulty which may emerge in trying to use direct incentives in isolation from other less direct forms of assistance. For example, without a minimal level of social overhead capital, industry is unlikely to show much interest in investing in an area. In addition this shotgun approach to identifying target regions invites an indiscriminate use of locational incentives to those cases in which they were deemed to be 'crucial' to assuring the location of the plant in the target region. However by virtue of the designation procedure the principal advantage of large segments of these areas may be the natural resource base. Investment by spatially-immobile, resource-based manufacturing industries in such locations could hardly be viewed as fundamentally dependent upon incentive policy.

In addition to the basic suitability of a region for manufacturing, the geographic scale at which a policy operates has a bearing on the impact that incentives have on manufacturing. Incentive policies have been formulated to encourage industry to locate in small scale ghetto areas within metropolitan areas, to redistribute manufacturing among local labour markets within major regions and to shift industry among major regions of a nation. Manufacturers operate in a distinct spatial context whose absolute and relative dimensions vary between industries and among firms within industries. Distinct differences in the ability of firms to make locational adjustments, depending upon distances involved, have been found. Large multi-plant corporations normally operate in a much broader action space than do smaller locally controlled businesses (Mueller and Morgan, 1962; Aharoni, 1966; Vernon, 1966). Thus the impact of an incentives policy will be affected by both the socio-economic characteristics of the target regions and the geographic dimensions of policy.

Nature of Inducement Policy

The third element of the policy environment concerns the form and administration of the inducement. The purpose of any policy initiative is to introduce new elements into the context of the investment decision. The varied nature of manufacturing industries suggests that any single inducement cannot help but be more attractive to certain industries and types of firms than others. Whereas pre-built rental factories have been found to offer an immediate advantage to some rapidly-growing small and medium-sized firms by making it possible for them to respond rapidly to market opportunities while maintaining adequate liquidity (Luttrell, 1962), policies which subsidize a particular factor of production such as labour or capital can create biases in favour of industries and technologies which use relatively large amounts of the subsidized factor (Harcourt, 1968; Hutton and Hartley, 1968). A broad range of policies has been utilized. These include not only inducements which have a direct pecuniary impact on the investment decision but also those which attempt to increase the absolute volume of manufacturing activity by extending credit to firms that are unable to obtain investment funds through normal channels

(Bianchi, 1970) and those which focus solely on improving the psychology of investment in target regions.

Given a particular inducement, the industrialist must determine its value in the context of his particular investment decision. It would be desirable to be able to calculate the specific quantitative effect of the incentive on the profitability of the investment (Ackley and Dini, 1959; Stober and Falk, 1969; Thomas, 1969; Scholefield and Franks, 1972). This type of evaluation is either impossible or highly problematical for certain types of incentives. For example, the psychological benefits of an incentive are impossible to measure. Further the real impact of certain forms of incentives such as 'tax holidays' and accelerated depreciation are not apparent until after the project is in production and unless the venture is successful no benefits may ever be realized. These difficulties have led some writers to suggest that incentives should be structured so that investors are aware of their magnitude prior to undertaking a project. This reasoning is partly responsible for the relative popularity of offering capital grants as an incentive.

Despite these difficulties investors must make estimates of the worth of an incentive. The simplest way to proceed is to compare the profitability of a project with and without incentive assistance. Various calculations which have been made indicate that even the most generous incentive programmes only improve the long-run profitability of a project by a few percentage points. Whether or not a benefit of this magnitude can be considered significant has been debated. On one hand, even an advantage of two per cent on a project which was expected to return 10 per cent would result in an increase in profits of twenty per cent. On the other hand, it has been argued that the error margin associated with such estimates may be so large that the potential benefit may be inconsequential. Moreover in cases where location in a target region involves high risk or substantial economic disadvantages, the potential benefit conferred by an incentive may be insignificant.

It could further be argued that the context of the comparison discussed above is inappropriate. The private industrialist should compare the profitability of the publicly assisted project with that of producing the output by the best alternative means whether this entail building the plant at another location, increasing capacity of pre-existing plants in the firm, having purchasing capacity controlled by other firms or by any other possible means. The relevant comparative context can only be determined in relation to the alternatives open to the particular manufacturer.

The administrative framework within which an incentive policy is handled represents a final matter of significance. Administrative involvement varies from a purely permissive stance, where industrialists' applications for incentives are simply declared eligible or ineligible in terms of the enabling legislation, to a highly discretionary one where each application is reviewed on its own merits. Although the latter view raises more controversial political and economic questions, it has the potential of allowing the administering agency to be very selective and thus capable of redirecting manufacturing in a more fundamental way. Over time the general trend in virtually all programmes has been to become more discretionary.

Incentives policies have been formulated by different levels of government (Brewis, 1962; Hale, 1969). Since the financial resources and responsibilities of governments vary, their capacity to provide incentives likewise varies. In the event of a war to attract industry it is likely that the richest governments would win. These are also the governments which already have the most prosperous manufacturing sectors. In countries where more than one level of government is involved in the administration of incentive programmes, competition for industry can be self-defeating. In an age of internationally mobile firms, the same problem can arise between countries. However, it appears virtually impossible for one government to abstain or withdraw from industrial promotion if parallel governments are actively pursuing industrial incentive policies.

The implications which inter-governmental competition holds for growth and change in the manufacturing sector are complex and unpredictable (Moes, 1962; Morss, 1966; Rinehart and Laird, 1972). Private industrialists will react to incentives in what they construe to be a manner consistent with achieving their business objectives. However despite this private rationality, it is recognized that public policy can indirectly contribute to inefficiency in manufacturing. A particular example can be taken from Canadian economic history where the imposition of a national tariff policy to encourage growth of domestic manufacturing led to the influx of large numbers of foreign producers who deemed it necessary to be represented in Canada. This has resulted in the evolution of a fragmented manufacturing sector with a large number of plants, in particular industries producing at inefficient scales of output (Daly, Keys and Spence, 1968; Eastman and Skykolt, 1970). The potential of well-intentioned interventionist policies to create undesirable side-effects must be guarded against.

The three elements comprising an incentives policy, the manufacturer, the target area and the inducement interact to create conditions which are particular to each manufacturing investment decision. The preceding section has been concerned with discussing these elements and some aspects of their interaction. The remainder of the essay will examine some empirical evidence pertaining to the functioning of incentive programmes in the light of this framework.

A.3. Incentive Programmes and the Performance of Manufacturing Industries

Consideration of the numerous ways in which incentives can affect investment decisions both directly and indirectly generates many hypotheses about the behaviour and performance of manufacturing industries. Testing of these hypotheses is hampered by the difficulties of attempting to isolate particular aspects of a multidimensional investment decision. Practical difficulties are often encountered because of data limitations which arise when attempting to assess the detailed impact of particular policies. However it is still necessary to examine the evidence relating to the impact of public policy on manufacturing growth and change. Only after the investment performance has been assessed with respect to a broad range of questions will it be possible to arrive at judgements on the ultimate desirability of incentives policy.

Three types of information have been of value in attempting to evaluate the impact of incentives on growth and change on the manufacturing sector. These include statistics generated through the administration of programmes general indicators of the performance of manufacturing industries and special surveys of companies receiving incentives. Each type of data suffers from particular deficiencies for the purpose at hand. All three types are used in the following pages to assess the extent of industry participation in the ADA programme, its locational impact and related structural impacts. A final section discusses the costs of incentive programmes. Comparative evidence dealing with other programmes is provided where it has been reported.

Industry Participation

It is commonly held that locational incentive programmes represent a relatively inconsequential factor in manufacturing investment decisions. However in Canada as elsewhere the number of industrial promotion programmes has increased dramatically in recent years. During the last decade all Canadian provinces developed programmes of industrial assistance. Although this assistance took a variety of forms, loans and loan guarantees represented the most common type of incentive. Between 1963 and 1967 provincial commitments to these programmes increased from $12·6 to £104·6 million. In relative terms this represented an increase from 3·5 per cent to 12·2 per cent of provincial indirect debt (Hopkinson, 1968).

Federal government expenditures were even greater. By the 1972–1973 fiscal year budget estimates for industrial incentives had climbed to $187·3 million.[1] Substantial federal financial involvement for industrial incentives followed the establishment of the Area Development Agency (ADA) in 1963. Between December 1963 and December of 1967 ADA approved projects involving a total investment of $1·8 billion.[2] Since ADA statistics relate only to investment intentions, it is impossible to provide a completely accurate estimate of the proportion of total Canadian manufacturing investment affected by ADA. However, if one arbitrarily allows for a one year lag between ADA approval of a project and the reporting of it in the annual federal government survey of investment, it appears that the ADA programme directly affected some 15 per cent of the $11·9 billion invested in manufacturing over the five year period from January 1964 to December 1968.[3]

Attempts to disaggregate this data on an annual basis reveal that the response to the programme was not uniform. The ADA programme began by offering 3 year tax holidays to participating firms. This was replaced by a capital grant scheme in August of 1965. The response rate was significantly higher during the capital grant phase. However because there were major changes in the listing of eligible areas during the latter phase, it is not possible to attribute the higher response rate totally to manufacturing investors expressing a preference for grants in contrast to tax holidays.

Disaggregation of the data also suggested that programme statistics probably overstated the relative importance of the incentives especially in the Atlantic region. Discrepancies between programme statistics and government investment surveys could arise because of differences in definitions of investment. In addition, some approved projects may not have begun by the end of 1968 while others may have been withdrawn. Thus a more conservative estimate of the proportion of manufacturing investment directly affected by the ADA programme would be 10 to 12 per cent. The corresponding percentage relating to manufacturing investment in eligible regions alone would of course be much higher. Even the more conservative estimate suggests that incentive policies are involved in a significant proportion of manufacturing investment activity.

Locational Impact

The principal purpose of incentives programmes is to alter locational preferences. Post-war studies of locational trends in Canada have found a tendency toward increasing regional concentration with dispersal apparent only in the form of suburbanization at the metropolitan scale (Slater, 1961; Hay, 1965). The ADA programme was aimed at reversing this trend by increasing the proportion of manufacturing activity in particular slow growth areas. In 1963, 35 areas representing about 8 per cent of the Canadian labour force became eligible for investment incentives. The expanded programme after August of 1965 included 17 per cent of the labour force. The areas, of varying sizes, represented a mixture of counties, census divisions and National Employment Service (NES) labour offices. Eligibility was determined by comparing employment and income data for all administrative units against norms established by ADA. Additions and deletions occurred as periodic reassessments of an area's eligibility was made.

The heterogeneous collection of eligible areas meant that there was no common set of employment or investment statistics which could be used to examine the pattern of manufacturing change in relation to the ADA policy. However, in Ontario and Nova Scotia, provincial investment surveys of new and expanding manufacturing activity did provide information on the number and location of manufacturing investment decisions.[4] The provincial surveys excluded very small investments but made it possible to distinguish between investment for at site expansions and new or branch plants. Investments which were included were not differentiated with respect to size. Using this information, it is possible to determine whether the programme of investment incentives affected the choice of location made by investment decision-makers. The total number of investment decisions involved in the analysis is shown in Table 4.1.

Ontario and Nova Scotia represent highly contrasting regions to which a uniform federal government policy is applied. The provincial units are very different in their industrial structures with Ontario representing the

Table 4.1. Investment decisions in study area

	1960–1968 All areas	1964–1968 All areas	1964–1968 Designated areas
Ontario			
Total	5,215	2,320	309
New and Branch	1,371	702	127
At Site	3,844	1,618	182
Nova Scotia			
Total	166	114	73
New and Branch	81	53	43
At Site	85	61	30

Source: Note 4.

manufacturing core of Canada and Nova Scotia a peripheral depressed area. The employment and income criteria which ADA used to designate areas resulted in 21 local areas being declared eligible for incentives in Ontario and 11 in Nova Scotia during the period of analysis. The eligible areas for Ontario and Nova Scotia are listed in Table 4.2.

Table 4.2. Designated areas in Ontario and Nova Scotia

Nova Scotia	Ontario	
New Glasgow	Brantford	Cornwall
Sydney	Windsor	Pembroke
Sydney Mines	Timmins	Wallaceburg
Amherst	Elliot Lake	Chatham
Springhill	Bracebridge	Parry Sound
Inverness	Sturgeon Falls	Owen Sound
Liverpool	Collingwood	Midland
Bridgewater	Haliburton	Parry Sound
Kentville	Manitoulin Island	Hawkesbury
Truro	Kirkland Lake	New Kiskeard
Yarmouth	North Bay	

To establish the pre-ADA manufacturing investment pattern, all investment decisions in the 1960–1963 period were allocated to the local policy area in which they were located. Then the share of total provincial manufacturing investment decisions occurring in each local policy area during this pre-programme period was multiplied by the total number of investment decisions recorded in the entire study area during the years that individual designated areas were eligible for investment assistance. This generated a value representing the expected number of investment decisions in an individual area during its period of eligibility based on the pattern of investment decision-making for the four years before the programme was introduced. If incentives have an impact on choice of location, one would expect to find the actual number of location decisions exceeding the expected in the designated areas during the years that the ADA programme operated.

The rationale for generating the distribution of expected location decisions merits attention. One can always ask in similar circumstances whether the base-period distribution, on which the expected values depend, is typical or stable. The balance of factors affecting investment decision-making is constantly changing (Fulton, 1971). However the introduction of the ADA policy did represent a distinctive new element to be considered in the investment decision. The 1960–1963 pattern represents the pre-ADA state of the system and the incentives were specifically designed to redirect manufacturing to particular target areas. The analysis simply allows one to determine whether eligible areas received a larger number of investment decisions after the introduction of the ADA programme than would have been expected based on the 1960–1963 distribution of decisions.

Interest in the geographic pattern of location decisions can be extended beyond the areas eligible for investment incentives. When the ADA programme was announced, representatives of municipalities in areas which were excluded from the programme but were adjacent to designated areas, raised strong objections, claiming that their jurisdictions were being placed at a competitive disadvantage in the attraction of new industry.

With respect to the functioning of ADA policy, adjacent areas can be treated as a separate group. Expected numbers of location decisions can be generated for the period that an area was adjacent to a designated area. In this case, if government policy has an impact on choice of location, one would hypothesize that the predicted number of location decisions should exceed the observed.

Because of ongoing additions and deletions to the list of eligible areas, a particular area could be effected by policy for a period ranging from zero to five years. Calculation of expected location decisions for designated and contiguous areas was based upon the number of years an area was in the relevant category plus one additional year in the case of designated areas to allow assisted projects time to appear in the provincial investment surveys. The lag period is arbitrary but no other feasible method of handling the problem existed.

A summary of the pattern of location decisions is presented in Table 4.3. In Ontario, results from 14 of 21 designated areas were in the predicted direction. Some of these 21 areas had very low levels of investment activity. In order to apply the Chi-square statistic to the distribution, these areas had to be aggregated. They formed a contiguous block in northeastern Ontario. Regrouping reduced the total number of designated areas to eleven. In nine of these areas, the number of observed investment decisions exceeded the expected. A Chi-square test indicated that the observed distribution was significantly different from the expected at the ·01 level. The two areas which behaved in a manner inconsistent with the hypothesis, in that expected decisions exceeded actual, contributed negligibly to this result. The test indicated that the number of location decisions recorded in the eligible areas was indeed significantly larger than would have been expected given the pre-ADA pattern of manufacturing investment decisions.

Table 4.3. Patterns of investment decision-making
Ontario

Regional groups	No. of areas*	Observed exceeds expected	χ^2 Value	Statistical significance
Designated	11	9	111·5	·01
Adjacent	23	14	63·8	·001
Neutral	21	7	114·8	·001

Nova Scotia

Regional groups	No. of areas	Observed exceeds expected	χ^2 Value	Statistical significance
Designated	9	3	23·5	·01
Adjacent	3	0	3·7	Insignificant

* A single area can appear in more than one category of region since its status with respect to ADA policy could change over time.

In Nova Scotia, only three of nine eligible areas recorded an excess of observed over expected investment decisions. However the Chi-square test indicated that the pattern of investment decision-making during the period of the ADA programme was significantly different than in the pre-ADA period and inspection of the data for individual areas revealed that the three areas that performed in a manner consistent with the hypothesis contributed over 80 per cent of the Chi-square value.

The analysis suggests that the availability of government incentives did have a positive effect on the number of investment decisions made in the designated areas. Inspection of the Chi-square calculations on an area by area basis for Ontario reveals that the impact was concentrated in a small number of the eligible areas. Older industrial centres, such as Windsor, Brantford and Chatham, appeared to derive a large measure of benefit. The areas in the Georgian Bay region, particularly Owen Sound, Midland and Collingwood, also recorded a significant increase in the number of investment decisions. In most areas, with the notable exception of Chatham, activity appeared to be related more to new and branch plant investments rather than expansions of existing facilities. Many areas, particularly in northeastern Ontario, had a limited industrial base when the programme was initiated and did not appear to attract a significantly large number of new investment decisions. In this respect, the success of the programme in the Georgian Bay region was notable since it represented the extension of significant manufacturing activity into an area which previously had little manufacturing activity (Yeates and Lloyd, 1970). At the same time, the improvement in economic conditions in areas such as Pembroke and Cornwall, which led to their removal from the list of eligible areas at an early date, did not appear to be related to an increase in manufacturing activity.

In Nova Scotia as well the positive locational effects of the policy appeared to be concentrated in a few areas. It should be noted that federal and provincial policies operating during this period had potentially countervailing effects in Nova Scotia. Under the federal programme the major metropolitan area of Halifax–Dartmouth was ineligible for assistance. At the same time, provincial authorities had been openly supporting the concentration of development efforts in a growth pole context. Thus, while provincial policy encouraged manufacturers to invest in Halifax–Dartmouth, the federal policy had the opposite effect.

A similar form of analysis was carried out for areas adjacent to designated areas. In Ontario, 13 out of 31 adjacent areas performed in the hypothesized manner recording an excess of expected investment decisions over actual. Regrouping of contiguous areas for statistical purposes reduced the total number of areas to 23. The Chi-square test revealed that the actual investment pattern in the latter time period was significantly different from that prior to the ADA programme. However the expected number of investment decisions exceeded the actual in only nine of the adjacent areas. The remaining areas which performed in a manner inconsistent with the hypothesis accounted for two thirds of the total Chi-square value. In Nova Scotia all three of the regrouped areas performed in the predicted direction, but the Chi-square test showed that the actual value was not significantly different from the expected. With respect to the adjacent areas, even in the Ontario case, where a significant modification of the investment pattern occurred, it was impossible to link the pattern of investment decisions to the programme of investment incentives.

Since the large relative gains in the designated areas were not compensated by losses in the adjacent ineligible areas, a review of the investment performance in the remaining neutral areas which had neither been eligible for incentives nor adjacent to eligible areas was undertaken. No areas in Nova Scotia fell into this category. In Ontario, trends in investment decisions in the neutral areas displayed considerable short-run volatility. A Chi-square test revealed that the distribution of investment decisions in the neutral areas changed significantly after the introduction of the ADA policy. Compared with the pre-ADA pattern, 15 areas had less than the expected number of location decisions. Areas in which the actual number of decisions fell short of the expected were twice as important as the reverse situation in determining the Chi-square value. Thus, in Ontario, gains recorded in the designated areas were compensated by losses, not in adjacent non-designated areas but in this third group of neutral areas. In particular, medium sized cities such as Kitchener and several NES areas in the Torontó region appeared to suffer the bulk of the losses.

Some of the apparent instability in investment patterns could well be accentuated by the shape and scale of the ADA policy regions. The administrative units represent relatively small areas when considered in the context of a manufacturing location decision. A relatively short-distance shift in the choice of location could remove a plant from a particular area. In many cases, it seems reasonable to expect that the location decision may have been framed in terms of the relative merits of a major manufacturing city on the one hand and a designated area on the other.

The analysis suggests that the incentives programme was associated with some intra-provincial reordering of locational choices. With respect to the designated areas, the increase in the number of location decisions was concentrated in a relatively small number of the eligible areas. This finding suggests that manufacturers did incorporate public policy into their location decisions at the local area scale. However the question of whether location policy has succeeded in bringing about any fundamental shifting of investment patterns at the scale of the major Canadian regions has not been confronted (Blake, 1972).

In 1969 the work of ADA was incorporated in the new Department of Regional Economic Expansion (DREE). The new programme was much more comprehensive. Not only were incentives potentially more generous but the programme also provided for greater administrative discretion and integration with a rather crude growth pole approach (Scace, 1970). The major target regions of the new policy were the Atlantic and Quebec. Table 4.4 shows regional investment patterns for the major Canadian regions. The Canadian experience with locational incentives can be interpreted as beginning in 1964. Increased government efforts coincided with the 1966 and 1970 investment years. The data suggest that policy is having some redistributive effect in the case of the Atlantic region. However, except for 1968, massive DREE expenditures in Quebec have failed to halt a decline in the proportion of

Table 4.4. Percentage distribution of manufacturing investment by region

	Atlantic	Quebec	Ontario	Prairie	B.C.
1960	5·9	25·9	47·1	10·7	10·4
1961	7·7	26·9	49·2	6·9	9·2
1962	4·4	27·3	52·0	6·0	10·5
1963	5·2	27·0	49·1	7·0	12·5
1964	5·9	25·7	49·4	7·4	12·9
1965	5·9	23·5	50·5	6·3	13·8
1966	8·2	23·5	48·7	5·9	13·6
1967	9·1	23·9	47·7	7·9	11·4
1968	7·9	27·3	45·5	10·0	9·3
1969	8·9	23·8	48·3	7·1	11·9
1970	11·1	19·3	50·4	8·0	11·1
1971	14·0	18·3	46·7	7·2	13·8
1972	11·0	21·4	47·3	8·0	12·3

Source: Note 3.

manufacturing investment entering the province in comparison with the years prior to the advent of incentive programmes.

In summary, some evidence of changes in investment patterns at the scale of the local employment office as well as at the level of the major Canadian regions were found. These shifts were positively related to the availability of locational incentives. This conclusion is reached quite apart from considerations of whether the expenditure has been efficient or has contributed to the solution of the regional problem in Canada. The interest here is simply with the effect of government policy upon the investment decision. The results suggest that policy has been sufficiently attractive to have an apparent impact upon locational choice. Two questions emerge from this finding. First to what extent have incentives been crucial in the reordering of locational preferences? Second, has incentives policy offered advantages to industrialists which have led to their participation in the programme for reasons quite independent of the locational issue? The following section turns to potential indirect impacts which a location of industry policy can have on the structural characteristics of manufacturing industries.

Structural and Temporal Impacts

The fact that patterns of manufacturing investment decisions are positively related to the availability of incentives in itself provides only weak evidence that incentives affect choice of location. The real impact must be assessed in terms of the proportion of total decisions in which choice of location is crucially dependent upon the incentive. The less discretionary an incentives policy, the greater the probability that the incentive will not be crucial in the location decision. However even if the incentive is not crucial to the choice of location for a particular project, it is incorrect to assume that the project would have proceeded in any case and that the incentive accrued as a windfall to the company (Economic Council of Canada, 1968). Manufacturers may find it to their advantage to participate in an incentives programme for reasons quite apart from locational incentives have implications for growth and change in the manufacturing sector which need to be investigated.

To illustrate potential indirect impacts of location of industry policies, three effects of policy on investment decisions will be discussed. First, it seems clear that incentives can affect the timing of investment. Second, incentives may affect industrial structure by influencing the scale of an investment. Third, because of characteristic differences in cost structures, incentives may bias investment in favour of particular industries and types of firms. Each of these possible effects can have serious ramifications for long-run change in manufacturing.

Manufacturers could use the ADA programme to influence the timing of investment in two ways. First, it can be argued that capital grants (or tax holidays) have the potential of increasing the effective rate of return on capital invested by a private industrialist. If calculation of the rate of return on an investment is based only upon the value of private funds risked on a project rather than the full investment including the incentive, projects which would be uneconomic if full costs were assessed may become marginally attractive. Frequently the effect may be to encourage a premature start on a project which has long run potential. However a firm able to operate in this way may gain important strategic advantages by building capacity in advance of market demand. Acceleration of investment plans caused by incentives would create excess capacity in the short run and could affect the competitive structure of an industry in the long run by heightening entry barriers. Second, the ADA programme provided generous accelerated depreciation privileges. This encourages fast write-off of plant and equipment and has been shown to contribute to economic instability through the bunching of investments (Kierans, 1971).

To determine the effect of policy on the timing of investment one could examine the relationship between the relative importance of incentives in financing the expansion of industrial capacity and capacity utilization rates. If the occurrence of lower utilization rates in particular industries coincided with widespread use of incentives, then it could be argued that a major impact of the incentive was the temporal acceleration of investment. Unfortunately although capacity utilization rates are quoted for individual industries periodically, there is no continuous source of information on this indicator which applies uniformly to all industries. Thus it was necessary to substitute the rate of growth of industrial production as a measure of capacity utilization.

The relative importance of incentives in the investment performance of an industry was found by calculating the ratio between each industry's share of ADA expenditure and its share of total manufacturing investment for the 1964–1968 period. Thus, each of the 17 industry groups identifiable in the ADA data could be ranked with the highest values indicating industries that received relatively more funds from the public sector than from the total pool of private manufacturing investment. The rank of each industry in terms of the change in the index of industrial production[5] was also calculated. Although rank correlation of the two indices did not result in a statistically significant negative coefficient, pulp and paper and petro-chemicals, which occupied the first two ranks on the investment index and consumed 50 per cent of ADA funds in absolute terms, ranked eleventh and eighth on the growth index respectively.

The pulp and paper industry experienced considerable excess capacity on a world wide basis during the period under review. A major impact of ADA incentives on this industry may well have been to accelerate investment and create excess capacity at least in the short run. The location of pulp and paper mills is very much bound to supplies of raw materials and thus incentives are unlikely to have much effect on choice of location. However it would clearly be to the advantage of pulp and paper producers to use public subsidies to increase capacity in anticipation of future market expansion. This should be regarded as an inefficient use of investment funds and is to be deplored on the basis of the distortions which are introduced into the manufacturing sector.

A second possible impact of incentives policies involves their effect on industrial structure. The number and size distribution of plants or firms can have a significant effect on performance in an industry (Bain, 1954; Caves, 1964). Incentives may provide manufacturers with additional financial capacity which may be used to build larger scale plants. Whereas larger scale plants are normally more efficient, this use of incentives may in some respects be applauded. However, the fact remains that it represents a misuse of locational incentives since no locational adjustment is involved. Moreover, the structural impact of incentives used in this manner by manufacturers cannot be ignored.

The employment size distribution of all ADA projects was significantly larger than the size distribution of all Canadian manufacturing industries.[6] This need not indicate that the ADA programme has contributed to the development of larger scale plants but may simply be an indication that smaller operations did not become involved to a significant extent in the ADA programme. However, in comparison with Canadian norms, ADA assistance was associated with relatively large-scale plants, sectorally in the pulp and paper industry, and regionally in the Atlantic provinces. At the other extreme, ADA projects appeared to be associated with relatively small scale operations in the food industry and in the Prairie provinces. This apparently random effect of ADA policy on industrial structure points up the need to consider the relationship between location and scale in formulating policy. Theoretically the two concepts represent interdependent components of the investment decision (Moses, 1958; Churchill, 1967; Bradfield, 1971; Hunter and Wendell, 1972). However the potential complexity of the relationship leaves the ultimate outcome of any individual case quite indeterminate and thus offers only limited insights for structuring policies.

A third possible structural impact of incentives is to introduce biases in investment preferences between sectors and among industries within sectors. Competitive capital markets are intended to allocate investment funds among competing uses. If government policy subsidizes investment in one sector such as manufacturing relative to other major productive sectors of the economy, the allocation process could become distorted. Although the allocation of investment among major sectors of the economy can be affected by a great variety of factors, it is of interest to examine the pattern for manufacturing during the period of growth of incentive programmes.

The data in Table 4.5 indicate that aggregate investment performance can display significant year to year fluctuations. However in both absolute and relative terms, the introduction of new incentive policies was followed by distinct surges in the level of investment in manufacturing in 1964, 1966 and 1970. This relationship again suggests that location of industry policy can have structural side-effects which in this case may contribute to instability in the growth of the manufacturing sector.

The potential impact of incentives will also vary among industries within the manufacturing sector depending upon the nature of the incentive. Following an

Table 4.5. Manufacturing investment as a per cent of total investment

	Total investment (mill $)	Manufacturing investment (mill $)	Per cent
1960	8,262	1,178	14·3
1961	8,172	1,085	13·3
1962	8,738	1,231	14·1
1963	9,393	1,358	14·5
1964	10,944	1,831	16·7
1965	12,865	2,340	18·2
1966	15,090	2,194	19·3
1967	15,322	2,534	16·5
1968	15,455	2,199	14·2
1969	16,927	2,600	15·4
1970	17,798	3,223	18·1
1971	19,788	2,949	14·9
1972	20,760	2,877	13·9

Source: Note 3.

early experiment with tax holidays, the ADA programme reverted to capital grants. Thus it could be hypothesized that industries and technologies that were relatively capital-intensive would find the policy more attractive. The existence of this policy bias has been debated in other nations as well (Chisholm, 1970).

The level of activity associated with the ADA programme increased substantially after the incentive was changed to a capital grant. Projects initiated under the capital grant phase of the programme represented an investment of $38,000 per job created. Data on capital stocks per employee in Canadian manufacturing indicate that ADA assisted projects were distinctly capital intensive (Economic Council of Canada, 1965; Hood and Scott, 1957).

When the ADA operations were examined by industry group, the two groups which received the most assistance from the programme, petro-chemicals and pulp and paper, also ranked first and second in terms of capital intensity. Rank correlation of the relative importance of the ADA incentive with capital intensity for the 17 broad industry groups produced a coefficient of ·36. Although the relationship was in the expected direction, it just failed to be statistically significant at the 5 per cent level. However, one could not help but note the absolute magnitude of incentive assistance which flowed to the very capital intensive industries. The ADA programme did exhibit some bias toward the capital-intensive industries. This represents yet another structural impact resulting from a location of industry policy.

This section has discussed selected structural impacts of locational incentives policy on investment performance. Conceptually it is evident that locational incentives can be incorporated into the investment decisions of manufacturers for reasons quite apart from the choice of location. Although data limitations precluded extensive testing of hypotheses concerning possible structural impacts of locational incentives, the fragmentary evidence available suggests that the effects can be substantial. It is likely that a significant proportion of ADA incentives had no effect on locational choice. In addition indiscriminate use of location of industry policy can affect industrial structure adversely. The potential effects of government policy on manufacturing need to be carefully assessed in the light of long run implications for the health of the manufacturing sector.

Costs of Location of Industry Policy

The focus of concern to this point has been with the actual and potential impacts of locational incentives on investment decisions. The question of the costs of policy constitutes a vital extension of this theme. The costs of policy may be assessed at several levels. This essay has adopted the perspective of the private investment decision-maker. Industry spokesmen in Canada have expressed concern about the potentially adverse effects of locational incentives on productive efficiency. In general, the conventional wisdom has been to regard incentives as subsidies and thus a threat to economic efficiency (Scott, 1950; Gray, 1964). However, an economically efficient allocation of resources is only guaranteed by free market operations if the restrictive conditions of perfect competition hold (Buchanan, 1952). Since manufacturing investment decisions are rarely made under these kinds of conditions, the claim that subsidy will inevitably produce inefficiencies cannot be sustained. This is not to deny that an inappropriate use of incentives can create inefficiencies in manufacturing industries. If inefficient productive capacity is encouraged by incentives, costs to industry will accrue in the form of lower standards of performance and profit levels.

However, to view the costs of public policy only from a private perspective represents too restricted a view. Locational incentives represent programmes of broad social significance which must account for externalities omitted from private investment decisions. Although such analysis extends beyond the scope of this essay, costs and benefits ought to be measured from the broader spatial and temporal perspective of government and society as a whole. Moreover, programmes of this nature may justifiably incorporate equity and distributional goals in addition to efficiency objectives. Incentives may be viewed as compensation payments from the public sector to the private sector. Prudent policy would seek to ensure that transfers to private producers are smaller than the costs which would fall on society as a whole in the absence of the jobs and output generated by incentive payments.

The process of enumerating and measuring pertinent costs and benefits represents a massive undertaking at both conceptual and technical levels and is bound to generate controversy. Simple measures of the direct monetary costs of incentives which are normally attempted only scratch the surface of the problem. Standard indicators, such as costs per job created, indicate that the ADA programme has been expensive relative to British and American programmes. British studies have pointed up the difficulty of attempting to use

128

manufacturing as a policy instrument to cure unemployment problems (Miernyk, 1966; Thirlwall, 1967). However other comprehensive examinations of incentive programmes have suggested that such policies can be beneficial to society (Miller, Gaskins and Liner, 1969; Sazama, 1970).

The purpose of this essay is not to provide a broad social evaluation of location of industry policy. Rather the major concern is with the impact of government policy on manufacturing growth and change. Such analyses must be regarded as on-going tasks. Locational incentive policies need to be articulated in particular development contexts. The Canadian experience with the ADA programme has demonstrated that the formulation and administration of incentive policies is a delicate business. Locational incentive programmes are being practised at such a large scale that their effect on the growth performance of manufacturing cannot be ignored. It is apparent that the effects can extend beyond influencing locational choice and can have an impact on industrial structure. Moreover because of the intricate and specific nature of an investment decision, the actual impact of an incentive on a manufacturer may not be predictable.

The experience with the ADA programme illustrates the basic dilemma of interventionist location-of-industry policies. The objectives of these programmes are attempting to satisfy two distinct sets of goals. On one hand, location-of-industry policy deals with broad social issues of regional balance. At the same time, policy should be concerned with encouraging development of a competitive manufacturing sector. Governments are placed in the unenviable position of being damned if they do or damned if they don't. The less administrative discretion exercised in allocating location incentives, the greater the probability of misuse of public funds. However, acceptance of the principle of public sector administrative discretion is not easily won in parts of the economy where private sector activity has normally prevailed. Another approach, which has been attempted in some western countries, involves selective direct government participation in manufacturing production. However discussion of this issue takes one beyond the realm of spatial and economic analysis into political philosophy. Approaches to structuring locational incentives have been experimental throughout their relatively brief history. The best hope of such social experimentation is that a well-founded monitoring system be established and used. Only then can the impacts of such programmes be seriously evaluated and the lessons of experience be applied in moving on to new programmes.

Notes

1. The Minutes of Proceedings and Evidence of the House of Commons Standing Committee on Regional Development are a valuable source of current information concerning policies of the Department of Regional Economic Expansion in Canada.
2. ADA data, supplied by the Programme Co-ordination Division, provided a cumulative summary of active applications from December 1963 to December 1967.

3. Investment figures are taken from the government publication 'Private and Public Investment in Canada' (Catalogue No. 61-205, Queen's Printer, annual).
4. Data on the number and location of investment projects were based upon the following provincial surveys:
   Ontario, Ontario Industrial Review, Ministry of Industry and Tourism, annual
   Nova Scotia, Economics and Development Division, Department of Trade and Industry, annual
5. Industry growth rates were calculated from the federal government 'Index of Industrial Production'. (Catalogue No. 61-005, monthly).
6. The employment size distribution of ADA projects by industry group was reported in the ADA programme statistics. Comparable data for all Canadian manufacturing is found in the federal government publication 'Manufacturing Industries of Canada: Type of Organization and Size of Establishment' (Catalogue No. 31-210 annual).

References

Ackley, Gardner and Dini, Lamberto (1959), Tax and Credit Aids to Industrial Development in Southern Italy, *Banco Nazionale del Lavoro*, **25**, 339–368.

Aharoni, Yair (1966), *The Foreign Investment Decision Process*. Cambridge, Mass.: Harvard University Press.

Bain, Joe S. (1954), Economies of Scale, Concentration and Entry, *American Economic Review*, **44**, 15–39.

Bianchi, Tancredi (1970), Credit Incentives: Reflections Suggested by Italian Experience, *Review of Economic Conditions in Italy*, **24**, 377–391.

Blake, Christopher (1972), The Effectiveness of Investment Grants as a Regional Subsidy, *Scottish Journal of Political Economy*, **19**, 63–71.

Bradfield, M. (1971), A Note on Location and the Theory of Production, *Journal of Regional Science*, **11**, 263–266.

Brewis, T. N. (1969), *Regional Economic Policies in Canada*, Macmillan.

Brewis, T. N. (1962), Regional Development: The Need for a Federal Policy, *The Business Quarterly*, **27**, 41–45.

Bridges, B. (1965), Industrial Incentive Programs, State of Wisconsin: Dept. of Resource Development.

Buchanan, James (1952), Federal Grants and Resource Allocation, *Journal of Political Economy*, **60**, 208–217.

Cannon, James B. (1969), An Analysis of Manufacturing as an Instrument of Public Policy in Regional Economic Development: the Canadian Area Development Agency Program 1963–1968, unpublished Ph.D. dissertation, University of Washington.

Caves, Richard E. (1964), *American Industry: Structures, Conduct and Performance*. Englewood Cliffs, N.J.: Prentice-Hall.

Chisholm, M. (1970), On the Making of a Myth? How Capital Intensive is Industry Investing in the Development Areas, *Urban Studies*, **7**, 289–293.

Churchill, Gilbert A. (1967), Production Technology, Imperfect Competition and the Theory of Location: a Theoretical Approach, *Southern Economic Journal*, **34**, 86–100.

Cumberland, John H. and Von Beek, Frits (1967), Regional Economic Development Objectives and Subsidization of Local Industry, *Land Economics*, **43**, 253–264.

Dales, John H. (1966), *The Protective Tariff in Canada's Development*. University of Toronto Press.

Daly, D. J., Keys, B. A. and Spence, E. J. (1968), *Scale and Specialization in Canadian Manufacturing*. Economic Council of Canada, Staff Study No. 21. Ottawa: Queen's Printer.

130

Eastman, Harry C. and Stykolt, S. (1967), *The Tariff and Competition in Canada*, Macmillan.

Eckhaus, R. S. (1961) The North-South Differential in Italian Economic Development, *Journal of Economic History*, **20**, 285–317.

Economic Council of Canada (1968), *The Challenge of Growth and Change*. Ottawa: Queen's Printer.

Economic Council of Canada (1965), *Towards Sustained and Balanced Economic Growth*. Ottawa: Queen's Printer.

Fulton, M. (1971), New Factors in Plant Location *Harvard Business Review*, **49**, 4–17.

George, Roy E. (1970), *A Leader and A Laggard: Manufacturing Industry in Nova Scotia, Quebec and Ontario*. University of Toronto Press.

Gray, Ralph (1964), Industrial Development Subsidies and Efficiency in Resource Allocation, *The National Tax Journal*, **17**, 167–172.

Hale, C. W. (1969), The Optimality of Local Subsidies in Regional Development Programs, *Quarterly Review of Economics and Business*, **19**, 35–51.

Harcourt, G. C. (1968), Investment Decision Criteria, Investment Incentives and the Choice of Technique, *The Economic Journal*, **78**, 77–95.

Hay, Keith A. J. (1965), Trends in the Location of Industry in Ontario, 1945–1959, *Canadian Journal of Economics and Political Science*, **31**, 368–381.

Helliwell, John F. (1968), *Public Policies and Private Investment*. Clarendon Press.

Hood, W. and Scott, A. D. (1957), *Output, Labour and Capital in the Canadian Economy*. Royal Commission on Canada's Economic Prospects. Ottawa: Queen's Printer.

Hopkinson, Richard (1968), *Government Financial Assistance for Industrial Development in Canada*. National Industrial Conference Board.

Howard, R. S. (1968), *The Movement of Manufacturing Industry in the United Kingdom 1945–1965*. London: H.M.S.O.

Hunter, A. P. and Wendell, R. E. (1972), Location and Production—a special case, *Journal of Regional Science*, **12**, 243–247.

Hutton, J. P. and Hartley, K. (1968), A Regional Payroll Tax, *Oxford Economic Papers*, New Series, **20**, 417–426.

Kierans, Hon. Eric (1971), Contribution of the Tax System to Canada's Unemployment and Ownership Problems, unpublished paper delivered at Canadian Economics Association annual meeting St. John's, Newfoundland.

Konings, M. (1971), La Politique régionale: données statistiques—Objectifs—Choix des régions à aider—Instruments, *Cahiers Econ. Bruxelles*, **51**, 327–392 and **52**, 545–579.

Laird, William E. and Rinehart, James R. (1967), Neglected Aspects of Industrial Subsidy, *Land Economics*, **43**, 25–31.

La Marca, N. (1970–1971), Evolution of the Policy for the Industrialization of southern Italy, *Review of Economic Conditions in Italy*, **24**, 33–45; **24**, 145–162; **24**, 212–227; **25**, 27–40.

Law, David (1964), Industrial Movement and Locational Advantage, *Manchester School*, **32**, 131–154.

Luttrell, W. F. (1962), *Factory Location and Industrial Movement*. London: National Institute of Economic and Social Research.

Miernyk, William H. (1966), Experience Under the British Local Employment Acts of 1960 and 1963, *Industrial and Labour Relations Review*, **20**, 30–49.

Miller, Stanley, Gaskins, D. and Liner, C. (1969), Evaluation of the ARA–EDA Loan Program, *Papers and Proceedings of the Regional Science Association*, **23**, 201–215.

Moes, John E. (1961), The Subsidization of Industry by Local Communities in the South, *Southern Economic Journal*, **28**, 187–193.

Morss, E. (1966), The Potentials of Competitive Subsidization, *Land Economics*, **42**, 161–169.

Moses, Leon N. (1958), Location and Theory of Production, *Quarterly Journal of Economics*, **72**, 259–272.

Moxon, J. W. (1972), The Industrial Development Certificate System and Employment Creation, *Urban Studies*, **9**, 229–233.

Mueller, Eva and Morgan, J. N. (1962), Location Decisions of Manufacturers, *American Economic Review, Papers and Proceedings*, **52**, 204–217.

Novacco, Nino (1971), Regional Policy for the Development of Southern Italy: 1960–1980, *Review of Economic Conditions in Italy*, **25**, 271–298.

Prescott, John R. and Lewis, William C. (1969), State and Municipal Incentives: A Discriminant Analysis, *National Tax Journal*, **22**, 399–407.

Rinehart, James R. and Laird, William E. (1972), Community Inducements to Industry and the Zero-Sum Game, *Scottish Journal of Political Economy*, **19**, 73–90.

Sazama, Gerald W. (1970), A Benefit-Cost Analysis of a Regional Development Incentive: State Loans, *Journal of Regional Science*, **10**, 385–396.

Sazama, G. W. (1970), State Industrial Development Loans: a general Analysis, *Land Economics*, **46**, 171–180.

Scace, A. R. A. (1970), Regional Incentives: An Improvement?, *Canadian Tax Journal*, **17**, 48–53.

Scholefield, H. H. and Franks, J. R. (1971), Taxation Commentary: What Has Happened to Investment Incentives, *Journal of Business Finance*, **3**, 54–62.

Scott, Anthony D. (1950), A Note on Grants in Federal Countries, *Economica*, **17**, 416–422.

Slater, David W. (1961), Trends in Industrial Location in Canada, *Resources for Tomorrow Conference Papers*. Ottawa: Queen's Printer.

Springate, David (1972), Regional Development Incentives Grants and Private Investment in Canada, unpublished DBA thesis, Harvard Business School.

Stober, W. and Falk, L. (1969), The Effect of Financial Inducements on the Location of Firms, *The Southern Economic Journal*, **36**, 25–35.

Tabb, William K. (1969), Government Incentives to Private Industry to Locate in Urban Poverty Areas, *Land Economics*, **45**, 392–399.

Thirlwall, A. P. (1967), The Impact of the British Local Employment Acts of 1960 and 1963, *Industrial and Labour Relations Review*, **20**, 667–671.

Thomas, R. (1969), The Financial Benefits of Expanding in the Development Areas, *Bulletin, Oxford University Institute of Economics and Statistics*, **31**, 77–87.

Vernon, R. (1966), International Investment and International Trade in the Product Cycle, *Quarterly Journal of Economics*, **80**, 190–207.

Wonnacott, R. J. and Wonnacott, P. (1967), *Free Trade Between Canada and the United States*. Cambridge, Mass.: Harvard University Press.

Yeates, M. H. and Lloyd, P. E. (1970), *Impact of Industrial Incentives: Southern Georgian Bay Region, Ontario*. Geographical Paper No. 44. Ottawa: Queen's Printer.

Part II
Methodological Considerations

5 A Behavioural Approach to Industrial Location

DAVID F. WALKER

It is quite clear that there has been a considerable swing towards a more behavioural viewpoint in industrial geography since McNee (1960) wrote his plea for 'a more humanistic economic geography'. From the mid-1960's especially, the assumptions of normative economic location theory have been questioned and found wanting. In conjunction with such criticisms, case studies of the behaviour of enterprises in changing economic environments have been completed (for example, Steed, 1968; Fleming and Krumme, 1968), and attempts have been made to conceptualize the decision-processes used by firms (for example, Stafford, 1971; Townroe, 1969; Dicken, 1971). In general, therefore, much more attention has been focused on the actual behaviour of manufacturing firms and their managements. The argument of this essay is that we are now in a position to integrate the findings of such studies more fully with the traditional work. Integration is necessary for adequate modelling of locational change, which is a reflection both of changing circumstances and the reaction of firms to them. The concept of 'adaptation' is proposed as a framework, and the simulation model as an appropriate device for the study of some of the complex interrelationships which are involved.

5.1. The Limitations of Industrial Location Theory

It is not appropriate to attempt here a detailed review of the limitations of industrial location theory but it is useful to outline some of the difficulties that have been pointed out. Theorists differ in viewpoint and in the assumptions they make. There are, however, underlying similarities of approach, mainly reflecting the economic background of the writers. Their analyses usually assume a perfectly competitive market and optimizing behaviour. Normally also, they deal with static conditions and have deterministic solutions. For the study of locational dynamics, the main problems arise through the treatment of the time dimension and through the assumptions made about the behaviour of 'economic man'.

Two aspects of the time dimension are commonly neglected. The first of these is the cost of finding and developing a new site. Frequently, large

135

136

expenses are required to collect the necessary information for a thorough search, as well as in the purchasing and development of the land, and the building of the factory. Costs are also incurred because of the interruption to production (especially in the case of a relocation) and the time expended in bringing a new site into commercial production (Dalhousie University, 1963; Whitman and Schmidt, 1966). These costs tend to discourage firms from considering new locations, expecially relocations, unless they are facing major problems at their existing sites. Thus they encourage locational inertia. The second aspect of the time dimension that has been neglected is the fact that locational decisions inevitably involve a large element of risk or uncertainty. Such decisions involve the provision of fixed capital with several years' life-span, but the future conditions facing the firm cannot be known for certain. This particular topic has recently received a thorough discussion (Webber, 1972). Most of these difficulties have been recognized by other writers and some attempts have been made to deal with them. It is not possible to review such work here (but see Walker, 1971, pp. 10–59, for a fuller discussion).

The economic man assumption has come under heavy fire of late. The assumption involves economic actors optimizing (usually with respect to financial goals), having complete knowledge of the relevant facts necessary to achieve their goals, and having the computational ability to calculate the optimal solution to problems. These qualities have been shown to be unrealistic for many if not all economic decisions. Goals are not always entirely economic and may be multiple, especially in large organizations. Individuals and firms rarely have the knowledge or ability to optimise, even if they wish to. In general, it has been recognised that a variety of economic behaviour may be expected both from person to person and for the same person over time. Pred's concept of the behavioural matrix illustrates this recognition (Pred, 1967, p. 25; 1969). The matrix categorizes economic actors on the basis of knowledge and ability to use the knowledge. Over time, if economic conditions remain similar, more and more actors may be expected to approach perfection in knowledge and ability, but major changes or parametric shocks would throw them back to being low on both scores.

5.2. Adaptation

The concept of adaptation focuses specifically on goals and the methods of attaining them over a period of time. It would seem, therefore, to offer scope in dealing with problems outlined in the previous section. It has in fact been utilized in a large number of disciplines.[1] Certain features seem to be common to all of these uses. Firstly, there is some *goal* or *objective* to which the adaptor, be it man or machine, is working. As long as the goal is reached, the adaptor has *stability*, which does not necessarily imply an absolutely fixed condition but more often allows slight variation. Thus, the goal is often to keep certain variables within set limits. Stability is achieved because the adaptor has *adaptive mechanisms*, which allow a variety of responses to match a variety of environmental conditions. The adaptor is *self-regulating*: no external interference is necessary to modify its behaviour under changed circumstances. The major aspects of relevance for the study of industrial location can be illustrated by discussion of three uses of the concept of adaptation; homeostasis, complex adaptive systems, and biological evolution.

The contemporary view of adaptation has been very greatly influenced by the work of Walter Cannon, a physiologist who coined the term, homeostatis. He was impressed by the ability of the human body to withstand considerable variation in external conditions. Cannon (1932) claimed that:

> 'The co-ordinated physiological processes which maintain most of the steady states in the organism are so complex and so peculiar to living beings . . . that I have suggested as special designation for these states, "homeostasis". The word does not imply something set and immobile, a stagnation. It means a condition which may vary, but which is relatively constant'. (p. 24).

Cannon's belief that a new term for the process was needed reflects the recognition that, in organisms, the equilibrium which is maintained in relation to the external environment is brought about by mechanisms which react in a variety of ways to changing circumstances in order to achieve some goal. The organism has a need to keep certain internal conditions, such as body heat, within specific limits. This stability is achieved because there is a feedback of information between the organism and the environment and because of the ability of certain adaptive mechanisms to respond in a variety of ways to a variety of conditions.

When Cannon suggested the term, homeostasis, to describe a process which he found applicable to studies of the higher animals, he thought that it 'may present some general principles for the establishment, regulation and control of steady states, that would be suggestive for other kinds of organization—even social and industrial—which suffer from disturbing perturbations' (Cannon, 1932, pp. 24–25). A little more than a decade after he wrote these words, the interest in concepts of control, information, maintenance of stability, adaptation and self-regulation had become so great amongst a number of workers in several fields that a new science, cybernetics, was being born. Weiner (1961), one of the originators, describes this field as the study of 'control and communication in the animal and the machine'. Ashby argues that its two great virtues are that: (1) 'It offers a vocabulary and a single set of concepts suitable for representing the most diverse types of system'; and (2) It provides a method for tackling highly complex systems (Ashby, 1964, p. 4). One development, which led to the founding of cybernetics and which has become increasingly important since, is the recognition that many features formerly considered applicable only to organisms may also be applied to machines.[2] Naturally, this aspect of adaptation has particularly interested engineers although Ashby's *Design for a Brain* is one of the best experiments in this direction.

The focus of this early work was on the individual as an adaptor. There are many cases, however, in which individuals combine into composites, such as firms, communities or societies. Such groups often develop some common modes of behaviour: a society has widely-accepted fashions or ethics, an organization its commonly-followed business goals. As such viewpoints and actions change, so the society or organization is adapting. Possible methods of adaptation are, however, very much more varied for composites than they are for individuals. The main reason for this is the possibility of structural changes. An individual organism cannot modify its internal structure to any important extent. If environmental conditions changed suddenly, it would not be possible to rearrange one's skeleton or internal organs as an adaptive response. A society, however, can make equivalent changes. Under threat of invasion, the members can change their function, switching to the production of war materials and to military service. A revolution in a society might lead to a complete rearrangement of the political power structure. This ability to change structure has led Buckley (1968, p. 490) to suggest that composites of people be termed 'complex adaptive systems'. [This potentiality for structural change, however, is not often fulfilled in society. Even seemingly major modifications often prove to be little more than a change of personnel rather than a change of organizational arrangements.] Another feature of complex adaptive systems, is that learning by the composite a a whole can take place not only by the learning of individuals but also by changes of personnel. Wise management can increase the knowledge of the firm by attracting experienced men from elsewhere. In contrast, the loss of a few key people could take a significant portion of the firm's knowledge out of the system.

The adaptation possible for complex adaptive systems is comparable to such adaptation of individuals as can only be made over a long-term period through processes of evolution. These processes are based on the slight differences, genetically-produced, that exist in individual organisms. Individuals are not all equally capable of coping with the environment: over a period of time, the most-adapted types tend to survive, the less suited breed less and die more easily. This selectivity assures the survival of the structures best suited to the environment not because of changes in any individual but because of the suitability of particular qualities (Dobzhansky, 1968). Differences in the type of organism which survives are based on both the nature of the initial population, that is its genetic attributes, and on the nature of the environment. Thus a fairly stable environment would encourage organisms with a narrow range of specialized reactions while a more varying one requires a greater variety of responses and a fuller ability to choose the most suitable.

In biology, adaptation through evolution is often associated with competition. The idea of the survival of the fittest in the struggle for life is important, If there were no competition, relatively poor quality adaptation would suffice, provided it ensured survival. The stiffer the competition, the greater the necessity for improvements. Such competition is an unconscious process in the sense that it arises without one individual being conscious of other, specific individuals as competitors. Most early human ecologists thought of it in this way too (Hollingshead, 1961, pp. 109–110; Hawley, 1961, p. 146). A similar idea is involved in the economists' concept of perfect competition, in which a kind of 'invisible hand' regulates the market process. No one person, whether buyer or seller, is able to affect the market price and each, therefore, behaves only with respect to given cost, price, and demand conditions. There is no concern for individual competitors. In human affairs, however, there are many occasions when competition is not impersonal. The markets in economics are often oligopolistic. In human ecology also, a purely biological conception of competition is now usually considered inadequate (Hollingshead, 1961; Quinn, 1961, p. 139). Competition can reasonably be considered as a process in which men as individuals or composites attempt to gain use or control of scarce resources. There is little advantage in limiting the concept on the basis of motivations or methods of the competitors. In addition, it should be noted that co-operation is important in the process of biological evolution, in many social processes and in the business world. Full-scale, 'cut-throat' competition is not always the best way to advance.

5.3. Adaptation by Manufacturing Firms

As one type of human organization, a manufacturing firm possesses adaptive qualities. Primarily through the decisions of its management, it works towards a goal or goals in an economic environment, which in most cases changes fairly frequently. It has some adaptive mechanisms which operate more or less homeostatically, that is they are built into its structure and function automatically. An increased demand, within certain limits, can be supplied by the same labour force and the same machines. A decline of sales due to an aggressive competitor will frequently provoke, in the sales and publicity departments, an almost automatic response designed to meet the threat. In the realm of material supplies, a firm may easily respond to rising costs at one source by switching to another, which has become relatively cheaper.

Such external changes may, however, be too extreme for an homeostatic mechanism to deal with. A firm is then forced to make full use of its flexibility as a complex adaptive system. Adaptation may be purely organizational, involving changes in personnel without any physical modification. On the other hand, it could include a modernization programme or expansion at the current site, a relocation, or establishment of some type of branch plant or subsidiary development. The alternative to structural change is decline and, possibly, extinction. If a firm fails to adapt, its better-adapted competitors will take over at its expense, eventually forcing it out of business.

The idea of adaptation is in fact not new to the industrial location literature. In 1950, Armen Alchian applied some evolutionary, biological concepts to economics. He suggested that the success of individuals or firms is a function both of the way they behave and the economic environment in which they exist. Thus, for example, a firm might choose a location more or less by chance but economic conditions could favour it and the firm would be adopted by the environment. Generally, however, firms attempt to adapt to these conditions so that, for example, if a new market developed at some distance away from the existing location, a new branch plant may be built to serve it. Alchian was not particularly concerned about the locational aspects of the survival of firms but Tiebout (1957) developed his idea into such a context. Several writers have since referred to this adaptive–adoptive approach in relation to industrial location and used it to help explain the locational dynamics of manufacturing in particular study areas (for example, Pred, 1966; Leblanc, 1969, pp. 6–11; Gilmour, 1972, pp. 83–86).

Not all types of adaptation affect the spatial organization of a firm directly. Price changes may often have no effect, while modifications to machinery or reorganization of personnel usually cause only minor spatial modifications. It is suggested that the term *spatial adaptation* be reserved for those types of adjustment in which a deliberate effort is being made to cope with the spatial dimension, for example, the price of inputs from various sources, the size of demand in different areas, or the cost of transportation changes. As a result of such environmental change, the firm may adjust its pattern of goods linkages to improve its profit record. One class of spatial adaptation may be termed *locational adaptation*. In this case, management decisions directly affect the location of the firm's production, that is through the building of new plants or the expansion or closing of existing ones.

5.4. An Adaptive Model of Location Decisions: The Individual Firm

Focusing initially on the individual firm an adaptive systems model is proposed as a framework for studying locational decisions. This is partly based on a model by Murphy (1965, pp. 12–31) and is illustrated by Figure 5.1. The adapting unit is a firm. Its economic strength and character are described by the structural system $(\mathbf{S})$, the firm's physical assets.[3] The nature of the adaptation is controlled by the firm's management through the decision-making function $(\mathbf{D})$. Outside the firm is an environment which includes all factors not within the control of the firm, such as the actions of suppliers, buyers, government departments and the whole range of events which comprise the general economic and social conditions of the society in which the firm is operating. In the model, factors in the environment affect the firm directly through the structural environmental vector $(\mathbf{U})$ and indirectly through the management by means of the decision-maker's environmental vector $(\mathbf{V})$.[4]

The economic condition of the firm at time $t + 1$ $(\mathbf{S}_{t+1})$ is some function of the structural environmental vector, the decision vector and its condition at time t (*a priori* structural state vector)

$$\mathbf{S}_{t+1} = \mathbf{T}_e(\mathbf{U}_t, \mathbf{D}_t, \mathbf{S}_t) \qquad t = 0, 1, 2, \ldots$$

The decision vector is some function of the decision maker's environmental vector, the historical information vector and the structural state vector of a previous time period.

$$\mathbf{D}_t = \mathbf{D}(\mathbf{V}_t, \mathbf{H}_{t-1}, \mathbf{S}_{t-1}) \qquad t = 0, 1, 2, \ldots$$

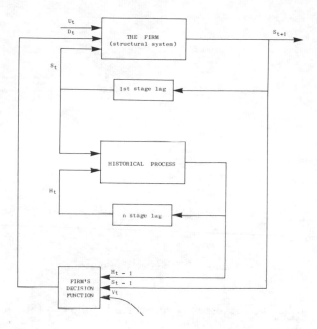

Figure 5.1. An adaptive process for a manufacturing
firm

The historical information vector contains the record of the firm's history. This
includes the effects of particular environmental changes and of management
decisions in the past. It is affected both by its predecessor and the immediate
past condition of the firm.

$$\mathbf{H}_t = \mathbf{T}_h(\mathbf{H}_{t-1}, \mathbf{S}_{t-1}) \qquad t = 0, 1, 2, \ldots$$

In Figure 5.1, the decision function is depicted as a 'black box'. That is, the
working of the function is unknown but, by observing outputs and inputs, one
can develop an ability to predict outputs from inputs. Figure 5.2 makes this
function more explicit, in a formulation which owes much to Miller, Galanter,
and Pribam (1960). A manufacturing firm has a broad general goal (or perhaps
more than one) for example, to make as much profit as possible or to attain a
high share of the market.[5] In order to achieve such goals, the decision-maker
must operationalize them. Some clearcut, specific objectives are established
which are expected to lead to their attainment. These operational goals will
depend partly on his own make-up but will be some function of the environ-
ment $\mathbf{V}_t$, the structural system $\mathbf{S}_{t-1}$ and the historical process $\mathbf{H}_{t-1}$. An example
of a general operational goal would be to attain an 8 per cent net profit per
annum. Subsidiary operational goals are likely to be drawn up in order to allow
a reasonable chance of attaining this objective. For instance, it may be decided
that a new branch plant is essential, a community with certain characteristics is
necessary for its success, and some specific site features crucial to its smooth

142

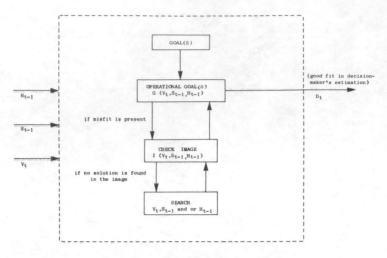

Figure 5.2. The decision unit

operation. In other words, a means-end chain is followed (Simon, 1957, pp. 62–66).

Having established operational goals, the manufacturer begins to look for ways of attaining them. He searches his image of the environment (Boulding, 1956, pp. 3–18) which, although it is a function of V_t, S_{t-1} and H_{t-1}, may be a very distorted function. As various possible solutions are evaluated, there is a considerable feedback between the operational goals and the image. The manufacturer is only able to test solutions in terms of expected results and this feature of the process makes it more complicated. If no solution is found from his image, the manufacturer may search elsewhere for one. In particular he would look at the environment but he may also be helped by a study of his historical information vector and even the immediate past history of his firm (S_{t-1}). Search procedures will modify the manufacturer's image and are likely to continue until a solution is found or until the decision-maker feels a solution is impossible, even after modifying both his image and his operational goals. In the case of the latter conclusion, the firm may accept a reduced profit level or, if it incurs losses, will probably go out of business.

Should the present state of the structural system (the firm's physical assets) satisfy the operational goals at any t_1, there is no need for the procedure to be initiated. New solutions are sought only if the operational goals are not being met, that is if there is a misfit (Alexander, 1966, Chapter 2). In such a case, the manufacturer looks for a solution which fits his goals to the environmental situation. Once such a solution has been found, he will apply it.

While operational goals may be quite frequently modified, the broader, more general business goals of a manufacturer are less likely to change. Thus in Figure 5.2, they are not modified by feedback. In the long run, however, they may be altered to some extent and this is recognized by the fact that they are contained within the decision function box rather than outside it. They are not isolated but may be influenced by **H, S** and **V**.

5.5. Some Empirical Evidence

Evidence related to the components of this model is spotty. There are numerous studies designed to trace which environmental (location) factors influenced the choice of location of specific firms, but investigations of decision-making procedures are less common. In general, however, this evidence is much more abundant now than it was five years ago.

On the subject of misfit variables (those factors encouraging firms to consider a change of location), a substantial difference of crucial variables might be expected by area. Nevertheless, several factors have shown up quite widely, perhaps because most studies have inevitably focused on old-established industrial areas, especially within cities. Keeble (1968) found that a large majority of North-West London firms which relocated elsewhere or established branches between 1940 and 1964 were undergoing expansion to service a growing market. Similar findings were obtained by Cameron and Clark (1966, pp. 71–74) for plants moving into areas qualifying for government assistance in the United Kingdom, and by Walker (1971, pp. 138–148) for the Maritime Provinces where the expansion of the regional marked proved a major attraction. In most cases negative factors were also present at existing sites, in particular, space or labour were in short supply at current locations.

Investigations which have attempted to find out about the goals of firms within the context of locational choice are few and far between, despite the clear importance of these in affecting the whole decision-making procedure. In the Maritime Provinces study, open-ended questions of senior executives revealed the goals listed in Table 5.1 (Walker, 1971, pp. 155–168). In circumstances where it was found that almost equal weight was given to two or more objectives these were allowed, so that there are more than one major goal per plant. The two categories of plant refer to newly-established ones, and those that were expanding or modernizing (upgrading). In this study, the replies were not subjected to systematic scrutiny but recently Stafford has suggested that interviews about the whole locational process could be analysed by means of content analysis (Stafford, forthcoming). He has followed this procedure with the aid of a psychologist. Such an approach may allow a better understanding of manufacturers' goals as related to locational choice. Some form of psychological analysis certainly seems to be necessary.

Locational adaptation tends to be an option that is considered only after other types of adaptation have been proved to be unsatisfactory. Because of the inconvenience, time and cost involved, even the development of a branch plant comes low on the list after various non-locational forms of adaptation and on-site expansion have been investigated. Relocation is recognized as a practical option even more rarely. A number of studies have focused on the overall adaptation by firms over a number of years (McNee, 1958; Steed,

Table 5.1. **Manufacturers' business goals in the maritime provinces**

	New plants		Upgrading plants	
Goals	Major goals	Secondary goals	Major goals	Secondary goals
High-Level Economic				
Maximum profit	18	1	3	0
High investment return	4	1	2	0
Growth	7	1	5	0
Increase sales or share of market	12	0	5	0
Lower-Level Economic				
Maintain sales or share of market	4	0	2	0
Good profit	8	5	3	3
Adequate living or profit	16	13	1	0
Cost reduction	1	0	0	0
To benefit the Corporate organization as a whole	11	0	0	0
Production of good quality products	4	0	0	1
Primarily Non-Economic				
Self-employment	12	1	0	0
To allow owner to live locally	4	14	0	0
To help community or area	9	2	1	2

1968; Fleming and Krumme, 1968). These have so far been mainly descriptive, and they have also tended to be confined to large multi-plant corporations.

The actual locational decision-making procedure used by manufacturers has been investigated by quite a large number of researchers recently. Outlines of the process have been suggested by Townroe (1971), Dicken (1971), Rees (1972), Stafford (1972) and others, while many earlier studies have provided data on aspects of these procedures (Ellis, 1949; Mueller *et al*, 1961; Luttrell, 1962; Cameron and Clark, 1966). It is easy to become bogged in the mass of empirical detail but the key features in the process from a geographical point of view seem to be the way in which areas were searched, and the information sources used by management to aid them in the procedure.

The size of the area considered for a location is related to the firm's goals, which may well restrict operations to a particular community, region or country. Some exceptionally thorough firms may go through a process starting with a spatial scale that involves choosing an appropriate country, then region, community and site, each scale involving a somewhat different set of location factors. In most cases, however, the search procedure is pretty sketchy at one or more of these scales. Moreover, the search level usually only starts with a comparison of cummunities and it seems to be rare for more than four or five communities or sites to be seriously considered. The procedure is not always as tidy as this discussion implies. In some industries, for example, the community is of no importance because site conditions are stringent. An oil refinery for example is likely to be located in terms of national and/or regional market conditions and specific site features, especially if it is based on imported petroleum.

The overall procedure, as well as that affecting each spatial scale, is likely to be considerably influenced by the method of information gathering. If companies rely heavily on the existing knowledge of the owner or executives, the likelihood is that the local area will weigh very heavily because of the characteristics of the mean information field (Abler *et al.*, 1971, pp. 413–416). Reliance on friends and fellow businessmen could well help to perpetuate existing locational features. Only a wide-ranging examination of data can be expected to allow a locational choice which is close to optimal. This, however, implies a large expenditure which may be beyond smaller firms. Empirical studies of the relationship between information sources and locational choice are fairly limited in number (Ellis, 1949, pp. 178–193; Luttrell, 1962, I, pp. 72–75; Walker, 1971, pp. 180–182). The evidence suggests a distinction between new firms, for which the owners rarely consult outside information sources to any great extent, and existing ones. Management of the latter frequently make use of government bodies at all levels, and occasionally use special studies or engage consultants.

5.6. Manufacturing Industry in the Aggregate

The focus on the individual firm in the previous sections is important in identifying some of the key aspects of locational adaptation. For the purpose of understanding the dynamic development of an industrial space economy, however, it is crucial to transfer these insights to the aggregate situation.

The Alchian–Tiebout, adoptive–adaptive approach provides a lead in this direction. An industry as a whole adapts to changing circumstances over time partly by means of the birth and death of firms and partly by modifications in the behaviour of the existing firms. Thus a number of firms can be seen to be placed in an environment which is common to all of them but which affects them selectively (tending either to adopt or not to adopt them) and which is responded to in a variety of ways (the method of adaptation being different for each).

It would greatly simplify the picture if the types of adaptation could in any way be generalized. Are there, for example, sufficient similarities in goals or search procedures amongst certain *groups* of firms to warrant some form of classification? It is not necessary that all firms in a group always adapt in the same way. Probabilities of particular forms af adaptation would be adequate to allow the modelling of expected changes. An empirical study along these lines suggests that there is indeed hope for generalization (Walker, 1971). As part of a study of procedures followed by managements in their search for a new site, a relatively crude scale was developed, which included components related to goals, area of search for the site, and number of information sources consulted. From this scale, six behaviour types were categorized with Number 1 indicating the most economically-oriented and most thoroughly-searched decision, and Number 6 being the case of no real search being made and non-economic motives being very strong (especially the desire to remain in a specific community).[6] The firms were classified on the basis of data that is relatively easily obtainable into seven categories:

Class 1 Small (under 15 employees) single-plant firms, controlled from the same community.
Class 2 Same type of firm as Class 1 with control from elsewhere in the province.
Class 3 Larger single-plant firm, controlled from the same community.
Class 4 Same type of firm as Class 3 with control elsewhere in the province.
Class 5 Branch of a firm with head office in the same region.
Class 6 Plant of a firm or organization with up to five plants.
Class 7 Plant of a multi-plant or multi-company concern.

Table 5.2 shows how locational adaptation cross-classified with plants type in this particular empirical study, conducted in connection with plants being located in the Maritime Provinces of Canada.

Table 5.2. Locational behaviour by plant type

Plant Type	Behaviour Type											
	1		2		3		4		5		6	
	No.	%	No.	%	No.	%	No.	%	No.	%	No.	%
1	1	2·4	2	4·9	1	2·4	18	43·9	7	17·1	12	29·3
2	0	0·0	0	0·0	2	50·0	1	25·0	1	25·0	0	0·0
3	0	0·0	1	11·1	3	33·3	5	55·6	0	0·0	0	0·0
4	0	0·0	1	20·0	0	0·0	1	20·0	3	60·0	0	0·0
5	0	0·0	1	50·0	0	0·0	0	0·0	1	50·0	0	0·0
6	2	40·0	3	60·0	0	0·0	0	0·0	0	0·0	0	0·0
7	7	38·9	6	33·3	1	5·6	2	11·1	2	11·1	0	0·0

More than 50 per cent of decision-makers in each of the first four classes were involved in relatively low-level decisions, concerned at best with a site comparison. All of the least economic decisions were made in connection with locally-controlled, small, single-plant firms. The fact that three of the five Class 4 firms failed to compare sites was unexpected but in two of three cases, there was a take-over of existing plants and, in a third, the owner already owned the land on which the plant was eventually built. The data for these four classes suggest, but are inadequate to prove, that locational behaviour improves from Class 1 to Class 7 plants. Plants in Classes 6 and 7 have been located with relatively greater care and it is worth noting that there are reasons for three of the four plants having low-level decisions. In one case, although the firm is a large multi-firm corporation, it is locally controlled; in another, government influence was very strong through incentives, and in the third case, the development was in essence an expansion, although performed under the guise of a new company. An extremely complicated classification scheme would be necessary to cover all possible details of these types.

Those cases which seem to be anomalous can mainly be related to special factors such as particularly strong government influence or to problems related to the classification (expected new plants proving to be take-overs or expansions in reality). No systematic variations arose which suggest that other attributes would be more useful for the purpose at hand than the ones chosen. The small numbers of plants in each industry group was a limitation in this study and possibly some useful relationship could be found if a much larger group of plants were available for analysis. As yet, the empirical evidence is inadequate to support the view that helpful classification is possible but there is good reason for optimism.[7]

5.7. An Adaptive Model of Locational Dynamics: The Aggregate Pattern

The argument of this essay leads logically to a model of locational change which specifies environmental conditions varying over time, and decision-makers adapting to these conditions. The decision-makers could be specified individually or in terms of probabilities, dependent upon some classification procedure. Major operational questions arise at this point. Just which features of the environment are important enough to be included? How may decision-making procedures be generalized in a meaningful way? And how do these two aspects interrelate? In this section, a specific model will be described in some detail.[8]

This model at present only deals with some types of locational adaptation and is, therefore, certainly incomplete. It covers the choice of a new site, which could however be next to an existing one. Thus it can consider expansion which involves the use of extra land but not modernization or reorganization. It is a simulation model which is very flexible, using no complex mathematical or statistical procedures.

The land area is specified in terms of sites and transportation routes. The sites may be combined into communities, counties or regions, each of which may be given a large number of attributes relevant to the locational decision-maker. These are listed in Tables 5.3 to 5.5.

It will be observed that some of these attributes are ones that can be easily specified quantitatively, for example wage rates, or hydro availability. Others, however, are less clearcut. For example, some type of scale must be developed to rate labour relations, educational facilities or the fire protection service. The details of how such scales could be set up are not considered here, as the use of the model has not progressed to the stage where this has been done. The three tables specify important location factors, recognizing the fact that these are not the same at every spatial scale. Each factor has a default option which sets a particular value for it if the model operator does not specify one. Thus, for example, it may be that a particular wage rate could operate over a whole region if different ones were not put in for communities. This allows most variables to be held constant so that experiments with just a few can be conducted very easily. In addition to the attributes listed, it is also possible to specify special attributes for a site or area.

Transportation routes are listed in terms of the sites that they run through. They may completely use up a site or allow at least some of the land to remain available. Their type is specified.

Table 5.3. Region attributes

Code	Value range	Units	Default	Meaning
1	⩾ 0	—	5	Labour relations (skilled)
2	⩾ 0	—	5	Labour relations (unskilled)
3	⩾ 0	—	5	Expectation of higher prod. (skilled)
4	⩾ 0	—	5	Expectation of higher prod. (unskilled)
5	⩾ 0	$1,000	0	Federal grant
6	⩾ 0	$1,000	0	Regional grant
7	⩾ 0	$1,000	0	Federal loan amount (maximum)
8	⩾ 0	years	0	Federal loan, Number of interest-free years
9	⩾ 0	%	0	Federal loan, Interest/year
10	⩾ 0	$1,000	0	Regional loan amount (maximum)
11	⩾ 0	years	0	Regional loan, Number of interest-free years
12	⩾ 0	%	0	Regional loan, interest/year
13	⩾ 0	—	5	Recreation rating
14	⩾ 0	—	5	Education rating
15	⩾ 0	%	15	Taxation
16	⩾ 0	10,000	0	Size of population

Firms in the model may operate or wish to locate one or more plants. Certain features of the firm are shown in Table 5.6. These allow classification when it is desired. When the firm's management decides to locate a plant, certain features of the plant are specified, reflecting their broad operational goals. In Table 5.7, these are indicated. Also shown there is an indication of the reason for looking for a new site, and whether a branch plant or relocation is being contemplated. These two features may be of some importance in affecting the search procedure.

Table 5.4. Community attributes

Code	Value range	Units	Default	Meaning
1	≥ 0	—	5	Unskilled labour relations
2*	≥ 0	1,000 men	1	Unskilled labour availability
3	≥ 0	¢/hr	250	Unskilled labour, average wage
4	≥ 0	—	5	Unskilled labour: expectation of higher prod.
5	≥ 0	—	5	Skilled labour: relations
6	≥ 0	—	5	Skilled labour: expectation of higher prod.
7*	≥ 0	100 men	1	Skilled labour type 1: avalability
8	≥ 0	¢/hr	600	Skilled labour type 1: average wage
9*	≥ 0	100 men	1	Skilled labour type 2: availability
10	≥ 0	¢/hr	600	Skilled labour type 2: average wage
11*	≥ 0	100 men	1	Skilled labour type 3: availability
12	≥ 0	¢/hr	600	Skilled labour type 3: average wage
13*	≥ 0	100 men	1	Skilled labour type 4: availability
14	≥ 0	¢/hr	600	Skilled labour type 4: average wage
15*	≥ 0	100 men	1	Skilled labour type 5: availability
16	≥ 0	¢/hr	600	Skilled labour type 1: average wage
17	≥ 0	$/u	1	Fuel cost/unit
18	≥ 0	$/u	1	Hydro cost/unit
19*	≥ 0	1,000 u	100	Hydro available units
20	≥ 0	$/unit	1	Water cost/unit
21*	≥ 0	1,000 unit	100	Water available units
22	≥ 0	—	5	Waste disposal rating
23*	≥ 0	1,000 units	100	Waste disposal available capacity
24	≥ 0	—	5	Education rating
25	≥ 0	—	5	Police rating
26	≥ 0	—	5	Fire protection rating
27	≥ 0	—	5	Recreational rating
28	≥ 0	$/site	300	Land taxation ($/site)
29	≥ 0	$/$1,000	10	Plant taxation ($/$1,000 plant value)
30	≥ 0	u $1,000	0	Maximum federal grant
31	≥ 0	$1,000	0	Maximum regional grant
32	≥ 0	$1,000	0	Maximum federal loan
33	≥ 0	years	0	Number free years federal loan
34	≥ 0	%	0	Annual interest federal loan
35	≥ 0	$1,000	0	Maximum regional loan
36	≥ 0	years	0	Number free years regional loan
37	≥ 0	%	0	Annual interest regional loan
38	≥ 0, 1	—	0	0 = may not have both Federal and Regional aid 1 = may have both Federal and Regional aid
39	≥ 1	10,000	50	Population size

* When a plant locates in a community, its requirements of this resource is subtracted from the available quantity.

Table 5.5. Site attributes

Code	Value range	Units	Default	Meaning
1	0, 1	—	1	1 = may combine with other sites 0 = may not combine with other sites
2	> 0	$100	50	Price
3	> 0	—	5	Water rating
4	> 0	—	5	Hydro rating
5	> 0	—	0	Soil type (rating)
6	> 0	—	5	Waste disposal rating
7	> 0	—	0	Actual zone (legal zone)
8	> 0	—	0	Current land use
9	> 0	1,000 sq. ft.	0	Vacant buildings space
10	> 0	$100/month	0	Vacant buildings rent
11	> 0	—	0	Current resident type

Table 5.6. Firm attributes

Code	Value range	Units	Default	Meaning
1	> 0	—	—	Type of firm
2	> 0	10 men	—	Employment size
3			Region	⎫
4			RLU	of ⎬ head office
5	> 0		Site	⎭
6				Age of firm
7	> 0			Number of plants

The firm's management decides how far away to search (i.e. it is specified by the model's operator or in terms of a probability). It may be only within the local community (i.e. where the head office is located) or it may be nationwide. According to the decision made, operational goals are set in terms of the attributes shown in Tables 5.3 to 5.5. Thus at a regional level, a population of greater than 500,000 may be mandatory and the only requirement. At community level, more features are likely to be required, perhaps minimum numbers of workers at certain skills with maximum wage rates, minimal levels on amenity and education, and maximum taxation rates. Finally at site level, the requirement would match the attributes in Table 5.5. Operational goals for the plant, then, may include specification of exact requirements, maxima, or minima.

As well as specifying the area of search and the operational goals applicable to a series of spatial scales, a search procedure must also be chosen. At any one scale, several options are available. Firstly, either a satisficing or optimizing approach may be taken. That is, the first site possessing the firm's requirements may be taken or the best of a number may be sought (Simon, 1959, pp.

151

Table 5.7. Plant attributes

Code	Value range	Units	Default	Meaning
1	> 0	—	—	Type of plant (SIC code)
2	> 0	$10,000	—	Value of plant (physical)
3	> 0	$10,000	—	Expected taxable income
4	> 0	$10,000	—	Max. total cost for location
5*	0, 1	—	—	Will use information source (regional)
6*	0, 1	—	—	Will use information source (community)
7	> 1	Sites	—	Number of sites required (width)
8	> 1	Sites	—	Number of sites required (depth)
9	> 1	—	—	Reason for search
10	0, 1	—	—	Branch of relocation

* 0 = NO, 1 = YES.

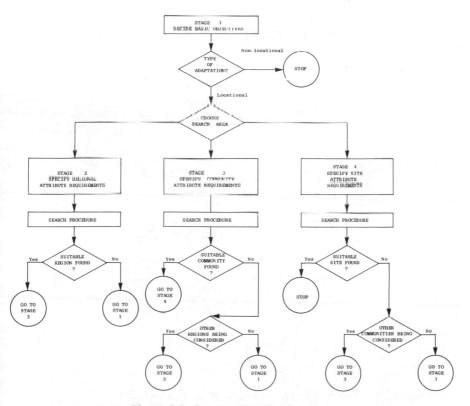

Figure 5.3. Computer model flowchart

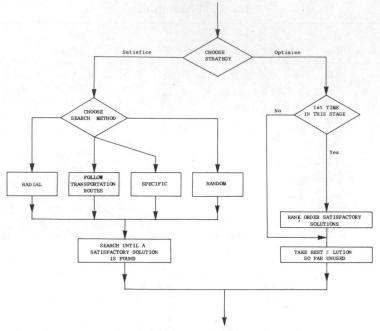

Figure 5.4. Search procedure in the model

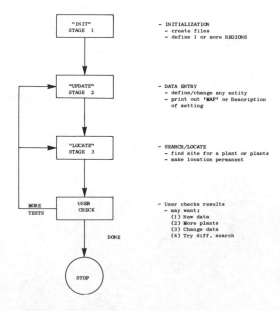

Figure 5.5. Organization of programs in the
computer model

262–264; Odnoff, 1965). If an optimal solution is required, the actual procedure of search does not matter very much but this is not true in the case of satisficing because the finding of the first suitable site will be dependent on the method used. In this model, decision-makers may search along one or more transportation routes for a specified distance, search gradually outwards from a particular location, or use an irregular procedure (for example, looking only at sites which have been suggested to them). A choice of these procedures, and of optimizing and satisficing, is available at each of the three spatial scales. Figures 5.3 and 5.4 provide a flow chart of the search procedure used in the model.

5.8. The Computer Model

The computer model has four basic programs, indicated by Figure 5.5. They require about 550 Bytes for execution. PL1 language is used but it would be possible to adapt to Fortran fairly easily.

Organization of the model revolves around its data structure. Data are stored as either full-word or half-word integers, or eight-byte character strings. They are organized into a number of files, shown in Table 5.8.

Table 5.8. Computer model file organization

File	Record length (bytes)	No. of records/2314 track
Region	80	40
Comm	188	22
Site-A	30	56
Site-P	612	10
Spec	160	27
Plants	110	34
Direc	254	20

Contents of each file are as follows:

Region	System status and regions
Comm	Communities and counties
Site-A	Sites
Site-P	For each sub-area, the SITE-P file points to every site within the area and indicates its attributes and availability.
Spec	Special attribute groups i.e. features which occasionally required by plants but are not indicated in the list of attributes for regions, communities or sites, as shown in Tables.
Plants	Firms and plants and their search requirements.
Direc	Directory of firm, county, community and special attribute group names.

The total size of each file depends on the size of area being considered, and the number of firms and plants. A detailed discussion of the model is available separately from the author.

5.9. The Potentialities of the Model

It is not yet possible to discuss results arising from the use of the model owing to the fact that it is not fully operational. What is clear at this stage is that there is considerable potential for its application in at least three ways: in experiments, as an aid to industrial development strategy, and for teaching purposes.

A major problem in social science is the difficulty of isolating variables in a real world situation in order to study them in ways comparable to the detailed experimental procedures of the natural sciences. A reasonably realistic computer model, however, provides scope for this type of work. In the context of industrial location, this could be particularly valuable for the study of interrelationships between decision-making procedures and the resulting spatial patterns of manufacturing plants. Important questions can be raised in this context:

In what ways is the locational pattern likely to vary according to the different goals that are pursued?

What is the effect of different decisions with respect to the size of the search area used when a new location is being sought?

Is it likely to make very much difference if decision-makers search along particular routes as opposed to fanning out in all directions, or looking only at specific places (e.g. based on advice or special information)?

How important is the initial location of the decision makers in affecting the subsequent pattern of industry?

In the simulation model, hypotheses related to these and similar questions can be tested under a variety of environmental conditions and over time periods of differing duration. In other words, very thorough examination is possible.

The answers to some of these questions, even though hypotheses are tested in somewhat abstract situations, could prove to be very helpful in facilitating the interpretation of locational trends. In this context, agencies responsible for industrial location may be aided. If the model can be used to give some indication of the way that present trends are leading, this would certainly be a valuable input into strategy concerned with development. It would point out the undesirable aspects requiring special treatment as well as those which were leading to future patterns consistent with the goals of the strategists.

Such use of a model in the development process assumes that real-world data are available. Data related to the environment required by the model are generally available, although not always in published form. It is reasonable to assume, at least for North America and Britain, that a development agency responsible for a particular area could obtain a high proportion of the required information. It is not as easy to find out how firms are conducting their decision-making. In most cases, it is expected that probabilities of particular types of behaviour would be used. These would be based either on surveys conducted specifically for an area or others conducted under similar circumstances. Certainly, a great deal of work would be necessary to set up the model for a particular area but it should not prove to be impossible. For any overall picture of the space economy, this model would have to be used in conjunction with other models which calculated the values of many of the inputs (e.g., population, land costs, changes in transportation routes, etc.). Development agencies could use such a model for regular business as well as long-term planning. When potential clients asked for information about locations possessing certain characteristics, the model could provide a print-out of such sites and also a large amount of extra information if it were required.

The final realm of potential use for this model is educational. It would allow students both to examine a fantastic variety of interrelationships and also to work with quite simple situations. It is possible for large numbers of the variables to be set to zero in such a way that very small amounts of computer time are needed to operate the model when only a few variables are being studied. Although this potential has not yet been thoroughly investigated, it is likely that the model can be made interactive, that is students could sit down at a terminal and interact with the computer, receiving answers very quickly to each input.

5.10. Conclusion

Studies of the development of an industrial space economy can be approached either at a macro-level with a focus on an examination *via* statistical procedures, or by means of a more behavioural method, emphasizing the role of individual manufacturing firms as agents in producing locational patterns. The two approaches are complementary. It is envisaged that at some stage it would be possible to examine output of the model discussed in this essay in a way which will allow direct comparison with such approaches as those suggested by Curry (1964, 1966) or by Norcliffe in the first essay of this volume.

The present essay has focused on the concept of adaptation as an appropriate framework for the study of the behaviour of firms in the context of changing environmental conditions. Key aspects of adaptation are the goals of the firm, the information sources used, and the method of searching for solutions. In the context of locational adaptations, the area of search is also very important. Beginning with an examination of individual firms, the emphasis switched to a model which incorporates numerous decision makers. Some indication of the potential uses of such a model has been provided. At this point in time no evaluation of the operation of the model can be made but the essay has offered a conceptual approach which offers hope both for abstract experimentation and real-world validation.

Acknowledgement

A grant from The Canada Council enabled the development of the computer model to be carried out.

156

Notes

1. For example in physiology (Cannon, 1932), engineering (Yovits and Cameron, 1960), biology (Ashby, no date), and economics (Murphy, 1965, pp. 1–11).
2. Beer, 1959, pp. 113–141 describes a large number of machines developed by various researchers.
3. The firm's physical assets include liquid assets, invested capital, land, buildings, and machinery. The liquid assets are used to pay for productive resources not owned by the firm, especially labour and management.
4. The vector terminology is used because this model has a mathematical structure and the vectors can be given values in an operational model.
5. For stylistic convenience and for simplification, the decision-maker is considered to be one person. Frequently, a number of people are involved. As the number of decision-makers increases, conflicts and compromises within the firm become more likely.
6. A Guttman scale was developed based on the following attributes:
   (1) Number of information sources.   Check if two or more sources from outside the firm were used.
   (2) Regional decision level.   Check if a comparative decision was made between regions.
   (3) Type of locational analysis.   Check if a detailed study was made.
   (4) Community decision level.   Check if a comparative decision was made between communities.
   (5) Site decision level.   Check if a comparative decision was made between sites.
   (6) Nature of business goals.   Check if these goals were entirely of an economic type.
   Managements were ranked on the basis of the positive checks on these attributes. They were then classified into behaviour types. Class 1 scored positively on all attributes, Class 2 on all but the first, Class 3 on all but the first three or four, Class 4 on only the last two, Class 5 on the last one, and Class 6 on none. Class 3 was a composite one because of the small numbers of plants involved.
7. This view was reinforced by discussion at a Symposium on 'The Spatial Organisation of the Firm' at the Annual Conference of the Institute of British Geographers, January 1973.
8. The author is indebted to Mr. Paul Wilson at the University of Waterloo for his invaluable work in the development of the computer model. He has been responsible for formulating its structure and writing the programmes.

References

Abler, R. *et al.* (1971), *Spatial Organization. The Geographer's View of the World.* Englewood Cliffs, N.J.: Prentice-Hall.

Alchian, A. A. (1950, Uncertainty, Evolution and Economic Theory, *Journal of Political Economy*, **58**, 211–221.

Alexander, C. (1966), *Notes on the Synthesis of Form.* Cambridge, Mass.: Harvard University Press.

Ashby, W. R. (1964), *An Introduction to Cybernetics.* London: University Paperbacks.

Ashby, W. R. (no date), *Design for a Brain.* Second Edition, London: Science Paperbacks.

Beer, S. (1959), *Cybernetics and Management.* London: English Universities Press.

Boulding, K. E. (1956), *The Image.* Ann Arbor: Michigan University Press.

Buckley, W. (1968), Society as a Complex Adaptive System, in Buckley, W. (ed.), *Modern Systems Research for the Behavioural Scientist.* Chicago: Aldine, 490–513.

157

Cameron, G. C. and Clark, B. D. (1966), *Industrial Movement and the Regional Problem*. University of Glasgow Social and Economic Studies, Occasional Papers No. 5. Edinburgh: Oliver and Boyd.

Cannon, W. B. (1932), *The Wisdom of the Body*. New York: Norton.

Curry, L. (1966), Chance and Landscape, in House J. W. (ed.), *Northern Geographical Essays in Honour of G. H. J. Daysh*. Newcastle-upon-Tyne: Oriel Press, 40–55.

Curry, L. (1964), The Random Spatial Economy: An Exploration in Settlement Theory, *Annals, Association of American Geographers*, **54**, 138–146.

Dalhousie University, Institute of Public Affairs and Nova Scotia Department of Trade and Industry (1963), *An Account of the Industrial Development, 1963*. Halifax, Nova Scotia: Dalhousie University Institute of Public Affairs.

Dicken, P. (1971), Some Aspects of the Decision Making Behaviour of Business Organizations, *Economic Geography*, **47**, 426–437.

Dobzhansky, T. (1968), Man and Natural Selection, in Cohen Y. A. (ed.), *Man in Adaptation*. Chicago: Aldine, **1**, 37–48.

Ellis, G. (1949), Postwar Industrial Location in New England, unpublished Ph.D. Thesis, Harvard University.

Fleming, D. K. and Krumme, G. (1968), The 'Royal Hoesch Union': Case Analysis of Adjustment Patterns in the European Steel Industry, *Tijdschrift voor Economische en Sociale Geografie*, **59**, 177–199.

Gilmour, J. M. (1972), *Spatial Evolution of Manufacturing: Southern Ontario 1851–1861*. Toronto: University of Toronto, Department of Geography.

Hawley, A. (1961), Ecology and Human Ecology, in Theodorson G. A. (ed.), *Studies in Human Ecology*. Evanston: Harper and Row, 144–150.

Hollingshead, A. B. (1961), A Re-examination of Ecological Theory, in Theodorson, G. A. (ed.), *Studies in Human Ecology*. Evanston: Harper and Row, 108–114.

Keeble, D. E. (1968), Industrial Decentralization and the Metropolis: The North-West London Case, *Transactions, Institute of British Geographers*, **44**, 1–54.

Leblanc, R. G. (1969), *Location of Manufacturing in New England in the 19th Century*. Dartmouth: Center for the Study of Social Change.

Luttrell, W. F. (1962), *Factory Location and Industrial Movement*. 2 vols. London: National Institute of Economic and Social Research.

McNee, R. B. (1958), Functional Geography of the Firm, with an Illustrative Case Study from the Petroleum Industry, *Economic Geography*, **134**, 321–337.

McNee, R. B. (1960), Toward a More Humanistic Economic Geography: The Geography of Enterprise, *Tijdschrift voor Economische en Sociale Geografie*, **51**, 201–206.

Miller, G., Galanter, E. and Pribram, K. H. (1960), *Plans and the Structure of Behavior*. New York: Holt, Rinehart and Winston.

Murphy, R, E., Jr. (1965), *Adaptive Processes in Economic Systems*. New York: Academic Press.

Mueller, E. *et al.* (1961), *Location Decisions and Industrial Mobility in Michigan, 1961*. Ann Arbor: Institute for Social Research, University of Michigan.

Odhnoff, J. (1965), On the Techniques of Optimizing and Satisficing, *The Swedish Journal of Economics*, **67**, 24–73.

Pred, A. R. (1966), *The Spatial Dynamics of United States Urban-Industrial Growth, 1800–1914*. Cambridge, Mass.: M.I.T. Press.

Pred, A. R. (1967), *Behavior and Location. Part 1*. Lund: G. W. K. Gleerup.

Pred, A. R. (1969), *Behavior and Location. Part 2*. Lund: G. W. K. Gleerup.

Quinn, J. A. (1961), The Nature of Human Ecology: Re-Examination and Re-definition, in Theodorson, G. A. (ed.), *Studies in Human Ecology*. Evanston: Harper and Row. 135–141.

Rees, J. (1972), Implications of Modelling the Industrial Location Decision Process, in Adams, W. P. and Helleiner, F. M. (eds.), *International Geography 1972*. Montreal: University of Toronto Press, 582–584.

158

Simon, H. A. (1957), *Administrative Behavior*. Second Edition, New York: Macmillan.

Simon, H. A. (1959), Theories of Decision-Making in Economics and Behavioral Science, *American Economic Review*, **49**, 253–283.

Stafford, H. A. (1971), The Geography of Manufacturers, in Board, C. *et al.* (eds.), *Progress in Geography IV*. London: Arnold, 183–215.

Stafford, H. A. (1972), Industrial Location Decision: Content Analysis of Case Studies, in Hamilton, F. E. I. (ed.), *The Industrial Firm and Location Decisions*, London: Wiley.

Steed, G. P. F. (1968). The Changing Milieu of a Firm: A Case Study of a Shipbuilding Concern, *Annals, Association of American Geographers*, **58**, 506–525.

Tiebout, C. M. (1967), Location Theory, Empirical Evidence and Economic Evolution, *Papers and Proceedings, Regional Science Association*, **3**, 74–86.

Townroe, P. M. (1969), Locational Choice and the Individual Firm, *Regional Studies*, **3**, 15–24.

Townroe, P. M. (1971), *Industrial Location Decisions: A Study in Management Behavior*. Occasional Paper No. 15. Birmingham: University of Birmingham, Centre for Urban and Regional Studies.

Walker, D. F. (1971), An Adaptive Framework for the Study of Industrial Location Decisions, unpublished Ph.D. Thesis, University of Toronto.

Webber, M. J. (1972), *Impact of Uncertainty on Location*. Cambridge, Mass.: M.I.T. Press.

Wiener, N. (1961), *Cybernetics*. Second Edition, New York: M.I.T. Press and Wiley.

Whitman, E. S. and Schmidt, W. J. (1966), *Plant Re-location: A Case History of a Move*. New York: American Management Association.

Yovits, M. C. and Cameron, S. (1960), *Self-Organizing Systems: Proceedings of an Interdisciplinary Conference on Self-Organizing Systems*. New York: Pergamon.

6 Allometry and Manufacturing Hierarchy: A General System Theory Approach to Manufacturing Employment and Industry Incidence

E. FREDERICK KOENIG
JOHN S. LEWIS
D. MICHAEL RAY

6.1. Introduction

Growth is a universal phenomenon exhibited by almost all systems, whether physical, biological, or social. Kenneth Boulding notes:

'It does not follow from the mere universality of growth phenomenon that there must be a single unified theory of growth that will cover everything from the growth of a crystal to the growth of an empire. Growth itself is not a simple or a unified phenomenon and we cannot expect all the many forms of growth to come under the umbrella of a single theory. Nevertheless all growth phenomena have something in common, and, what is more important the classification of forms of growth, and hence of theories of growth seem to cut across most of the conventional boundaries of science'. (Boulding, 1953, p. 326)

Ludwig von Bertalanffy has explicitly elaborated theories of growth within general system theory and notes the fundamental distinction between growth-in-time and relative growth (von Bertalanffy, 1960 and 1968). Von Bertalanffy notes the simplicity and generality of relative growth concepts. The relationship between the size of a component to its system, or some other system component, either through time with the growth of the system, or at one point in time for corresponding systems of different sizes, is very commonly logarithmically linear. The relationship is general and has been very widely applied in the biological sciences and, within the social sciences, to phenomena such as the division of labour in primitive societies, the growth of support to productive staff in industrial firms and to urbanization and economic linkages within national economies. The objective of this paper is to review and illustrate the concepts of relative growth, identifying the concept of allometry both in its simple form, the logarithmically linear growth of components when measured against system growth, and in its broadest sense, the study of size and its consequences. A three stage mathematical methodology is developed and applied to relate the relative growth of total manufacturing employment in Canadian cities in the post World War II period to their industrial structure as measured by scores in a direct factor analysis of a binary matrix indicating incidence of each industry type. The concept of allometry serves not only as a guide to structure the research problem, organize the data, select the analytic tools and evaluate the results, but also offers firm bonds with other disciplines, principally the biological sciences, where growth has been a central research interest. The geography of economic systems is inescapably dynamic; accelerating rates of social change and of population and economic growth, and their impact on human organization and physical environment will demonstrate increasingly the deficiency of the synchronic approach and hence the need for a deeper understanding of relative growth and the consequences of size.

6.2. On Growth and Form

Growth may be of two quite different types, simple and structural. Simple growth entails only an increase in size, but a limit is set to such growth by the structure, or level of organization, of the system for 'growth creates form, but form limits growth' (Boulding, 1953, p. 337). Conversely, structural growth, which entails the development and evolution of the form of the system, both spatial and sectoral, may promote new potential for continuing growth and enable the system to maintain its functionality through a much wider size range.

Examples of the close association between size change and structural transformations abound in the physical and social sciences. Von Bertalanffy (1964, p. 21) writes that 'it is a truism in engineering that any machine requires changes in proportion to remain functional if it is built in different size'. This so-called engineering principle has its counterpart in the principle of biological similarity which states that in order to remain functional the ratio of certain key system parameters must remain constant regardless of variations in absolute size (Boulding, 1953). In many cases the maintenance of this ratio demands a change in structure which is indicated by a change in the proportion of parts with size change. As Samuel Brody (1954, p. 580) has remarked, 'the organism changes geometrically so as to remain the same physiologically'. The appeal to invariance as a final cause of change may seem counter-intuitive, but grasping this fundamental concept is imperative to a fuller understanding of growth and its consequences.

John Friedmann (1969) has emphasized the importance of the relationship between size and structure to understanding the development of social systems at all geographic scales. He writes that 'development is distinguished from growth and is characterized as an innovative process leading to the structural transformation of social systems. Societies which fail to achieve such transformations either become arrested in their growth or start to degenerate as their internal order breaks down into increasingly unstable and random relations'

(p. 4). Continued system viability is achieved in this hypothetical case through a series of spatial transformations of core-periphery relations leading eventually to a nested hierarchy of five spatial sub-systems: world, continent, nation, region and city.

In examining the growth of Denmark, 1801–1950; Switzerland, 1850–1950; and Belgium, 1846–1939, Naroll and von Bertalanffy (1956) observed that the urban proportion of the national population tends to grow at a constant rate with increasing total population. In each case the observed ratio of the specific growth rate of urban population to that of total population was greater than one-to-one indicating the increasing urban character of national populations with increasing size. It is no surprise that the proportion of the population that was urban had increased during system growth, but the regularity with which the transformation had taken place may indicate the fundamental role which size plays in determining the internal form of nations.

The relationship between size change and its structural consequence in intra-urban systems has also been widely demonstrated. Thus Larry Smith (1961, p. 40) argues that population size is usually the primary factor affecting the distribution of facilities between the central business district (CBD) and other sections of metropolitan areas, although physical characteristics of a city, its absolute rate of growth and the timing of the period of rapid growth are not unimportant. The CBD's proportion of a city's food stores and major comparison shops is most sensitive, and its proportion of major offices and medical-dental offices least sensitive, to city size. Minimum employment requirements to serve basic needs have also been observed to comprise a regularly increasing proportion of city labour force as city size increases (Ullman and Dacey, 1968, pp. 175–194).

These examples illustrate the principle that the relationship between growth and form and between size and organization is both regular and pervasive. The implication of this relationship to geography is that the size of a system may well provide a more meaningful yardstick than either time or the age of the system to understanding its form. Conversely, important insights may be gained on the degree to which variations in size may be accommodated by structural transformation, both spatial and sectoral. These insights on the ability of systems to accommodate growth may be especially important given the present concern of many social sciences with such popular topics as pollution, the effects of crowding on social behaviour and other allied issues falling under the general heading of the limits to growth. The pessimistic outlook derived from ominous-looking exponential growth-curves might be alleviated if at least partial attention is given to the ways in which world systems might respond to ever more rapid increases in size.

Allometry: The Study of Size and its Consequences

To date, biologists have led in developing conceptual frameworks for dealing with size and its consequences. One of the most promising contributions is the concept of allometry. Indeed, in a comprehensive review paper Stephen Gould

(1966, p. 587) has defined allometry with precisely this emphasis: allometry is the study of size and its consequences. Allometry is concerned with the relative growth of the components of a system, rather than with the absolute growth-in-time of these components or of the system itself. The importance of allometry to understanding form and organization stems from the fact that fundamentally all form is the resultant of differential growth. Changes in form are thus an expression of the differing growth rates of components during system growth so that they comprise changing proportions of the system.

As D'Arcy Thompson (1919) noted in his classical work on growth and form, the form of a living system is an expression of the forces which were acting on that system during its growth. Von Bertalanffy (1951) considers form in a dynamic framework and notes, like Thompson, that organic forms are persistent and constant only in appearance. In reality they are an expression of a perpetual stream of events and are maintained in a continuous exchange among their components. A further complication is introduced to the system's dynamics as changes in the forces occur, e.g. changes in preference functions of buyers, transport technology or farming techniques. Such changes usually result in parameter adjustments. Von Bertalanffy (1960, p. 226) writes that 'breaks and jumps are frequently found in allometric plots so that all data cannot be fitted by a single regression line'. However, if these discontinuities can be connected with definable changes in the underlying process of growth, such as moulting or the attainment of sexual maturity in biological systems, or technological innovation in social systems, the allometric framework need not be discarded. Indeed, identification of inflection points in empirical studies may serve to suggest the need for closer scrutiny of the forces involved in system growth.

Mathematically, allometry is a ratio of two specific growth rates:

$$\alpha = \left(\frac{1}{y}\frac{dy}{dt}\right)\Big/\left(\frac{1}{x}\frac{dx}{dt}\right) \tag{1}$$

Huxley's seminal study gave currency to the remarkable finding that allometry is very often described by the simple power formula $y = bx^{\alpha}$, derived from (1) where y is a variable whose size is being related to some variable x representing another component of the system or the system itself, and α is the allometric coefficient. The significance of b, the value of y when x equals one, remains somewhat problematic (White and Gould, 1965, pp. 5–18). The logarithmic transformation of this power formula

$$\log y = \log \mathbf{b} + \alpha \log x$$

indicates that where this simple allometric relationship holds, the paired values of y and x plot along a straight line on log-log graph paper with the allometry indicated by the slope of the plot.

Three categories of simple allometry can be distinguished on the basis of the alpha value: positive allometry where y increases relative to x, negative allometry where y decreases with an increase in the absolute magnitude of x, and the special case of isometry in which form is unchanged with change in size. If the two variables have the same dimensionality, both being population or area of land, for instance, then positive, negative and isometric allometry are indicated by alpha values greater than, less than and equal to 1·0 respectively.

Finally, since the equation expresses only the ratio between relative growth rates, the stage phase or time element of the growth process is eliminated from direct consideration. As a result the equation can be used not only to examine the relative growth of one part compared to another in the same system as it develops longitudinally, but may also be used to examine the relative proportions of parts of different sized systems at one point in time. The latter is termed inter-specific, or cross-sectional, allometric analysis and is especially important given the difficulty of obtaining consistent time series data for small geographic units.

Size-required structural transformations: deductive examples of compensatory allometry

Stephen Gould (1966), as a palaeontologist with a particular interest in the role of absolute magnitude as a cause of trends in form alteration, writes that:

'... an artificial distinction between two types of size-correlated change in shape seems justified, at least in a heuristic sense. Certain shape alterations are mechanically required by size increase. Other regular allometric trends not casually related to absolute magnitude are nonetheless size-dependent in the sense that any variation in absolute magnitude implies a different shape. This is particularly important in phylogenetic size increase where extrapolation of ancestral trends into widened size ranges produces new shapes and corresponding new functions. In the first case, size increase requires form change; in the second, size increase permits the expression of new potentiality'. (p. 588)

The engineering principle and the principle of biological similarity represent cases in which size increase requires form alteration, or compensatory allometry. 'If physiological constancy is to be considered as a prime impetus for morphological allometry, we must know which physiological parameters remain constant over wide size ranges...' (Gould, 1966, p. 612). In many cases these parameters are easily identified and may be deduced from simple physical laws. As an example consider the square-cube law. Many biological system functions are dependent upon surface areas and, therefore, if the system is to remain functional as its size increases, the surface area of certain system components must grow in constant proportion to body volume. Structural changes must occur in order for the system to maintain physiological constancy as defined by constant area-to-volume ratios; area grows as the square of linear dimensions while the volume it encloses grows as the cube. If differential increase of surface area does not take place with size increase, i.e. if the system grows isometrically rather than allometrically, surface area will increase as volume to the two-thirds power. Hence isometric growth produces continually decreasing area-to-volume ratios where isometry is indicated by an alpha value of 0·67, which equals the ratio of the dimensions of area (2) and volume (3). This situation will eventually lead to system dysfunctionality.

An example of the square-cube law is provided by the development of vertebrate limbs. The strength of bones is proportional to cross-sectional area. The maintenance of geometrical similarity with size (volume) increase would lead to continually decreasing area-to-volume ratios. In order to compensate for size increase and to maintain constant area-to-volume ratios, therefore, differential increase of leg-bone thickness is required. An animal's legs must grow allometrically. If body volume (dimension 3) is represented by length L (dimension 1) and leg cross-section (dimension 2) is represented by leg width W (dimension 1) then leg width must grow as the 3/2 power of overall body length to maintain a constant area-to-volume ratio. That is:

$$\log W = \log b + 1\cdot5 \log L \qquad (2)$$

The size-required allometry of $1\cdot5$ in this example is thus greater than the isometric value of $1\cdot0$ for proportionate growth of two components of equal dimensionality.

Of course, if maintenance of constant area-to-volume ratios was the only criterion for shaping growth, other solutions would be equally satisfactory. In the previous example, for instance, the animal could have grown more legs during growth rather than differentially thickening the existing ones to compensate size increase. Allometry and geometry alone do not predict which solution will prevail. 'Some shape vectors are more size-limiting than others, and the determination of each involves many contingencies beyond the scope of allometric studies. Allometry does supply, however, certain very basic criteria by which each solution must be judged' (Dutton, 1972, p. 2). For instance, compensation by differential increase in leg thickness cannot be continued indefinitely. If equation (2) is extrapolated through a wide enough size range it is clear that eventually convergence will occur between leg width and body length setting an upper limit to this type of compensation. If the system is to grow beyond this size, other solutions are necessary. The evolution of the horse is an example. Departure from an $\alpha = 1\cdot5$ is achieved in this case by the transition to monodactyly with three small toe bones replaced by one larger and stronger hoof (Watson, 1949, p. 50).

The deduction of size-required allometries in biological and engineering systems has been facilitated by the time-honoured laws of physics which offer predictions that are both rigorous and readily-observed. No set of laws yet exists in the social sciences that permits size-required allometries to be deduced with corresponding exactitude and certainty. Yet some efforts have been made, whether implicitly or explicitly, to suggest changes in the organization of social systems required to maintain functionality. Most of these efforts resort to biological analogy. As an example consider the work of Mason Haire (1959). Haire partitions employment within a sample of four industrial firms into a production group, termed the internal, or 'inside' workers, and external workers that 'have to do primarily with things outside the firm. Purchasing and shipping employees, receptionists, and the like are outside' (Haire 1959,

p. 284). The general analogy is of a skeleton supporting a body. Thus:

'As the organization grows, its internal shape must change. Additional functions of coordination, control, and communication must be provided and supported by the same kind of force that previously supported an organization without these things. If the relationship were linear, there would be no problem. If each increment in size produced one increment (or one plus) in productive capacity and needed one increment of additional supportive function there would be no limit. However, in the organism, the proportion of skeleton needed to support the mass grows faster than the mass itself and puts a limit on size as a function of the environmental forces playing on it. Similarly, it is suggested that, as the size of a firm increases, the skeletal structure (needed to support it against the forces tending to destroy it) grows faster than the size itself, and hence comes to consume a disproportionate amount of the productive capacity of the organization. If this is so, it becomes important to identify the skeletal support of the firm, the forces it resists, and the rates at which the support must grow'. (Maire, 1959, pp. 274–275).

The square-cube law is then applied to deduce that the growth of the square root of the number of external employees should grow proportionately to the cube root of the number of internal employees. The actual results for the four firms are 0·72, 0·51, 0·50 and 0·97 (Haire, 1959, p. 285) and the differences between these values and the predicted value of 1·0 are attributed to the artifacts of the definition and the geometry of such social organizations.

Anatol Rapoport (1970) has noted that the use of analogy is fundamental in science and may provide valuable insight if made at a high order of generality. Thus all systems, biological or social, require functions of maintenance, defence, homeostasis, communication and the like. But direct analogy of the kind used in the Haire example is likely to prove naïve and sterile.

Friedmann's emphasis on the structural transformations required to achieve system development appears to offer an appropriate application of general system theory as endorsed by Rapoport. Structural transformation, as distinguished from simple growth, depends on the innovative capacity of the system which Friedmann (1969, pp. 10–11) relates to information exchange or communication in open systems. The implication is that population potential, or some other measure of accessibility to the aggregate population, must increase differentially with respect to population. However, no explicit parameters such as those derived from the square-cube law have yet been hypothesized relating changes in system structure, population potential, and population growth within Friemann's system theory framework.

Size-required Structural Transformations: Empirical Examples of Compensatory Allometry

Empirical attempts to identify changes in form required to adjust to increasing size have generally made only implicit use of general system theory. They include the classic input-output tables in which the technical coefficients set the allometries of the differential growth of the economic sectors as the economy grows. Another example is the fundamental notion of basic, non-basic city employment in which the number of workers required to meet a city's needs increases differentially with city size as measured, for example, in the

Ullman–Dacey technique (Ullman and Dacey, 1958). The size-required component of employment which is invariant among cities of any given size is then disregarded in comparing the performance of cities in competing for economic functions.

Explicit use of the allometric framework to measure size-required system changes suggests that important scaling constants can be derived directly for system components with equal alpha values. The methodology was first suggested in the biological sciences (Guerra and Gunther, 1957; Stahl, 1962).

'In Stahl's method, each variable is related to body weight by the allometric power function. Possible dimensionless terms are then located by inspection. Division of two simple allometric regressions with the same α value yields a number, dimensionless because the mass exponents are equal and invariant with change in body size. This number is the ratio of b values for the two regressions; since α is the same, it is also the ratio of y values at any x.' (Gould, 1966, p. 612).

In an empirical examination of the growth of the United States, 1870–1950, Dutton has derived an apparent constant which Woldenberg terms the Dutton number (Woldenberg, 1971, p. 14 after Dutton, 1971). The Dutton number is given by the formula:

$$\frac{E}{P_u} = \frac{8 \times 10^{-2} P_t^{1 \cdot 775}}{6 \cdot 72 \times 10^{-7} P_t^{1 \cdot 73}} = 1 \cdot 19 \times 10^5$$

where

E is the demographic energy of the
system, one unit of which is generated
by two people one mile apart,
P_u is the urban population of the system and
P_t is the total population of the system.

'This equation implies that each new urban person adds $1 \cdot 19 \times .10^5$ units of demographic energy to the system, and this apparently is true for all scales and through time. From 1798 to 1950, there is no trend. The Dutton number is thus one of the design criteria for the U.S. macrogeographic system as it increases in size through time. To preserve this number may optimize the functioning of the system; however, the shape of the system may be forced to change to maintain the Dutton number.' (Woldenberg, 1971, pp. 14–15).

Structural Change and Survival of the Fittest: Competitive Allometry

Many types of structural change are not mechanically required by size change. Rather they result from the differential capability of various components to compete for the resources available to the system. Rewriting the allometry equation (1) as

$$\frac{dy}{dt} = \alpha \frac{y}{x} \frac{dx}{dt}$$

shows that the component 'y' takes, from a change in the total system 'dx/dt', a share which is proportional to its actual proportion of the latter, 'y/x'. The alpha value is thus a partition coefficient which indicates the competitive ability that the component 'y' has in seizing its share of total growth. Structural transformations resulting from this differential competitive ability may allow the system to develop new functions as it progresses through wider size ranges and thus permits the expression of new system potentiality.

Many familiar geographic examples illustrate competitive allometry. Consider competition for land use in von Thunen's Isolated State (Hall, 1966, p. 217). The three grain-farming systems described there, the three-field, the improved and the crop alternation system, individually show complex patterns of expansion and decline with the changing radius of the plain. Combining the radii of all three grain-farming systems indicates, however, that the expansion of grain farming in competition with other land uses is simple allometric and slightly positive (Ray, 1972).

The competitive mechanism which specifies the locational character of the urbanization process accompanying development is illustrated by the familiar heartland–hinterland paradigm. 'Core regions (heartlands) are defined as territorially organized subsystems of society which have a high capacity for generating and absorbing innovative change; peripheral regions (hinterlands) are subsystems whose development path is determined chiefly by core region institutions with respect to which they stand in a relation of substantial dependency' (Friedmann, et al., 1970, p. 5). This autonomy-dependency interrelationship is fundamental to the paradigm and lies at the root of its internal (spatial) dynamics.

Initially, the heartland-hinterland pattern exists at the international (world) scale with regional economies of a colonial nature tied to their mother country abroad (Darwent 1969, p. 17). Successful translation of this export sector growth into 'residentiary' growth internal to the region leads to a shift of the pattern to the national scale. The region with the greatest initial advantages and achieving sustained growth becomes the economic centre or heartland at the national scale. 'The remainder of the country is thus relegated to a second-class, peripheral position. It is placed in a quasi-colonial relationship to the center . . .' (Friedmann and Alonso, 1964, p. 3). Such a shift can be thought of as a shift in the autonomy-dependency interrelationship among regions which is brought about by changes in the forces acting upon the system.

The colonial-mother country (international scale heartland-hinterland) relationship has been related to the staple export theory of growth in which exports depend on regional endowment and market accessibility (Perloff and Wingo, 1961, pp. 191–212; also see Gilmour essay). At this stage the force of development is externally induced. 'Spatial systems—even at the level of nation—are never completely closed to external influence. The paradigm therefore provides for the influence of exogenous core regions on urbanization processes and integration patterns' (Friedmann et al., 1970, p. 9). Initial settlements are usually founded along the coast (market accessibility) and serve as base camps for subsequent exploration and occupation of interior regions. These base camps also serve as quasi-commercial centres for surrounding, loosely defined hinterland areas and one is usually elevated to a loftier position and serves as the administrative capital of the new province. We thus see the emergence of fairly weak, yet important, political and economic forces tending to begin differentation between colonial regions.

'Residentiary' growth continues to increase as the demand for exports (externally induced force) decreases and a number of new cities are established for administrative control as well as for the provision of essential services to the surrounding countryside. Forces in the social overhead capital sector tend to parallel these increasing political and economic forces and the three sets in combination lead to clearly defined regional complexes of a nation now liberated from the mother country.

During the next period of growth economic forces play the most important role. This 'period is characterized by a cumulative process of industrialization and by dramatic shifts in the existing spatial patterns, reflecting the basic transformations taking place in the structure of the economy' (Friedmann, 1966, p. 9). One or two of the administrative capitals will typically receive most of the benefits of these economic forces and will achieve the threshold size for the production of a wide range of goods and services and will achieve the associated economies of scale (Ullman, 1958). At this point a clearly defined heartland-hinterland pattern can be discerned at the national scale.

Centripetal forces are then set in motion and leadership in finance, education, research and planning are added to the initial advantages of this new heartland (Ullman, 1958). Secondary manufacturing and service activity gravitate toward the heartland which becomes the centre of corporate control, channelling the flow of corporate profits from the hinterland to the heartland. This net flow creates an underlying shortage of capital in the hinterland and an associated heartland-hinterland disparity in interest rates (Keeble, 1967; Davis and Banks, 1965).

Centrifugal forces, which tend to reduce heartland-hinterland contrasts, include the spread effects of growing markets and improving technology at the centre that can benefit localities in the hinterland, the protection afforded hinterland industry by distance from the heartland and the increasing congestion of the heartland combined with special amenities which parts of the hinterland have to offer (Myrdal, 1957). At the national scale, however, Lasuen has found the centrifugal forces to be weaker than the centripetal (Lasuen, 1962).

This paradigm has been recently investigated within an allometric framework for Canada, 1851–1961 (Koenig, 1971). A summary of the results provides an introduction to the case study which follows. The heartland, which includes the provinces of Ontario and Quebec, the eastern periphery comprising all provinces east of Quebec and the western periphery, made up of all provinces west of Ontario, are identified by a county-level factor analysis. Each growth period indicates an inflection in the regional growth curves and has been related to changes in the system forces specified by the paradigm.

As an example consider the world-wide depression which followed 1873. This depression lasted for over twenty years and had various effects on different regions. The eastern periphery, with its major focus on external trade was the

Partition coefficients for Canadian regions: 1851–1961

Eastern periphery		Heartland		Western periphery	
Growth period	α Value	Growth period	α Value	Growth period	α Value
1851–1881	0·86372	1851–1891	0·97886	1871–1901	5·72303
1881–1901	0·12148	1891–1911	0·57423	1901–1921	2·94307
1901–1921	0·22342	1911–1931	0·90168	1921–1941	1·01385
1921–1961	0·53930	1931–1961	1·05359	1941–1961	0·86018

Note: A simple regression of the form; log y = log b + α log x is run in which; y = the population of the various regions, i.e. the heartland, the eastern periphery, and the western periphery, x = total Canadian population, α and b = empirically derived parameters.

first region to be hit. The great blow to this region exhibits itself in its partition coefficient from the period before 1881 to the period 1881 amd lasting until 1901. With its market virtually destroyed, the eastern periphery lost its power to compete for what little growth Canada was experiencing throughout the period of the depression. A more diversified economic structure enabled the heartland to hold on to its competitive edge until sometime between 1891 and 1901. The National Policy Tariff of 1879 was a powerful instrument for promoting domestic production in a wide range of goods and for diverting trade from international to interprovincial channels (Smiley, 1963, p. 67). The expansion of the rail network into the Canadian Shield was also important since it led to the discovery of many important mineral bodies such as the Sudbury basin. As a result Toronto began to be established as a world centre in mining finance (Robinson, 1969, pp. 14–36). The project of the transcontinental railway was taken up again in 1880 and by 1885, the railway to the Pacific was completed by the Canadian Pacific Railway Company. This project, along with land grants, gave the western periphery the best competitive advantage throughout the depressed period which lasted until 1896. 'The principal policies and expenditures of the Federal Government were designed to fill the empty spaces with people' (Smiley, 1963, pp. 68–69).

Allometric Analysis: A Final Caution

Ackoff has noted that:

'In the last two decades we have witnessed the emergence of the "system" as a key concept in scientific research. Systems, of course, have been studied for centuries, but something new has been added . . . the tendency to study systems as an entity rather than as a conglomeration of points is consistent with the tendency in contemporary science no longer to isolate phenomena in narrowly confined contexts, but rather to open interactions for examination'. (quoted in von Bertalanffy, 1968, p. 9). George Braziller, Inc. *from General Systems Theory* by Ludwig von Bertalanffy reprinted with the permission of the publisher, copyright 1968, George Braziller, Inc.

Allometry, a crucial aspect of general system theory, implies the importance of interdependence and interaction of system components during growth by focusing on the growth of components relative to the growth of other components or the system itself. Furthermore, these interdependencies are highlighted by downplaying fluctuations in the absolute growth of systems through time. However important allometry might seem, much painstaking research is still needed before the allometric framework of analysis makes its proper contribution to understanding urban and regional systems. The practitioner should therefore be warned against the light-handed application of this framework. The relation revealed by allometric analysis is not trivial, but previous frivolous application of the framework has nearly led to its demise (Scholl, 1954). It should be stressed that allometry should be employed to extend the more usual approaches to the study of growth, rather than in place of them and that, in any case, we should always 'take the allometric equation for what it really is: a highly simplified, approximate formula, which applies to an astonishingly broad range of phenomena, but is neither a dogma, nor an explanation for everything' (von Bertalanffy, 1968, p. 165).

6.3. The Mathematical Methodology

A three-stage mathematical methodology is presented for (1) the computation of simple allometries, (2) the measurement of system structure and (3) identifying the relationship between growth and form. Each of the three stages in the mathematical methodology may be based on well-known techniques, but modifications are presented to provide a methodology suited to coarse data. The use of a three-stage methodology is a new development in the study of relative growth, but it represents a natural extension of current research in other disciplines on system growth.

Computation of Alpha (α)

The relationship between the growth of a system component to the total system is most simply identified by plotting ordered pairs of data on log-log paper as illustrated in Figure 6.1. Where a constant relationship appears to exist, this relationship can be expressed mathematically as:

$$\log y = \log b + \alpha \log x$$

where y and x are the component and system respectively, and b and α are fitted parameters. This procedure is applied in the case study which follows, for which accurate measures of employment by sector were available.

Even though the simple allometric, $y = bx^\alpha$, may be appropriate to a given system, the practical analysis of growth can involve the fitting of observed data with errors of non-negligible magnitude in both measurements. This suggests that the modelling procedure should, for example, be based on regression analysis assuming the independent variable to be subject to error. The logical extension of this concern occurs when it is recognized that a whole system may have undergone abberations of growth in certain periods such as economic depression, social or technical revolution, imposition of protective tariffs, etc. In these circumstances a simple growth model cannot be expected to com-

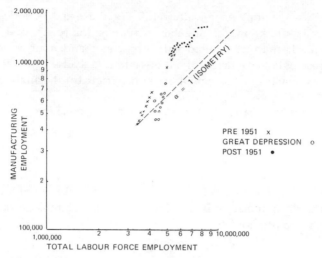

Figure 6.1. Structural change during system growth: Canada 1921–1969

prehend the 'slippage' that has occurred in the system: the parts do not maintain their 'normal' relationship to the whole. This slippage cannot be considered as an error in the usual statistical sense. One approach to this problem is to smooth the measure of the whole system through a separate model which could be generalized as:

$\hat{x} = f$ (time; exogenous variables; slippage).

The allometric model is then $y = b\hat{x}^\alpha$

A useful model in this two-stage procedure is the simple exponential $x = ce^{kt}$ which provides an accurate description for many population and aggregate economic series. Then

$$y = b(ce^{kt})^\alpha = re^{st}.$$

If the latter model is fitted directly as $\log y = \log r + st$ through regression analysis, the estimate of α is then s/k. It should be noted that this estimation of α is not equivalent statistically to the direct fitting *via* $\log y = \log b + \alpha \log x$. We have interposed a prior modelling step which must be assessed separately.

Measurement of System Structure

The alpha is a descriptive measure of relative growth. A parsimonious description of system structure is also necessary prior to an examination of the relationships between growth and structure. This description has usually been obtained by factor analysis.

Factor analysis is applied with the fundamental motive of extracting generalized interpretations of data structures (e.g. Rummel, 1970; Horst, 1965; and Harman, 1967). Occasionally, however, the standardization of the data implicit to analyses based on correlations or covariances is inappropriate, or, as in the case study which follows, correlations of any sort would be dubious measures of association. As an alternative to the usual varieties of factor analysis a procedure known as singular decomposition (e.g. Good, 1969) has been adopted. It may be applied with objectives and interpretations very similar to those of factor analysis and it has additional advantages in simplicity and directness which make it seem more appropriate for the analysis of coarse data.

An arbitrary $m \times n$ matrix X of rank k can be expressed as

$$X = e_1 L_1 R_1' + e_2 L_2 R_2' + \ldots + e_k L_k R_k' \ldots \tag{3}$$

where the **L** are orthonormal 'left' vectors of m components, the **R** are orthonormal 'right' vectors of n components and the e are positive scalars, the singular values. Each summand on the right side of (3) is an $m \times n$ matrix of rank one. The decomposition is developed through a simple iterative procedure based on the relations

$$\mathbf{XR} = e\mathbf{L} \text{ and } \mathbf{L'X} = e\mathbf{R'}.$$

The procedure derives the largest singular value and associated vectors, which are extracted from the matrix, then the next largest and so on, in a parallel manner to the successive determination of eigenvalues and vectors of a correlation or covariance matrix as in factor analysis. The singular decomposition procedure becomes the 'spectral decomposition' in terms of eigenvalues and vectors only if X is square symmetric. The decomposition has an important least-squares property:

minimizing

$$\sum_i \sum_j (x_{ij} - el_i r_j)^2$$

with respect to the m parameters l_i and the n parameters r_j and the scalar e subject to the restrictions:

$$\sum_i l_i^2 = 1, \qquad \sum_j r_j^2 = 1$$

leads to the first singular value and vectors of X. In a statistical framework the first model postulated would be

$$x_{ij} = el_i r_j + \text{error}$$

which is a non-linear type with the parameters subject to restrictions; additional orthogonal terms (decompositions) may be evaluated for their contribution (decreasing) to the model and included if significant.

In application, with the objective of summarizing the data structure, the decomposition procedure is continued until by some criterion a satisfactory approximation to the data matrix has been obtained. Hopefully this is accomplished with a matrix of much lower rank than the original, i.e. with p terms of (3) where $p \ll k \leqslant \min(m, n)$.

A convenient reference to the degree of approximation is based on the fact that

$$\sum_{i=1}^{k} e_i^2 = \sum_i \sum_j x_{ij}^2;$$

The ratio $\sum_{i=1}^{p} e_i^2 / \sum\sum x_{ij}^2$ may be interpreted as the percentage of variance (of the matrix elements about the origin) which is 'explained' by the first p decompositions.

A very simple example illustrates the decomposition: following equation (3),

$$X = e_1 L_1 R_1' \qquad\qquad\qquad + e_2 L_2 R_2'$$

$$\begin{bmatrix} 2 & 0 \\ 1 & 3 \\ 4 & 2 \end{bmatrix} = 5\cdot358 \begin{bmatrix} 0\cdot305 \\ 0\cdot475 \\ 0\cdot826 \end{bmatrix} [0\cdot819 \quad 0\cdot574] + 2\cdot301 \begin{bmatrix} -0\cdot499 \\ 0\cdot818 \\ -0\cdot286 \end{bmatrix} [-0\cdot575 \quad 0\cdot818]$$

$$= \begin{bmatrix} 1\cdot340 & 0\cdot938 \\ 2\cdot084 & 1\cdot463 \\ 3\cdot622 & 2\cdot540 \end{bmatrix} + \begin{bmatrix} 0\cdot660 & -0\cdot939 \\ -1\cdot082 & 1\cdot539 \\ 0\cdot377 & -0\cdot538 \end{bmatrix}$$

Here $\sum\sum x_{ij}^2 = 34\cdot000 - (5\cdot358)^2 + (2\cdot301)^2 - 28\cdot708 + 5\cdot295$ and the first singular approximation explains $28\cdot708/34 = 0\cdot844$ or 84·4 per cent of the variance: the second absorbs the remainder of the original rank two matrix.

The interpretation of a decomposition analysis may proceed along lines very similar to that of factor analysis or, more accurately, principal components analysis. If typically the columns of the matrix represent variables and the rows observation units, the right decomposition vectors may be interpreted as factor loadings and the left vectors as factor scores. The similarity is more than superficial: if the columns are standardized to mean zero and variance one, the right vectors are the principal components of the correlation matrix. However, there are fundamental differences that are important. When applied to raw data, as in this study, the singular values directly reflect the scaling inherent in the data, and their significance must be judged relative to the aggregate variance of the original matrix. The distinction between scores and loadings is now purely arbitrary. Commonly the first singular value and vectors resemble a 'size' factor explaining 65–90 per cent of the variance. The primary interest in the interpretation usually lies in subsequent approximations.

Singular decomposition extends to higher dimensions, i.e. to multi-way contingency tables. In three dimensions, for example, the least-squares property is the minimization of

$$\sum_i \sum_j \sum_k (x_{ijk} - ea_i b_j c_k)^2$$

With each singular value there are three associated vectors, one for approximating the data along each dimension. It is interesting to contrast this procedure with the 'three-mode' factor analysis which is much more involved (Tucker, 1964; Cant, 1971). The data are splayed into three two-way tables which are each subjected to a standard factor analysis. The sets of loadings are then used to generate a 'core' matrix which represents the final distillation of the data. Although this procedure potentially offers a more succinct description of the data, it necessarily assumes that covariances or correlations may be appropriately defined along each of the three dimensions. The less sophisticated decomposition procedure offers a direct description of the data and frequently permits a more immediate interpretation of features of the data that would be obscured in other types of analysis.

Growth and System Structure

The relationship between growth and system structure could be postulated simply as

$$\alpha = b_0 + b_1 S_1 + b_2 S_2 + \ldots$$

where the S_i are scores vectors from a singular decomposition or factor analysis, and the α is the vector of relative growths determined from an allometric analysis. The b coefficients are then estimated using multiple regression analysis. The scores vectors are mutually orthogonal but if they are derived through singular decomposition they will not be uncorrelated since they describe the raw rather than standardized data. In this case, preferably $b_0 = 0$, i.e. the regression plane is forced through the origin; the contribution of each structural score vector to the explanation of growth could then be evaluated independently. If the data demand that $b_0 = 0$, the interpretation of the fitted equation follows the usual lines in dealing with correlated data: the significance of each variable is expressed in terms of its incremental contribution such as the 'null t' value of the coefficient.

6.4. The Case Study: The Hierarchy of Manufacturing Centres in Canada: 1911 to 1961

Manufacturing in the Canadian Economy

Canada's economic development has always been profoundly influenced by external economic forces because of the country's heavy dependence on international trade and foreign investment, and on immigration and international business and labour organizations. These relationships and the history of Canadian economic development have been best explained, perhaps, by the staple export theory and the economic role of codfish, fur, square-timber and other forest products and of wheat. Nevertheless, manufacturing has grown at an average annual rate of 4·7 per cent since Confederation in 1867 compared with 3·5 per cent for Canada's GNP over this same period (Economic Council of Canada, 1966, p. 18). Corresponding to the increasing relative contribution of manufacturing to GNP, manufacturing has had a positive employment allometry since Confederation although the Great Depression interrupted a period of rapid growth that persisted until 1950, and growth since 1950 has been more erratic but generally slower (Figure 6.1). The primary industries remained dominant until 1910 when manufacturing output equalled about 42 per cent of the value of the primary industries, but by the late twenties, manufacturing was, for the first time in Canada, more important than the primary industries taken together, even though mining was beginning its spectacular rise (English, 1968).

Manufacturing has substantially increased its dominance over the primary industries in the post World War II period, maintaining about one quarter of the national labour force, whereas agriculture's share fell from 24·8 to 7·4 per cent between 1946 and 1966, and the share of all the primary industries fell from 28·6 to 10·5 per cent over the same twenty year period. Furthermore, the structure of manufacturing industry has changed substantially in Canada since the turn of the century and secondary manufacturing has outstripped the processing industries, despite the importance of Canada's resource production. Three particularly rapid periods of growth of Canada's secondary manufacturing industry have been identified: 'the first decade of this century, when the opening of the western wheat economy and the rapid expansion of the railways gave impetus to the capital goods industries; the boom in the last half of the 20's; and the war and post-war expansion' (Canada, 1957, pp. 232–233). The common element in each of these periods has been a strong domestic market.

There is some agreement among economists that the threshold market for any substantial range of manufacturing activity is about ten million people (Robinson, 1960). The Canadian population reached the ten million mark by the end of the twenties, but was spread from Halifax, Nova Scotia, more than 800 miles from Toronto, to Vancouver, more than 2,000 miles from Toronto. More significantly, then, the population of Ontario and Quebec grew from six million in the 1920's to twelve million in the early sixties, bringing the domestic market within four to five hundred miles of Toronto up to the threshold market. English (1968, p. 86) comments that as a result, 'perhaps from the twenties, certainly since World War II, the staple theory no longer deserves pride of place in the explanation of Canadian economic growth'. Attention needs to be focused rather on manufacturing.

Manufacturing Employment and the Manufacturing Belt

Manufacturing employment in Canada stood at one and a quarter million in 1961, but it has always been unequally distributed across the country, and the two heartland provinces, Ontario and Quebec, which had 63 per cent of the 1961 population, had 81 per cent of the workers in manufacturing (Figure 6.2). Furthermore, just two census divisions, Montreal and Toronto, with almost a quarter of a million manufacturing employees each, together had one third of Canada's total.

Of the twelve census divisions which had over 15,000 manufacturing employees in 1961, only three are in the peripheral provinces. These three, all

176

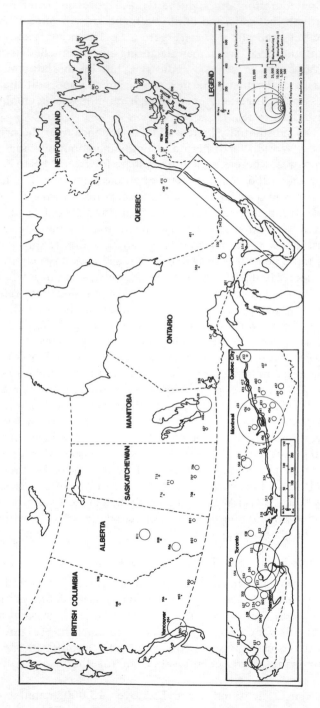

Figure 6.2. Distribution of manufacturing employment: 1961

Map Codes

Codes	County name	Predominant city
425	Ile de Montreal	Montreal
554	York	Toronto
904	B.C. 4	Vancouver
620	Man. 20	Winnipeg
504	Carleton	Ottawa
553	Wentworth	Hamilton
447	Quebec	Quebec City
811	Alta 11	Edmonton
806	Alta 6	Calgary
510	Essex	Windsor
208	Halifax	Halifax
528	Middlesex	London
550	Waterloo	Kitchener-Waterloo
905	B.C. 5	Victoria
706	Sask. 6	Regina
546	Sudbury	Sudbury
526	Lincoln	St. Catharines
311	St. John	St. John
711	Sask. 11	Saskatoon
547	Thunder Bay	Port Arthur
001	Nfld. 1	St. John's
455	St. Maurice	Trois Rivieres
533	Ontario	Oshawa
457	Sherbrooke	Sherbrooke
511	Frontenac	Kingston
522	Lambton	Sarnia
501	Algoma	Sault Ste. Marie
422	Hull	Hull
502	Brant	Brantford
314	Westmoreland	Moncton
538	Peterborough	Peterborough
545	Stormont	Cornwall
552	Wellington	Guelph
411	Chambly	Jacques–Cartier
505	Cochrane	Timmins
419	Drummond	Drummondville
517	Halton	Burlington
551	Welland	Welland
802	Alta. 2	Lethbridge
454	St. Jean	St. Jean
203	Cape Breton	Sydney
707	Sask. 7	Moose Jaw
415	Chicoutimi	Chicoutimi
456	Shefford	Granby
518	Hastings	Belleville
406	Beauharnois	Valleyfield
521	Kent	Chatham
607	Man. 7	Brandon
412	Champlain	Cap-de-la-Madelaine
005	Nfld. 5	Corner Brook

178

Map Codes (Cont.)

Codes	County name	Predominant city
462	Terrebonne	St. Jerome
801	Alta. 1	Medicine Hat
530	Nipissing	North Bay
509	Elgin	St. Thomas
453	St. Hyacinthe	St. Hyacinthe
437	Megantic	Thetford Mines
544	Simcoe	Barrie
534	Oxford	Woodstock
537	Perth	Stratford
315	York	Fredericton
808	Alberta 8	Red Deer
403	Arthabasca	Victoriaville
536	Peel	Brampton
103	Queens	Charlottetown
426	Joliette	Joliette
524	Leeds	Brockville
450	Rimouski	Rimouski
514	Grey	Owen Sound
448	Richelieu	Sorel
542	Renfrew	Pembroke
432	Levis	Levis
452	Saguenay	Sept–Iles
908	British Columbia 8	Prince George
903	British Columbia 3	Penticton
429	Lac-St. Jean	Alma
459	Stanstead	Magog
307	Madawaska	Edmundston
204	Colchester	Truro
606	Mantiboa 6	Protage la Prairie
708	Saskatchewan	Swift Current
909	British Columbia 9	Prince Rupert
902	British Columbia 2	Trail
716	Saskatchewan 16	North Battleford
401	Abitibi	Val-D'or
910	British Columbia 10	Dawson-Creek
520	Kenora	Kenora
205	Cumberland	Amherst
532	Northumberland	Cobourg
906	British Columbia 6	Kamloops

in the western periphery, contain the cities of Vancouver, Winnepeg and Edmonton. The other nine census divisions are all located in the two central provinces and are confined in a belt stretching across southern Ontario and the lower St. Lawrence Valley from Windsor to Quebec City (White, *et al.*, 1964; Ballabon, 1956).

The Canadian manufacturing belt, in part, forms a northward extension of the United States manufacturing belt, and of three distinct manufacturing districts that may be recognized, two are direct extensions of districts in the

United States. The most important of the three is the Golden Horseshoe area, adjacent to upstate New York and extending from Niagara to Toronto around the western end of Lake Ontario. The predominant industries in the Golden Horseshoe district are steel, with more than half of Canada's production from the Hamilton mills, flour milling, the automotive industry and, associated with power from Niagara, electro-chemical and electro-metallurgical industries.

The Windsor area, one of the outstanding automotive centres of the entire British Commonwealth, as well as a centre for agricultural implements, is distinct in industrial structure from the Golden Horseshoe area and is an extension of the southern Michigan automotive district. The middle St. Lawrence district, which includes Montreal and surrounding areas, is geographically separated from the two other manufacturing districts and is the only district of North American manufacturing regions to lie entirely outside the United States. Montreal is Canada's largest single industrial centre and important for the manufacture of machinery, railway equipment, aircraft, clothing, textiles, food and tobacco products. The remainder of the middle St. Lawrence district is noted for its resource-based industries, particularly pulp and paper, Canada's largest industry, and aluminum.

Maxwell's Functional Classification of Canadian Cities

An indication of the importance of manufacturing activity in the Canadian economy is provided by J. W. Maxwell's functional classification of Canadian cities (Maxwell, 1965; Maxwell *et al.*, 1972). Maxwell uses the Ullman–Dacey technique to classify by their basic employment urban centres with populations over 10,000. The results, using the 1961 census data, indicate that sixty-six cities out of a total of one hundred and ten have more basic employment in manufacturing than in any other single function and that in thirty-six of these, which are termed manufacturing I cities, more than half the basic employment is in manufacturing (Table 6.1). Mapping the results of the analysis reveals a fundamental difference between the cities in the densely populated heartland region of the St. Lawrence Lowlands and Southern Ontario, and the cities in the hinterland. Heartland cities are more specialized, and emphasize manufacturing to a greater degree than do cities in the periphery. The latter, except for a few resource-oriented manufacturing centres, are diversified and have an important involvement with functions associated with distance such as wholesale trade and transportation. The only heartland cities in which manufacturing is not a dominant function are Asbestos, Kingston, Ottawa, Pembroke, Quebec, Thetford Mines, Trenton and Valleyfield, that is, eight out of a total of fifty-two heartland cities. Twenty-two of the fifty-two hinterland cities have manufacturing as a dominant function, but only six of these, Arvida, Jonquiere, Kenogami, Port Alberni, Sault Ste. Marie and Trail, are classed as manufacturing I centres.

Furthermore, heartland cities with ratings of manufacturing I are, with but three exceptions, focused on Toronto and Montreal respectively and comprise integrated manufacturing districts with high levels of industrial linkage among

Table 6.1. A functional classification of Canadian cities: 1961

Region	Central Place[1]	Trans-portation	Manufacturing I	Manufacturing II	Manufacturing Total	Extraction	Total
Atlantic	5	1	0	6	6	2	14
Quebec	3	2	16	4	20	5	30
Heartland	2	0	13	2	15	2	19
Hinterland	1	2	3	2	5	3	11
Ontario	4	2	18	13	31	2	39
Heartland	4	0	17	12	29	0	33
Hinterland	0	2	1	1	2	2	6
Prairie	10	2	0	1	1	2	15
British Columbia	2	2	2	6	8	0	12
Total	24	9	36	30	66	11	110

Note: 1 Central place functions include community service, government service, wholesale trade, public utilities and personal service.
Source: Maxwell, *et al.*, 1972.

industries. By contrast, cities with a manufacturing I status in the hinterland have isolated locations, are usually dominated by a single industry and are resource-oriented primary manufacturing centres.

Industry Incidence: 1961

Given the prominence of manufacturing as a dominant function in Canadian cities, and the clear differences in the industrial structure of heartland and hinterland cities, is it possible to determine a more detailed manufacturing hierarchy? Ideally, such a hierarchy would be based on employment data by manufacturing type, as indicated by the three digit codes of the Standard Industrial Classification, through time so that the development of the hierarchy could be determined. Frequent changes in census listings of manufacturers, continouus changes in the boundary definitions of census divisions and cities, and the restrictions on the release of data imposed by the Statistics Act combine to reduce the information available (Gilmour, 1966). The procedure adopted in this case study is to employ the McInnis' (1969) classification to achieve a consistent industrial classification, 1911 to 1961, for fifty-four SIC groups which together accounted for 63·6 per cent of the national manufacturing employment in 1911 and 69·1 per cent in 1961. Unfortunately, no solution has been found for cases of missing employment data, deleted to avoid disclosure, employment in single firms or for changes in boundaries. Accordingly, industry incidence only is recorded for the sixty-two cities listed in the census tabulations for both 1961 and 1911, with three levels of incidence distinguished; a zero indicating no employment, a half indicating less than ten employees and a one indicating more than ten.

If total city employment is plotted against the number of manufacturing types occurring a semi-logarithmically linear plot is obtained for both 1911 and 1961 (Figure 6.3). The exceptions in the 1961 case are either the largest metropolitan centres, in which employment is boosted by industry types not recorded in this analysis, or for smaller centres identified by Maxwell as non-manufacturing. The relationship of employment to industry types is, then, simple allometric. But the allometry is changing, and any given number of industrial functions is generating less employment in 1961 than in 1911, providing an aggregate measure of a half-century of capital–labour substitution.

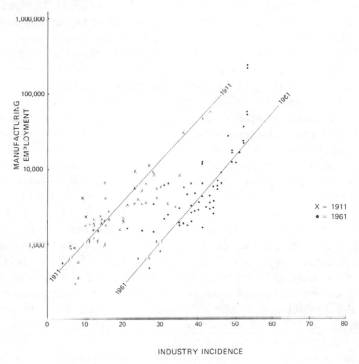

Figure 6.3. Manufacturing employment *vs.* industry incidence: 1911 and 1961

The presence of a single and simple allometric relationship for the entire observed range of employment and industry incidence argues that no clear hierarchy of manufacturing centres can be identified from industry incidence alone. Hence, industry-type is also considered in deriving the hierarchy. The method presented is quite arbitrary and is not likely to be of general use, but such descriptive attempts are often, as is true in this case, invaluable in understanding the results of more sophisticated methods such as factor analysis. Indeed, the factor analysis suggests that the hierarchy established is a balanced weighting of aggregate incidence and industry type.

The Manufacturing Hierarchy: 1961

A two-step procedure is adopted to define the manufacturing hierarchy: first, industries are ranked by ubiquity and divided into five sets, the fully ubiquitous, occurring in all cities over 10,000 and four equal-range ubiquity classes; second, cities are allocated to a five-level hierarchy according to minimum incidence-requirements set for each level of the hierarchy on each set of industries (Table 2). The fully ubiquitous industries are dairy products, saw and planing mills, furniture, printing and publishing, and scientific and professional equipment. The least ubiquitous set are carpet, mat and rug (occurring in 43·6 per cent of the cities), wooden box (40·3), fish products (35·5), sugar refineries (29·0), and cordage and twine (25·8). The four cities in Canada that have all the industries, including all of the most sporadic set, namely, Montreal, Toronto, Hamilton and Vancouver, are classed as metropolitan I centres. Progressively lowering the minimum incidence-industry mix requirements permits the classification of metropolitan II centres, Quebec City, Windsor, Winnipeg and Ottawa, manufacturing I and II centres, and finally, local centres.

The manufacturing employment ranges particularly, but also the range of aggregate industry incidence for the lower levels of the hierarchy, partially overlap. Population is not perfectly correlated with number of industry types, and, more important, the incidence of industry types with increasing population size is not perfectly ordered (Table 2). Furthermore, there is no definitional relationship between the five-level hierarchy obtained and Maxwell's two-level hierarchy. Nevertheless, the metropolitan I and II and manufacturing I groups are, with few exceptions, classed as manufacturing I centres by Maxwell, and the manufacturing II and local centres as manufacturing II.

The geographic pattern of the hierarchy is as expected. The manufacturing I centres in the heartland tend to cluster within one hundred miles of Montreal and Toronto, which, though only 340 miles apart, are the centres of clearly separated manufacturing districts; Windsor is, in fact, the only high-order representative of the third manufacturing district. No manufacturing clusters occur in the periphery where the most important distinction is between the western periphery, with a metropolitan I and II centre, and four manufacturing I centres, compared with a single manufacturing I centre, Halifax, in the eastern periphery.

Manufacturing Employment in 1911 and the Changing Incidence Pattern

The geographic distribution of manufacturing employment in 1961 differs in two respects from the 1911 distribution (cf. Figures 6.2 and 6.4). The Montreal and Toronto manufacturing districts are already evident by 1911, but these two cities are not as dominant, together accounting for 21·8 per cent of the national work force in manufacturing compared with 34·9 per cent in 1961. The disparity between the eastern and western periphery is much less obvious. Vancouver with 9,777 manufacturing employees in 1911 and Winnipeg, 11,565, were already much larger than Halifax, 5,716, or Saint John, 5,907.

Table 6.2. A manufacturing hierarchy of Canadian cities and industrial incidence: 1961

City[1]	Code[2]	Industry group[5] A	B	C	D	E	Population (1961)	Maxwell functional Classification[6] 1961	% of all industries occurring in: 1961	1911
Metropolitan I Centres[3] [4]										
* Montreal	425	1 1 1 1	1 1 1 1	1 1 1 1	1 1 1 1	1 1 1 1	2,109,509	MI	100·0	77·4
* Toronto	554	1 1 1 1	1 1 1 1	1 1 1 1	1 1 1 1	1 1 1 1	1,824,481	MI	100·0	81·1
Vancouver	904	1 1 1 1	1 1 1 1	1 1 1 1	1 1 1 1	1 1 1 1	790,165	MII	100·0	43·4
* Hamilton	553	1 1 1 1	1 1 1 1	1 1 1 1	1 1 1 1	1 1 1 1	395,189	MII	100·0	67·9
Minimum class incidence for all industries in each group[7]		100%	100%	100%	100%	100%				
Metropolitan II centres										
* Quebec City	447	1 1 1 1	1 1 1 1	1 1 1 1	1 1 1 1	1 1 1 0	357,568	G.S.	98·1	52·8
* Windsor	510	1 1 1 1	1 1 1 1	1 0 1 1	1 1 1 1	1 1 1 1	193,365	MI	98·1	41·5
Winnipeg	620	1 1 1 1	1 1 1 1	1 1 1 1	1 1 1 1	1 1 1 1	475,989	T	98·1	50·9
* Ottawa	504	1 1 1 1	1 1 1 1	1 1 1 1	1 1 1 1	1 1 1 0	429,750	G.S.	96·2	52·8
* St. Catharines	526	1 1 1 1	1 1 1 1	1 1 1 1	1 1 1 1	1 1 0 1	95,577	MI	94·3	45·3
Minimum class incidence for all industries in each group		100%	100%	90%	90%	50%				
Manufacturing I centres										
* London	528	1 1 1 1	1 1 1 1	1 1 1 1	1 1 1 0	1 1 0 1	181,283	MII	92·5	66·0
Calgary	806	1 1 1 1	1 1 1 1	1 0 1 1	1 1 1 1	1 0 1 1	279,062	Ex.	92·5	26·4
Edmonton	811	1 1 1 1	1 1 1 1	1 1 1 1	1 1 1 1	1 1 0 0	337,568	G.S.	92·5	26·4
* Sherbrooke	457	1 1 1 1	1 1 1 1	1 1 1 1	1 1 1 1	0 0 1 0	70,253	MII	90·6	30·2
* Kitchener-Waterloo	550	1 1 1 1	1 1 1 1	1 1 1 1	1 1 1 0	1 1 0 0	154,864	MI	90·6	54·7
* Brantford	502	1 1 1 1	1 1 1 1	1 1 1 1	1 1 0 1	1 1 0 0	56,929	MI	86·8	49·1

Table 6.2—Continued

City[1]	Code[2]	A	B	C	D	E	Population (1961)	Maxwell functional classification[6] 1961	% of all industries occurring in: 1961	1911
Manufacturing I centres—continued										
* Peterborough	538	1 1 1 1	1 1 1 1	1 1 1 1	1 1 0 1	1 0 0 0	49,902	MI	86·8	47·2
Halifax	208	1 1 1 1	1 1 1 1	1 0 0 1	1 1 1 0	1 1 1 1	183,946	G.S.	84·9	43·4
* Granby	456	1 1 1 1	1 1 1 1	1 1 1 1	0 1 0 1	1 1 0 0	31,463	MI	84·9	22·6
* Welland	551	1 1 1 1	1 1 1 1	1 0 1 1	0 1 1 1	1 0 0 0	36,079	MI	84·9	54·7
* Hull	422	1 1 1 1	1 1 1 1	1 1 0 1	1 0 1 1	0 1 0 1	56,929	(8)	83·0	28·3
* St. Jean	454	1 1 1 1	1 1 1 1	1 1 1 1	0 0 1 0	1 0 0 0	34,576	MI	83·0	20·8
* Guelph	552	1 1 1 1	1 1 1 1	1 1 1 1	1 1 1 0	1 0 0 0	41,767	MI	83·0	45·3
Regina	706	1 1 1 1	1 1 1 1	1 1 1 1	1 1 0 0	0 0 0 1	112,141	G.S.	81·1	15·1
Saskatoon	711	1 1 1 1	1 1 1 1	1 1 1 1	1 1 0 0	0 0 0 1	95,526	C.S.	81·1	13·2
* St. Hyacinthe	453	1 1 1 1	1 1 1 1	1 1 1 1	1 0 0 0	0 0 0 1	22,351	MI	79·3	28·3
* Drummondville	419	1 1 1 1	1 1 1 1	1 1 1 1	1 0 1 0	1 0 0 1	39,307	MI	77·4	20·8
* Oshawa	533	1 1 1 1	1 1 1 1	1 1 1 1	1 0 0 0	1 1 0 0	80,918	MI	77·4	28·3
Minimum class incidence for all industries in each group		100%	90%	66%	50%	33%				
Manufacturing II centres										
* Trois-Rivieres	455	1 1 1 1	1 1 1 1	1 1 1 1	0 1 1 1	0 0 0 0	83,659	MI	83·0	28·3
* Belleville	518	1 1 1 1	1 1 1 1	1 1 1 0	1 1 0 1	0 0 0 0	30,655	MII	81·1	30·2
St. John	311	1 1 1 1	1 1 1 1	0 0 0 0	1 0 1 0	0 1 1 1	95,563	MII	77·4	56·6
* Joliette	426	1 1 1 1	1 1 1 1	1 1 0 1	0 1 1 0	0 0 0 0	18,008	MII	77·4	24·5
* Cap-de-la-Madeleine	412	1 1 1 1	1 1 1 1	1 1 0 0	1 0 1 1	0 1 1 1	26,925	(9)	75·5	17·0
* Chatham	521	1 1 1 1	1 1 1 1	0 0 1 0	1 1 1 1	1 0 1 1	29,826	MII	75·5	22·6
* Kingston	511	1 1 1 1	1 1 1 1	0 1 0 1	0 1 0 0	0 0 0 0	63,419	C.S.	73·6	37·7
Sudbury	546	1 1 1 1	1 1 1 1	0 1 1 1	0 1 0 1	0 0 0 0	110,694	Ex.	73·6	00·0

Industry group[5]

City	Code	100%	66%	50%	33%	0%	Population	Class		
*Valleyfield	406	1 1 1 1	1 1 1 1	0 1 0 1	0 0 1 1	0 0 0 0	29,849	P.U.	71·7	15·1
Levis	432	1 1 1 1	1 1 1 1	0 0 0 0	1 0 0 0	1 1 0 0	15,112	(10)	71·7	22·6
*St. Jerome	462	1 1 1 1	1 1 1 0	0 1 1 1	0 1 0 0	0 1 0 0	24,564	MI	71·7	22·6
*St. Thomas	509	1 1 1 1	1 1 1 1	1 1 1 0	1 1 1 0	0 0 0 0	22,469	MII	71·7	30·2
*Stratford	537	1 1 1 1	1 1 1 1	1 1 1 1	0 1 1 0	0 0 0 0	20,467	MII	71·7	37·7
Moncton	314	1 1 1 1	1 1 1 1	1 1 0 0	0 1 0 0	0 0 1 0	55,768	T	69·8	30·2
*Cornwall	545	1 1 1 1	1 1 1 1	1 1 1 1	0 1 1 0	0 1 1 0	43,639	MI	69·8	28·3
North Bay	530	1 1 1 1	1 1 0 1	1 1 1 0	1 0 1 0	1 0 1 0	23,781	T	67·9	24·5
Victoria	905	1 1 1 1	1 1 1 1	1 1 0 0	1 0 1 1	1 1 1 0	154,152	G.S.	67·9	26·4
Chicoutimi	415	1 1 1 1	1 1 1 1	0 0 0 0	0 0 0 1	0 0 1 0	31,657	MII	66·0	17·0
*Owen Sound	514	1 1 1 1	1 1 1 0	1 1 1 0	1 0 0 0	0 0 0 0	17,421	MII	66·0	37·7
*Woodstock	534	1 1 1 1	1 1 1 0	1 0 1 1	0 1 1 0	0 0 0 0	20,486	MI	66·0	17·0
Thunder Bay	547	1 1 1 1	1 1 1 1	1 0 0 0	1 1 0 0	0 0 1 0	93,251	T	66·0	20·8
*Sarnia	522	1 1 1 1	1 1 1 1	1 0 1 1	1 1 1 1	0 0 0 0	61,293	MI	60·4	17·0
*Sorel	448	1 1 1 1	1 1 1 0	0 0 1 1	1 0 1 1	0 0 0 0	17,147	MI	58·5	18·9
Truro	204	1 1 1 1	1 1 0 1	1 1 0 0	0 1 1 0	0 0 0 0	12,421	MII	56·6	24·5

Minimum class incidence for all industries in each group

		100%	66%	50%	33%	0%				

Local centres

City	Code	100%	<66%	<50%	0%	0%	Population	Class		
*Brockville	524	1 1 1 1	1 1 1 1	1 0 0 1	0 0 0 0	0 1 0 0	17,744	MII	60·4	35·9
Sault Ste. Marie	501	1 1 1 1	1 1 1 1	0 0 0 0	1 0 0 1	0 0 0 0	58,460	MI	58·5	24·5
Brandon	607	1 1 1 0	1 1 0 1	0 1 1 0	1 0 0 0	0 0 0 0	28,166	C.S.	56·6	28·3
Sydney	203	1 0 0 1	1 0 0 0	1 0 0 0	0 0 0 0	0 0 1 0	33,617	MII	52·8	11·3
Moose Jaw	707	1 1 1 1	1 1 1 1	0 0 1 0	0 0 1 1	0 0 1 0	33,206	T	52·8	7·6
Fredericton	315	1 0 0 1	0 0 0 0	1 0 0 0	0 0 0 0	0 0 0 0	19,683	G.S.	50·9	22·6
*Thetford Mines	437	0 1 1 1	0 0 0 1	0 0 0 1	0 0 0 1	0 0 0 0	21,618	EX.	50·9	11·3
Lethbridge	802	1 1 1 1	1 0 0 0	0 0 1 0	1 0 0 0	0 0 0 1	35,454	WT	47·2	15·1
Charlottetown	103	1 0 0 0	1 0 0 0	0 1 0 0	0 0 1 0	0 0 1 0	18,318	C.S.	45·3	22·6
*Pembroke	542	1 1 1 1	1 1 0 0	0 1 0 0	0 0 0 1	0 1 0 0	16,791	G.S.	39·6	13·2
Medicine Hat	801	1 1 1 1	1 1 1 0	0 0 0 0	1 0 0 1	0 0 0 0	24,884	MII	39·6	15·1

Minimum class incidence for all industries in each group

		100%	<66%	<50%	0%	0%				

186

Notes for Table 6.2

1. The 62 cities in the analysis were those for which compatible data could be obtained back to 1911, and also all of which had a population of over 10,000 in 1961.
2. The first digit of the location code indicates province as follows: 0—Newfoundland, 1—Prince Edward Island, 2—Nova Scotia, 3—New Brunswick, 4—Quebec, 5—Ontario, 6—Manitoba, 7—Saskatchewan, 8—Alberta, 9—British Columbia. The next two digits indicate the provincial country or census division and also are used to identify the cities. See code list to Figure 6.2.
3. Five levels of manufacturing centres were identified on the basis of incidence on industry incidence as follows:
    (a) industries are ranked by incidence from most ubiquitous (100% occurrence) to most sporadic (25·8 occurrence).
    (b) industries are grouped into 5 equal-range sets:

    >A. 100%
    >B. 81·5–99·9
    >C. 62·9–81·5
    >D. 44·3–62·9
    >E. 25·8–44·3

    (c) the cities are classified by setting a minimum industry incidence for each industry set. These minimum class incidences are indicated for each level of the manufacturing hierarchy in the table (see note 7).
4. *Denotes cities within the Canadian heartland as defined by Maxwell (1965).
5. (a) In the complete analysis 54 industries are used of which 20 are individually indicated in the above table and are described in their respective grouping as follows: (from Standard Industrial Classification Manual, DBS 1960).

SIC		Respective Description
Group A:	105, 107†	Dairy factories, processed cheese;
	128, 129, 131†	Biscuits, Bakeries, Confectionery;
	251	Sawmills;
	286, 288†;	Commercial printing, Publishing.
Group B:	101	Slaughtering and meat processing;
	374	Pharmaceuticals and medicines;
	294	Iron foundries;
	365	Petroleum refining.
Group C:	174	Shoe factories;
	193, 197†	Wool yarn, Wool cloth;
	311	Agricultural implements;
	201	Synthetic textile mills.
Group D:	221	Canvas products;
	323	Automobiles;
	297	Copper and alloy rolling and casting;
	295	Smelting and refining.
Group E:	216	Carpet, mat and rug;
	256	Wooden box;
	111	Fish products;
	133	Sugar refineries.

† denotes where two or more Standard Industrial Codes were combined into a single grouping for analysis.

(b) The total list of industries sequenced by ubiquity and listed by SIC code are:
Group A: (105, 107), (128, 129, 131), 251, (261, 264), (268, 288).
Group B: 101, (376, 377) 374, 112, 143, (243, 244), 291, (268, 331, 332, 334, 338), 356, 379, 271, 294, (231, 239), 321, 353, (161, 163), 365, 273.
Group C: 306, 124, 246, 174, 351, 375, 341, 383, (151, 153), 326, 328, (193, 197), 311, 179, 201.
Group D: 221, 305, 323, 247, 183, 297, 327, 295, 172.
Group E: 216, 256, 111, 133, 213.
Note: Bracketed SIC's denote industries which were combined into a single grouping for analysis.

6. Maxwell's 1951 functional classification system (revised Greig and Meyer, 1972) is based on 1961 occupation data and is for cities over 10,000 in 1961. Cities in which manufacturing is the dominant function are subdivided into two classes: Manufacturing I in which more than 50 per cent of the excess employment is in manufacturing and Manufacturing II in which manufacturing still dominates but is less than 50 per cent. The following city classifications are used with their corresponding abbreviations in the table: Manufacturing I—MI, Manufacturing II—MII, Government Service—G.S., Community Service—C.S., Wholesale Trade—W.T., Public Utilities—P.U., Extraction—Ex., and Transportation—T.
7. This indicates that Metropolitan I centres have all industries, whereas Metropolitan II centres may have as few as 50 per cent of the industries in Group E.
8. Hull is included with Ottawa.
9. Cap-de-la-Madeleine is included with Trois-Rivieres.
10. Levis is not classified.

But Calgary, 2,486, and Edmonton, 1,960, were small, not only in comparison with Halifax and Saint John, but particularly in comparison with their 1961 manufacturing employment of 13,064 and 17,477 respectively. Vancouver's manufacturing employment grew to 57,485 and Winnipeg's to 38,537. In contrast, manufacturing employment in Halifax grew to only 7,472 and in Saint John to 6,744.

Slower relative employment growth in manufacturing industry in the Atlantic provinces was associated with a slower increase in industry incidence (Table 6.3). Whereas the Atlantic provinces ranked ahead of Alberta and

Table 6.3. Mean per cent occurrence of industries by province and regions: 1911 and 1961

| Region | Mean per cent occurrence by industry[1] | | |
	1911 %	1961 %	Net gain[2] %
Atlantic	28·51	59·00	30·49
P.E.I.	22·64	45·28	22·64
N.S.	26·42	64·78	38·37
N.B.	36·48	66·94	30·46
Quebec	26·97	77·80	50·83
Ontario	38·90	77·50	38·60
Prairie	24·11	72·33	48·22
Man.	39·62	77·36	37·74
Sask.	11·95	71·70	59·75
Alta.	20·76	67·93	47·17
British Columbia	34·91	83·97	49·06

Notes for Table 6.3
1. Mean per cent provincial occurrence is calculated by summing the per cent occurrence of the 54-industry set (see Table 6.2, Note 5) for each city greater than 10,000 and dividing by the number of cities.
   As an example consider Nova Scotia. In 1911, three cities had populations greater than 10,000. Halifax had 23 of the 54 industries (43·39%), Truro had 13 of the 54 (24·53%) and Sydney had 6 of the 54 (11·32%). The mean per cent provincial occurrence is therefore 26·42%.
   Mean per cent regional occurrence is calculated by summing the mean per cent provincial occurrences and dividing by the number of provinces in the region.
2. Net gain is the difference between the mean per cent occurrences of industry types in 1911 and 1961.

Table 6.4. Net changes in industrial incidence, 1911 to 1961; cross tabulated by region

Industry Group	Canada Absent[2]	Canada Gains[3]	Canada % Gain[4]	Atlantic Absent	Atlantic Gain	Quebec Absent	Quebec Gain	Ontario Absent	Ontario Gain	West Absent	West Gain	ICQ[5] Atlantic	ICQ Quebec	ICQ Ontario	ICQ West
A[1]															
105,107 dairy products	6	6	1·0	2	2	0	0	2	2	2	2	1·0	1·0	1·0	1·0
128, 129, 131 bakery, biscuits, confectionery	21	21	1·0	4	4	8	8	4	4	5	5	1·0	1·0	1·0	1·0
251 saw and planing mills	1	1	1·0	0	0	0	0	1	1	0	0	1·0	1·0	1·0	1·0
286, 288 printing and publishing	8	8	1·0	1	1	5	5	1	1	1	1	1·0	1·0	1·0	1·0
B															
101 slaughtering and meat processing	38	37	0·97	4	4	13	12	14	14	7	7	1·03	0·95	1·03	1·03
374 pharmaceuticals and medicines	46	43	0·93	6	3	13	13	17	17	10	10	0·65	1·08	1·08	1·08
294 iron foundries	9	1	0·11	1	-3	2	2	2	0	4	2	-3·0	9·09	0·0	4·55
365 petroleum refining	61	51	0·84	7	6	17	14	26	22	11	9	1·02	0·98	1·01	0·98
C															
174 shoe factories	31	17	0·55	2	0	8	5	12	7	9	5	0·0	1·15	1·05	1·02
193, 197 primary woollen textiles	38	17	0·45	3	-1	13	8	11	3	11	7	0·73	1·27	0·60	1·40
311 agricultural implements	41	20	0·49	7	0	10	3	15	10	9	7	0·0	0·61	1·35	1·59
201 synthetic textile mills	62	40	0·65	7	1	17	14	27	19	11	6	0·22	1·26	1·08	0·85

D

Code	Industry															
221	canvas products	47	24	0·51	7	2	15	6	19	11	6	5	0·57	0·78	1·14	1·96
323	automobiles	58	34	0·59	7	3	17	7	23	18	11	6	0·73	0·69	1·32	0·93
297	copper and alloy rolling and casting	52	25	0·48	7	2	16	9	20	10	9	4	0·60	1·17	1·04	0·92
295	smelting and refining (non-ferrous)	54	24	0·44	6	-1	15	10	22	7	11	7	0·39	1·52	0·73	1·43

E

Code	Industry															
216	carpet, mat and rug	55	20	0·36	6	0	16	5	22	9	11	6	0·0	0·86	1·14	1·53
256	wooden box	32	-5	-0·16	4	0	7	-3	14	-2	7	0	0·0	2·69	0·88	0·0
111	fish products	54	16	0·26	1	0	16	3	27	7	10	4	0·0	0·73	1·0	1·54
133	sugar refineries	56	12	0·21	6	1	16	4	26	5	8	2	0·81	1·19	0·90	1·19

Notes for Table 6.4

1. The industries are those selected for Table 6.1.
2. Absent indicates the number of cities in which an industry did not occur in 1911.
3. Gain indicates the net gain (or loss) in the number of cities with the industry from 1911 to 1961.
4. % Gain is the percentage gain in the industry occurrence and is computed as Absent/Gain × 100.
5. The Change quotient is the ratio of the % gain in each region and the Canada % gain.

For the purposes of these computations $0/0 = 1\cdot0$ and $x/0 = 0$.

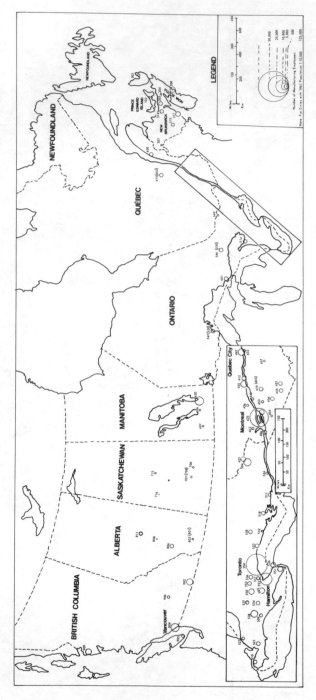

Figure 6.4. Distribution of manufacturing employment: 1911

Saskatchewan in 1911, they were the lowest ranking in the country by 1961. Two spatial growth gradients, the heartland-hinterland gradient (national scale) and the east-west gradient, both discriminate against growth in the Atlantic provinces. The two gradients are evident in the changing regional industrial structure (Table 6.4). Some industries show an east-west trend in incidence 1911 to 1961, including the manufacture of agricultural implements, canvas products, carpets, mats and rugs, and fish products. Others have become increasingly heartland industries, including synthetic textile mills and copper and alloy rolling and casting.

Multivariate Analysis

A more explicit examination of the spatial and sectoral components of employment growth in manufacturing industry is provided by the three stage mathematical methodology described earlier. The city manufacturing employment figures (y) for twelve selected years from 1951–1969, tabulated from the annual Census of Manufactures, are regressed separately for each city against the Canada total (x) for the corresponding twelve years. Each city's relative

Table 6.5. Relative growth rates in manufacturing employment by region: 1951–1969

Region[1]	No. of cities[2]	Mean alpha[3]	Heartland sub-regions[4]	
Periphery	16	0·604		
Atlantic	5	0·211	Montreal District	0·988
Quebec	1	0·489	Other Quebec	0·545
Ontario	4	0·624	Southwestern Ontario	1·155
West	6	0·936	Eastern Ontario	0·520
Heartland	39	0·872		
Quebec	16	0·767		
Ontario	23	0·946		
Total	55			

Notes for Table 6.5
1. The heartland-hinterland boundary accords with Maxwell (1972); the heartland is shown in the inset, Figures 6.2 and 6.4, with the exception of Owen Sound (514) and Pembroke (542).
2. The number of cities is reduced from 62 to 55 in order to maintain compatability with a comprehensive study of which this is part.
3. A mean alpha value of 1·0 indicates that regional employment is proportional to national growth and is thus the special case, isometry. The Montreal district provides an example of isometry, although Montreal itself has an alpha of only 0·296 for the period, 1951 to 1969, indicating substantial industrial relocation into surrounding cities. Southwestern Ontario has a slightly positive allometry although the range of city allometries is 2·045 with St. Thomas having the highest growth rate (2·349) and Oshawa (1·734), Stratford (1·684) and Kitchener-Waterloo (1·363) the next highest, and Welland having the lowest allometry (0·304). Windsor (0·520), St. Catharines (0·728) and Sarnia (0·774) have the next lowest values. Toronto's rate is nearly isometric (0·988).
4. The Montreal district includes all cities within a 50 mile radius of Montreal. Eastern Ontario includes all cities east of Toronto.

growth rate is indicated by the regression coefficient (α) in the equation $y = bx^a$. This alpha value measures growth during the second, slower growth period following World War II (Figure 6.1). Ideally, an additional alpha value should have been computed for the preceding, faster growth period, but satisfactory employment data are unavailable.

The relative growth rates repeat the patterns identified in the descriptive analysis. A clear east to west gradient is evident for the growth rates, with the Atlantic region having the lowest and the western region the highest mean regional allometries (Table 6.5). The heartland allometry is close to one, the special case, isometry: the overwhelming concentration of manufacturing in the heartland makes it the nation's pace-setter so that its allometry is never likely to vary substantially from isometry. Nevertheless, substantial variations do occur within the heartland and, surprisingly, the lowest allometries tend to occur in the corridor linking Montreal and Toronto. The fastest relative growth rates tend to occur southeast of Montreal and southwest of Toronto creating a downward-transitional region in what one would expect to be a development corridor (Table 6.5 and 6.6). The Windsor district, too, is a lagging region with one of the lowest allometries in southwestern Ontario.

Can these patterns of post World War II employment growth in manufacturing industry be related to the contemporary industrial structure? There is no convenient procedure for relating the alpha values directly to the binary matrices of industry incidence. But city scores on the industry incidences for

Table 6.6. Simple correlations of relative growth of manufacturing employment 1951 to 1969 with distance from regional metropolitan centres

Cities in	Simple correlation of alpha values with distance from					Population potential 1961
	Vancouver	Winnipeg	Toronto	Montreal	Halifax	
Atlantic region	−92	−94	−98	−97	−35	30
Quebec	20	22	31	16	−22	−32
Ontario	04	10	−20	22	16	05
Western Canada	07	−27	−17	−16	−15	02
Canada	−06	−23	−17	09	24	03

1. Leading decimals are omitted. Obvious cautions apply in interpreting such tables but certain points are clear. Quebec alpha values tend to increase with distance from Toronto ($r = 0.31$) and Ontario alpha values tend to increase with distance from Montreal ($r = 0.22$) emphasizing the comparatively low alpha values between Canada's two major manufacturing centres. The prevailing pattern of post World War II manufacturing growth has increased east to west from Halifax ($r = 0.24$) to the prairies and Winnipeg ($r = −0.23$). There is no correlation between relative growth in manufacturing employment in Canada and population potential. In Quebec however, there is a strong negative correlation ($r = −0.32$) and relative employment growth rates tend to increase with distance from Montreal ($r = 0.16$), the city of highest population potential in Canada in 1961. Only in the Atlantic region is the rate of relative employment growth directly related to the population potential ($r = 0.30$).

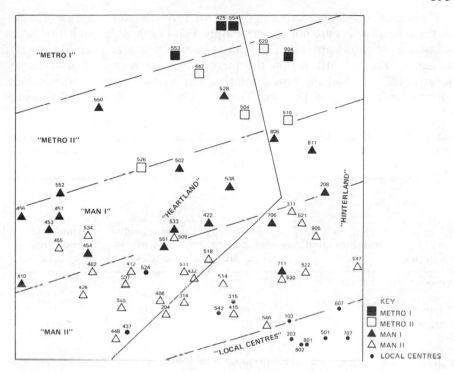

Figure 6.5. Factor analysis of manufacturing incidence matrix 1951 and 1961: factor score II *vs.* factor score III

1951–1961 can be obtained by singular decomposition, or direct factor analysis, of the two matrices, interfiled so that for each city in the analysis the occurrence of each of the fifty-three industries is recorded for both 1951 and 1961. Four direct factors are extracted. The first is a data transformation factor which scales the data according to aggregate incidence, and it may be thought of as a size factor. The city scores for factors II (vertical axis) and III (horizontal axis) are plotted in Figure 6.5. In combination, these two factors order the cities according to their rank on the descriptive hierarchy and distinguish between heartland and hinterland cities. Heartland-type industries are indicated by high negative scores on the textile and clothing industries, principally cotton yarn and cloth, SIC 183, primary woollen textiles, 193 and 197, synthetic textile mills, 201, and hosiery and knit goods, 231 and 239, paper box and bag manufacturing, 273, and iron foundaries, 294. Periphery-type industries, identified by high positive scores on factor III, include slaughtering and meat packing, 101, fish products, 111, canvas products, 221, boatbuilding, 328, railway equipment, 326, clay products, 351, and petroleum refining, 365. The fourth factor contrasts the regional distribution of the manufacture of rubber products, 161 and 163, agricultural implements, 311, and automobiles, 323, with fish products, 111, shipbuilding, 327, and pulp and paper, 271.

The simple correlations between the relative growth rates and the city scores on these four factors are not encouragingly high (Table 6.7). No nation-wide relationship occurs between employment growth and hierarchy (Factor II), though in the Atlantic region the larger cities, as measured by industry occurrence, have had the fastest relative employment growth, whereas the opposite is occurring in Quebec. These results may indicate a relationship

Table 6.7. Simple correlations of relative growth rates in manufacturing employment 1951 to 1961 with city scores on direct factor analysis of industry incidence 1951 to 1961

	Factor			
	I	II	III	IV
			heartland–	regional
	data		hinterland	contrasts in
	transformation	manufacturing	industry	industrial
Cities in	(size)	hierarchy	contrasts	structure
Atlantic region	68	79	−01	37
Quebec	−55	−45	−40	−11
Ontario	−12	02	−31	−43
Western Canada	15	18	−48	−07
Canada	−06	00	−23	−31

Note for Table 6.7
1. Leading decimals are omitted. Exact identification of the factors is complex but the names are suggestive of their dominant character. Compare the correlations of Factor II in this table and their correlations with population potential in Table 6.6; the values above are higher for the Atlantic region and Quebec, but the pattern of correlations is the same. Growth rates are negatively associated with hinterland-type industry.

between the structure of the urban hierarchy and hierarchial distribution of employment growth. Ontario cities, with a well-developed hierarchy, display no relationship between rank and growth; Quebec cities, with a marked relative absence of cities in the 100,000 to 250,000 population size range, exhibit an inverse relationship; the Atlantic region, with a relatively small proportion of population in cities of 100,000 and above, has a positive relationship. The relative growth of manufacturing employment in Canada may be promoting a more balanced urban hierarchy.

Stronger relationships are exhibited between employment growth rates and industry structure (Factor IV). in general, heartland-type industries have generated the greatest relative employment growth, with the exception of the Atlantic provinces where growth has been size-dominated. The regional contrasts identified by factor IV attribute significant relative employment growth in the Atlantic provinces to the fish products, shipbuilding, and pulp and paper industries, but, in Ontario, as for the country generally, to the manufacture of rubber products, agricultural implements and automobiles.

These relationships should be examined further using industry-mix, regional-share data.

The combined contribution of the factors to explaining relative growth in manufacturing employment in the post World War II period is small but significant. The empirical relationship between growth and structure is given by the equation:

$$\alpha = 2.945 - 2.094\,S_1 - 0.551\,S_2 - 0.173\,S_3 - 0.201\,S_4$$

$$(2.92)\ (-2.14) \qquad (-2.03) \qquad (-2.11) \qquad (-2.52)$$

where

α = relative growth of manufacturing employment 1951–1969 and

S_1–S_4 = factor scores from direct factor analysis of industry incidence matrix 1951 and 1961.

The null 't' values are given in parentheses.

The multiple coefficient of determination (R^2) is 0.22, which is all that could be expected given the simple correlations of the alpha values with the factor scores. A higher R^2 could no doubt be achieved by extracting more factors from the incidence matrices or by applying the model regionally. But, on the one hand, these empirical results do serve to illustrate a useful methodology to measure the impact of structure on growth. On the other hand, regional submodels, incorporating additional factors, would call for more elaboration and knowledge of industry structure in Canada than can be provided at present.

The multiple regression model reiterates the relationship evident in the simple correlation matrix, with the exception that size and hierarchy are related to growth once the heartland-hinterland and regional contrasts in industrial structure are accounted for. It is not the cities with the greatest industry incidence that tend to have the fastest employment growth rates. Size (S_1) and alpha are inversely related (partial correlation = -0.29). Size (S_1) and hierarchy (S_2) are collinear ($r = 0.95$), but with the size factor accounted for, city employment growth depends on level in the manufacturing hierarchy.

6.5. Conclusions

Growth creates form; the form of a system is an expression of the relative growth rates of components during system growth. Changes in system form reflect differences in the relative growth rates of components so that they comprise changing proportions of a system. The manufacturing component of the Canadian space-economy has clearly changed since Confederation in 1867, both in its contribution to GNP and employment vis-a-vis other sectors of the economy, and in its spatial distribution and internal sectoral configuration. Manufacturing employed similar proportions of the labour force in each Canadian province at Confederation. By 1911, an incipient manufacturing belt is evident, with industrial concentrations occurring in the Toronto and Montreal regions. Regional disparities have increased in the subsequent half century to 1961, with the increasing dominance of the Toronto and Montreal districts, and an east to west growth gradient.

Allometry emphasizes the regularity of the relative growth rates of system components rather than the actual growth-in-time of these components. The size of a system component tends to maintain a simple relationship to the size of other components or to the system itself longitudinally through time with the growth of the system, or cross-sectionally, at one point in time, for corresponding systems of different sizes. Thus, the population growth of metropolitan centres has maintained a logarithmically linear relationship with the population growth of Canada during the period 1901–1961, and the logarithm of manufacturing employment has a linear relationship with the number of industry types in each Canadian city over 10,000 in 1911 and 1961.

Certain regular proportional adjustments are required by size change, while others are the result of the differential competitive ability of the system components which is determined in part by their position in the overall pattern of system interdependencies. In both cases, the evolving spatial form of the system may be considered as an expression of the forces acting on that system during its growth. Socio-economic system forces are extremely complex, but their net effect can be measured by the relative growth rates of system components. The regularity of net system response may result from the consistency of system forces operating during growth, the interdependence of the forces, with a change in one evoking a response in others, and/or the articulation of the system which may set limits to growth.

The degree to which form limits growth is examined in the case study through the use of a three stage mathematical methodology. Relative employment growth in manufacturing is related to industrial structure with the significance of each underlying structural component expressed in terms of its incremental contribution to relative employment growth. In general, relative employment growth is limited by the number of industrial establishments present, with the exception of the Atlantic provinces, the position of a city in the overall manufacturing hierarchy, the presence of hinterland-type industries and the absence of key regional industries such as pulp and paper or automobiles.

A great deal of further research is needed to examine the relationship between growth and form in geographic systems. Allometry, emphasizing the regularity of the relative growth rates of system components rather than the actual growth-in-time of these components, provides a simple and interpretable framework within which geographers can proceed in this effort. The deduction of size-required proportional adjustments needs detailed elaboration. Further improvements in the measurement of allometries might also be made. This paper presents only the rudiments of a new conceptual and methodological tool for examining structural changes and for identifying the degree to which form limits growth in dynamic and complexly interacting systems. More detailed analysis utilizing better data is encouraged so that the full implication of this approach can be better assessed.

References

Ballabon, M. B. (1950), Area Differentiation of the Manufacturing Belt in Central Canada, Unpublished Ph.D. dissertation, Department of Geography, McGill University.

Bertalanffy, Ludwig von (1960), Principles and Theory of Growth, in Nowinski, Wiktor, W. (ed.), *Fundamental Aspects of Normal and Malignant Growth.* Amsterdam: Elsevier Publishing Co., 137–259.

Bertalanffy, Ludwig von (1964), Basic Concepts in Quantitative Biology of Metabolism, in Locker, A. (ed.), *Quantitative Biology of Metabolism—First International Symposium.* Helgolander Wissenschaftliche Meeresuntersuchungen, **9**, 5–37.

Bertalanffy, Ludwig von (1968), *General System Theory.* New York: George Braziller.

Boulding, Kenneth E. (1953), Toward a General Theory of Growth, *Canadian Journal of Economics and Political Science,* **19**, 326–340.

Brody, Samuel (1945), *Bioenergetics and Growth.* New York: Reinhold.

Canada (1957), *Royal Commission on Canada's Economic Prospects: Final Report.* Ottawa: Queen's Printer.

Cant, R. G. (1971), Changes in the Location of Manufacturing in New Zealand 1957–1968: An Application of Three-Mode Factor Analysis, *New Zealand Geographer,* **37**, 38–55.

Darwent, D. F. (1969), Growth Poles and Growth Centres in Regional Planning—A Review, *Environment and Planning,* **1**, 5–32.

Davis, P. G. and Banks, L. (1965), Interregional Interest Rate Differentials, *Monthly Review* (August). New York: Federal Reserve Bank of New York.

Dutton, Geoffrey, (Forthcoming), The Shape of Urban Systems—An Allometric Perspective, Discussion Paper, Ottawa: Ministry of State for Urban Affairs.

Economic Council of Canada (1966), *Third Annual Review—Prices, Productivity and Employment.* Ottawa: Queen's Printer.

English, H. E. (1968), The Canadian Industrial Structure: An Essay on its Nature and Efficiency, in Leack, R. H. (ed.), *Contemporary Canada.* Durham, N. C.: Duke University Press, 81–103.

Friedmann, John and Alonso, William (eds.), (1964), *Regional Development and Planning.* Cambridge, Mass.: M.I.T. Press.

Friedmann, John (1966), *Regional Development Policy—A Case Study of Venezuela.* Cambridge, Mass.: M.I.T. Press.

Friedmann, John (1969), A General Theory of Polarized Development, Los Angeles: U.C.L.A. School of Architecture and Urban Planning, M.S.

Friedmann, John, McClynn, Eileen, Stuckey, Barbara and Chung-Tong Wu (1970), Urbanization and National Development: A Comparative Analysis. Los Angeles: U.C.L.A. School of Architecture and Urban Planning, M.S.

Gilmour, J. M. (1966), The Joint Anarchy of Confidentiality' and Definitional Change, *The Canadian Geographer,* **10**, 40–48.

Good, I. J. (1969), Some Applications of the Singular Decomposition of a Matrix, *Technometrics,* **2**, 823–831.

Gould, S. J. (1966), Allometry and Size in Ontogeny and Phylogeny, *Biological Review,* **41**, 587–640. Published by Cambridge University Press, New York.

Guerra, E. and Gunther, B. (1957), On the Relationship of Organ Weight Function, and Body Weight, *Acta. Physiol. Lat. Am.,* **7**, 1–7.

Haire, Mason (1959), Biological Models and Empirical Histories of the Growth of Organizations, in Haire, M. (ed.), *Modern Organization Theories*. New York: Wiley, **1**, pp. 272–306.

Hall, Peter, G. (ed.), (1966), *Von Thunen's Isolated State*. Translated by Carla M. Wartenberg. New York: Pergamon Press.

Harman, H. H. (1967), *Modern Factor Analysis*. Chicago: University of Chicago Press.

Horst, P. (1965), *Factor Analysis of Data Matrices*. New York: Holt, Rinehart and Winston.

Huxley, Julian (1932), *Problems of Relative Growth*. London: Methuen.

Keeble, D. E. (1967), Models of Economic Development, in Chorley, R. J. and Haggett, P. (eds.), *Models in Geography*. London: Methuen, 243–302.

Koenig, E. F. (1971), Heartlands, Hinterlands, and Allometric Growth, unpublished Master's Thesis, State University of New York at Buffalo.

Lasuen, J. R. (1962), Regional Income Inequalities and the Problems of Growth in Spain, *Papers and Proceedings, Regional Science Association*, **8**, 169–191.

Maxwell, J. W. (1965), The Functional Structure of Canadian Cities: A Classification of Cities, *Geographical Bulletin*, **7**, 79–104.

Maxwell, J. W., Greig, J. A. and Meyer, H. G. (1972), The Functional Structure of Canadian Cities: A Classification of Cities, Canada, Department of the Environment, Mimeo.

McInnis, R. M. (1969), *A Consistent Industrial Classification of Canadian Work Force Statistics, 1911–1961*. A report to Department of Manpower and Immigration, Canada, Mimeographed.

Myrdal, Gunnar (1957), *Rich Lands and Poor*. New York: Harper.

Naroll, R. S. and Bertalanffy, Ludwig von (1956), The Principle of Allometry in Biology and the Social Sciences, *General Systems*, **1**, 76–89.

Perloff, Harvey S. and Wingo, Lowden, Jr. (1961), Natural Resource Endowment and Regional Economic Growth, in Spengler, J. J. (ed.), *National Resources and Economic Growth*. Washington, D. C.: Resources for the Future, Inc.

Rapoport, A. (1970), The Search for Simplicity, Paper presented at the Symposium on General System Theory in Honour of Ludwig von Bertalanffy, Geneseo, N.Y.

Ray, D. M. (1972), The Allometry of Urban and Regional Growth, Discussion Paper No. B. 72.10. Ottawa: Ministry of State for Urban Affairs.

Robinson, A. (ed.) (1963), *The Economic Consequences of the Size of Nations*. London: Macmillan.

Rummel, R. J. (1970), *Applied Factor Analysis*. Evanston: Northwestern University Press.

Scholl, D. A. (1954), Regularities in Growth Curves, Including Rhythms and Allometry, in Boell, E. J. (ed.), *Dynamics of Growth Processes*. Princeton: Princeton University Press, pp. 224–242.

Smiley, D. V. (ed.) (1963), *The Rowell-Sirois Report: Book 1*. Toronto: McClelland and Stewart.

Smith, L. (1961), Space for the CBD's functions, *Journal, American Institute of Planners*, **37**, 40.

Stahl, W. R. (1962), Similarity and Dimensional Methods in Biology, *Science*, **137**, 205–212.

Thompson, D'Arcy (1919), *On Growth and Form*. Cambridge University Press.

Tucker, L. R. (1964), The Extension of Factor Analysis to Three-Dimensional Matrices, in Frederiksen, N., and Gulliksen, H. (eds.), *Contributions to Mathematical Psychology*. New York: Holt, Rinehart and Winston.

Ullman, Edward L. (1958), Regional Development and the Geography of Concentration, *Papers and Proceedings, Regional Science Association*, **4**, 179–198.

Ullman, E. L. and Dacey, M. F. (1960), The Minimum Requirements Approach to the Urban Economic Base, *Papers and Proceedings, Regional Science Association*, **6**, 175–194.

Watson, D. M. S. (1949), The Evidence Afforded by Fossil Vertebrates on the Nature of Evolution, in Jepson, G. L., Simpson, G. G., and Mayor, E. (eds.), *Genetics, Paleontology, and Evolution.* Princeton University Press.

White, J. F. and Gould, S. J. (1965), Interpretation of the Coefficient in the Allometric Equation, *American Naturalist,* **99,** 5–18.

White, L., Foscue, E. J. and McKnight, T. L. (1964), *Regional Geography of Anglo-America.* Englewood Cliffs, N.J.: Prentice-Hall, Inc.

Woldenberg, Michael (1971), Allometric Growth in Social Systems, *Harvard Papers in Theoretical Geography,* No. 6.

7 Three-mode Factor Analysis as Applied to Industrial Location Data

GARTH CANT

Studies of change in the location of industrial establishments represent a special case of the more general problem of the analysis of phenomena whose distribution in space varies over time. Horst (1963, 1965), Gould (1967, 1969) and Berry (1968) in their discussions of general field theory and the analysis of two dimensional data matrices have all suggested that techniques of factor analysis may be extended to incorporate an additional dimension. Where similar observations are made for the same locations at a number of different points in time it is thus possible to use factor analysis to describe temporal changes in geographical patterns. A number of procedures for three-mode factor analysis have been developed by Tucker (1963, 1964, 1966) and applied to educational and psychological problems by Tucker (1965, 1967) and Levin (1965). Such techniques can be applied to changes in industrial location in cases where information is recorded at regular intervals for a common set of spatial units.

Gould (1967, p. 53) sets out the metaphysical background for such studies by noting that we can collect and arrange large quantities of geographical information into rectangular arrays called matrices. It is sometimes possible by the use of mathematical techniques such as factor analysis to identify patterns of relationship which can be given geographical interpretation. In Figure 7.1a, for example, a data matrix is formed by describing a number of farms in terms of the crops grown on each (Henshall and King, 1966). The correlations between these crops are calculated (Figure 7.1b) and entered into a principal components form of factor analysis which reduced the larger number of crops to a smaller number of crop combinations (Figure 7.1c). As a further step it is possible to calculate a matrix of factor scores (Figure 7.1d) which rates each of the original farms in terms of these new crop combinations. King (1969, pp. 174–184) uses data for crop acreages in the counties of Ohio State to provide a worked example of this type.

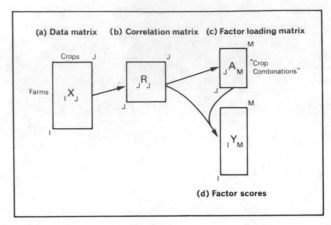

Figure 7.1. Two-mode factor analysis as applied to agricultural data

To extend the traditional two-mode factor analysis to incorporate temporal changes it is necessary to visualize a sequence of rectangular matrices stacked alongside each other to form a three-dimensional matrix (Gould, 1967, p. 84). A recent study of changes in the location of manufacturing industry in New Zealand used as a framework for analysis the number of workers employed in each of 20 industries in the 23 employment districts for the eleven years up to 1967/1968 (Cant, 1971). The general procedure is shown in Figure 7.2 and described below.

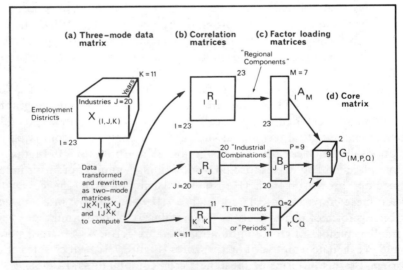

Figure 7.2. Three-mode factor analysis as applied to manufacturing
employment data

The data are entered into the three-mode data matrix X_{IJK} where I is the number of employment districts, J is the number of industries and K is the number of years (Figure 7.2a). If any transformation of the data is required it may be made at this point. Each of the three modes are treated separately by rewriting the data into the appropriate two-mode matrix and calculating the matrix of intercorrelations for that particular mode (Figure 7.2b). To obtain the I-mode correlation matrix, for example, the numbers in each employment district are written separately for each industry and each year into the 220 by 23 matrix $_{JK}X_I$ and the 23 by 23 correlation matrix $_IR_I$ calculated. The three correlation matrices are next used to calculate the factor loading matrices shown in Figure 7.2c. In the 1971 study, a principal components form a factor analysis was used and the 23 employment districts were reduced to seven 'regional components', the twenty industries to seven 'industrial combinations' and the eleven years reduced to two 'change through time' components. In the final stage of the analysis a reduced 'core matrix' was computed to show the structural relationships between each of the three reduced modes (Figure 7.2d).

As a practical application of three-mode factor analysis the 1971 results were modest in achievement. The factor analyses of the three separate modes were successful in that they gave a good indication of the main structural and locational relationships and are significant in that they confirmed that these had persisted right through the study period with very little change. The final stage of the study was less successful in that the factor scores in the core matrix were unstandardized and very difficult to interpret. In th light of experience gained in this initial study an alternative operational procedure is now suggested.

7.1. Operational Procedure

The procedure described here is designed to take advantage of a series of standard programs prepared by Cooley and Lohnes (1971) for analysis of the traditional two mode data matrices. The strategy followed is devised to permit maximum flexibility and range of choice in the selection and rotation of factors for each of the three modes and then, in a final sequence of operations, to reduce the three-mode data matrix to a core matrix of standardized factor scores (Figure 7.3).

(1) Rewrite the three-mode data matrix X_{IJK} into each of the two-mode matrices $_{JK}X_I$, $_{IK}X_J$ and $_{IJ}X_K$.

(2) From $_{JK}X_I$ $_{IK}X_J$ and $_{IJ}X_K$ calculate the correlation matrices $_IR_I$, $_JR_J$, $_KR_K$ (Program CORREL).

(3) From $_IR_I$, $_JR_J$, $_KR_K$ calculate and select principal components M, P and Q and corresponding factor loading matrices $_IA_M$, $_JB_P$ and $_KC_Q$ so that $M < I$, $P < J$ and $Q < K$ (Program PRINCO).

Note: Unless $MP > K$ it will not be possible to compute the core matrix in 5 (e) below.

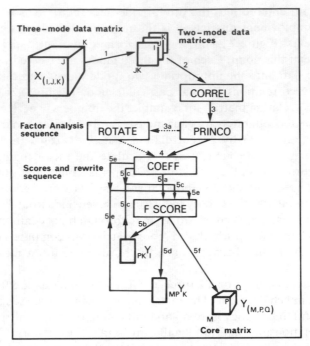

Figure 7.3. A program sequence for three-mode factor analysis using Cooley and Lohnes packing programs

(3a) (Optional) Any or all of the factors in $_IA_M$, $_JB_P$ and $_KC_Q$ may be rotated by any orthogonal rotation to obtain new factor loadings for these matrices (Program ROTATE).

(4) From $_IA_M$, $_JB_P$ and $_KC_Q$ calculate the coefficient matrices $_ID_M$, $_JE_P$ and $_KF_Q$ which will be used for the computation of factor scores in 5 (Program COEFF).

(5) Select the modes which retain the greatest proportion of the variance in the original data and reduce the data matrix to a core matrix of factor scores by the following sequence. In Figure 7.3 and the listing below we assume that the variance retained in $J > I > K$.

(a) Reduce the data matrix $_{IK}X_J$ to the standardized factor scores matrix $_{IK}Y_P$ using the coefficients matrix $_JE_P$ (Program FSCORE).

(b) Rewrite the scores in $_{IK}Y_P$ into the matrix $_{PK}Y_I$ and calculate the means and standard deviations for all Y_I.

(c) Reduce the factor scores matrix $_{PK}Y_I$ to the standardized factor scores matrix $_{PK}Y_M$ using the coefficients matrix $_ID_M$ (Program FSCORE).

(d) Rewrite the scores in $_{PK}Y_M$ into the matrix $_{MP}Y_K$ and calculate the means and standard deviations for all Y_K.

(e) Reduce the factor scores matrix $_{MP}Y_K$ to the standardized factor scores matrix using the coefficients matrix $_KF_Q$ (Program FSCORE).

(f) Rewrite the scores in $_{MP}Y_Q$ into the core matrix Y_{MPQ}.

It is possible either to transform the original data while they are still contained in the three-mode matrix or to standardize each mode separately after the values are rewritten into the two-mode data matrices. In the procedure outlined above the latter operation is done automatically since the factor scores are standardized each time Program FSCORE is used. Decisions regarding transformation of the original data remain a matter of individual choice and in the following worked examples the results from two separate analyses of the same original data are compared. In the first one the untransformed employment figures are used while in the second these raw figures are transformed into location indices.

7.2. The New Zealand Data Matrix 1951–1970

The present examples are both concerned with changes in the location of manufacturing in New Zealand during the decades of the 1950's and 1960's. The raw data used are the numbers employed in each of the 10 provinces (Figure 7.4), cross classified according to 20 industrial groups for 19 consecutive years. Employment figures are used in preference to value of production, net value added or value of plant and equipment since the use of the latter information is constrained by the disclosure regulations. Compared with the

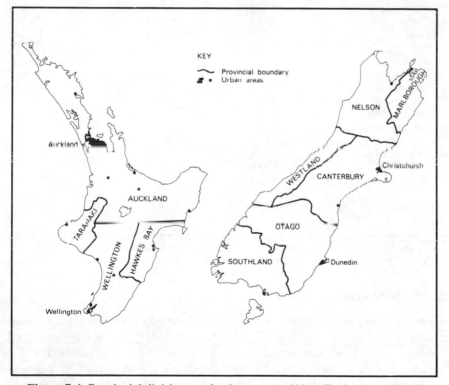

Figure 7.4. Provincial divisions and urban areas of New Zealand 1951–1970

previous study (Cant, 1971) the time sequence is longer but the areal mesh is coarser since the publication of figures for employment districts is a more recent innovation. The early figures are taken from the annual volumes of *New Zealand Official Yearbook* while the more recent figures are also available in the annual *Statistics of Industrial Production*. The numbers employed in each industry and in each provincial district vary considerably in magnitude (Table 7.1). Total employment in manufacturing has increased from 144,370 in 1951/1952 to 241,650 in 1969/1970. These figures do not include a number of activities such as dressmaking, boot repairs and railway workshops and exclude all persons engaged in factories in a purely distributive basis.

Table 7.1. Employment in manufacturing in New Zealand by industry groups and by provinces, 1969–1970

	Industry Group			Province[1]	
1	Food	41,585	1	Auckland	112,638
2	Beverages	2,824	2	Hawkes Bay	9,882
3	Tobacco	1,147	3	Taranaki	6,468
4	Textiles	15,304	4	Wellington	46,262
5	Footwear	27,446	5	Marlborough	1,526
6	Wood products	14,703	6	Nelson	3,813
7	Furniture	5,484	7	Westland	1,194
8	Paper	8,843	8	Canterbury	37,763
9	Printing	15,273	9	Otago	14,822
10	Leather	2,288	10	Southland	7,281
11	Rubber	4,122			
12	Chemicals	6,829		Total	241,650
13	Petroleum and coal	663			
14	Non-metallic minerals	8,672			
15	Basic metals	2,761			
16	Metal products	15,240			
17	Machinery	17,618			
18	Electrical	9,218			
19	Transport	32,589			
20	Miscellaneous	9,041			
	Total	241,650			

[1]A fourfold subdivision of Auckland Province has been published since 1960 but this has been reaggregated for the present study to retain comparability with earlier years.

7.3. The New Zealand Space Economy

Contemporary spatial patterns of manufacturing in New Zealand are best understood in the context of the larger space economy which has developed since the advent of planned settlement in the 1840's. Traditionally the economy has been dependent on the production and export of primary products and the most characteristic urban settlements have been the provincial cities located at a convenient port of entry and servicing a rural hinterland (Rimmer, 1967). In the middle decades of the nineteenth century first timber (from the Auckland Province) then gold (from Otago and Westland) and wool (from the tussock grasslands of Canterbury, Otago, Marlborough, Wellington and Hawkes Bay) were the dominant exports. Later, with the advent of refrigeration in the 1880's and 1890's and the clearing of the North Island forests, there was intensive development of grassland farming and a swing towards the production of meat and dairy products. Exotic plantations were established in the central North Island in the 1930's and as a result forest products have recovered much of their former importance during the last two decades.

The development of a fully integrated economy came slowly; the provinces of Auckland and Wellington were not linked by rail, for example, until 1908. With successive changes in the importance of the various forms of primary production different regions expanded at different rates (Cant and Johnston, 1972). As the centre of gravity swung southwards from the northern forests to the southern grasslands and goldfields, four regional centres, (Auckland, Wellington, Christchurch and Dunedin) developed metropolitan functions. More recently, as the balance of primary production and population has tilted northwards, the importance of the last two has diminished. Peripheral regions in the south have declined and a number of new regional centres have developed within the Auckland Province (Figure 7.4).

The New Zealand economy which developed during the period 1880–1930 is best described as pastoral-commercial. Pastoral products were processed and exported from the nearest provincial seaport and the metropolitan centres of Auckland, Wellington, Christchurch and Dunedin provided a range of more specialized commercial and social service functions. From the late 1930's onwards the transition was made to a pastoral–industrial economy as the proceeds from pastoral exports were increasingly used to finance imports of the capital goods and raw materials needed to sustain a growing manufacturing sector. The greatest expansion of market-oriented, import-substitution industrial growth has taken place in the metropolitan centres, particularly Auckland and Wellington. McDonald (1970) describes this as the

'typical pattern of industrializing primary produce exporting countries; outlying regions specialize in producing internationally competitive primary commodities; their exports finance imports into the central region which balances its account by selling the products of their protected manufacturing industries and services to outlying regions.' (p. 153).

7.4. The Pastoral–Industrial Economy

It is thus characteristic of the New Zealand economy that while most of its exports derive from pastoral products, a high proportion of its workforce is employed outside the primary sector and a large proportion of its population live in urban areas. In 1952 pastoral products represented 95·7 per cent of all exports by value but the number employed in all primary industry was 136,000 as compared with 143,000 in manufacturing and 566,000 in the labour force as a whole (*New Zealand Official Yearbook*, 1956, p. 297 and p. 1047). Eighteen years later in 1970 pastoral products still contributed 82·1 per cent of all exports and forest products added a further 5·5 per cent. (*New Zealand Official Yearbook*, 1971, p. 631). Employment in the primary sector had increased slightly to 144,000 while that in manufacturing had more than doubled to 303,000 in a total labour force of 1,077,000 (*New Zealand Official Yearbook*, 1971, p. 907). Between 1951 and 1971 the proportion of people living in urban areas increased from 72·7 per cent to 81·5 per cent of total population (*New Zealand Census of Population and Dwellings*, 1971, 1, p. 3). New Zealand is well described as a 'small yet prosperous ex-colony' (Johnston, 1971) with a strong pastoral base and a population which is both urbanized and industrialized.

Example 1: Untransformed Data Matrix

In the first example the entries in the cells of the three-mode data matrix are the numbers of workers employed in each industry in each province for each year. In view of the large number of observations ($10 \times 20 \times 19 = 3,800$) and the magnitude of some of the entries (there were 14,740 employed in the food industry in Auckland in 1969/1970, for example) the possibility of storage overflow was recognized. To guard against this all entries were reduced by a factor of 10^{-2} before computations were commenced. The operational procedures outlined above were followed through; the factor loading matrices were obtained for each of the three modes (Tables 7.2, 7.3, and 7.4) and the core matrix of factor scores was obtained (Table 7.5). As an additional aid to the interpretation of the factor loading matrices the factor score matrices for each separate mode were also calculated. The latter are not reproduced in full but are shown graphically where appropriate (for example in Figure 7.5).

Regional Components (I-Mode): The principal components analysis of the I-Mode matrix produced three factors which together account for 93 per cent of the variance in the data. These were rotated by varimax rotation to give the factors shown in Table 7.2.

The original 10 provinces are thus reduced to three provincial components. A study of the factor loadings in Table 7.2 and an examination of the factor scores suggests that Factor I_1 is a regional component; the provinces of Southland, Hawkes Bay, Taranaki, Nelson and Marlborough are all important sources of pastoral products while in the case of Otago we know that the decline in the former metropolitan role of Dunedin has been offset by a continued expansion of the pastoral base (Ministry of Works, Town and Country Planning Branch, 1967). Highest factor scores on this factor are recorded by the food processing, non-metallic minerals, and transport industries all of which are closely linked to the pastoral economy. It is interesting to note that the large provinces of Auckland, Wellington and Canterbury, all of which also have important pastoral industries, have intermediate loadings while Westland, with limited scope for food production, has a very small factor loading.

Table 7.2. Provincial components derived from untransformed data. I-mode factor loadings obtained by varimax rotation.

	Province	Factor		
		I_1 Regional	I_2 Forestry	I_3 Metropolitan
1	Auckland	0·39	0·33	**0·81**
2	Hawkes Bay	**0·90**	0·02	0·40
3	Taranaki	**0·83**	0·13	0·46
4	Wellington	0·29	0·18	**0·90**
5	Marlborough	**0·60**	0·28	**0·68**
6	Nelson	**0·70**	**0·58**	0·31
7	Westland	0·07	**0·97**	0·15
8	Canterbury	0·34	0·11	**0·90**
9	Otago	**0·55**	−0·01	**0·75**
10	Southland	**0·92**	0·16	0·33
Per cent variance accounted for		38·6	15·5	38·9

Note: The signs for Factor I_1 have been reversed in Table 7.2 and Table 7.5 to simplify interpretation and description. Factor loadings greater than 0·50 are bold.

Factor I_3 which accounts for a similar proportion of total variance is identified as a metropolitan component with high loadings for the provinces which contain four main centres and for Marlborough. The industries which score most highly on this factor include footwear, textiles, metal products, machinery and printing. Marlborough is a very small region with a relatively high proportion of its workforce employed in the footwear and machinery industries.

Factor I_2 identifies two small regions where forest processing and transport are particularly important activities. Auckland province which contains most of the wood industries associated with the exotic forests of the North Island has an intermediate loading on this factor.

Industrial Combinations (J-Mode): The seven largest principal components accounted for 99·3 per cent of total variance in the J-mode data. These seven factors were rotated by varimax rotation and the corresponding coefficients matrix was selected as the point of entry for stage 5 of the operational procedure previously described. After the core matrix had been computed the three smallest factors were discarded. The four factors which remain account for 92·2 per cent of the variance (Table 7.3).

Table 7.3 contains one very large general factor, with high loadings on a wide range of industries, and three special factors which load heavily on one or two industries only.

Factor J_1 (General) loads heavily on a number of industries which are important in all provinces; these include processing (food and wood products), non-metallic minerals, machinery and transport, all of which are closely linked to primary production, together with consumer industries such as beverages, furniture and printing which tend to serve provincial rather than national or overseas markets. Among the other industries which have high loadings on J_1 are the paper and petroleum industries, both of which have their largest establishments in the Auckland Province.

Table 7.3. Industrial combinations derived from untransformed data. J-mode factor loadings obtained by varimax rotation.

		Factor			
		J_1	J_2 Tobacco and chemicals	J_3 Rubber, electrical & textiles	J_4 Metal industries
	Industry	General			
1	Food	**0·86**	0·13	0·37	0·22
2	Beverages	**0·91**	0·13	0·29	0·21
3	Tobacco	0·04	**0·99**	0·08	0·02
4	Textiles	0·45	0·15	**0·75**	0·21
5	Footwear	**0·84**	0·22	0·45	0·18
6	Wood products	**0·95**	0·02	0·23	0·18
7	Furniture	**0·88**	0·17	0·38	0·18
8	Paper	**0·89**	0·07	0·16	0·28
9	Printing	**0·71**	0·39	0·41	0·26
10	Leather	**0·83**	−0·04	0·49	0·16
11	Rubber	0·33	0·09	**0·92**	0·15
12	Chemicals	**0·70**	0·46	0·35	0·25
13	Petroleum and coal	**0·77**	0·21	0·18	0·27
14	Non-metallic minerals	**0·88**	0·00	0·40	0·19
15	Basic metal	0·59	0·06	0·33	**0·72**
16	Metal products	**0·83**	0·15	0·31	0·29
17	Machinery	**0·79**	0·14	0·39	0·34
18	Electrical	**0·62**	0·30	**0·53**	0·28
19	Transport	**0·77**	0·31	0·40	0·25
20	Miscellaneous	**0·73**	0·16	0·31	0·42
	Per cent variance accounted for	56·4	9·0	18·6	8·2

Note: The signs in Factors J_1, J_2 and J_4 have been reversed in Tables 7.3 and 7.5 to assist interpretation and description. Factor loadings greater than 0·50 are bold.

The factor scores for this 'general' industrial factor are plotted in Figure 7.5(a). While these emphasize the wide range and balance of industrial activity in the Auckland Province the falling off of the curve over the final three years indicates a move here towards greater specialization. Increasing specialization is also evident in the case of Taranaki and Canterbury, the two provinces which record the largest negative scores for the closing years of the period covered by the study.

Factor J_2 (Tobacco and chemicals) loads heavily on tobacco and has a moderately high loading for chemicals. Both of these industries rely on a proportion of imported raw materials and serve national markets. The tobacco industry is concentrated in a very small number of establishments located in

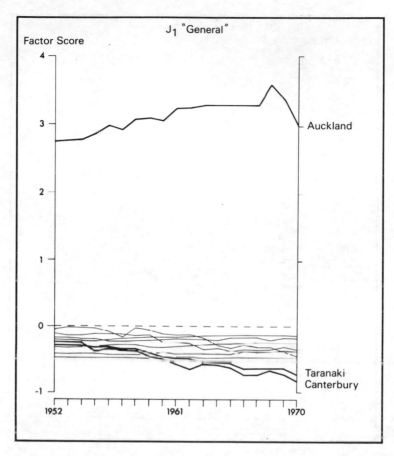

Figure 7.5a. Factor scores for J mode rotated factors obtained from untransformed data

Wellington, Auckland and Hawkes Bay and the pattern of factor scores in Figure 7.5(b) shows the effect of a major locational shift from Wellington to Hawkes Bay.

Factor J_3 (Rubber, electrical and textiles) links together a group of industries which produce for national and overseas markets as well as for local demand. In this instance the Province of Canterbury has the highest scores followed by Auckland, Wellington and Otago.

Factor J_4 is termed 'Metal Industries' since it has the highest loading for basic metals and includes the machinery, miscellaneous and metal products industries among its intermediate loadings. The pattern of factor scores in Figure 7.5(d) indicates that there has been a major development of this component during the period. The reflects the expansion of basic metal industries in Taranaki from the mid 1950s and the opening of the Glenbrook Steel Mill in the Auckland Province in 1968.

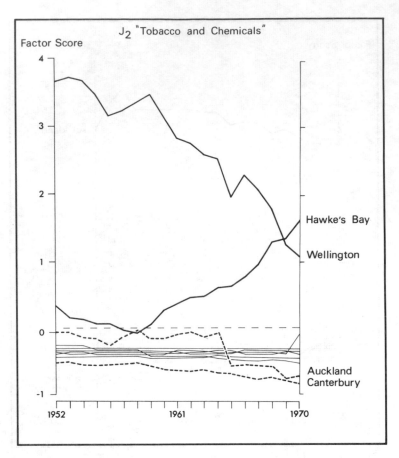

Figure 7.5b. Factor scores for J mode rotated factors obtained from untransformed data

Time Trends (K-mode): Reference to studies in the field of vocational training (Tucker, 1967) might lead us to anticipate that an analysis of the occasions mode for industrial location data would produce a series of factors which identify successive periods of economic development. Such, however, is not the case either in the 1971 study (Cant, 1971, pp. 48–49) or with the present results (Table 7.4). In each case a very large general factor with high loadings on all years indicates that the time period covered is too short for any major locational or structural changes to be apparent. Rotation of the factors in Table 7.4 offered no improvement in that this produced two large factors with almost equal variance, the first the mirror image of the second; one with factor loadings increasing steadily from year 1 to year 19 and the other with loadings diminishing in similar manner.

Factor K_1 is thus described as the 'continuing pattern'. The high proportion of variance accounted for and the fact that K_1 loads heavily on each of the 19

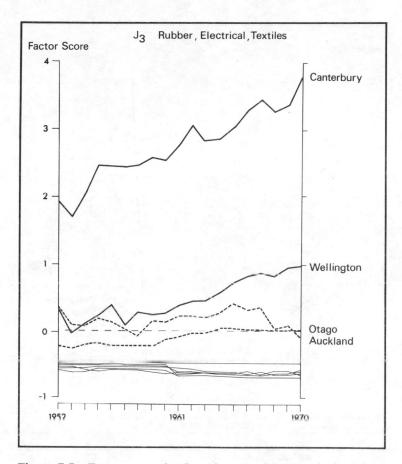

Figure 7.5c. Factor scores for J mode rotated factors obtained from untransformed data

years both serve to emphasize the high degree of continuity that has character-ized the locational and structural relationships in the period since 1950.

Within this larger continuity some changes can be recognized. Factor K_2 suggests that distinctions may be made between the 1950's (shown with negative loadings in Table 7.4) and the 1960's (with positive loadings). Examination of the factor scores suggests that the regions most affected by these changes in emphasis are Auckland, Marlborough and Hawkes Bay. The actual nature of these distinctions is best considered however in the discussion of the core matrix to which we now turn.

Core Matrix. The core matrix in Figure 7.5 is partitioned into two time-trend slices. The first of these, K_1, shows the continuing pattern of relationship between industrial combinations and provincial types. Both the 'general industrial' factor J_1 and the special character factors J_2, J_3 and J_4 record higher

214

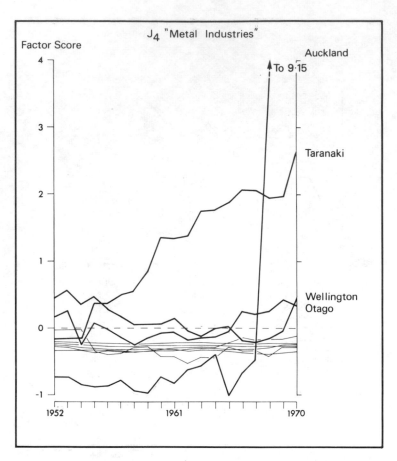

Figure 7.5d. Factor scores for J mode rotated factors obtained from untransformed data

scores for the 'metropolitan' factor, I_1, than for the regional factor, I_3. This does not, however, imply a complete dichotomy between the regional centres and the metropolitan centres. It has been noted already that the 'general industrial' factor combines together both primary production-based and consumer industries oriented to the local market. The higher score for this industrial combination supports the earlier contention that the four main urban areas continue to act as provincial service centres for large and productive rural hinterlands. In addition to this they have each developed their own particular mix of special metropolitan functions.

The lower slice of the core matrix shown in Table 7.5 enables us to identify a number of minor structural and locational changes which distinguish the 1960's from the 1950's. The largest of these is a shift in the tobacco and chemical combination from a metropolitan to a regional location. Reference back to Figure 7.4 and to the original data indicates that this is largely the result of the

Table 7.4. Time trends derived from untransformed data. Factor loadings for K-mode principal components.

	Year	K_1 Continuing pattern	K_2 1950's vs 1960s
1	1951–1952	0·92	−0·38
2	1952–1953	0·90	−0·41
3	1953–1954	0·90	−0·43
4	1954–1955	0·89	−0·45
5	1955–1956	0·88	−0·47
6	1956–1957	0·87	−0·49
7	1957–1958	0·89	−0·46
8	1958–1959	0·89	−0·45
9	1959–1960	0·87	−0·47
10	1960–1961	0·89	0·24
11	1961–1962	0·92	0·39
12	1962–1963	0·91	0·40
13	1963–1964	0·91	0·41
14	1964–1965	0·91	0·41
15	1965–1966	0·91	0·41
16	1966–1967	0·91	0·41
17	1967–1968	0·90	0·42
18	1968–1969	0·90	0·43
19	1969–1970	0·90	0·43
	Per cent variance accounted for	80·8	17·9

Note: The signs in Factor K_1 have been reversed in Tables 7.4 and 7.5 to assist interpretation and description.

Table 7.5. Core matrix of factor scores obtained from analysis of untransformed data.

		I_1 Regional	I_2 Forest Processing	I_3 Metropolitan
K_1	*Continuing Trend*			
J_1	General industries	−1·07	−1·00	0·87
J_2	Tobacco and chemicals	−0·86	−1·50	1·06
J_3	Rubber electrical and textiles	−2·34	−1·13	2·06
J_4	Metal industries	−0·41	−1·07	0·42
K_2	*Contrast 1950s vs 1960s*			
J_1	General industries	−0·13	0·59	−0·02
J_2	Tobacco and chemicals	0·83	0·24	−0·63
J_3	Rubber electrical and textiles	0·24	−0·30	0·04
J_4	Metal industries	0·31	0·35	0·31

expansion of tobacco manufacturing in Hawkes Bay and (at the very close of the period) in Nelson at the expense of Wellington and Auckland. The expansion of 'general industries' in the 'forest processing' regions is largely the result of diversification in Nelson Province which received a major boost when a motor assembly plant was opened in 1965. 'Metal industries' show positive scores in all three regional types but here again the impact is localized; basic metals have expanded in both Taranaki and Auckland and there has been a smaller expansion of other metal industries in Nelson and in Hawkes Bay. While changes such as these may represent the beginnings of new developments in smaller regions such as Hawkes Bay, Nelson or Taranaki there is as yet no evidence to suggest that any permanent long term trends have been established.

Example 2: Location Indices

It is widely recognized that the use of unweighted employment figures may overemphasize the importance of larger industries and larger statistical divisions. To counteract this Linge (1957), following Florence (1929) has used a 'location factor' which takes the number employed in any one industrial division for any one statistical area and weights it according to the total number employed in that industrial division and the total number employed in that statistical area. In the study cited above, Cant (1971) extended this concept to the three-mode situation using a 'location index' which measures the degree of concentration of employment in each cell of the three mode matrix (Appendix A). Any time and place concentration of a particular activity in any one province for any one year is indicated by a value greater than unity while industries with a less than proportionate share have values less than unity. In the case of the tobacco industry in 1951–1952, for example, Hawkes Bay and Wellington had location indices of 6·3 and 5·1 respectively indicating a very high degree of concentration, Auckland had a value of 0·2 indicating that this industry employed a less than proportionate share of the Auckland labour force, and the remaining regions scored 0 indicating a complete absence of this activity. In contrast the location indices for Food Processing and for Printing cluster towards the unity value indicating a more even distribution of these activities.

In this second worked example the location indices were calculated and entered into the cells of the three-mode data matrix. The analysis was carried out as before and the results are presented in Tables 7.6, 7.7, 7.8 and 7.9. A detailed interpretation of these is not intended, however; instead it is intended to focus attention on the nature of the factors obtained and make certain comparisons with the previous sequence of results shown in Tables 7.2, 7.3, 7.4 and 7.5.

Provincial Components and Industrial Combinations. Both the principal components analysis (results not reported here) and the varimax rotations shown in Tables 7.6 and 7.7 produced *I* and *J*-mode factors which were strongly bi-polar.

Table 7.6. Provincial components derived from location indices. *I*-mode factor loadings obtained by varimax rotation

Province	I_1 Primary servicing	I_2 Special A Auckland *vs* Hawkes Bay–Wellington	I_3 Special B Otago–Canterbury *vs* Wellington Hawkes Bay
1 Auckland	0·19	**0·81**	−0·06
2 Hawkes Bay	0·19	**0·76**	−0·43
3 Taranaki	0·10	0·42	−0·28
4 Wellington	−0·33	**−0·64**	−0·49
5 Marlborough	**0·68**	0·08	−0·03
6 Nelson	**0·92**	0·00	−0·01
7 Westland	**0·74**	0·09	−0·08
8 Canterbury	−0·20	0·12	**0·74**
9 Otago	0·13	−0·06	**0·75**
10 Southland	**0·79**	0·16	0·05
Per cent variance accounted for	27·3	18·7	16·2

Note: The signs for Factor I_3 have been reversed in Table 7.6 and Table 7.9.

Even the first general factor, the 'primary servicing' factor I_1 shown in Table 6, has negative loadings for two of the larger provinces. Factors I_2 and I_3 are even more strongly bi-polar the one contrasting Auckland with Wellington and Hawkes Bay, the other contrasting Otago and Southland with Wellington and Hawkes Bay. In Table 7.7 the seven factors shown account for a lesser proportion of total variance than the four factors reported in Table 7.3. The four largest of these are so strongly bi-polar that both their positive and negative attributes call for separate verbal description; Factor J_5, for example, distinguishes provinces where 'Wood and Beverages' are important from those where 'Food and Chemicals' are important. In such cases the negative attributes are given their own subtitle at the foot of the column of factor loadings.

Time Trend for Location Indices. Analysis of the K-mode data matrix again produced a large general factor which loads strongly on all years and which is interpreted as a 'continuing trend' (Table 7.8). The second factor is similar but not identical to Factor K_2 in Table 7.4. Whereas the use of untransformed data suggested a fairly marked change in structural relationships between 1959–1960 and 1961–1962 the use of location indices suggests a more gentle transition. For this reason we interpret K_2 in Table 7.8 as a '1953 to 1970 trend'.

218

Table 7.7. Industrial combinations derived from location indices. J-mode factor loadings obtained by varimax rotation

Industry	J_1 Light consumer	J_2 Basic metal and machinery	J_3 Food	J_4 Printing and tobacco	J_5 Wood and bevs.	J_6 Furn. and tobacco	J_7 Paper
1 Food	−0·28	0·13	**0·58**	−0·29	**−0·64**	0·20	−0·02
2 Beverages	−0·06	−0·05	0·21	0·10	**0·77**	0·28	−0·30
3 Tobacco	−0·17	0·06	0·18	**0·61**	−0·14	**0·60**	−0·10
4 Textiles	**0·88**	−0·05	−0·03	0·20	0·02	0·04	−0·02
5 Footwear	0·25	0·33	**−0·81**	0·10	0·05	0·05	−0·07
6 Wood products	−0·29	−0·08	0·13	−0·14	**0·86**	−0·24	−0·12
7 Furniture	0·26	−0·07	−0·07	0·06	−0·05	**0·86**	0·04
8 Paper	0·21	−0·01	−0·01	0·00	−0·16	0·04	**0·94**
9 Printing	0·13	0·04	−0·21	**0·86**	0·17	0·07	0·01
10 Leather	**0·87**	0·04	−0·12	−0·14	−0·15	0·08	0·33
11 Rubber	**0·55**	−0·03	**−0·58**	−0·10	−0·21	0·09	−0·15
12 Chemicals	0·24	0·28	−0·04	**0·54**	**−0·59**	0·11	−0·05
13 Petroleum and coal	0·32	0·25	−0·31	**0·53**	−0·26	−0·02	0·40
14 Non-metallic minerals	−0·02	**−0·85**	0·13	−0·29	−0·04	−0·07	0·01
15 Basic metals	0·15	**0·63**	0·12	0·00	−0·34	−0·42	−0·21
16 Metal products	**0·63**	−0·14	−0·18	0·44	−0·21	−0·07	0·47
17 Machinery	−0·18	**0·75**	−0·39	−0·18	−0·24	−0·11	0·13
18 Electrical	**0·71**	0·06	−0·28	0·49	−0·23	0·05	0·14
19 Transport	**−0·69**	**−0·56**	−0·09	−0·03	0·00	−0·34	−0·18
20 Miscellaneous	−0·09	0·06	**−0·86**	0·23	−0·20	0·00	0·23

	Transport	Non-metallic minerals	Foot-wear rubber and misc.		Food and chemical		
Per cent variance accounted for	19·0	11·6	13·1	12·4	13·1	8·1	8·4

Note: The signs for Factors J_1, J_4, J_5 and J_6 are reversed in Tables 7.7 and 7.9 to simplify interpretation.

Table 7.8. Time trends derived from location indices. Factor loadings for K-mode principal components.

	Year	Factor K_1 Continuing pattern	Factor K_2 Trend 1953–1970
1	1951–1952	**0·90**	−0·33
2	1952–1953	**0·90**	−0·38
3	1953–1954	**0·90**	−0·39
4	1954–1955	**0·94**	−0·31
5	1955–1956	**0·94**	−0·30
6	1056–1957	**0·94**	−0·30
7	1957–1958	**0·94**	−0·26
8	1958–1959	**0·97**	−0·15
9	1959–1960	**0·96**	0·03
10	1960–1961	**0·99**	0·06
11	1961–1962	**0·99**	0·09
12	1962–1963	**0·98**	0·15
13	1963–1964	**0·98**	0·19
14	1964–1965	**0·97**	0·23
15	1965–1966	**0·96**	0·25
16	1966–1967	**0·95**	0·28
17	1967–1968	**0·94**	0·32
18	1968–1969	**0·93**	0·34
19	1969–1970	**0·88**	0·41
Per cent variance accounted for		89·3	7·5

Note: The sign for Factor K_1 is reversed in Table 7.8 and Table 7.9 to simplify interpretation.

Core Matrix for Location Indices. The core matrix is again partitioned into two time slices for ease of presentation. In order to simplify description of the bi-polar factors the positive aspects of these are named at the top and left of the table while the negative aspects are named at the bottom and right (Table 7.9).

The problems of interpretation that arise from the use of location indices are readily apparent when the core matrix is displayed in this way. Take, for example, the very high score of 2·57 recorded in the cell identified by the intersection of K_1, J_1 and I_3. This indicates that there is a very strong and continuing relationship between J_1 and I_3. Such a relationship, however, can arise in at least two different ways; either because there is a concentration of light consumer industries in 'Special type B' provinces at the Otago–Canterbury end of the scale or (following both sets of negative loadings) because there is a concentration of the transport industry in 'Special type B' provinces such as Hawkes Bay and Wellington. Reference to the original data suggest that the score is a composite of both these concentrations.

In contrast to the example just cited, an examination of the industries and provinces involved in the largest score in the K_2 slice in Table 7.9 suggests that the negative score in cell J_6 I_1 reflects a single change, that of internal

Table 7.9. Core matrix of factor scores obtained from analysis of location indices

	I_1 Primary Servicing	I_2 Special A Auckland	I_3 Special B Otago-Canterbury	
K_1 *Continuing Pattern*				
J_1 Light consumer	−0·86	0·49	**2·57**	Transport
J_2 Basic metal and machinery	**−1·37**	0·53	−0·72	Non-metallic minerals
J_3 Food	0·72	**−1·45**	0·47	Footwear, rubber and miscellaneous
J_4 Printing and tobacco	−0·80	−0·76	**−1·72**	Food and chemicals
J_5 Wood and beverages	0·81	0·75	−0·46	
J_6 Furniture and tobacco	0·10	−0·53	−0·80	
J_7 Paper	−0·11	0·82	−0·17	
K_2 *Trend 1953 to 1970*				
J_1 Light consumer	−0·87	0·20	−0·84	Transport
J_2 Basic metal and machinery	**−1·20**	**1·28**	**−1·28**	Non-metallic minerals
J_3 Food	−0·15	−1·17	**1·08**	Footwear, rubber and miscellaneous
J_4 Printing and tobacco	**1·24**	−0·09	0·06	Food and chemicals
J_5 Wood and beverages	**−2·10**	0·06	**−1·03**	
J_6 Furniture and tobacco	**−3·18**	0·82	−0·66	
J_7 Paper	−0·02	−0·42	−0·02	
	(Wellington Canterbury)	Hawkes Bay Wellington	Wellington Hawkes Bay	

reorganization within the furniture industry and a consequent reduction in the numbers employed in this industry in all provinces but especially in the smaller provinces.

These and similar problems of interpretation can only be resolved by reference back to the original entries in the three-mode matrix. Instead of reducing the original data to a few simple structural relationships this second analysis raises a larger number of empirical questions that can only be answered by further detailed investigation. As in the 1971 study 'the results are consistent with the data but the illumination tends to proceed from the data to the results' (Cant, 1971, p. 52).

7.5. Conclusion

The results of this study confirm that the main structural and locational patterns which characterize manufacturing industry in New Zealand have persisted through the period from 1951 to 1970. On the basis of the results presented here two types of manufacturing centre can be recognized. At the lower level there are the regional centres which combine a range of primary servicing industries with consumer industries oriented to their regional market. At the upper level are the smaller number of metropolitan centres which, in addition to their regional function, have developed a selection of manufacturing activities oriented to national and overseas markets. At the beginning of the period the latter activities could be characterized as import replacement industries but by the late 1960's the expansion of industries such as basic metals, paper and wood products indicate a small but significant change in emphasis.

Within the overall pattern a number of locally-important changes are taking place. In part these are concealed in the present analysis by the use of provincial data which incorporates a number of independent regional centres into the very large Auckland and Wellington Provinces. Even so there is evidence that at least one of the metropolitan centres is losing some of its manufacturing functions while some of the regional centres are developing new industries to serve national markets. Some industries are moving out of high rent locations in Wellington, the national capital and other industries are moving northwards from Dunedin and Christchurch. Regional centres which have gained new functions include Napier in Hawkes Bay, New Plymouth in Taranaki, and Nelson. Throughout the period Auckland has continued to expand in the scale and range of its industrial activities. At the same time there are new developments in other provinces which can be cited as evidence to encourage those who favour policies of balanced regional development; the most significant of these are the expansion of basic metals, machinery and electrical industries in Taranaki, the tobacco, metal products and electrical industries in Hawkes Bay and the rubber and electrical industries in Canterbury.

From the viewpoint of operational experience the results of the two examples presented here suggest that the computational routine shown in Figure 7.3 has eliminated some of the problems encountered in the previous study. The separation of the three modes during the initial stages of the operation has given greater flexibility and provided a series of intermediate outputs which are of assistance in the selection of factors and the choice of rotation procedures. The calculation of the core matrix by means of the sequence of standardized factor score operations involves some loss of symmetry but it has produced results which are much simpler to interpret.

A comparison of the two examples makes it clear that some of the difficulties of interpretation encountered in the earlier study (Cant, 1971) are related to the use of the location index in conjunction with factor analysis. The transformation of the raw data into location indices means that we have closed the number system involved and may, as a result, have introduced correlations where the original data were uncorrelated (King, 1969, p. 179; Krumbein, 1962, p. 2230). In the present example, where there are only 10 provinces and 20 industries, these artificial correlations have almost certainly made some contribution to the particular factor patterns reported. Apart from this more serious limitation, the problems involved in the interpretation of a core matrix formed by a number of bi-polar factors suggests that the use of variables which are likely to produce such factors should be avoided where possible. Although the location index will continue to be a useful tool in its own right our experience now suggests that it is not an appropriate transformation to use in three-mode factor analysis.

The results obtained from the untransformed employment figures appear to be a much more useful and valid simplification of a complex real world situation. Their limitations reflect the coarseness and lack of regularity in the particular data mesh chosen for study (Table 7.1). The use of raw data for the number of workers employed (or other simple criteria such as added value, or value of plant and equipment) will provide the research worker with a sound base for analysis provided that an appropriate industrial division/statistical area mesh can be established. The provincial divisions reported on here are not fully satisfactory but they represent the best that have been published in New Zealand for the period covered by the present analysis. The operational success of the exercise suggests that the method of analysis can now be extended to unpublished data and larger and better-partitioned data matrices.

Appendix A

Calculation of Location Indices for Three-mode Data Matrix

$$l_{ijk} = \frac{\dfrac{N_{ijk}}{\displaystyle\sum_{i=1}^{I}\sum_{j=1}^{J} N_{ijk}}}{\dfrac{\displaystyle\sum_{j=1}^{J} N_{ijk}}{\displaystyle\sum_{i=1}^{I}\sum_{j=1}^{J}\sum_{k=1}^{K} N_{ijk}}}$$

224

Where N_{ijk} is the number employed in industry j in province i for year k; there are I regions, J industries and K years and l_{ijk} is the location index for industry j in province i for year k.

References

Berry, B. J. L. (1968), A Synthesis of Formal and Functional Regions using a General Field Theory of Spatial Behaviour, in Berry, B. J. L. and Marble, D. F. (eds.), *Spatial Analysis: A Reader in Statistical Geography*. Englewood Cliffs, New Jersey: Prentice-Hall, 419–428.

Cant, R. G. (1971), Changes in the Location of Manufacturing in New Zealand 1957–1968. An Application of Three-Mode Factor Analysis, *New Zealand Geographer*, **27**, 38–55.

Cant, R. G. and Johnston, R. J. (in press) Regional Development Patterns, in Johnston, R. J. (ed.), *Urbanisation in New Zealand*. Wellington: Reed.

Cooley, W. W. and Lohnes, P. R. (1971), *Multivariate Data Analysis*. New York: Wiley.

Florence, P. S. (1929), *The Statistical Method in Economics and Political Science*. London: Kegan Paul.

Gould, P. R. (1967), On the Geographical Interpretation of Eigenvalues, *Transactions, Institute of British Geographers*, **42**, 53–86.

Gould, P. R. (1969), Methodological Developments Since the Fifties, in Board, C. *et al.* (eds.), *Progress in Geography*, **1**, 1–50.

Henshall, J. D. and King, L. J. (1966), Some Structural Characteristics of Peasant Agriculture in Barbados, *Economic Geography*, **42**, 74–84.

Horst, P. (1963), Multivariate Models for Evaluating Change, in Harris, C. W. (ed.), *Problems of Measuring Change*. Madison, Wisconsin: University of Wisconsin Press, 104–121.

Horst, P. (1965), *Factor Analysis of Data Matrices*. New York: Holt, Rinehart and Winston.

Johnston, R. J. (1971), Regional Development in New Zealand: The Problems of a Small Yet Prosperous Ex-Colony, *Regional Studies*, **5**, 321–331.

King, L. J. (1969), *Statistical Analysis in Geography*. Englewood Cliffs, New Jersey: Prentice-Hall.

Krumbein, W. C. (1962), Open and Closed Number Systems in Stratigraphic Mapping, *Bulletin, American Association of Petroleum Geologists*, **46**, 2229–2245.

Levin, J. (1965), Three-Mode Factor Analysis, *Psychological Bulletin*, **64**, 442–452.

Linge, G. J. R. (1957), The Location of Manufacturing in New Zealand, *New Zealand Geographer*, **13**, 1–18.

Linge, G. J. R. (1960), The Concentration and Dispersion of Manufacturing in New Zealand, *Economic Geography*, **36**, 326–343.

McDonald, T. K. (1970), *Regional Development in New Zealand*. Wellington: New Zealand Institute of Economic Research.

Ministry of Works, Town and Country Planning Branch (1967), *Otago Region*. Wellington, New Zealand: Government Printer.

New Zealand Census of Population and Dwellings (Five yearly), Wellington: Government Printer.

New Zealand Official Year-book (Annual), Wellington: Government Printer.

New Zealand Statistics of Industrial Production (Annual), Wellington: Government Printer.

Rimmer, P. J. (1967), The Changing Status of New Zealand Seaports, *Annals, Association of American Geographer*, **57**, 88–100.

Tucker, L. R. (1963), Implications of Factor Analysis of Three-Way Matrices for Measurement of Change, in Harris, C. W. (ed.), *Problems of Measuring Change.* Madison: University of Wisconsin Press, 122–137.

Tucker, L. R. (1964), The Extension of Factor Analysis to Three-Dimensional Matrices, in Frederiksen, N. and Gulliksen, H. (eds.), *Contributions to Mathematical Psychology.* New York: Holt, Rinehart and Winston, 109–127.

Tucker, L. R. (1965), Experiments in Multi-Mode Factor Analysis, in *Proceedings of the 1964 Invitational Conference on Testing Problems.* Princeton, New Jersey: Educational Testing Service, 46–57.

Tucker, L. R. (1966), Some Mathematical Notes on Three-Mode Factor Analysis, *Psychometrika,* **31,** 279–311.

Tucker, L. R. (1967), Three-Mode Factor Analysis of Parker-Fleishman Complex Tracking Behaviour Data, *Multivariate Behavioural Research,* **2,** 139–152.

8 A Procedure for Forecasting Changes in Manufacturing Activity*

LYNDHURST COLLINS

'... the question is not one of, "should geographers forecast?" but, "how should geographers forecast?"' Haggett, 1972, p. 441.

The underlying philosophy for developing predictive models reflects Alfred Marshall's viewpoint that 'Man's prerogative extends to a limited but effective control over natural development by forecasting the future and preparing the way for the next step.' Models and techniques for analysing current changes and for forecasting future changes in manufacturing activity are not new and have been reviewed and synthesized elsewhere by Hamilton (1967). Hamilton has shown for example that both *structural* and *spatial* aspects of the industrial landscape can be and have been fruitfully analysed with a view to developing predictive models. His discussion shows, however, that most of these models have been based on aggregative methods for quantitatively describing urban–industrial relationships. In particular, one group of models based on input–output analysis has been confined largely to national and regional estimates of inter-industry flow patterns for which aggregate data are more readily available than on a small area basis. Forecasted changes in these flow patterns resulting from new inputs in the export sector are used to predict changes in total output of individual sectors in the various regions. Essentially the input-output family of models is structural and aspatial in character: structural in that the predictions provide coefficients or measures of changes in total output by sector or area; aspatial in that the models do not accommodate actual spatial shifts or relocation of manufacturing activity.

Although Hirsch (1963) has emphasized the usefulness of applying input-output models to urban areas, and several studies, including the classic input-output survey by Artle (1965) of Stockholm, have shown the feasibility of applying the technique to metropolitan areas, by and large input-output

---

* The material for this essay is taken from a pilot study prepared for Statistics Canada: L. Collins (1972).

models on their own seem limited through lack of suitable disaggregated data for small area analysis.

More generalized and more suitable for small area analysis are the Economic Base models developed in part to estimate the increase in total employment which would result from an increase in the 'basic' activities in an urban area. The expected increase in total employment is given by multiplying the increase in basic activities by a 'multiplier'—the basic/non basic ratio—calculated from the existing employment structure. Dissatisfaction with the technical difficulty of distinguishing between basic and non-basic industries has encouraged successive refinements by Alexandersson (1956), Morrissett (1958), and finally by Ullman and Dacey (1960) all of whom independently developed the Minimum Requirements approach to urban-industrial analysis. Morrissett hypothesized that the employment ratios or the minimum percentage of employment expected in a given industry in any city are related to city size and that as cities grow their industrial structures will evolve along the 'contour lines' of the industry profiles. Assuming the validity of such an hypothesis it would be possible to forecast *structural* changes in urban areas. To this end Ullman and Dacey added regression techniques to the minimum requirements approach and though they emphasize the 'speculative' nature of extrapolations derived from the procedure the authors do provide yet another model for predicting structural change in conjunction with urban growth.

Some of the more successful models have been the allocation models developed in association with transportation studies based on elaborate computer simulations for evaluating the possible impact of planned highway networks on the internal spatial structures of adjacent urban areas. More recently the notion of developing simulation models for demonstrating the utility of a probabilistic approach for analysing the dynamic properties of spatial patterns exhibited by intraurban retail establishments has been explored by Pred and Kibel (1970). This concept of analysing the spontaneous evolution of modern industrial patterns in the framework of stochastic process models seems appropriate so long as industrial location is not strictly and scientifically planned (Hamilton, 1967). Of those stochastic process models readily available to geographic research Hamilton suggests that Markov chain models seem to have the most potential for tracing trends in industrial location and that although much more research is needed before satisfactory models of interregional migration can be presented, Markov chain models, possibly when combined with input-output analysis may offer a solution to the problem.

The aims of this essay are to examine the validity of adopting Markov chain analysis to the study of manufacturing activity, to elaborate the technical procedure and the underlying assumptions of Markov chain analysis, and to assess the ability of a Markov model to describe actual changes in the landscape. These changes refer to both structural and spatial aspects.

8.1. The Markov Procedure

Markov chains are particular cases of Markov processes which in turn are a subset of stochastic processes. More specifically Markov chains are stochastic processes in which the future development depends only on the present state, but not on the past history of the process or the manner in which the present state was reached. State in the present context may refer to either the locations of manufacturing establishments in a spatial system 'spatial states', or to the size of plants in terms of, say, employment of productive capacity, 'structural states'. Formally, in a Markov chain a system of states changes according to some probability law with time t in such a manner that the system changing from a given state S_i at time t_{0+1} depends only on the state S_i at time t_0 and is independent of the states of the system at times prior to t_0. If the state of the system at time t_{0+1} is only dependent on the state of the system at time t_0 plus some independent random component, the process is referred to as a first-order Markov chain; in a second-order Markov chain the state of the system at time t_{0+2} would depend on the states of the system at both time t_0 and t_{0+1}.

The transition probabilities, the p_{ij}'s which give the probability that the process will move from state S_i to state S_j are given for every pair of states. The 'set' of probabilities describes the process as it moves through any finite number of steps. For computational efficiency the transition probabilities are best represented in the form of a transition matrix P.

$$
P = \begin{array}{c} \\ S_1 \\ S_2 \\ S_3 \\ \\ \\ S_n \end{array}
\begin{array}{ccccc}
S_i & S_2 & S_3 \ldots S_n & \\
p_{11} & p_{12} & p_{13} & p_{1n} \\
p_{21} & p_{22} & p_{23} & p_{2n} \\
p_{31} & p_{32} & p_{33} & p_{3n} \\
\vdots & & & \\
p_{n1} & p_{n2} & p_{n3} & p_{nn}
\end{array}
$$

where

$$
\sum_{j=1}^{n} p_{ij} = 1
$$

and $p_{ij} \geqslant 0$ for all i and j.

The elements of P denote the probability of moving from state S_i to S_j in the next step. Since the elements of this matrix must be non-negative and the sum of the elements in any row is 1, each row is called a probability vector and the matrix P is a stochastic matrix (Kemeny and Snell, 1967). If for some power of the matrix P there are only positive entries the transition matrix is described as regular. For regular Markov chains two important theorems relating to the existence and uniqueness of an equilibrium solution are provided by Kemeny and Snell (1967, p. 70).

(1) If P is a transition matrix for a regular Markov chain then
    (i) the powers of P approach a matrix A
    (ii) each row of A is the same probability vector α
    (iii) the elements of α are all positive.

(2) If P is a regular transition matrix for a regular Markov chain and A and α are as in theorem 1, then the unique vector α is the unique probability vector such that $\alpha P = \alpha$. The matrix A is defined as the limiting matrix.

In terms of analysing the spatial rearrangement of manufacturing activity in an isolated region, which can be viewed as a closed system, consider a constant sample of manufacturing establishments distributed in three towns possessing varying degrees of industrial attractiveness. Assume that at time t_0, 20 per cent of the total number of plants of the three towns are located in town A, 20 per cent are in town B, and 60 per cent are in town C. Thus the initial state of the system can be represented by the initial distribution vector $p^{(0)}$—which is:

$$p^0 = (20, 20, 60).$$

Assume also that the probability of a manufacturing establishment's relocating from one state (town) to any other state during a specified time period is described by the following transition matrix:

		S_1 (Town A)	S_2 (Town B)	S_3 (Town C)
	S_1 (Town A)	0·6	0·2	0·2
$P =$	S_2 (Town B)	0·3	0·4	0·3
	S_3 (Town C)	0·2	0·2	0·6

The matrix shows that the probability of a plant's remaining in town A during a given time period is 0·6, whereas the probability of a plant's moving from town A to town B is 0·2, and so on. Given this initial transition matrix it is now possible to compute the transition probabilities after 1, 2, 3, ..., n stages by calculating the relevant power of the matrix. Thus after two stages:

		S_1	S_2	S_3
	S_1	0·46	0·24	0·30
$P =$	S_2	0·36	0·28	0·36
	S_3	0·30	0·24	0·46

and after four stages:

		S_1	S_2	S_3
	S_1	0·3880	0·2496	0·3624
$P =$	S_2	0·3744	0·2512	0·3744
	S_3	0·3624	0·2496	0·3880

These matrices display a rapid convergence towards some average state of the system which is represented by the limiting or A matrix:

$$
\begin{array}{cccc}
 & S_1 & S_2 & S_3 \\
S_1 & 0{\cdot}3750 & 0{\cdot}2500 & 0{\cdot}3750 \\
A = S_2 & 0{\cdot}3750 & 0{\cdot}2500 & 0{\cdot}3750 \\
S_3 & 0{\cdot}3750 & 0{\cdot}2500 & 0{\cdot}3750
\end{array}
$$

In the present context the notion of equilibrium can be defined as that distribution for which the average number of plants entering a given town per period equals the average number of plants leaving it. The concept of equilibrium is thus statistical in nature for the industry or system and dynamic for the individual plant (Adelman 1958). This equilibrium distribution, however, should not be viewed as a *forecast* of the future state of the industry but rather as the expected pattern if current trends are allowed to continue unhindered. Thus, the expected proportion of plants in any one town at the end of each time period is derived by multiplying the P^n transition matrix by the initial distribution vector $p^{(0)}$. After two stages, for example, the expected proportion of plants in each town is given by

$$p^{(0)}P^2$$

The limiting probability, a_j, of being in state S_j is independent of the starting state and represents the fraction of the time that the process can be expected to be in state S_j during a large number of transitions and after a large number of steps from $p^{(0)}$. This arises from the law of large numbers for regular Markov chains. In our example this means that after a large number of time periods 37·5 per cent of the plants will be in town A, 25 per cent will be in town B and 37·5 per cent will be in town C.

8.2. Markov Probabilities

In the example so far the transition probabilities have been assumed but for models of real world situations such probabilities must be estimated; *a priori* there are underlying fixed probabilities for each event but since these are not known and cannot be derived theoretically they must be estimated from empirical evidence. Several alternative estimating procedures are available though the particular method adopted usually depends on the quality of the data. Where only aggregate data in the form of say frequency distributions for two or more points in time are available statistical estimation techniques involving the use of linear and quadratic programming solutions are commonly employed (Lee, Judge and Zellner, 1970).

Where observations on individual transitions from one state to any other are available, Anderson and Goodman (1957) provide the maximum likelihood technique for estimating the probabilities. Maximum likelihood estimates of the p_{ij}'s are obtained by dividing the number of times micro units move from S_i

to S_j by the total number of occurrences of S_i; the total number of occurrences and individual movements are obtained from empirical observation. Thus

$$P = [p_{ij}] = \left[\frac{f_{ij}}{\sum\limits_{j=1}^{n} f_{ij}} \right] \geqslant 0$$

where f_{ij} is the number of movements of the sample elements from state S_i to S_j. Transition probabilities derived in this way can be subjected to statistical tests for determining the specific order of the chain.

The partial dependence or Markov property of a transition matrix, for example, can be tested with the maximum likelihood ratio criterion. This tests the null hypothesis that a stationary transition matrix is of 'zero-order', that is $p_{ij} = p_j$ for all i, against the alternative of a first-order chain. For this test it is necessary to know the actual number of observations for all cells; these observations are represented in a 'tally' matrix. The tally matrix for our hypothetical three-town example is given in Table 8.1.

Table 8.1. Tally matrix

	S_1	S_2	S_3	Marginal totals
S_1	120	40	40	200
S_2	60	80	60	200
S_3	120	120	360	600
	300	240	460	1,000

Using this matrix we test for the Markov property with the ratio criterion:

$$\lambda = \prod_{i,j} (\hat{p}_j/\hat{p}_{ij}) f_{ij} \tag{1}$$

where the marginal probability

$$\hat{p}_j = \sum_i f_{ij} \Big/ \sum_i \sum_j f_{ij} = f_{.j}/f_{..}$$

and

$$\hat{p}_{ij} = f_{ij} \Big/ \sum_j f_{ij} = f_{ij}/f_{i.}$$

and f_{ij} is the number of observations in each cell. The required statistic is $-2 \log \lambda$ which under the null hypothesis has an asymptotic Chi-square distribution with $(n-1)^2$ degrees of freedom. Equation (1) may be written as

$$-2 \log \lambda = 2 \sum_{i=1}^{n} \sum_{j=1}^{n} f_{ij} \log \frac{f_{ij} f_{..}}{f_{i.} f_{.j}}$$

(The logarithms are Naperian.)

In the three-town example $-2 \log \lambda = 165\cdot8$ which is greatly in excess of the tabled value of Chi-square for four degrees of freedom so that the hypothesis of an independent trials process would be rejected. The Markov property alone, however, provides no indication of the specific-order of the chain. Such additional information is obtainable only from cubic or three way tally matrices. The cubic matrix (Table 8.2.) for our example shows that of the 40

Table 8.2. Cubic matrix for a first-order Markov chain

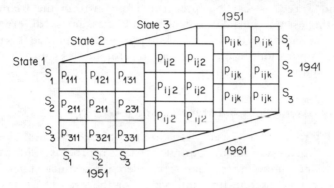

plants which moved from S_1 to S_2 between 1941 and 1951 (p_{12} in Table 8.1.), 28 remained in their location during the 1951–1961 period (p_{122} in Table 8.2.), two returned to S_1 (p_{121}) and ten relocated to S_3 (p_{123}). Given this information we can test the null hypothesis that the chain is first-order against the alternative that it is second-order. The null hypothesis is that $p_{1jk} = p_{jkl}$ for j, $k = l$. The likelihood ratio criterion for testing this hypothesis is:

$$\lambda = \prod_{i,j,k=1}^{n} (\hat{p}_{jk}/\hat{p}_{ijk})^{f_{ijk}}$$

where

$$\hat{p}_{jk} = \sum_{j} f_{ijk} \bigg/ \sum_{i} \sum_{k} f_{ijk} = f_{\cdot jk}/f_{\cdot j \cdot}$$

and

$$\hat{p}_{ijk} = f_{ijk} \bigg/ \sum_{k} f_{ijk} = f_{ijk}/f_{ij \cdot}$$

Under the null hypothesis, $-2 \log \lambda$ is asymptotically χ^2 with $n(n-1)^2$ degrees of freedom. If for our three town example $-2 \log_e \lambda$ is less than the tabled value of Chi-square with $n(n-1)^2$ degrees of freedom the data could then be considered as typifying a first-order Markov chain.

Although this procedure provides a statistical rationale for adopting a Markovian framework it does not prove that the observations represent those of a first-order Markov chain; the procedure provides only statistical boundaries of acceptance or rejection. If the methodology is adopted, therefore, the analyses and 'forecasts' can be interpreted only within the framework of several limiting assumptions. Since each postulate assumes a different level of importance depending on the variables and processes examined it is necessary to assess the implications of these assumptions for studies concerned with the dynamics of manufacturing activity.

8.3. Markov Assumptions and Manufacturing Activity

Four basic interdependent assumptions are recognized, the first being one of definition or classification. In discontinuous Markov processes, for example, it must be assumed that the system is typified by distinct states and that transitions occur at discrete time intervals. For the present context there is ample evidence to suggest that manufacturing establishments relocate once, twice, or many times during their existence (Figure 8.1.). Moreover several studies of industrial relocation (Ellis, 1949; McLaughlin and Robock, 1949; Keeble, 1965) have recognized the tendency of plants to relocate over a considerable range of distance so that spatial states of origin and destination typified by well defined geographic areas are clearly descernible (Figures 8.2. and 8.3.). But the selection and delimitation of the states, as with any formal regionalization of the landscape, calls for subjectivity which will in varying degrees affect the transition probabilities. Ideally for example, the most appropriate system would be one comprising as states the smallest areal units for which data are available, in this case the individual municipalities (townships and urban centres), but they are too numerous for computational feasibility. In the following analysis such a classification of states would require a matrix of the order 500×500. Operationally, therefore, it is necessary to aggregate the smallest areal units or municipalities into spatial groups. Conceptually, for the analysis of plant relocation several alternative grouping methods can be proposed though the combinations of the number and size of states within any one system are innumerable. One alternative is the regionalization of contiguous municipalities on the basis of their economic viability measured by a variety of factors. A second alternative, and one that is implicitly suggested by studies concerned with decentralization (Keeble, 1968) is a system of states based on a series of concentric distance bands radiating outwards from the core of industrial activity. Yet another alternative is the grouping of locations according to their industrial attractiveness or similarities in which case the system need not be spatially continuous as it would be in the first two alternatives. In such a system, at least in terms of existing migration theory, the probability of a plant's moving from one state to another would be a

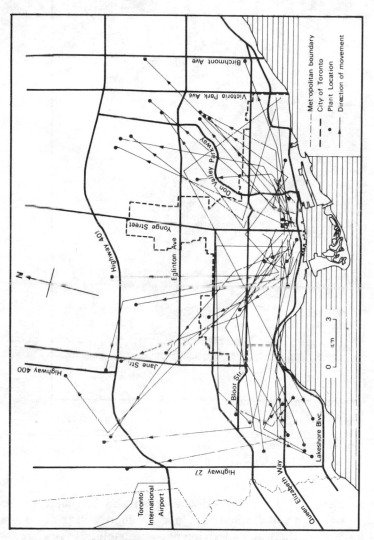

Figure 8.1. Relocation paths of <3 manufacturing plants in metropolitan Toronto, 1945–1966

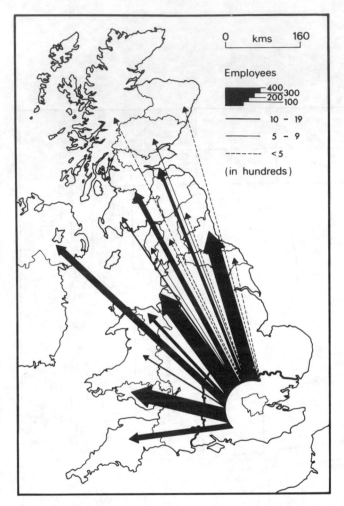

Figure 8.2. Manufacturing movement to the peripheral
areas from South East England, 1945–1965
Source: D. E. Keeble (1972), Industrial Movement in the
United Kingdom, *Town Planning Review*, **43**, 14

function of the characteristics of the individual plant and the characteristics of
both the states of origin and destination. Since it is impossible to evaluate in a
conceptual framework the true underlying fixed probabilities associated with
such movement it is necessary to estimate them from actual observation as
outlined in the preceding section.

The same problem arises in a dynamic analysis of industrial structure. States,
in this case, would refer to establishment size categories, represented by
employment, value added, or some other viable measure of productive
capacity. Here, however, the system of states must be continuous within the

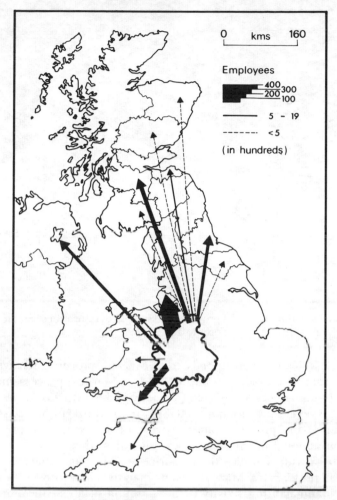

Figure 8.3. Manufacturing movement to the peripheral areas from the West Midland, 1945–1965
Source: D. E. Keeble (1972), Industrial Movement in the United Kingdom, *Town Planning Review*, **43**, 14

limits of the actual range of the size criteria examined, though the upper and lower bounds must be subjectively determined. The size of the state will affect the estimated transition probabilities, but the degree of affect can be determined more easily for structural than for spatial states by an iterative procedure with a change of limits for each iteration. Generally, the smaller the states the greater is the tendency for the appearance of 'noise' elements in the off-diagonals of the matrix, whereas the larger the states the more pronounced is the main diagonal. The size of the states and the method of classification do, of course, depend largely on the quality of the data. But if we show that a

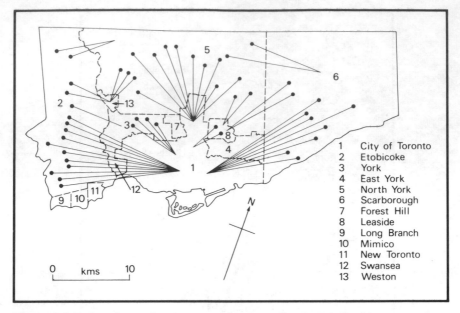

Figure 8.4. Relocation paths of a proportional sample of relocations in metropolitan Toronto 1961–1962

particular classification corresponds to a Markov process then we cannot arbitrarily treat a coarser classification as a Markov process unless the condition of 'lumpability' is satisfied (Kemeny and Snell 1967, p. 194).

Usually, however, data are not available for an arbitrarily fine classification so that even if the process examined were of an exact Markov type, the classification adopted might include several states whose patterns of movements are disparate because of industrial mix and age characteristics. A fundamental problem of Markov chain analysis, therefore, at least when applied to manufacturing activity is the adoption of a classification scheme which is good enough to enable a reasonably simple model to fit the data.

The second assumption relates to the specific order of the chain. In a first-order chain we assume that in the absence of information about the history of the process it is possible to deduce the future development of the process from knowledge of its present state only. It should be clear, however, that the ability to verify statistically this assumption *depends* on the initial classification of states. Moreover this assumption has severe limitations for a spatial analysis of manufacturing activity since a very long time period would be required to obtain a sufficiently large sample of plants which have changed spatial states more than once. Nevertheless, several studies of intra-urban location (Reeder, 1954; Kerr and Spelt, 1965; and Martin, 1966) have shown that the location of a plant will be dependent upon its existing location though not necessarily on previous locations—the essential property of a first-order Markov chain. Thus it may be reasonable to hypothesize that the pattern of industrial location for S_j

at time t is a function of the industrial location pattern at time $t - 1$ plus some component of change which may be defined by a set of probabilities (Harvey, 1967).

The first-order assumption also has significant implications for structural analyses in which the dependence or Markov property is translatable in terms of a size-dependent stochastic process describing the structural evolution of manufacturing establishments. This implies that the underlying determinants of change in the size distribution of plants during one period may be represented by a probability of a plant's movement from one size category to another. The structural model adopted in this study assumes that of those economic factors—such as entrepreneurship, financial structure and position, ability to introduce technological change, and profits—which may determine the growth pattern of manufacturing plants, *size,* measured in terms of employment, is the most important summary criterion. By using this variable the first-order assumption can be statistically verified for the structural model.

A third limiting restriction of Markov chain models for the analysis of manufacturing activity is the concept of stationarity. This implies a constant relationship among the transition probabilities throughout the predictive period. For studies of other phenomena this may not be a severe restriction since its limitations can be overcome by manipulating two independent sets of transition matrices; Pattison (1965), for example, used both first-order and sixth-order chains to traverse transition periods separating rainfall cycles. In the present context the hypothesis of stationarity is dependent on the first-order property which is assumed in statistical tests for stationarity; similarly statistical tests for the first-order property are predicated on the constancy of the parameters. Acceptance of the stationarity hypothesis for a long-term prediction of industrial activity may not always be justifiable since technological change could have a significant impact on existing trends. On the other hand, there is no evidence to suggest that any technological innovation so far has profoundly affected the spatial distribution of manufacturing during the short-term period. Factors likely to have the greatest impact on the spatial rearrangement of manufacturing activity include the construction of new motorways, airports, or government policy, but the influence of such factors is only asserted gradually. Technological changes may well influence the size structure of industry to a greater degree but again there is little evidence to suggest that even this is substantial in the short term. In this study the constancy of the trends over a five year period is tested, and lends credence to the assumption of stationarity.

The last assumption relates to the nation of uniform probabilities for all individual components of each cell or state in the matrix. The degree of uniformity will inevitably depend on the initial classification system though in some cases the assumption is not always tenable. Sociological studies of occupational mobility, for example, suggest a marked negative correlation between length of time in any one state and the tendency to move out of that state. Such observations have encouraged the adoption of a 'mover-stayer' dichotomy (Blumen, Kogan, and McCarthy, 1955) in which one transition matrix and a second matrix represents those who possess relative occupational stability. It is unlikely, however that a mover-stayer dichotomy is applicable to the analysis of industrial activity since there is no theoretical reason or empirical evidence to suggest a correlation between the length of time a plant remains in a location and the likelihood of its relocating. But there are other difficulties for the analysis of manufacturing activity. In terms of size, for example, a plant employing 200 employees locating in a country town is unlikely to satisfy the notion of uniform probabilities for such a state but as part of a large industrial complex it might well do so. Similarly in terms of state content a factory manufacturing lawn mowers is more likely to relocate than a plant manufacturing rubber tyres; in Ontario between 1961 and 1965 mobility indices for twenty 2-digit industries ranged from 0·40 for rubber products to 1·82 for machinery industries. (The mobility index is calculated by dividing the percentage of relocations in each industry by the percentage of all establishments in each industry.) It may also be that plants in urban areas are more likely to relocate than plants in rural locations or vice versa; so far no study has provided any indication of such a difference. It has been shown however that branch plants do have a higher propensity to relocate than other types of plants (Ellis, 1949). Conceivably, other sub-groups within the broader aggregate categories could be distinguished as having a higher/lower propensity to relocate.

The four Markov assumptions, then, are interdependent in that the basic classification will not only influence the Markov property but also the stationarity and uniformity properties of the transition probabilities. When applied to manufacturing activity the severity of the constraints depends on whether the analysis is structural or spatial since the concept of stationarity is not so rigid for spatial as it is for structural patterns. Therefore, the results of the following Markov analyses in the study of manufacturing activity must be interpreted only within the framework of these assumptions.

8.4. A Markov Model of Manufacturing Activity

The data used in the development of the model are taken from the annual Census of Manufactures for the Province of Ontario compiled by Statistics Canada for the years 1961–1965. For each of these years there are approximately 12,000 observations which are organized into four groups. The first comprises all those establishments which remain in the same municipal location for the five year period and constitutes the constant sample (approximately 7,000) of permanent establishments. The second and third groups are annual births—those plants which appeared for the first time in the five year period—and annual deaths—those plants which ceased operation during the period; each group comprises approximately 4,000 observations. The last group consists of over 400 plants which relocated from one municipality to another during the five year period.

241

Table 8.3. Spatial matrix 1964–1965

	Toronto	Toronto suburbs	Large urban	L.U. suburbs	Small urban	Rest of Ontario
Toronto	0·9539	0·0401	0·0005		0·0017	0·0035
Toronto suburbs	0·0051	0·9801	0·0008			0·0137
Large urban		0·0012	0·9902	0·0073		0·0012
L.U. suburbs			0·0671	0·9253	0·0074	
Small urban	0·0009	0·0029	0·0004		0·9876	0·0079
Rest of Ontario	0·0007	0·0052	0·0076	0·0007	0·0181	0·9743

Table 8.4. 1961–1962 Structural probability matrix for permanent establishments in Ontario

No. of employees		1	2	3	4	5	6	7	8	9	10	11	12	13	14
2–3	1	0.7375	0.2228	0.0294	0.0086	0.0017									
4–6	2	0.1475	0.6530	0.1674	0.0244	0.0055		0.0011	0.0011						
7–10	3	0.0085	0.1681	0.5883	0.2132	0.0183	0.0024	0.0012							
11–17	4	0.0011	0.0157	0.1265	0.6585	0.1825	0.0090	0.0045	0.0022						
18–27	5		0.0025	0.0038	0.1648	0.6388	0.1660	0.0203	0.0038						
28–43	6		0.0014	0.0027	0.0096	0.0984	0.6940	0.1803	0.0123	0.0014					
44–67	7					0.0052	0.0873	0.7068	0.1867	0.0140					
68–105	8			0.0020			0.0061	0.1086	0.6967	0.1660	0.0184	0.0020			
106–165	9							0.0052	0.1016	0.7318	0.1484	0.0130			
166–256	10								0.0034	0.1092	0.7201	0.1638	0.0034		
257–398	11								0.0059	0.0059	0.0941	0.7588	0.1235	0.0118	
399–618	12							0.0101			0.0101	0.1111	0.7071	0.1515	0.0101
619–960	13												0.0755	0.8491	0.0755
961–	14												0.0169	0.0847	0.8983

Analyses of the relocation patterns provide the rationale for adopting a system of spatial states that gives emphasis to the varying degrees of industrial attractiveness exhibited by groups of urban areas rather than to the alternative systems associated with distance bands or economic regions. The analyses reveal a marked tendency for plants to relocate from the city of Toronto (Figure 8.4.) to its suburbs and to other centres; from the metropolitan cities of Hamilton, Windsor, Ottawa, and London, to their respective suburbs; and from smaller to larger urban centres. With maximum likelihood techniques we can estimate the transition probabilities for these states for each year. The transition matrix for 1964–1965 is shown in Table 8.3.

Similar transition matrices for changes in size for all establishments in the constant sample of permanent establishments can be estimated for each year (Table 8.4.). For the structural matrices 14 size categories are used. The number of categories, or rather the upper limit of the highest category is limited for reasons of confidentiality but the actual widths of the class intervals are calculated so that the resulting frequency distribution provides the 'best fit' to the lognormal model. Earlier work has shown for example, that the lognormal distribution can be interpreted in terms of Gibrat's Law of Proportionate Growth which in turn is governed by a simple Markov process (Collins, 1973).

Following the procedure outlined in the preceding sections we can test both the spatial and structural sets of annual matrices for the Markov property (Table 8.5.). In both cases we can reject the null hypothesis and consider the

Table 8.5. Test of Markov property for structural and spatial matrices

Realization	$-2 \log \lambda$	D.F. $(n-1)^2$
	Structural matrices	
1961–1962	20,444	169
1962–1963	21,803	169
1963–1964	22,959	169
1964–1965	22,520	169
	Spatial matrices	
1961–1962	980	25
1962–1963	954	25
1963–1964	1,026	25
1964–1965	973	25

two sets of matrices as realizations of two separate Markov chains. Because of the relatively short time period there is not a sufficient number of observations with which to test the spatial matrices for the first-order property, and must in this instance be assumed. For the structural data, however, four cubic matrices can be provided and when tested the resulting values (Table 8.6.) of $-2 \log \lambda$ are less than the degrees of freedom so that the null hypothesis is not rejected and the change in a plant's employment structure is considered to typify a first-order Markov process.

Table 8.6. Test of first-order property for structural matrices

Realization	$-2 \log \lambda$	D.F. $n(n-1)^2$
1961–1963	697·62	2,366
1962–1964	631·21	2,366
1963–1965	607·78	2,366
1961–1965	610·16	2,366

That the transition probabilities in each of the four matrices of each set are stationary can be tested with the minimum discrimination information statistic—the m.d.i.s. Formally, a null hypothesis is postulated that the four annual matrices are realizations from the same set of transition probabilities of a first-order Markov chain. Following the procedure outlined by Kullback, Kupperman, and Ku (1962) the indices are given by:

Component due to	Information	D.F.
(i) homogeneity	$2 \sum\limits_{k=1}^{r} \sum\limits_{i=1}^{n} f_{ki\cdot} \log \dfrac{f_{\cdots} f_{ki}}{f_{k\cdot\cdot} f_{\cdot i\cdot}}$	$(r-1)(n-1)$
(j/i) conditional homogeneity	$2 \sum\limits_{k=1}^{r} \sum\limits_{i=1}^{n} \sum\limits_{j=1}^{n} f_{kij} \log \dfrac{f_{kij} f_{\cdot i\cdot}}{f_{ki\cdot} f_{\cdot ij}}$	$n(r-1)(n-1)$
(i/j) homogeneity	$2 \sum\limits_{k=1}^{r} \sum\limits_{i=1}^{n} \sum\limits_{i=1}^{n} f_{kij} \log \dfrac{f_{\cdots} f_{kij}}{f_{k\cdot\cdot} f_{\cdot ij}}$	$(r-1)(n^2-1)$

The components due to each information statistic for the structural matrices are shown in Table 8.7. The (i) component measures the lack of homogeneity among the initial distributions (1961–1964), and the (j/i) component measures that of the transitions to the final distributions (1962–1965) from the corresponding initial distributions. The (i, j) component is the sum of these two. In Table 8.7 the three information components are not significant; this implies that the difference between the various independent realizations within the set are small enough to be attributed to chance or random fluctuations. By

Table 8.7. Test of homogeneity for four annual structural matrices

Component due to	Information	D.F.
(i) homogeneity	31·36	39
(j/i) conditional homogeneity	384·43	546
(i, j) homogeneity	415·79	585

statistical inference the set of realizations are accepted as homogeneous and as representing the same first-order Markov chain. A similar conclusion is reached for the spatial matrices, the information components of which are shown in Table 8.8. but in this the validity of the results is predicated on the first-order assumption.

Table 8.8. Test of homogeneity for four annual spatial matrices

Component due to	Information	D.F.
(i) homogeneity	12·6	15
(j/i) conditional		
homogeneity	74·2	90
(i, j) homogeneity	86·8	105

One convenient way to compress all the information contained in the set of both structural and spatial matrices is to compute an 'average' or representative matrix. Such a matrix can be calculated by summing the elements of the original annual tally matrices and by re-estimating the transition probabilities. Thus the average transition probabilities are given by

$$p_{ij} = \sum_k f_{kij} \Big/ \sum_k \sum_j f_{kij}$$

Powering of the average structural or spatial matrix and multiplication by the respective initial distribution vectors of state probabilities provides 'forecasts' of the change in numbers, or proportions of the total, in each state; since in the present case we are dealing with a constant sample the totals would remain the same for each year.

In real world situations, however, plants are continually going out of business and new plants are starting operations so that the totals vary annually. By recording the actual number of births and deaths in each year for each state for both structural and spatial matrices average birth and death vectors can be estimated for each model. In the structural matrix for those plants which ceased operations between 1961 and 1965 the average death probabilities for each of the 14 size categories can be represented by the following *column* vector:

$d = (0·27386, 0·19417, 0·14486, 0·14401, 0·08576, 0·06634, 0·05016,$
    $0·03559, 0·02427, 0·00647, 0·00323, 0·00161, 0·00161, 0·00080)$

This vector is combined with the average structural matrix by computing a new average tally matrix for the whole population of establishments on the basis of equivalent proportions to the constant sample. The numerical values of the death vector are arranged alongside the S_1 column of the new 14×14 average tally matrix for the whole population and the new probabilities of the 14×15 transition matrix are re-estimated.

The initial *row* vector of the 14 average birth probabilities is:

$$b = (0{\cdot}24930, 0{\cdot}22160, 0{\cdot}15927, 0{\cdot}13296, 0{\cdot}09002, 0{\cdot}05678, 0{\cdot}04016,$$
$$0{\cdot}02077, 0{\cdot}01662, 0{\cdot}00554, 0{\cdot}00277, 0{\cdot}00104, 0{\cdot}00138, 0{\cdot}00173)$$

The main difficulty in this case is one of assigning a value to the element S_{00} which acts as an initial reservoir of potential entrants who may or may not enter the system through S_0. Once assigned, the value of this reservoir is summed algebraically with the elements of the tally vector for births and a new row vector of birth probabilities is computed. When tested against the observed distributions for 1961–1965 the best results were obtained from a reservoir of 900,000 though Adelman (1958) has shown that for the equilibrium vector any large number will provide the same result. The same procedure is adopted for the spatial matrix and the resulting transition matrices for the population of establishments are shown in Tables 8.9. and 8.10.

Annual totals for all establishments in Ontario and Toronto derived from successive powering of the two models are plotted in Figure 8.5. Trend lines are also presented for individual industries such as foods and beverages, and metal fabricating; the estimated size distribution vectors for the metal fabricating industry are listed in Table 8.11. In theory estimated size distribution vectors can be obtained for each point on the curvilinear line for each industry in each state. In practice, however, it would be unrealistic to attach too much significance to the results of a Markov model based on such a small number of observations as the latter exercise would require.

8.5. Concluding Remarks

The procedure outlined in this essay provides a statistical framework for analysing the dynamics of manufacturing activity in terms of the establishment but the procedure could also be used to analyse changes in the locational patterns of industrial employment. Although Hamilton (1967, pp. 401–402) has suggested that Markov chain models seem to have the most potential in tracing trends in industrial location no claim is made here that this is in fact true. The essay does show, however, that there is a strong theoretical and statistical rationale for adopting a Markovian framework for analysing the locational dynamics of manufacturing activity. Moreover the tests indicate that the power of the model to predict for short term periods is extremely good.

What is urgently required now is the application of several techniques, such as those employed by Sant (1973), to the same body of data for comparative purposes. In a comparative framework, however, the particular attraction of Markov models is that they accommodate in a compact matrix format not only the processes of birth, growth, and death, but also that of migration. In this respect Rogers (1968, p. 5) has earlier emphasized that the basic matrix structure of a Markov model avoids the necessity of replicating the analysis over as many spatial units as comprise the study area so that in generalizing the processes involved the technique provides insight which may not be so readily

Table 8.9. Average spatial matrix with birth and death vectors for all establishments in Ontario 1961–1965

	Deaths	Toronto	Toronto suburbs	Large urban	L.U. suburbs	Small urban	Rest of Ontario
Births	0·99920	0·00016	0·00022	0·00007	0·00002	0·00019	0·00015
Toronto	0·06076	0·91306	0·02259	0·00012		0·00108	0·00239
Toronto suburbs	0·06424	0·00343	0·02602	0·00026		0·00103	0·00502
Large urban	0·05776	0·00046	0·00074	0·93822	0·00603	0·00186	0·00093
L.U. suburbs	0·08086			0·05728	0·81604	0·01348	0·03235
Small urban	0·05670	0·00030	0·00150	0·00030	0·93578	0·93578	0·00543
Rest of Ontario	0·05265	0·00021	0·00169	0·00034	0·00034	0·01232	0·03246

Table 8.10. Average structural matrix for all establishments with birth and death vectors in Ontario 1961–1965

	0	1	2	3	4	5	6	7	8	9	10	11	12	13	14
0	0·9988	0·0003	0·0002	0·0002	0·0002	0·0001									
1	0·2089	0·6226	0·1493	0·0149	0·0039	0·0004									
2	0·1225	0·1043	0·6143	0·1405	0·0151	0·0023	0·0005	0·0003	0·0003						
3	0·1051	0·0071	0·1263	0·5947	0·1534	0·0106	0·0023	0·0006							
4	0·0896	0·0008	0·0088	0·0997	0·6409	0·1478	0·0086	0·0025	0·0010	0·0003					
5	0·0645		0·0009	0·0045	0·1204	0·6431	0·1535	0·0113	0·0018						
6	0·0575		0·0010	0·0007	0·0085	0·0918	0·6835	0·1486	0·0078	0·0007					
7	0·0491			0·0008	0·0016	0·0083	0·0890	0·6834	0·1591	0·0075	0·0008				
8	0·0418			0·0005	0·0005	0·0019	0·0104	0·0954	0·7021	0·1381	0·0071	0·0019			
9	0·0334				0·0006		0·0012	0·0036	0·0746	0·7403	0·1403	0·0060			0·0005
10	0·0128							0·0008	0·0032	0·0895	0·7634	0·1279	0·0024		
11	0·0105						0·0013	0·0013	0·0026	0·0039	0·0802	0·7622	0·1340	0·0039	
12	0·0092							0·0023			0·0023	0·0970	0·7644	0·1155	0·0092
13	0·0158								0·0039				0·0827	0·7953	0·1024
14	0·0119													0·0356	0·9526

Table 8.11. Expected size distribution vectors for metal fabricating 1962–1970–1975

Size categories

Year	1	2	3	4	5	6	7	8	9	10	11	12	13	14
1962	156	197	199	213	181	144	99	69	50	35	27	15	6	2
1970	172	247	269	297	266	207	169	122	76	59	52	31	15	7
1975	180	260	280	320	300	232	186	149	90	64	58	35	17	9

attainable by other methods of analysis. Another attraction of Markov models is their inherent stochastic properties which represent the dynamic element in statistical analysis (Bartlett, 1953, p. 1). These properties allow a multiplicity of variables to be embraced by a random component, thereby considerably simplifying the computational procedures.

In summary, the steps outlined above show how the various Markov matrices could be assembled and combined to form a general three dimensional model in which it would be possible to ascertain the probability of a plant's changing a specified number of size categories in relocating from one state to another or more simply the probabilities of plants in specified industries relocating from state to state. Such a model would serve to generalize and describe in a neat statistical format both the structural and spatial dynamics of manufacturing activity of an area.

References

Adelman, I. G. (1958), A Stochastic Analysis of the Size Distribution of Firms, *Journal, American Statistical Association*, **53**, 893–904.

Alexandersson, G. (1956), *The Industrial Structure of American Cities*. Lincoln, Nebraska: University of Nebraska Press.

Anderson, T. W. and Goodman, L. A. (1957), Statistical inference about Markov chains, *Annals, Mathematical Statistics*, **28**, 89–109.

Artle, R. (1965), *The Structure of the Stockholm Economy, Toward a Framework for Projecting Metropolitan Community Development*. Ithaca, New York.

Bartlett, M. S. (1953), *An Introduction to Stochastic Processes*. Cambridge University Press.

Blumen, I., Kogan, M. and McCarthy, P. J. (1955), *The Industrial Mobility of Labor as a Probability Process*. Ithaca, New York: Cornell University Press.

Collins, L. (1972), *Industrial Migration in Ontario*. Ottawa: Statistics Canada.

Collins, L. (1973), Industrial Size Distributions and Stochastic Processes, in Board, C. *et al.* (eds.) *Progress in Geography*, Vol. V, London: Arnold, 119–165.

Ellis, G. (1949), Why New Manufacturing Establishments Located in New England: August 1945 to June 1948, *Monthly Review of the Federal Reserve Bank of Boston*, Vol. XXXI, 1–12.

Haggett, P. (1972), *Geography: A Modern Synthesis*. London: Harper and Row.

Hamilton, F. E. I. (1967), Models of Industrial Location, in Chorley, R. J. and Haggett, P. (eds.), *Models in Geography*. London: Methuen, Chapter 10.

Harvey, D. W. (1967), Models of the evolution of spatial patterns in human geography, in R. J. Chorley and P. Haggett (eds.), *Models in Geography*, London: Methuen and Co. Ltd.

Hirsch, W. Z. (1963), Application of Input–Output Techniques to Urban Areas, in Barna, T. (ed.), *Structural Interdependence and Economic Development*. Geneva: Chapter 8.

Keeble, D. E. (1965), Industrial Migration from North-West London, 1940–1964, *Urban Studies*, **2**, 15–32.

Keeble, D. E. (1968), Industrial Decentralization and the Metropolis: The North-West London Case, *Transactions, Institute of British Geographers*, **44**, 1–54.

Keeble, D. E. (1972), Industrial Movement and Regional Development in the United Kingdom, *Town Planning Review*, **43**, 1–25.

Kemeny, J. G. and Snell, J. L. (1967), *Finite Markov Chains*. Princeton, New Jersey: D. Van Nostrand Co.

Kerr, D. P. and Spelt, J. (1965), *The Changing Face of Toronto*. Department of Mines and Technical Surveys, Ottawa: Geographical Branch, Memoir II.

Kullback, S., Kupperman, M. and Ku, H. H. (1962), Tests for Contingency Tables and Markov Chains, *Technometrics*, **4**, 572–608.

Lee, T. C., Judge, G. G. and Zellner, A. (1970), *Estimating the Parameters of the Markov Probability Model for Aggregate Time Series Data*. Amsterdam: North-Holland.

Martin, J. E. (1966), *Greater London: An Industrial Geography*. Bell's Advanced Economic Geographies, London: G. Bell and Sons.

McLaughlin, G. E. and Robock, S. (1949), *Why Industry Moves South*. Washington: National Planning Association.

Morrissett, I. (1958), The Economic Structure of American Cities, *Papers and Proceedings, Regional Science Association*, **4**, 239–256.

Pattison, A. (1965), Synthesis of Hourly Rainfall Data, *Water Resources Research*, **1**, 489–498.

Pred, A. R. and Kibel, B. H. (1970, An Application of Gaming Simulation to a General Model of Economic Locational Processes, *Economic Geography*, **46**, 136–156.

Reeder, L. G. (1954), Industrial Location Trends in Chicago in Comparison to Population Growth, *Land Economics*, **30**, 177–182.

Rogers, A. (1968), *Matrix Analysis of Interregional Population Growth and Distribution*. Berkeley: University of California Press.

Sant, M. E. C. (1974, forthcoming), *Industrial Movement and Regional Development*, London: Pergamon.

Ullman, E. C. and Dacey, M. F. (1964), The Minimum Requirements Approach to the Urban Economic Base, *Papers and Proceedings, Regional Science Association*, **6**, 175–194.

Part III
Empirical Studies

9 Industrialization in Nineteenth-Century St. Petersburg: The Role of Linkages in Shaping Location Patterns

JAMES H. BATER

From the mid-nineteenth-century comment, 'Petersburg grows not by the year, but by the house' (Grech, 1851, pp. iii–iv), it may be surmised that the recent addition of industrial functions to those of a court-administrative nature was having a perceptible effect on the rate of urbanization. But in terms of urban industrial expansion, this was just the beginning. The subsequent tempo of growth is illustrated by the following statistics. St. Petersburg in 1852 had a population of 330,000 with approximately 19,300 engaged in industrial occupations.[1] By 1914, the population, including the official suburban population, exceeded 2,124,000 and nearly one-tenth was employed by industry (Kruze and Kutzentov, 1957, p. 105; Kandaurov, 1914). The industrial structure at this date was characterized by a predominance of the textile and metalworking groups, by large scale factories, by foreign productive techniques and by foreign investment. Six decades of rapid industrialization had wrought substantial, if not to say dramatic, changes in the city's economy.

How this process of industrialization was manifested in spatial terms is a question that has been little studied outside the work of Pokshishevskiy (1931 and 1950). Given the scale and complexity of the issue, it is possible in this preliminary examination to discuss in detail only one facet of the process—the role of industrial linkage in shaping industrial location patterns during the period from 1867 to 1913 (Bater, in preparation). Before outlining the hypotheses to be evaluated and discussing the data sources and procedures used, it is appropriate that the characteristics of the industrial structure and the nature of intra-urban goods movement be considered, if only briefly. The latter consideration is of particular interest inasmuch as the spatial ramifications of industrial linkage are frequently assumed to involve minimization of distance friction. Therefore an appreciation of the facilities and costs of intra-urban goods transfer is an essential prerequisite to the formulation of hypotheses pertaining to industrial linkage at the urban scale.

255

9.1 The Nature of the Industrial Structure

From the middle of the nineteenth century, industry in the capital of the Russian Empire was dominated by the textile and metalworking sectors, with the latter assuming pride of place after 1890 (Figure 9.1). Accounting for over 77,000 workers in 1913, the metalworking industries employed almost twice

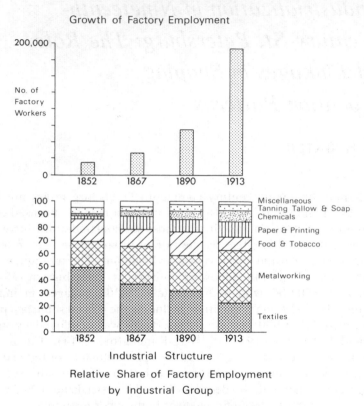

Figure 9.1. Changing industrial structure

the number engaged by the textile factories. The food and tobacco products and paper and printing groups ranking third and fourth until 1890, had also changed relative position by 1913. In that year the paper and printing group with 23,000 workers was marginally greater in terms of employment than the food and tobacco group. Both changes in relative position were attributable in some measure to government policies. After 1890, the government became totally committed to a programme of industrialization, and in this endeavour the metalworking industries especially were accorded substantial benefits, primarily through the media of protective tariffs, direct subsidies, and state orders (Gerschenkron, 1947). The impost of tariffs served to foster the use of domestic raw materials in virtually every sector. But for some industries the higher costs resulting from the shift to supplies of domestic raw material contributed to the closure of factories—especially of the smaller scale operations. For example, in 1914 after decades of rising import duties, only one sugar refining factory remained in operation, having successfully made the transition from imported cane to domestic beet sugar. At mid-nineteenth century, sugar refining had been the most important industry in the food and tobacco products group. In the printing and publishing sector, the growth was in large part attributable to the recently-awakened demand for the printed word owing to a growing general level of literacy and the gradual relaxation of censorship, coupled with a burgeoning mercantile-administrative demand during the years from 1890 to 1913. While tariffs affected adversely all industries to a greater or lesser extent, entrepôt manufactures were specially vulnerable, and many of the industries in the textile and food and tobacco products industrial group fell into this category. However, if particular industries were reduced in importance as a result, others absorbed, or passed on, higher costs, and growth rates in all groups were high. For the metalworking and paper and printing groups however, relative gains were unequalled.

The Industrial structure of St. Petersburg was also characterized by large scale factories, especially in the textile and metalworking industries (Figure 9.2). Mean factory employment had increased steadily from mid-nineteenth

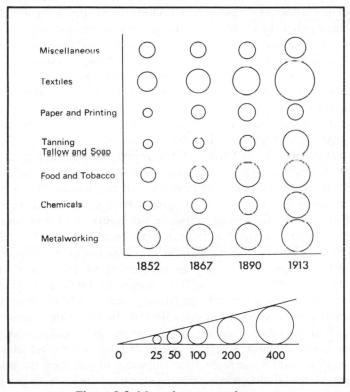

Figure 9.2. Mean factory employment

century and by 1913 the figures for the above two groups were 510 and 274 respectively. There are a number of reasons for the large size of productive unit in the city. The development of oligarchic control, for instance, had been responsible for the growing scale of production units in many industries. In the manufacture of tobacco products and in the textile group the number of smaller plants was steadily reduced through attrition or amalgamation. Secondly, out-of-date, labour-intensive practices often coexisted with the latest productive techniques in the most advanced factories, and in the less technically advanced, the former were usually dominant. And finally, it has been suggested that the paucity of managerial and entrepreneurial talent in Russia was compensated for by 'bigness of plant and enterprise' (Gerschenkron, 1960, p. 50). Whatever the reason, or combination of reasons, employment in Russian factories in general, and St. Petersburg factories in particular, was notably higher than that common elsewhere.

9.2 Intra-Urban Goods Movement

An earlier study of the relationship between mobility, as reflected by the journey to work, and public transportation in St. Petersburg, provided sufficient evidence to suggest that personal mobility remained quite limited throughout the 1860 to 1914 period (Bater, 1973, pp. 85–103; 1974, pp. 66–91). This applied to all socio-economic groups considered, from factory workers to management and professionals. In view of the evidence of limited personal mobility, some knowledge of the nature of intra-urban goods movement assumes even greater significance as background for the formulation of hypotheses concerning the role of industrial linkage in shaping patterns of manufacturing through time.

The first major technological innovation adopted for the express purpose of facilitating goods movement within the city was the horse tram. The initial tram-line was constructed in 1860 on Vasil'yevskiy Island and was intended to transfer goods from the port to the customs complex.[2] (For place-names see Figure 9.3.) While subsequent lines were constructed in order to accommodate intra-urban passenger as opposed to goods traffic, the shipment of wares continued as an auxiliary service between the hours of 11 p.m. and 9 a.m.[3] Because the auxiliary service was initially little used, the company concerned suggested to the City Council in 1867 that daytime use of the tram system for goods transfer be permitted. But as movement of wares was originally restricted to the night hours in order to minimize daytime congestion, the proposal was deemed unacceptable. In consequence, the large scale transfer of wares from the port, on Vasil'yevskiy Island, to the main point of goods interchange with the interior regions of the country, the Nikolayevskiy railroad station, was handled almost solely by a host of horse-drawn vehicles (Figure 9.3). The tariff levied for the night-time shipment of wares on the horse tram from the port to the Nikolayevskiy railroad station, 1–1½ kopecks per *pud*, was apparently competitive, and, therefore, did not constitute a principal deterrent

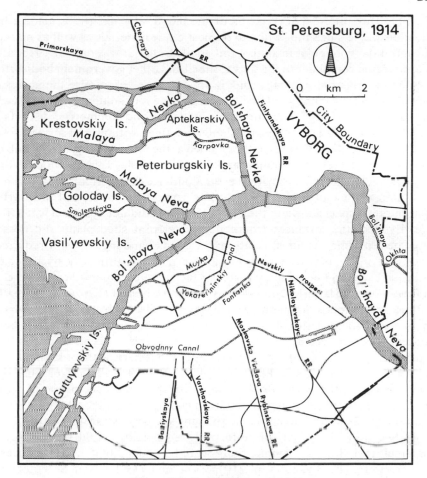

Figure 9.3. St. Petersburg 1914

to its use.[3] Probably of greater importance in this connection were the facts that night work in the commercial and industrial sectors of the city's economy was not common, and that the horse-drawn vehicle offered greater flexibility than the tram.

During the 1870's and early 1880's, the volume of goods moving through the city between the port and the railroad stations (Nikolayevskiy in particular) increased steadily, despite the declining relative position of the capital as a Baltic port.[4] Although the completion of new port facilities on Gutuyevskiy Island in 1885 served to re-direct a substantial volume of through traffic, this was only a temporary respite from the growing congestion on city streets (Figure 9.3). The traffic generated by the rapidly expanding industry and commerce often entailed shipment through the city simply because there was no direct rail access from the terminals in the southern reaches of the urban area to the important industrial and commercial districts in the northern part of the city. The discriminatory tariffs of the late 1880s and 1890s made a bad situation worse since the switch to domestic raw materials as well as markets enhanced the volume of incoming rail goods traffic. It was only in 1913, after years of futile complaint to the City Council and other government bodies, that a group of industrialists finally took it upon themselves to raise the necessary capital to construct a ring rail line connecting the four southern terminals with the suburb of Vyborg.[5] The important industrial and commercial districts on Vasil'yevskiy and Petersburgskiy Islands remained without rail service.[6]

In the distribution of wares, either landed at the port or brought in by rail, the waterways had a relatively minor, and diminishing role. This situation resulted from the fact that even during the seven month ice-free period water transport was often neither the most practical nor expeditious method of intra-urban distribution, especially when the recipient plants did not possess a waterfront site. Even in the instances where non-waterfront sited plants did possess separate wharfing facilities, costly extra goods handling was still required.[7] Thus, the movement of wares within the city was primarily by road, the principal exception being the transfer of fuels, either imported coke and coal, or fuel wood (and latterly Donetsk coal) from the interior (Kruze, 1957, p. 81).

Intra-urban goods shipment by road was complicated by two factors. Firstly, there was a comparative shortage of bridges, which resulted in traffic being concentrated on certain routes. The degree of this concentration has been indicated by Nikitin (1904, p. 71) who noted that Paris with 14 kilometres of river had 34 bridges, but St. Petersburg with 135 kilometres of river—had only 54 bridges. By the early 1900's congestion had reached the point where goods-moving vehicles were banned from many principal thoroughfares in the central city, the diversions adding to the time and cost of transfer (Orlov, 1913, p. 4). Secondly, the impact of motorized transport by World War I was only marginal; in 1913, for example, there were less than 2,600 motor-vehicles in St. Petersburg (Petrov, 1957, p. 910). As noted by G. Dobson, St. Petersburg was the last major European city to be so 'invaded', and '. . . leaving out of account a few commercial motor vans and lorries recently introduced, the conveyances still widely used for the carriage of heavy goods are of the most non-descript and antediluvian kind (Dobson, 1910, p. 131). The impression made on foreigners by Russian conveyances had altered little over the past half century or so.

The absence of an intra-urban rail network coupled with the growing congestion and rising haulage charges certainly must have increased the costs of production for many factories in the city. The scale of increase in production cost cannot be determined, but the relative cost of intra-urban haulage charges can at least be inferrred from the comments of the owners of the one remaining sugar refinery. In 1912 they complained of having to pay about 6 kopeks per *pud* to have beet sugar hauled by road from Gutuyevskiy port to their plant in Vyborg district (Figure 9.3). To put this cost into perspective, it represented 30 per cent of the charge per *pud* to ship beet sugar by sea from Odessa to St. Petersburg (Orlov, 1913, p. 6).

9.3 Hypotheses and Procedures

The exploratory hypotheses to be evaluated in this examination of industrialization in St. Petersburg are based on the general notion that during a period of rapid industrialization brought about by market expansion greater specialization results, not only in respect to the division of labour within the factories, but also in terms of the function of individual plants, especially the smaller ones, and that immediacy of contact with suppliers and customers is essential for economic viability [Lampard, 1954–1955, p. 88]. It is therefore postulated that from 1867 to 1913 the distribution of factory production will

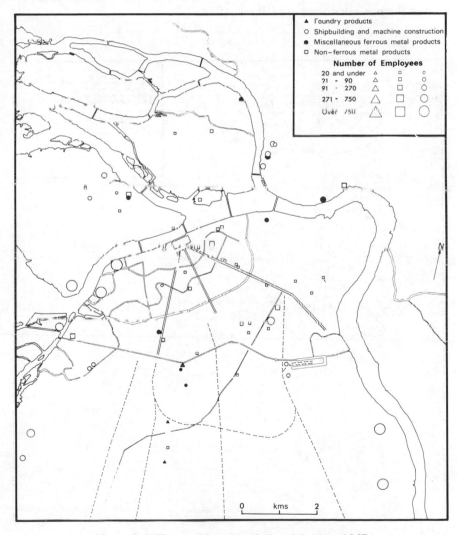

Figure 9.4. The metalworking industrial group 1867

evince a proclivity for increased clustering as opposed to dispersal. It is further hypothesized that this tendency to minimize 'distance friction' within the urban area will be greatest for the smaller scale establishments where presumably economies derived from spatial proximity to firms engaged in the same or related productive processes are of more importance than in the case of large plants, where scale economies can be substituted for localization economies. The idea that minimization of distance friction would be an underlying locational factor is supported by the fact that intra-urban goods movement during the fifty-odd years under review was increasingly time consuming and costly. Additionally, the evidence of low levels of personal mobility would argue for spatial proximity so as to render less difficult interpersonal contact, at least in the pre-telephone era (Bater, 1974).

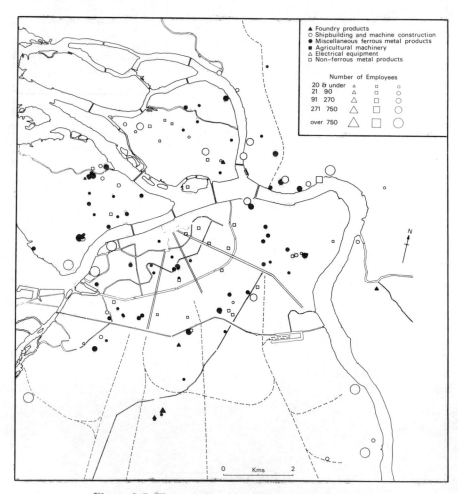

Figure 9.5. The metalworking industrial group 1890

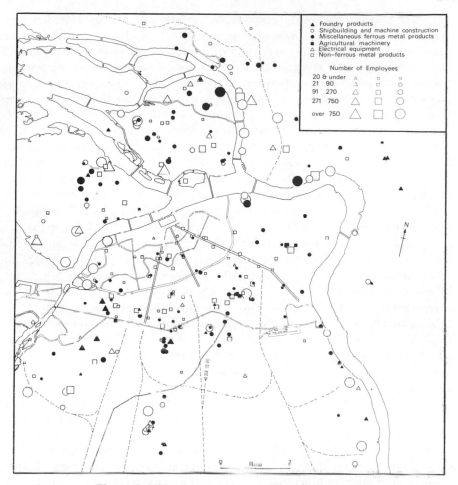

Figure 9.6. The metalworking industrial group 1913

The number of factories and workshops in St. Petersburg totalled several thousand by the early 1900's, hence it was necessary to limit the analysis and discussion to only a selected segment of the industrial structure. For the purpose of this paper, the degree of spatial proximity of cognate industries through time, was examined for the metalworking industrial group. This group was selected because it was the largest employer by 1913 and consisted of a full range of plant scales (Figures 9.4, 9.5 and 9.6).

Data Base and Measures of Spatial Association

A combination of factory statistics, city directories, and large scale base and street maps permitted the precise location of factories within the area outlined in Figure 9.4 and provided individual factory employments for 1867, 1890 and 1913.[8] These years were selected for the following reasons. For each year the last, and presumably most complete, in a series of factory statistics was available. Secondly, these years corresponded well with city directories and street maps. Finally, each year was in a period characterized by economic expansion rather than depression, a consideration of no small importance when the analysis was based on employment data. Although not entirely satisfactory, factories were defined as establishments employing more than five workers. Handicraft production, with one exception, was not included in the study.

As the analysis was concerned with changing patterns of manufacturing through time, objective and comparable measures of distributional characteristics were required. To measure spatial association, the Pearson product moment coefficient of correlation was employed. To operationalize this part of the analysis the following procedures were used. At a fair copy scale of 1: 12,600 a quarter kilometre grid was placed over the study area (11·3 by 13·3 kilometres). The total employment in all industries, not just the industrial group discussed here, was noted for each of the years 1867, 1890 and 1913. Since many grid squares had few employees, particularly in the peripheral areas, several systems of regions based on different combinations of quarter kilometre sections were devised. The problem, as Artle has noted, is to seek a compromise '. . . between the two extremes, the very large and "too" heterogeneous areas on the one side and very small and "too" homogenous on the other. . . .' (Artle, 1965, p. 121). A system of 44 regions was selected in which employment variance amongst the regions, and between the years, was minimized.[9] In examining the distribution of industry, a five-fold factory size classification was adopted (Figure 9.4).

In the initial correlation analysis a fairly broad industrial classification was used in order to obtain an overview of spatial association through time. This analysis was of total employments in each of the 44 regions for six industrial categories and therefore excludes reference to variations in association according to the factory size classes. For each year, a matrix of correlation coefficients for four, and after 1890 for six, categories of metalworking was compiled. A second correlation analysis was undertaken for 1913 using the five-fold plant size system. In this instance, employment totals over the 44 regions for six categories of metalworking and using a five-plant employment size groups was the basis for the matrix of correlation coefficients. A final correlation analysis involved a detailed industrial classification (15 categories) for the 1913 data. In this case, a 90 and under, and, over 90 workers, factory size class system was utilized. Within the limits of the factory size classification, 90 employees was the most satisfactory threshold for broadly separating the smaller scale from the larger, more mechanized factories. The regional system, factory size classes and assignment of individual factories to industrial groups are of course arbitrary and the results of the analysis have relevance only in relation to this particular system.

The correlation analysis provided a measure of spatial association *between* industries on various levels of dis-aggregation according to employment size classes, but to fully evaluate the hypotheses some indication of the spatial characteristics of the total distribution of industries was required. For this task a form of the nearest neighbour distance measure was adopted. The problems encountered in the use of nearest neighbour method are well documented and need not be discussed here in detail (Dacey, 1962, pp. 54–75). To measure distributional characteristics, Cowie has devised a graphic version of the nearest neighbour distance measure. This has advantages over the calculation of the nearest neighbour statistic in that it accommodates independence of area and depicts the total distribution, which brings out the existence of eccentrically located points (factories) (Cowie, 1967). Deviation from the Y axis, which represents complete clustering, is of particular importance in this study because the hypotheses are fundamentally concerned with the degree of spatial grouping of theoretically functionally-linked industries. To be more incisive in both describing patterns and establishing an empirical basis for assessing hypotheses, the third nearest neighbour was used as the basis for measurement. In this case a minimum of four establishments must be proximate for a high degree of clustering to be registered graphically. The procedure was simple. The straight line distance to the third nearest neighbour of all factories, according to the five-fold factory size classification, was determined.[10] These distances were then cumulated and plotted on ordinary graph paper. By visually comparing the curves, it is possible to discern differences in degree of clustering between factory size groups and through time.

A Nearest Neighbour Analysis of Locational Change   An examination of the distribution of the metalworking industries in 1867, as portrayed by Figure 9.4, does not result in any appreciation of spatial order, either within or between factory size classes. This aspect of the pattern, however, is brought out palpably in Figure 9.7a. From this graph it is evident that the first two size classes evince respectively the greatest degrees of clustering. The initial section of the 91–270 size class curve, indicating a clustered pattern, reflected the group of factories in Vyborg district (Figures 9.3 and 9.4). The shape of the tail end of the curve on the other hand, as in the case of the largest class interval, revealed considerable dispersal of plants within the urban area. Figures 9.4, 9.5 and 9.6 depict the locational changes which occurred during a period of nearly five decades. The alterations in spatial grouping, by size class of factory, are presented in Figures 9.7b and 9.7c. A visual inspection of these graphs prompts the following observations. In 1890 the distances between establishments were least for the two smallest size classes, but there was no clear, consistent relationship for increased distance between plants with an increase in scale. During the period of rapid growth after 1890, the metalworking industries continued to evidence some discernible spatial order. From Figure 9.7c it is apparent that the three smallest factory size classes exhibited a tendency to agglomerate, with the 20-and-under size class establishments being marginally the most highly clustered. As in the case of the distribution of metalworking factories in 1890, there was no consistent distance–order relationship, such that the distances separating plants increased progressively from small to large

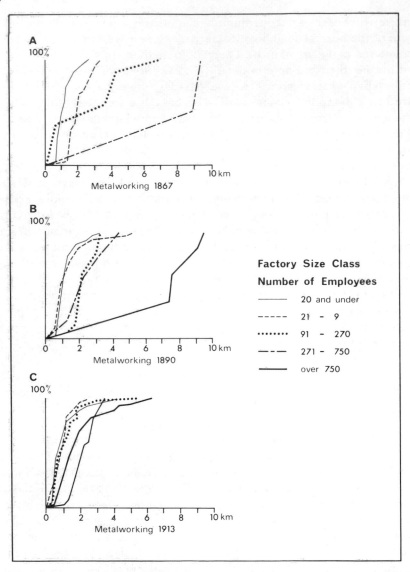

Figure 9.7. Nearest neighbour graphs

factory size class. Nonetheless, the hypothesis that the smaller scale plants would manifest a greater degree of clustering than the larger scale operations was supported. The other hypothesis to be tested concerned the temporal aspects of intra-urban clustering. It was postulated that the smaller scale plants particularly would tend to be increasingly clustered during the period under review. This aspect of locational dynamics is also portrayed by the graphs of Figure 9.5. By visually comparing the graphs it is obvious that the distributions were increasingly clustered through time, especially for the two smallest size classes (and by 1913 the third factory size class as well).[11] For the two largest size class distributions the pattern had altered from relatively dispersed before the 1890's to fairly clustered by 1913.

A Correlation Analysis of Spatial Linkage

The computation of simple coefficients of correlation using a generalized industrial classification and aggregate industrial employments for the metalworking group gave little indication of spatial associations for 1867 and 1890. Indeed, as Table 9.1 shows, there was just one spatial association statistically significant at the one per cent level. By 1913, diversification of the industrial structure and precipitous expansion in the metalworking sector had given rise to little additional evidence of spatial association. At this date, the matrix had two statistically significant correlations at the one per cent level. In terms of the hypothesized increase in spatial association of cognate industries through time, this particular correlation analysis offered at best only tenuous support.

Table 9.1. Correlation matrix—metalworking group* 1867, 1890, 1913

		1	2	3	4	5	6
Foundry products	1						
Shipbuilding and machine construction	2				0·19 ___ 0·28		0·14
Miscellaneous ferrous metal products	3				0·41		0·50
Non-ferrous metal products	4						
Agricultural machinery (post-1890)	5						
Electrical machinery (post-1890)	6						

Notes to Table 9.1
* Positive values only (+0·1) and over. (+0·38 and over statistically significant at one per cent level).

1867—no positive values over +0·1
1890—0·19
___
1913—0·28

When the five-fold factory size classification was used in analysis of the 1913 data, the correlations were only infrequently statistically significant at the one per cent level (Table 9.2). The shipbuilding and machine construction category, the most important in terms of number of establishments and total employment (Figure 9.6), had six such correlations. The spatial relation between the first and second size classes of the agricultural machinery category (+0·49), reflected a concentration of the few plants around the Nikolayevskiy railroad station. Statistically significant spatial ties typically were not among the small scale production units, but were either between small and large scale plants (e.g. in non-ferrous metalworking between the fifth and the second (+0·38)), or between the large scale units, as in the case of electrical equipment, where there was a +0·76 tie between the fourth and fifth size classes. Although the analysis for this study was restricted to 1913, in fact the general lack of spatial association did not constitute a change from the situation in 1867 or 1890. Thus, when a generalized industrial classification was employed, there was very little evidence in support for the conjecture that the greatest correspondence would be between the patterns of the smaller scale operations.

In a final assessment of the inter-industry linkage hypotheses, the generalized classification was dropped and simple coefficients of correlation were calculated for the fifteen industries enumerated in Table 9.3 and portrayed in Figure 9.8, in terms of a 90-and-under and over-90 workers factory size breakdown. This classification permitted a more incisive analysis of the suggested spatial aspects of industrial linkage than was possible under the generalized six category breakdown. The linkages portrayed in Table 9.3 provided a measure of support for the argument that the small scale production units would display a greater degree of spatial proximity than the large plants. In total there were seven ties statistically significant at the one per cent level for the 90-and-under workers size class as compared with four for the over-90 size class. To some extent the spatial bonds between the patterns of the small production units reflected juxtaposition in the central city, for instance between scientific equipment and non-precious decorative wares, +0·69.

While details of actual inter- and intra-industry commodity flows cannot be obtained, several of the spatial associations revealed in the correlation analysis would seem to have had a functional basis. One example at the 90-and-under employment level was the spatial tie between ferrous and non-ferrous castings and pipe rolling, plumbing and heating equipment. (Additionally, there were ties between the 90-and-under worker distribution and the over-90 workers general machine construction and pipe rolling plumbing and heating equipment.) Plant production data indicated that castings required in the manufacture of plumbing and heating fixtures frequently comprised a part of the output (Kandaurov, 1914). For some of the ties between the small and large scale plants there was also some evidence of a functional link. An instance was that between the small scale plants of the other fabricated metal wares category and electrical equipment. Again plant production data for the former category

Table 9.2. Correlation matrix—metalworking group* 1913

			1	2	3	4	5	6	7	8	9	10	11	12	13	14	15	16	17	18	19	20	21	22	23	24	25	26
Foundry products	a	1		23				29												21					11		16		
	b	2								13											16								
	c	3				21										24						26					17		
Shipbuilding and machine construction	a	4					33	36	49						23			66		27	36							21	38
	b	5						21	33	30				10	20		37	43											10
	c	6							32	35					31	14	17	16		19	15							39	45
	d	7								33							20	20		17									24
	e	8									12					45			17				23						
Agricultural machinery	a	9										49			11				28		16			55					
	b	10											32		20						34	43						26	19
	c	11												11		19						20							
Non-ferrous metal products	a	12													22	17	21		32										
	b	13													38	22	23	13						14					
	c	14														23									28				
	d	15														12	23												
	e	16															35							24	21		11		
Miscellaneous ferrous metal products	a	17																18		40									
	b	18																	19		38					33	35	37	
	c	19																		20					28	66	48		
	d	20																			21						12		
	e	21																				22							
Electrical equipment	a	22																					23						
	b	23																						24					
	c	24																							25			76	
	d	25																								26			
	e	26																											

Notes to Table 9.2

* Positive values only (+0·1) and over. (+0·38 and over statistically significant at one per cent level).

Factory Size Class Employment:
a— 20 and under
b— 21– 90   d—271–750
c— 91–270   e—over 750.

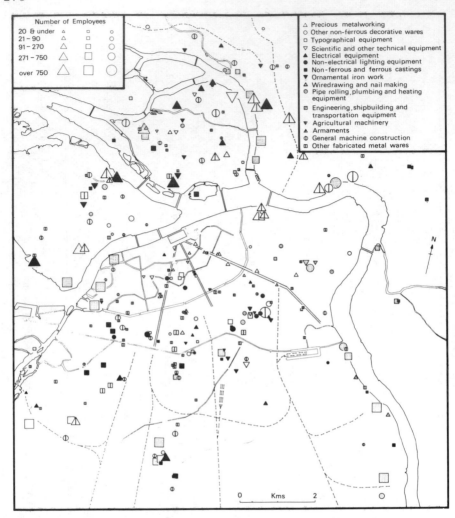

Figure 9.8. The metalworking industrial group–detailed classification 1913

revealed that simple electrical fixtures constituted a minor part of the diver-sified output of a quite substantial number of plants. In this connection, it is of interest to note that between the large and small scale plant categories within a single industry, the only spatial tie statistically significant at the one per cent level was that between the two distributions in electrical equipment manufac-turing (+0·38). Here the link is clear, for component manufacture for assembly in the large plants was an important part of production. But generally, in the small scale metalworking plants a repair function as opposed to specialized manufacture was more characteristic.

Table 9.3. Inter-industry coefficients of correlation statistically significant at the one per cent level

	90 and under workers	<90 and >90	Over 90 workers
1. Agricultural machinery	1	1	1	1
2. Ferrous and non-ferrous castings	2	2	2	2
3. Ornamental iron works	3	3	3	3
4. General machine construction	4	4	4	4
5. Other fabricated metals	5	5	5	5
6. Pipe rolling, heating and plumbing	6	6	6	6
7. Electrical equipment	7	7	7	7
8. Typographical equipment	8	8	8	8
9. Armaments			9	9
10. Precious metals	10	10	10	10
11. Scientific instruments	11	11	11	11
12. Non-precious decorative wares	12	12	12	12
13. Non-electric lamp equipment	13	13	13	13
14. Wiredrawing and nail making	14	14	14	14
15. Transportation, engineering and shipbuilding	15	15	15	15

A Rationalization of Measures of Spatial Linkage

The foregoing correlation and nearest neighbour analyses provided a basis for evaluating certain theoretical spatial consequences of industrial linkage. A measure of support was provided for the argument that the small scale metalworking plants would exhibit the greatest degree of spatial association. To a certain extent, the greater degree of linkage between patterns of the small production units, was a reflection of the greater need for spatial proximity due to specialization in the productive process. However, specialization in the context of St. Petersburg's industrial structure was different in degree from that found in many other cities where the process of urban industrialization has been observed. In fact specialization, in terms of the physical separation of a particular stage of a given productive process (i.e., components manufacture), or in terms of a narrow, perhaps single type of production, was generally the exception in the small scale plants in all industries of the capital. And this characteristic in large measure mirrored the comparatively backward nature of the industrial structure on the eve of World War I. This point might be sharpened through the examination of two specific small scale metalworking processes, one of a workshop nature, the other a factory production.

In some cities, a high degree of concentration has been observed for workshop manufacture of items of gold and jewellery, which to a certain extent at least, was the spatial reflection of a highly developed division of workshop functions (Wise, 1951, pp. 59–72). The distribution of gold and jewellery workshops in 1912, Figure 9.9, is instructive, for it refutes any notion of a highly concentrated pattern. Two or three points may be made in this regard. In

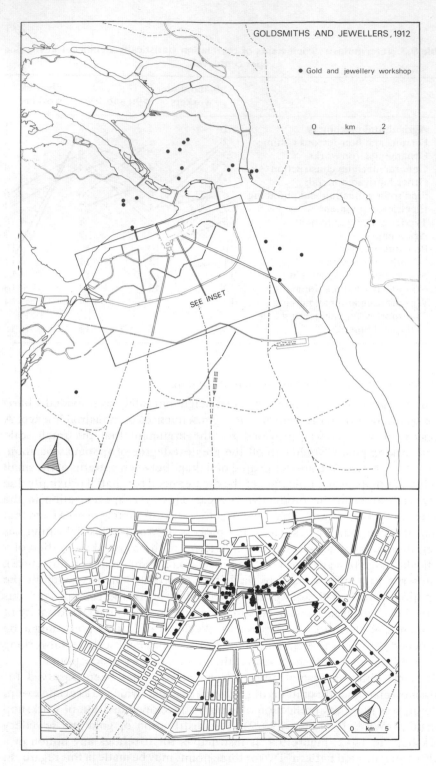

Figure 9.9. Goldsmiths and jewellers 1912

terms of the actual production process, it was common for as many functions as possible to be incorporated into individual workshops. A speciality such as gold beating for example, had been highly developed at mid-nineteenth century, but by 1912 it was in marked decline as this function had been assumed by the larger workshops. The tendency to adopt a broader range of functions at the workshop level was a reflection of the pressure to move into a larger scale unit, for factory production of gold and jewellery wares had made notable gains at the expense of the small workshop after 1880 (Kireyev, 1957, p. 121). This adoption of a broad range of production functions was frequently a necessity in St. Petersburg, because of the lack of a large, skilled artisan class on which to rely. To take a different industry to illustrate this point, the manufacture of guns at the state plant at Sestrorctsk, 8 kilometres to the northwest of St. Petersburg, was held down during the 1890's because all components had to be fabricated in the plant. It was remarked that '. . . if some of the minor parts could be worked elsewhere the production at the plant could be doubled (Labzin, 1893, p. 151). St. Petersburg could not provide the necessary production facilities. The fact that specialized handicraft production of all types was considered second best by those Russians in a position to purchase such wares did little to encourage the development of workshop production (Von Laue, 1960–1961, pp. 353–367), despite the fact that in some cases domestic production was of a quality comparable to the best of European workmanship (Labzin, 1893, p. 152). Thus, to return to the manufacture of gold and jewellery wares, workshops tended in large number to concentrate on the cheaper and simpler lines. The lack of specialization in function and frequently in quality, was reflected spatially, as this manufacture in 1912 was concentrated only in the sense of being located dominantly in the central city, within the triangular area delimited by the Nevskiy and Voznesenskiy Prospects (Figure 9.8). The distribution does not warrant 'quarter' as a descriptive term.

A brief consideration of a 'specialized' factory production, where the small scale operation was common, will also serve to bring into focus the nature of the productive process in St. Petersburg. For this purpose, the manufacture of typographical equipment has been selected. As remarked above, production in individual plants was not specialized to a high degree. In terms of type founding, the Bertgol'd factory on Meshchanskaya Street, established in 1895, was the largest operation in the city. In 1913, 175 persons were employed in the factory. But in addition to type founding, for which there was nearly an insatiable demand, owing to the city's burgeoning printing and publishing sector, the factory also produced on a considerable scale such items as rulers and copper and bronze ornaments. The Leman factory (200 workers), established in 1854, had been engaged in the manufacture of typographical equipment since the 1880's and was probably the most highly specialized. In 1913, production included type founding, engraving plates, all fittings for typo-lithographic work, and the manufacture of printing presses. The company had its own retail outlet. Smaller operations in this industry, such as the Mark Frants company, 25 employees (located on Stolyarnyy Pereulok), the Lange plant, 20 employees (on Serpukhovskaya Street), the Kaplan establishment,

15 employees (Gorokhovaya Street), and the Nilyander works, with 20 workers (Bol'shaya Vul'fova Street, Peterburgskiy Island), were concerned with both type founding and general repair work, and in certain cases even the production of simple typographical equipment. In not a single plant was production specialized to the extent of being concentrated on one of the above manufactures within the typographical equipment sphere. This tendency of course was even more pronounced in the larger scale units. Indeed, at the large scale end of the production continuum, vertical integration was often nearly complete.[12] Additionally, where the state did not constitute the principal market, a mercantile function was the common adjunct to factory production.[13] In short, independence, rather than inter-dependence, was still very much the keynote of manufacturing at all scales in St. Petersburg in the early 1900s.

9.4. Summary and Tentative Conclusions

The role of industrial linkage has often been assigned considerable importance as a factor in industrial location. In this preliminary study this facet of industrial location has been examined for one important sector of St. Petersburg's industrial structure during a period of rapid urban-industrial expansion. It was argued that because intra-urban goods movement was increasingly time consuming and costly and because there was evidence of limited personal mobility, there would be a tendency in locational decisions to minimize distance friction. It was hypothesized that from 1867 to 1913 the distribution of factory production would become increasingly clustered. It was further postulated that the clustering would be greatest for the smaller scale establishments. In evaluation of these hypotheses two measures of spatial association were employed. Firstly, in the analysis of the total pattern of a single industrial group, a form of the nearest neighbour distance measure was adopted. The graphic presentation of cumulative third nearest neighbour distances provided a description of degree of spatial clustering which was amenable to visual comparison and assessment. Through this medium, the argument that smaller scale plants would display greater proclivity for clustering was accorded some support. Additionally, there was support for the hypothesis that the degree of clustering would increase from 1867 to 1913. Secondly, a basic for evaluation of the hypotheses was obtained by means of correlation analyses. Results of the analysis of spatial linkage using industry employment totals for a generalized industrial classification revealed few statistically significant associations and provided only tenuous support for the first hypothesis. Employing a five-fold factory size classification, in the case of the 1913 data, did not corroborate the findings of the nearest neighbour analysis, in that the distributions of the smaller scale production units displayed fewer spatial ties than the large scale operations. When a detailed industrial classification of the 1913 data was coupled with an under-90 and over-90 employees factory size class system the hypothesis that the smaller scale units would evince the greatest degree of association was accorded some support.

While these data relate solely to the industrial classification and regional system used in the correlation analyses, the results tend to corroborate the argument of a contemporary observer: 'The very distribution of Petersburg factories, in relation to one another, is to such a degree inconvenient . . .' the delivered prices of raw materials and manufactured goods are raised to artificially high levels due to excessive haulage (Nikitin, 1904, pp. 76–77). These remarks imply that inter-industry commodity flows were lengthy, and, therefore, that the spatial impact of industrial linkage was not reflected in proximity of factories.

The lack of strong association between patterns of industries in the metal-working group was at least in part attributable to the nature of St. Petersburg's industrial centres where the process of urban industrial growth has been observed, for example, London, New York and Birmingham, the physical separation of, and specialization in, the various stages of the productive process, was not characteristic. Indeed, as noted above, independence of individual units, as opposed to inter-dependence, was still the keynote in 1913. And among the smaller scale units the repair function was dominant. It is in fact quite probable that this aspect of intra-urban industrial location is yet another manifestation of a process of industrialization that was in contra-distinction to patterns of behaviour applicable in the West.[14]

In conclusion, the need for localization economies, that is, the minimization of distance friction and hence the ultimate expression on the urban landscape of pronounced proximity of the small scale production units was not highly developed in the cases considered. Since industrial linkages were not common-ly expressed through spatial proximity, it may be suggested that the added cost of intra-urban goods transfer in overcoming distance friction was a minor consideration as a factor in site selection. In light of this suggestion, the role of other location factors such as land cost, rent, zoning, and labour availability and mobility deserve examination in order that the process of nineteenth century intra-urban industrial location be better comprehended.

Notes

1. Narodonaseleniye S. Peterburga v 1852 godu, *Vestnik Imperialisticheskago Geograficheskago Obshchestva* (1852), Vol. II, pp. 62–63. The population figure includes 33,600 suburban inhabitants, and see Kryukov, 1853, pp. 179–186.
2. Obozreniye Promyshlennosti i Torgovli v Rossii, *Vestnik Promyshlennosti* (1860), No. 10, p. 2.
3. Konno-Zheleznaya Doroga, *Izvestiya S. Peterburgskoy Gorodskoy Obshchey Dumy* (1867), No. 5, p. 234, and p. 246. A *pud* equals 36 pounds.
4. See, Zapiska Kommissiy o Severnykh Zheleznykh i Vodnykh Putyakh, Znacheniye Peterburga vo Vneshney Torgovle Rossii, *Isvestiya S. Peterburgskoy Gorodskoy Dumy* (1899), No. 23, pp. 294–295.
5. K Proyektu Okruzhnoy Dorogi v S.P., *Torgovo-Promyshlennaya Gazeta* (1913), No. 51, p. 3.
6. See Figures 9.4, 9.5 and 9.6 which indicate the importance of metalworking in these districts.

7. In some cases wharfing facilities were several kilometres distant from the factory.
8. Unless otherwise indicated, the sources used were as follows. For 1867: *Fabriki i Zavody v S. Peterburgskoy Gubernii v 1867 Godu*, No. 6 (St. Petersburg, 1868); *Vseobshchaya Adresnaya Kniga S. Peterburga* (St. Petersburg, 1867–1868); M. I. Musnitskim, *Plan S. Peterburga 1867–8*, 1:12,600. For 1890: P. A. Orlov, S. G. Budagov, *Ukazatel' Fabrik i Zavodov Yevropeyskoy Rossii* (3rd ed., St. Petersburg, 1894); Adresnaya i Spravochnaya Kniga G. S. Peterburg (St. Petersburg, 1895); V. Tyapin, *Plan G. S. Peterburga s Pokazaniyem Naimenovaniya Vsekh Ulits i Nomeratsii Domov 1890*, 1:23,300. For 1912: D. P. Kandaurov (1914); *Ves' Peterburga na 1912g. Adresnaya i Spravochnaya Kniga G. S. Peterburga* (St. Petersburg, 1912). The latter includes large scale street maps for each district.
9. For each of the three years, variance was comparable (approximately 10·5 times).
10. See Figure 4 for class intervals.
11. In order to complement conclusions drawn from the visual inspection of the graphs a slightly different procedure was adopted in a further examination of the change in pattern from 1890 to 1913 of the metalworking group. In each case the first nearest neighbour statistic was calculated by factory size class. The results were as follows:

Metalworking Group	1890	1913
Size Class 1	0·86	0·73
2	0·87	0·94
3	1·21	0·90

12. A few examples will suffice. The iron ore mine in Olonets *guberniya*, brought into operation in the 1890s by the Putilov Plant, was providing some of the pig iron requirements of the plant in the 1900s. Within the plant productive facilities were broad enough to render the factory independent of other plants in the capital. Factory departments ranged in type from the metallurgical, in which there was a separate section devoted to the production of all machine tools required in the plant, railroad equipment, steam engine manufacture to artillery, to name only a few. *K. Stoletiyu Putilovskago Zavoda 1801–1901gg.* (St. Petersburg, 1902), pp. 41 *et passim*. In the case of the Siemens–Halske factory, in addition to the assembly of equipment manufactured in foreign branches of this organization, even the high grade copper ore required for the manufacture of electrical wire was obtained from the company owned mine in the Caucasus. (See A. Voronov (1896).)
13. Typical in this respect was the San-Galli factory. Shortly after the establishment of a small metal fabrication plant on Ligovka in 1853, F. San-Galli opened up a shop on the Nevskiy Prospect for the retail sale of the factory's product (metal grates and fireplaces, washbasins, bedsteads, etc.). By 1913 the company employed 1,000 persons in the manufacture of a wide range of metal wares and machinery, much of which was marketed through company retail outlets in St. Petersburg (two on the Nevskiy Prospect) and in Moscow (on the Kuznetskiy Most). *Curriculum Vitae Zavodchika i Fabrikanta Frantsa Karlovicha San-Galli* (St. Petersburg, 1903), pp. 12–16.
14. In this general context a comment by A. Gerschenkron (1961) in a review of Rashin's (1958) work is of interest. With reference to the data gathered by Rashin on the movement of factories to the villages in order to secure a labour supply (especially pronounced in the central industrial district) Gerschenkron noted that, 'If it was cheaper to move the factory to the workers rather than the other way around . . . the external economics of established industrial centres, must have been rather low'. In the preceding discussion, the analysis of the location of the metalworking industry within one of the most highly concentrated industrial centres in Russia, suggests that the same comment may be equally applicable.

References

Artle, R. (1965), *The Structure of the Stockholm Economy, Toward a Framework for Projecting Metropolitan Community Development.* Ithaca.

Bater, J. H. (1973), The Development of Public Transportation in St. Petersburg, 1860–1914, *Journal of Transport History,* New Series, Vol. II, No. 1, 85–103.

Bater, J. H. (1974), The Journey to Work in St. Petersburg, 1860–1914, *Journal of Transport History,* New Series, Vol. II, No. 2, 66–91.

Bater, J. H. (in preparation), *St. Petersburgh: Two Centuries of Change,* a forthcoming volume in the series, Studies in Urban History, edited by Professor H. J. Dyos and published by Edward Arnold, London.

Cowie, S. R. (1967), The Cumulative Frequency Nearest Neighbour Method for the Identification of Spatial Patterns, University of Bristol, Department of Geography, Discussion Paper.

Dacey, M. F. (1962), Analysis of the Central Place and Other Point Patterns by Nearest Neighbour Methods, in K. Norburg (ed.), *Proceedings IGU Symposium in Urban Geography, Lund,* 54–75.

Dobson, G. (1910), *St. Petersburg,* London.

Gerschenkron, A. (1947), Rate of Industrial Growth in Russia since 1885, *Journal of Economic History, Supplement,* 7, 144–174.

Gerschenkron, A. (1960), Problems and Patterns of Russian Economic Development, in C. E. Black, *The Transformation of Russian Society,* Cambridge, Mass., 50–67.

Gerschenkron, A. (1961), The Expansion of the Labor Market in Capitalist Russia 1861–1917, *Journal of Economic History,* Vol. 21, 208–216.

Grech, A. (1851), *Ves' Peterburg v Karmane.* 2nd ed., St. Petersburg.

Kandaurov, D. P. (1914), *Fabrichno-Zavodskiya Predpriyatiya Rossiyskoy Imperii (Isklyuchaya Finlyandiya).* Petrograd.

Kireyev, N. V. (1957), Promyshlennost, *Ocherki Istorii Leningrada,* Leningrad, Vol. II, 75–125.

Kruze, E. E. (1957), Transport, Torgovlya, Kredit, in *Ocherki Istorii Leningrada,* Leningrad, Vol. III, 61–103.

Kruze, E. E. and Kutsentov, D. G. (1957), Naseleniye Peterburga, in *Ocherki Istorii Leningrada,* Leningrad, Vol. III.

Kryukov, P. (1853), *Ocherk Manufakturno-Promyshlennykh Sil Yevropeyskoy Rossii,* St Petersburg

Labzin, N. F. (1893), The Metal Industries, *The Industries of Russia, Manufactures and Trade.* St. Petersburg, Vol. I, 144–162.

Lampard, E. (1954–1955), History of Cities in the Economically Advanced Areas, *Economic Development and Cultural Change,* Vol. III, 81–136.

Nikitin, A. (1904), *Zadachi Peterburga,* St. Petersburg.

Orlov, N. M. (1913), *S. Peterburgskiy Sakharo-Rafinadnyy Zavod, L. E. Kenig-Nasledniki,* St. Petersburg.

Petrov, N. N. (1957), Gorodskoye Upravleniye i Gorodskoye Khozyaystvo Peterburga, *Ocherki Istorii Leningrada,* Leningrad, Vol. III, 887–913.

Pokshishevskiy, V. V. (1931), Leningrad, Opyt Vnutrigorodskoy Krayevednoy Kharakteristiki, *Sovetskoye Krayevedeniye,* No. 6, 14–24.

Pokshishevskiy, V. V. (1950), Territorial'noye Formirovaniye Promyshlennogo Kompleksa Peterburga v XVIII–XIX Vekakh, *Voprosy Geografii,* 20, 122–162.

Rashin, A. G. (1958), *Formirovaniye Rabochego Klassa Rossii, Istoriko-Ekonomicheskiye Ocherki.* Moscow.

Von Laue, T. (1960–1961), Imperial Russia at the Turn of the Century, *Comparative Studies in Society and History,* Vol. III, 353–367.

Voronov, A. (1896), Sostoyaniye Elektrotekhnicheskoy Promyshlennosti v Rossii, *Fabrichno–Zavodskaya Promyshlennost' i Torgovlya Rossii*, 2nd ed., St. Petersburg, 574–584.

Wise, M. J. (1951), On the Evolution of the Jewellery and Gun Quarters in Birmingham, *Institute of British Geographers: Transactions and Papers*, No. 15, 59–72.

10 Industrial Activity in the Parisian Agglomeration: A Study of Recent Change in Location and Structure*

JEAN BASTIÉ

The Parisian industrial complex comprises by far the most important and most diverse industrial region of France. It contains over a quarter of the national man-power engaged in industry with a total of 1,650,000 workers and is hallmarked by its high value of production, by its potential for innovation and inventiveness and by its radial influence. All branches of industry are represented with the exception of mining, heavy iron working, and the manufacture of textiles from natural raw materials.

The numerous advantages are typical of traditional urban and metropolitan industrial areas where the complex infrastructure and installations have long since been amortized. Power and raw materials can be easily moved to meet fluctuations in demand by several integrated modes of transport while the cost of transportation is minimized by the close proximity of linked industries. The wide range of activities has given rise to increasing specialization and to the development of subcontracting specialists who perform a regulating role at times of peak demand. The agglomeration also benefits from the large pool of male and female labour which is experienced in a variety of skills and used to the old traditions of work but which is also adaptable to new methods. Finally the agglomeration is the traditional centre of scientific research for the development of new techniques, is the country's main source of capital and has a high market potential. At a more local level within the agglomeration there are distinct pockets of intense industrial activity centred around giant factories such as Renault at Billancourt with 35,000 workers. Around this factory, which is the largest in France, 'swarm' innumerable small and medium-sized enterprises which range from new modern factories to small family craftshops. Some are very old and long established and although new ones appear daily many disappear—just as quickly. As a unit the whole industrial area comprises a complex bundle of interrelationships which not only unite the industrial

---

* Translated from the French by M. G. Pearson (University of Edinburgh).

279

activities but also link them to other sectors. The production of luxury goods, for example, is related to tourism whereas industries dependent on government contracts are linked to government offices. Similarly experimental industries and those which produce artistic goods are linked to education, research and cultural activities.

Although nearly all branches of French industry are represented in the Parisian agglomeration some industries are more concentrated than others (Table 10.1). Altogether the agglomeration accounts for 28 per cent of the national labour force, the same proportion of establishments employing more than 200 workers (approximately 1,200), and for the same proportion of the national value added. It should be noted however that the industrial manpower accounts for less than half (44 per cent) of the area's active population. The 'Industrial tertiary' sector (industrial employment which is not directly productive) is much more fully developed than anywhere else in France. Most of this employment is found in head offices, warehouses, commercial services, laboratories and research services. Whereas almost 70 per cent of the national manpower engaged in industrial activity are actual production workers only 60 per cent are so classed in the Parisian complex where activity tends to concentrate on the most advanced and delicate stages of manufacture. Therefore, there is a marked concentration of highly skilled workers and technicians in the Parisian agglomeration. This means that the total wage bill, and hence purchasing power, is much greater than one would expect on the basis of the number of workers.

Table 10.1

Industry	% National total (No. of est. with more than 200 workers)	Total No. of employees	% of employment in Parisian agglomeration
Printing and publishing	55	100,000	6
Chemicals	37	150,000	9
Metallurgical	35	730,000	44·2
Building and public works	22·5	290,000	17·5
Food and beverages	18	70,000	4·2
Textile and clothing	16	165,000	10
Miscellaneous	28	150,000	9
		1,655,000	100·0%

10.1. Historical Background

Industrial development of the Parisian complex took place principally during the last two-thirds of the nineteenth century. The railway, in lowering the cost of transport, and by its characteristic radial pattern with Paris at the centre of the web, reinforced the polarizing potential of the capital which had earlier been established by the radial road network. The nineteenth-century industrialization of Paris was founded on an already well-established trade in luxury goods. One of the earliest 'new' industries was chemical production born partly from the availability of a plentiful supply of urban waste. Gradually the process of industrialization accelerated towards the end of the nineteenth century with the growth of metallurgy resulting from the rapid extension of the railway network beyond the Paris basin and with the introduction of metal frameworks in the construction industry. By the turn of the century Paris had also established itself as a centre for the electrical industries, motor cars, and aircraft all of which acted as important propulsive industries for related activities. During the First World War, because of the occupation in the industrial regions of the north and east, Paris became the main arsenal of France which further ensured its industrial pre-eminence. Given this economic environment, the state, for reasons of external economies, encouraged other manufacturing activity in the agglomeration so that the growth had a cumulative effect.

Since then, this pre-eminence has not been questioned, by the economic crises of the area in the 1930's, by the Second World War and the area's occupation, by later attempts (especially at the end of 1954) to decentralize manufacturing activity, by increasing tertiary activities, or by the national acceleration of technical progress and industrial production which quadrupled between 1938 and 1972. Without doubt the most important industrial sector contributing to this unrivalled position is that comprising the metallurgical industries which accounts for 730,000 workers and 43 per cent of the national value added. Of particular importance in this sector has been car manufacturing.

10.2. Location Patterns

Several facts emerge concerning the distribution of the various branches of industrial activity within the Parisian Agglomeration (Figure 10.1). First and foremost, the dominant industrial zones which are situated closest to the navigable waterways and railways are dominated by the oldest and heaviest industries. Formerly these sites were favoured by a variety of important factors: proximity to Paris, numerous railways, rivers and canals, good and flat building land, and easy access to other industrial areas in the country. Thus, such areas as Levallois-Perret, Clichy, Saint-Owen, Asnieres, Saint Denis, La Courneuve, and Aubervilliers (Figure 10.2) were among the first to be industrialized and through time have developed into the major zones of heavy industries with the greatest densities of large industrial establishments.

To some extent this heavy industrial activity excludes the lighter industries, especially the electrical and electronic activities which are found mostly on the east of the right bank in Paris and in the neighbouring south-east suburbs. Most

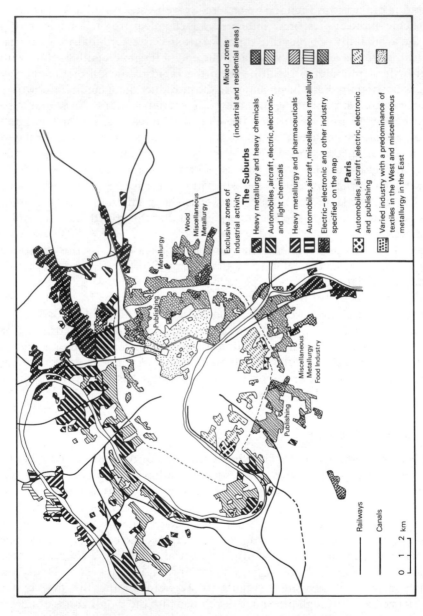

Figure 10.1. Types of industrial zones

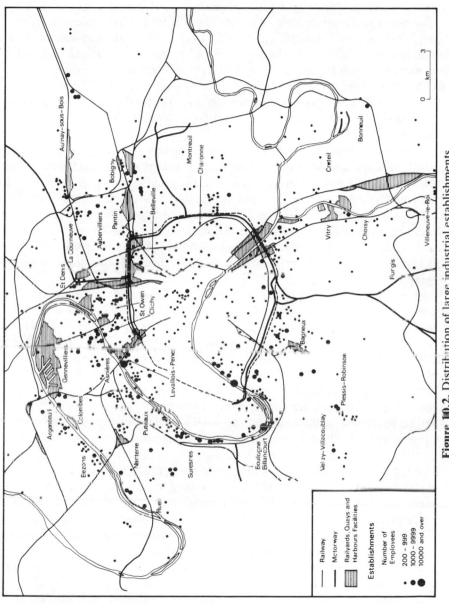

Figure 10.2. Distribution of large industrial establishments

of the remaining industrial sectors are dominated by the motor car and related industries (engines, lighting fixtures, and aircraft components).

Industries which may be termed specifically Parisian producing 'articles de Paris'—jewellery, games and toys, pharmaceutical products (soap, beauty products and perfumery), musical instruments, works of art, precision instruments, and cultural material (books, magazines, records and films)—also remain important and tend to be concentrated in the city of Paris or within the inner suburbs; such locations are in fact determined largely by access to the tourist trade, research, education, entertainment, fashion and artistic activities—all of which are non-industrial but are the basis of the Parisian scene To a large extent then these industries can only survive as they do in or close to the centre of Paris.

The spatial pattern of industrial activity in the Parisian agglomeration remains, perhaps more than in any other urban area, as a historical legacy of the second half of the nineteenth century. Specifically, the individual location of each establishment, factory, or workshop depends on the nature of the industry, the type of establishment, the stature and age of the enterprise, the location of the clientele, the net effect of polarizing and repelling forces, and on local by-laws controlling the locations of dangerous or noxious activities. Collectively however, these locations can be grouped into three distinct geographic types.

First, old industrial districts near the city centre comprise unsuitable and often delapidated buildings, many of which were formerly middle and upper class seventeenth-century mansions, as for example in Le Marais. Typically in such areas are found industries employing traditional skills for making ready-to-wear clothing, expensive hand made jewellery and fine metal work.

Second, peripheral core areas and the inner-suburbs contain industries which date for the most part from the second half of the nineteenth century or from the beginning of the twentieth. In such areas, for example at Belleville, Charonne, and Levallois-Perret, custom-built industrial premises lie adjacent to cheerless dwelling houses for the working class population.

Finally, there are sectors in which large factories, mainly concerned with heavy industries, are located along rail sidings or on private quays along waterways (rivers and canals). These factories were established at the end of the nineteenth or the beginning of the twentieth centuries and are mainly in the inner suburbs. Here, the characteristic landscape is one of high brick chimneys, gasholders, long ugly black buildings with asymmetric roofs and interminable windowless walls. These areas such as Plaine Saint-Denis and Ivry-Port are almost entirely industrial in function.

These three types of area represent a process of 'spontaneous' location and did not progress very much in the first half of this century. Throughout this time, industrial zoning in urban plans concerned with the Parisian complex remained either as an affirmation of the status quo or as a pious hope of the planners.

10.3. Post-War Developments

Between 1928 and 1945 industrial activity stagnated in the Parisian complex. But by 1954 there had been a massive increase in the population and the physical area of the complex increased considerably. These changes were accompanied by a great surge in economic growth and technical progress which together with increasing pressure of public authorities, particularly in the years since 1960, have led to an appreciable evolution in new industrial locations. By 1968 for example, if we exclude the construction industry and public works for reasons of their temporary locations which contained 33,000 establishments and employed 300,000 workers, the Parisian complex contained 85,000 establishments, of which 17,000 employed more than 10 people giving a total employment of 1,350,000.

New developments in the localization of such activities in an urban environment can be described in terms of a five-fold classification.

(1) The least important ones are expansions *in situ*, or more rarely contractions, which do not involve any change in the function of the establishment.

(2) Changes in the function of the establishment which may become more oriented to tertiary or wholesaling activities. Such a change may reflect a change of ownership.

(3) The disappearance and birth of establishments *in situ* which may be described as a process of natural replacement.

(4) Changes which involve the movement of plants out of the agglomeration from the centre. Sometimes the reverse movement occurs.

(5) Dispersion which represents a change in the spatial pattern of establishments within the agglomeration. Usually movements are outwards towards the periphery though centrifugal movements sometimes occur.

Thus, changes in the spatial pattern of establishments directly influence the location of industrial employment and the commuting patterns. Land which is given up by one form of employment is usually occupied very quickly by other enterprises offering similar or different forms of activity. The development of new industrial sites therefore, especially those which attract 'migrant' establishments influences the whole organization of urban space. Spatial patterns then can only be understood in terms of the underlying processes such as regrouping, rapid expansion, the swarming of establishments, increasing concentration, absorption, fusion or more rarely the division of enterprises. Such processes result from (1) technological demands—the requirement for more space, the development of new manufacturers, introduction of new processes, or the need to leave unsuitable buildings; (2) economic needs—to realize for example, the full value of the land; and (3) local government policy decisions—whereby residential developments require removal because of noise and other public nuisances.

In many cases where a firm is forced to relocate from its original site the choice of a new location is not the result of careful selection. For the small and medium-sized firms in particular the location decision is seldom preceded by a preliminary study and in most cases the new location is at the nearest available open space or free building. Obviously these basic requirements vary according to the particular function of the establishment and to the specific type of industry but in general such trends are quite clear. In most cases of dispersion, for example, relocations are made in an outwards direction along the same radial axis so that the new location is a direct function of the old.

10.4. Processes of Change

With aggregate data it is difficult if not impossible to isolate the effects of decentralization from those of dispersion, of natural replacement, or from those of the merging and regrouping of companies. Furthermore, it would be extremely difficult for so long a period and for such a large area to study each individual establishment to assess the effects of the respective processes on the employment for small areas. Yet another difficulty of using aggregate data is the problem of defining the reasons for decentralization. For example, in the case of a Parisian company establishing a branch plant outside the agglomeration there is no way of determining whether the process results from a desire to decentralize operations or whether the company has been forced to expand outside the complex for reasons of lack of space at or near the parent plant. Despite these difficulties an attempt is made in the following sections to assess the relative impact of the respective processes.

Birth-Death Differentials

The birth rate of new industrial establishments employing more than ten employees in or near the centre has been very low. But in the suburbs the birth rate of such plants is considerably higher than one might expect; since 1954 for example, in addition to the 300 discussed later which have located in the industrial zones, a further 600 have been located outside the zones.

It is also estimated that between 1954 and 1972 almost one quarter (5,000) of the plants with more than 10 employees in 1954 have ceased operations at their original sites without either dispersing or decentralizing. There are several reasons for these closures.

Many products have lost their markets while some firms have suffered from obsolete methods of production, insufficient productivity, regrouping and merges, difficulties of adaptation through shortage of capital, lack of suitable land for expansion, advancing years of the chief executive and from urban redevelopment. The disappearance of factories, however, does not always imply a cessation of production. Sometimes the same firm will replace manufacturing activities with retail outlets for its products, service facilities or even research laboratories. In other cases one firm replaces another with or without demolishing the original building. In the latter case the old building is usually refitted to the specifications of the incoming firm so that a foundry, for example, can be replaced by a workshop for the manufacture of plastic goods.

In most cases closure of a firm is followed by demolition and only rarely are new industrial buildings erected on the cleared site; usually it is more profitable to use the land for other purposes. Thus in Paris, between 1954 and 1971, 3,230,000 square metres of floor space were demolished (Figure 10.3). During the same period only 840,000 square metres of new industrial land was developed. Of this, the slaughter houses of la Villette accounted for 94,000 square metres of the demolished sites and their reconstruction for 365,000 square metres of the new developments. Between 1954 and 1971 the total industrial floor space of Paris decreased from 12,300,000 square metres as land covering 640 hectares by 2,400,000 square metres (20 per cent) and accounted for the loss of 2,125 enterprises. Demolition also occurred in the inner suburbs but as yet the amount cannot be estimated.

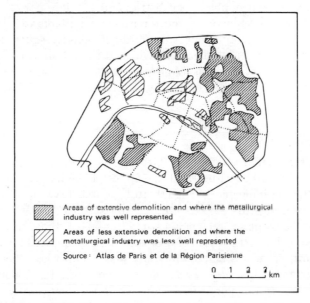

Areas of extensive demolition and where the metallurgical industry was well represented

Areas of less extensive demolition and where the metallurgical industry was less well represented

Source : Atlas de Paris et de la Région Parisienne

0 1 2 3 km

Figure 10.3. Demolition of industrial buildings in Paris between 1960 and 1966

Throughout this period there was only 7,600,000 square metres of new construction in Paris. Of this 70 per cent was residential, 17 for offices, commercial or public service and only nine for industrial use and four for garages. Thus industry is inevitably declining in the central areas—that is Paris and the inner suburbs. The main reason is that it cannot compete for space with other land uses. On the Champs-Elysses for example, a square metre of ground at the end of 1971 realized a value of 30,000 francs (3 million old francs); even on the outskirts land was valued at 3,000 francs per square metre which is too high for most industrial establishments to pay.

Dispersion

This can be spontaneous or forced (for example, by urban renewal) and can lead to locations in isolation or industrial districts (Z.A.E.) organized by companies or quasi-public organizations (e.g. Chambre de Commerce et d'Industrie de Paris, S.C.E.T., S.E.M.E.A.S.O. dans l'Ex-Seine-et-Oise). At one time, such dispersion mainly involved the large companies such as Simca to Poissy, Renault to Flins, C.E.A. to Saclay and then I.B.M. and S.N.E.C.M.A. to locations near Corbeil. In the last twenty years this process has created about a hundred industrial districts in the Paris region and there are more than twenty others under construction (Figure 10.4). These districts have 1,300 plants, including about 1,000 which have moved from Paris and its inner suburbs. At the end of 1971 these plants contained 130,000 jobs of which 100,000 resulted from transfers out of the most densely-settled part of the agglomeration. On an average there were eleven plants per district and 100 jobs per plant. It can be estimated that dispersion involved about 6 per cent of plants and 12 per cent of jobs of the industrial employment of the most densely settled part of the agglomeration. The most important district, Plessis-Robinson, employs only about 1,000 workers in 37 plants. Nanterre-des-Groyes has more plants (57) but only 3,500 workers. At the end of 1971 three-quarters of the districts had less than a thousand jobs.

Decentralization

About 2,900 activities actually left Paris between 1953 and 1972, involving the movement of 2,120 firms and 2,240 establishments. The dominant direction of flow is indicated in Figure 10.5. If one takes into account that several of the large firms have continued to establish many branch plants elsewhere in the country one can estimate that of those establishments employing more than 10 people, 13 per cent have accounted for at least one provincial plant. For plants employing more than 200 workers this percentage probably rises to fifty. Over the last twenty years decentralization has removed an average of 8,000 jobs per annum from the Parisian agglomeration; at the same time 25,000 new jobs annually were created in the rest of the country. From 1954 to 1971 therefore, 450,000 new jobs were developed outside the Parisian complex, while 160,000 were removed from that complex. Of the provincial operations, 65 per cent represent extensions to branch plant operations and hence have never removed any employment from the central area, 25 per cent are relocations of manufacturing operations. Very few firms (10 per cent) relocated their complete operations including head offices. It can be estimated that, as a result of decentralization, scarcely 200 industrial enterprises and about double that number of establishments with more than ten workers (or approximately 3 or 5 per cent) disappeared from the Paris agglomeration.

Of all those establishments which have disappeared from their initial locations in the central area—Paris and its inner suburbs—between 1954 and

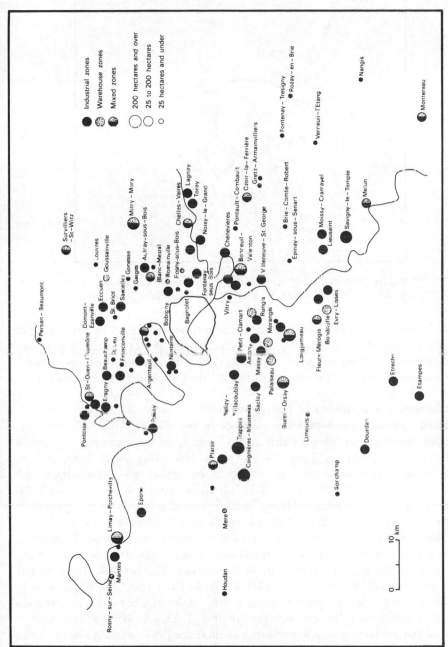

Figure 10.4. New and planned zones of industrial and warehouse activity

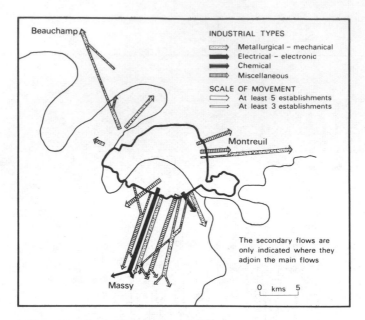

Figure 10.5. Industrial dispersion (1962–1966). Principal directions of industrial relocations within the Parisian agglomeration

1971, 70 per cent have actually gone out of business (deaths), 18 per cent have relocated elsewhere within the agglomeration (dispersed), and 12 per cent have moved out completely (decentralized). For the agglomeration as a whole, deaths have accounted for 85 per cent of the disappearances and decentralization for 15 per cent.

Changes in the number of job opportunities have been different and more marked than the corresponding changes in the number of establishments. Employment in the whole Parisian agglomeration for example, increased between 1954 and 1972 by 50 per cent expanding from 2,600,000 to 3,900,000. This increase was due entirely to the tertiary sector which increased from 950,000 to 2,225,000. Industrial employment, however, has been characterized by its great stability and remained throughout the period at approximately 1,650,000 (including construction and public works).

This stability in number however, masks important structural changes. Non-productive workers in the industrial sector—industrial tertiary—have increased continuously and it is estimated that in 1972 it reached 30 per cent of the total industrial employment (500,000); in Paris itself the proportion is estimated to be 40 per cent. On the other hand the number of establishments has continued to decline throughout the period. This means that the average size of the remaining establishments has increased substantially; in 1972 the average employment size was 15. This low figure reflects the extremely large number of very small plants (about 115,000 in the whole complex), many of which are craft shops; 32,000 are family concerns with no outside employment and 50,000 have between 1–5 employees. For the Parisian agglomeration as a whole the locational changes in industrial employment are listed in Table 10.2.

Table 10.2. Evolution of the location of industrial employment

Expansion of establishments existing in 1954	+400,000
Creation of dispersed establishments	+100,000
Creation of establishments in the Z.A.E.	+30,000
Decrease of establishments existing in 1954	−60,000
Disappearance of establishments excluding those involved in decentralization	−250,000
Industrial decentralization	−200,000
Dispersion outside the complex but in the Parisian region	−20,000

If we add the employment of the establishments dispersed from the interior of the complex to the Z.A.E. (80,000) to those in establishments which have moved inwards either to the central area or to the inner suburbs outside the Z.A.E., then it is estimated that between one third and one half of the 1954 employment (1,650,000) had a different location in 1971. In the city of Paris and its inner suburbs industrial employment decreased by 200,000 between 1954 and 1971 from 1,200,000 to one million. Half of this loss is attributed to dispersion and half to decentralization. Employment losses due to deaths (which equalled the combined losses of dispersion and decentralization) were offset by new employment opportunities and especially by expansion in the industrial tertiary sector of existing establishments.

From the above discussion it can be seen that changes in the spatial pattern of industrial activity within the Parisian complex can be interpreted only in terms of the particular structure and functions of the respective activities. In general there are three main groups of factors. First, new developments in manufacturing processes consequent upon scientific and technological discoveries, have led to significant increases in productivity among certain industries. The introduction of such techniques because of the large capital investment requirement has encouraged structural changes in the organization of activity which has normally resulted in increased spatial concentrations. Second, the development of new requirements, and tastes resulting from actual changes in the way of life and from the desire to try new products as a result of the publicity on most mass media has decreased the demand for many products but at the same time has markedly increased that for others. In order to meet this demand manufacturers have been forced to substitute artificial materials for primary materials; plastics for metal, synthetic textiles for wool and cotton. Finally with increasing size the Parisian agglomeration has simultaneously become more attractive for some enterprises while less attractive for others. For many industries increasing size means greater economies of scale whereas for others, increasing size means greater congestion and less ability to compete for land with low rent. Nevertheless there is still a remarkable degree of inertia especially among the large industrial establishments, many of which still occupy the sites that they occupied in 1914. During the last two decades, however, there are positive traces of this inertia breaking down.

10.5. A Summary of Recent Developments and Trends

Industrial activity in the Parisian agglomeration is becoming less varied. Already well-established industries such as metallurgy are becoming more important while those that are smaller (for example wood and clothing) are declining even further. Nevertheless, some new industries, such as electronics and plastics have made considerable advances. One of the most striking features is the increasing concentration of firms and establishments, with a decline of workshops and the disappearance of many small firms. This has been paralleled by a marked decrease in the number of production workers, and a corresponding increase in office employment within manufacturing firms, and of better qualified employees.

Manufacturing in the old Parisian industrial core has been reduced through deaths, dispersion, and decentralization, resulting in significant changes to the townscape. Old industrial quarters have been replaced by new residential areas and to a lesser extent modern offices. Most of the outward movement of plants, especially the medium and small ones from the central area has been not to the large isolated industrial complexes (Poissy, Flins and Saclay), but to the new zones of economic development in the suburbs where they have been encouraged to locate by local cooperatives or para-public bodies. Such locations have benefited from the improved road networks for heavy loads. Industry, therefore, is becoming much less dependent on railways and water transport so that many of the hitherto disadvantages of congestion have been removed. The net result is a wide dispersion of industry, each small grouping providing the surrounding population with employment that minimizes commuting. Each industrial zone, however, is exclusively industrial with light functional buildings, parking places, lawns and no long bare walls with high brick chimneys. The new industrial landscape presents an entirely different perspective to that which stigmatized the social literature of the last century.

In relocating, the more technically-advanced firms are the most particular in their selection of a new location and display an acute awareness of their environment. Relocations to the surrounding country (decentralization) are tending to decrease, especially among the large enterprises. It is now more a matter of the provinces industrializing rather than relying on decentralization from Paris, which provides all the more reason for a deconcentration of decision-making powers. The various public bodies involved in industrial location are pursuing increasingly more sensible policies with respect to decentralization, dispersal and the creation of industrial districts.

Without doubt, the Parisian region comprises the most complex industrial organization in France—more so even than the non-metropolitan industrial regions of Lorraine and the North. The Parisian region remains unrivalled as the industrial heartland and finds strength in its ability to adapt quickly though its weakness lies in its inability to stop spreading towards a breaking point of congestion. Today, however, there are safeguards in that its development is no longer a natural and spontaneous process, but results more from planning measures guided by public authorities.

11 Manufacturing Decentralization and Shifts in Factor Costs and External Economies

W. F. LEVER

Much of the analysis of locational decision-making by manufacturers has relied upon studies made at one point in time. These cross-sectional studies have been made either within an optimizing, cost-minimizing or profit-maximizing framework which imputes economic rationality to the entrepreneur or within a satisficing, behavioural framework often depending upon personal or questionnaire approaches to the entrepreneur. Studies of changes in manufacturing location over time are much fewer in number, they tend to follow the behavioural approach and they tend to concentrate upon relatively long-distance interregional movements. At the short-distance, intra-urban scale, most of the studies of industrial location have been cross-sectional, usually involving an empirical exercise designed to rank in importance factors taken into consideration in the locational decision. Dynamic models of shifts in industrial location at the intra-urban scale are relatively scarce and until recently have tended to take a long-run historical perspective. Models such as those of Pred (1966) and Moses and Williamson (1967) for example have explained shifts in manufacturing location largely in terms of changes in transport technology and costs resulting from the increasing use of road transport. More recently, following a suggestion by Hamilton (1967) a number of stochastic models based on the Markov process have been developed to reproduce shifts in manufacturing within cities (Collins, 1972; Lever, 1972). Whilst such models were relatively successful, their major weakness was that they failed to consider seriously the underlying costs and revenues of alternative locations and were thus causally weak (Smith, D. M. 1971). This study represents a first attempt to examine shifts in operating costs of industries at the intraurban level and to use them to explain the movement of manufacturing establishments in two of Britain's major metropolitan areas—Glasgow and Birmingham. The results are presented firstly in the form of inter-industry comparisons of the impact of changes in different operating costs and secondly as comparisons between the two separate urban economies in terms of locational shifts achieved both by the migration of industrial plants and by differences in the relative birth and death rates of industrial plants. Shifts in manufacturing location due to the relative rates of expansion or decline, measured in terms of employment, of firms located in different parts of the city are not included in the analysis which therefore focuses solely upon manufacturing establishments rather than other measures such as output or employment about which it is much more difficult to obtain data.

11.1. The Data Base

The data on establishments are drawn primarily from directories of the Glasgow and Birmingham areas for 1959 and 1969. A 20 per cent sample of all manufacturing establishments was taken by identifying the fifth, tenth, fifteenth, etc., establishments which are listed firstly by manufacturing process and then alphabetically. As a result the establishments included in the study formed a stratified random sample in which industries with five or more establishments in 1969 were certain to be represented. Although the Glasgow area directories cover an area larger than the continuous built-up area of Glasgow, coverage of a number of physically separate towns such as Paisley and Renfrew was less than complete and these towns were omitted from the survey. Similarly, although the Birmingham area directories covered an area which included the Black Country to the north-west and Sutton Coldfield to the north-east again coverage of these towns appeared to be incomplete and they too were omitted from the study. In both cases it was possible to check the accuracy of the directory data against an independent source. In the case of Glasgow data on establishments employing ten or more persons have been collected in the form of the Glasgow University Register of Industrial Establishments from Department of Employment statistics (Firn, 1970). In the case of Birmingham data made available to the West Midland Regional Study (1971) by the Board of Trade were used to check the directory data. In both cases the lists of firms in the directories were remarkably complete with more than 90 per cent of the firms listed by Department of Employment or Board of Trade sources. It was impossible to check on firms employing less than ten persons however for whilst the directories listed many such small firms official sources were not available as a cross-check. As a result of this sampling process a list was compiled of 419 establishments in Glasgow and of 812 establishments in Birmingham in 1969. By referring to the corresponding directories for 1959 it was possible to allocate each of these 1,231 establishments to one of three types. These were 'stayers' when the establishment was found at the same address in both years, 'movers' when the establishment was found at two different addresses in the two years, and 'new firms' when the establishment was listed in 1969 but not in 1959. These 'new firms' are of two types. There are some which were established spontaneously within Glasgow or Birmingham and there are others which have moved into Glasgow or Birmingham either as branch plants of non-local companies or less commonly as total 'lock, stock and barrel' moves. In some cases the directories record the previous location or head office of such immigrant firms but, as they do not do so in all cases, all 'new' firms whether spontaneous or immigrant had to be classified into a common group. In order to document fully shifts in the patterns of manufacturing establishments it is also necessary to list those establishments which went out of existence (or emigrated from Glasgow or Birmingham) in the period 1959–1969.

Such a list was compiled by reversing the sampling procedure described above. A 20 per cent sample of establishments in the 1959 directory was made and traced in the 1969 directory. Those which could not be found, after allowing for changes in name, takeovers and changes in product, were assumed either to have gone out of business or to have left the city and were therefore classified as deaths. In consequence, in addition to the 1,231 live firms in the study the distribution of the 124 deaths in Glasgow and the 224 deaths in Birmingham was also taken into account.

In order to make the data easier to handle spatially all locations were expressed in terms of the kilometre square grids shown in Figure 11.1. The 16×21 km square grid representing Glasgow and the 20×20 km square grid representing Birmingham have areas of 197 square kilometres and 264 square kilometres respectively. The Glasgow area comprises the city of Glasgow and the contiguous towns of Barrhead, Clydebank, Bearsden, Milngavie, Bishopbriggs, Cambuslang and Rutherglen whilst the Birmingham area comprises the city of Birmingham and Oldbury and Smethwick in the west and Solihull in the south-east. The outer solid lines effectively mark the limits of the continuous built-up areas except to the north-west Birmingham where an arbitrary boundary was drawn to separate Birmingham from the Black Country towns. Two gaps occur in the Glasgow grid representing six kilometre squares in Springburn and Pollok which are wholly given over to non-urban uses such as parks and golf courses and one such gap occurs in the Birmingham grid coinciding with the large areas of parkland between Edgbaston and Moseley south-west of the city centre.

In Figure 11.1 the 419 Glasgow establishments and the 812 Birmingham establishments have been distributed on the grids by their 1969 locations. In both cases the numbers of establishments peak sharply at the city centres with squares H12 and I12 in Glasgow containing 77 establishments and squares H10 and I10 in Birmingham containing 126 establishments. From these central peaks there is a steady decline in most directions until on the urban periphery there are blocks of squares which have no manufacturing establishments. These largely coincide with major housing areas such as Drumchapel and Castlemilk in Glasgow and Selly Oak and Hall Green in Birmingham. Exceptions to this gradual decline in the numbers of manufacturing establishments with distance from the city centres are most likely to occur where peripheral industrial estates have been established such as that at Hillington in Glasgow (H5) and the Birmingham Factory Centre at King's Norton (Q8 and Q9). Table 11.1 demonstrates the regular decline in manufacturing establish-

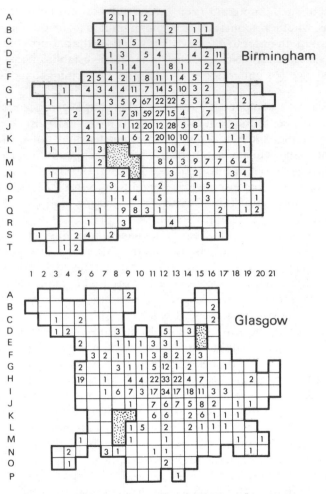

Figure 11.1. Distribution of sample firms, Birmingham
and Glasgow, 1969

ment densities in the two cities. That in Glasgow declines from 26·5 per square kilometre at the city centre—here defined as the nearest grid intersection point to the land value peak—to 0·4 per square kilometre near the city periphery whilst that in Birmingham declines from 43·8 per square kilometre to 1·0 per square kilometre, eight kilometres from the city centre (Diamond, 1962). Establishment densities in Birmingham appear to be consistently twice as high as those in Glasgow. This difference in the number of establishments per square kilometre may reflect absolute differences in employment density measured in workers per square kilometre or it may reflect differences in average establishment size. There were 212,000 employees in manufacturing in Glasgow and

Table 11.1. Distribution of sample manufacturing establishments, 1969

Mean distance from city centre (km)	0·5	1·5	2·5	3·5	4·5	5·5	6·5	7·5
Glasgow: est. per sq. km.	26·5	8·8	4·0	2·0	1·5	0·5	0·4	—
Birmingham: est. per sq. km.	43·8	16·3	9·8	3·4	2·4	1·4	0·9	1·0

422,000 in Birmingham recorded by the 1966 Sample Census and 2,095 and 4,060 establishments respectively. The average size of establishment in Glasgow is 101 employees and in Birmingham it is 104 employees. Employment densities per square kilometre therefore must be approximately twice as great in Birmingham as in Glasgow either by employing twice as many workers per net acre of manufacturing land or by taking a higher proportion of all land for manufacturing use (Davidson, 1970).

In addition to the dominant pattern of employment decline with distance from the city centre, a secondary locational feature is the attractiveness of radial routes from the city. In the Glasgow map the main roads south, south-east and east from the city centre to Kilmarnock, Carlisle and Edinburgh are particularly noticeable as attractors of industry whilst in the Birmingham map the roads south-west, south and south-east to Bristol, Warwick and Coventry are the most obvious.

11.2. Manufacturing Decentralization

Of the 1,231 firms in the survey, 302 were classified as new, leaving 929 who had been in existence in both 1959 and 1969. Of these 681 (73·2%) had remained in the same location throughout the decade and 248 (26·8%) had relocated at least once during the decade. Figure 11.2 illustrates the relative losses or gains of kilometre square in both cities. The overriding tendency is for central squares to experience net losses of manufacturing establishments whilst the outer suburban areas tend to receive a wide scatter of decentralizing manufacturing establishments. The central area of net loss in Glasgow is highly concentrated upon one square, H12, which experiences a net loss of 21 sample firms. In contrast the central area of net loss in Birmingham is rather larger with five kilometre squares (H10, H11, I10, I11 and J11) jointly experiencing a net loss of 31 manufacturing establishments. In the Birmingham case there appears to be a zone in which losses are broadly counterbalanced by gains (marked 0 in Figure 11.2) but in the Glasgow case there appears to be a marked switch from a zone of net loss to a zone of net gain.

The overriding impression created by Figure 11.2 is that in both cities manufacturing establishments are decentralizing either in single long moves or in a succession of short moves. This confirms at the establishment level what is already known to be true of most major cities from employment data. For

300

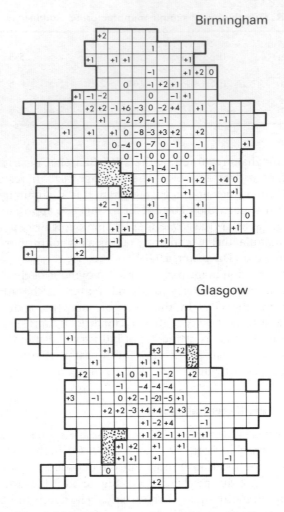

Figure 11.2. Net gains and losses from migration, Birmingham and Glasgow, 1959–1969

example in two contrasting studies Tulpule (1969) found that the average distance of a manufacturing worker's place of work from the centre of London rose from 10·33 kilometres in 1951 to 11·83 kilometres in 1961 and Hoover and Vernon (1959) found that New York City's share of manufacturing employment in the New York Metropolitan Region fell from 63·0 and 36·8 per cent in 1939 to 55·4 and 25·9 per cent in 1956 in small plant industries and large plant industries respectively.

Most of the studies of the costs of industrial movement refer firstly to long distance movement and secondly to the establishment of branch plants at some distance from the major manufacturing plant (Luttrell, 1962; Board of Trade, 1968). Total relocations where a firm has closed in one location and re-established itself in another are much less common than branch plant creations and have as a result excited less study and those studies which have been made have dealt with long distance moves (Hague and Newman, 1952; Hague and Dunning, 1954). Nevertheless the costs of short-distance moves within the city are not too dissimilar involving as they do the acquisition of a new site and premises, the interruption to production and possibly the retraining of labour when the move is sufficiently long distance to cause a substantial turnover in the labour force.

Where the costs of intra-urban movement are great the pressures to relocate must be substantial before relocation occurs especially where the manufacturing establishment concerned is small or where the manager is of a 'satisficing' disposition (Simon, 1957). In some cases the decision to relocate is forced upon the manufacturer by external circumstances such as urban redevelopment which are beyond his control. Evidence from a study of manufacturing establishments in four Comprehensive Development Areas in Glasgow (Cameron and Johnson, 1969) suggests that relocation due to clearance is untypical of intra-urban relocation as a whole. Of the 39 establishments studied 37 chose to stay close to the city centre largely for reasons of access to labour or to market and only two chose to relocate at some distance from the centre of the city. In a study of the relocation of manufacturing establishments, predominantly in metal working, in the West Midlands (Smith, B. 1971) however the 49 establishments affected by redevelopment behaved more like the other establishments than did their Glasgow counterparts.

Nevertheless it is more common for relocation decisions to be taken for reasons internal to the manufacturing establishment as such moves in Glasgow and Birmingham appear to make up over 90 per cent of all intra-urban movement. By far the most important of such internal reasons for relocation is growth. In Townroe's (1971) study of relocating firms in the West Midlands and the North East, 73 per cent said that growth was the main reason for relocation, in Keeble's (1968) study of north-west London the figure was 80 per cent and in the West Midland Regional Study (1971) the figure was 48 per cent. Expansion in this context may mean one or both of two things—the need for more space and the need for more labour. The inability to acquire more space particularly in central city areas may be the result either of planning constraints upon industrial expansion or of the inability to purchase sufficient land because of high land prices or rents. The inability to acquire more labour basically reflects the inability to pay sufficiently high wages to draw sufficient labour to the existing site. Thus in the studies cited above the inability to attract labour or the high cost of labour were mentioned by 21 per cent of the manufacturing establishments relocating from north-west London and by 3 per cent of the West Midlands manufacturing establishments. The high price of land or high rents were cited by 15 per cent of the north-west London establishments but the West Midlands studies did not specifically distinguish between 'space for expansion' as a motive for relocation and 'high price of land or high rents'.

Whilst the costs of space and labour are the major motives for relocation particularly amongst expanding firms their ability to form the basis of a model of manufacturing decentralization is weak unless the prices of space and labour vary systematically with the urban area. Of the three major factor costs it is possible to assume that at the intra-urban level the cost of capital, measured in terms of interest rates, does not vary. American studies (Chinitz, 1961; Smith, D. 1971) have demonstrated that inter-regional differences in interest rates may affect the industrial locational decision but over the much shorter intra-urban distances of British conurbations and the greater uniformity amongst sources of capital it is reasonable to omit the cost of capital in a model of manufacturing decentralization.

11.3. Space and Labour Costs

Data on the cost of labour at different locations within cities are relatively scarce and much of what does exist relates to American experience. Rees and Shultz (1970) in their study of Chicago found that wage rates paid to all types of labour varied inversely with distance from the city centre. The rationale between the higher cost of labour in the city centre was that plants located there were most distant from the peripheral residential areas and workers had to be compensated by higher wages for their longer journeys to work. Data from the New York Metropolitan Regional Study (Segal, 1960) were less conclusive but there were some industries such as food processing, radio and electronic equipment manufacture and shipbuilding in which peripheral establishments held a marked labour cost advantage over central establishments. Lastly from the same study Hoover and Vernon (1959) present evidence from the building and construction industries that wage rates in the non-central counties were on average 2-3 per cent lower than in central New York and in some peripheral counties the difference was as great as 6 per cent. Evidence of differences in labour costs at the intraurban scale in Britain appears to bear out these American findings. A study of wage rates in the engineering industries of Birmingham and Glasgow (Mackay et al., 1971) demonstrates the wide range of weekly earnings and wage rates paid by different plants to workers in the same occupations. There appears to be no strength in the argument that the higher levels of unionization in Britain guarantee uniformity in labour costs to manufacturers either at the regional or at the intra-urban scale. The number of plants in the survey are small (25 in Birmingham, 27 in Glasgow) but there is some evidence to support the American finding that central city plants are at a labour cost disadvantage to their peripheral or suburban counterparts (Boddy, 1973). In terms of the overall trend of labour costs at different locations within cities the only time series data available are that of Segal (1960) covering the period 1947–1955. These figures indicated that wage rates in the city centre and in the suburban periphery were converging to the common mean but if the more recent findings of Rees and Schultz (1970) which directly associate wage rates with access to residential population are correct the increased outward movement of residential population in both British and American cities should increase the centre-periphery labour cost differential.

Data on the cost of land are much more readily available than on the cost of labour at the intraurban scale. General models of city land values characterize them as a negative logarithmic curve sloping away from a sharp peak at the city centre (Clark, 1967). Knos (1962) for example, in his study of land values in Topeka found that distance from the city centre explains 65 per cent of the variance in plot land values. Data from the Estates Gazette (Stone, 1970) show that in the early sixties land prices per acre in Greater London averaged £32,200 within five miles of the city centre, £17,100 between five and ten miles out and £8,400, £7,400 and £4,700 with each additional five miles from the centre. Comparable figures for Birmingham were £9,700 at the city centre, £7,000 and £4,600. More recent data for London (National Building Agency, 1968) indicate that per acre land prices have now risen for the same five zones to £90,000, £45,000, £33,000, £20,000 and £22,000. These figures indicate that the rate of increase of land prices in British cities during the 1960's appears to have been fairly uniform within cities at about 25–30 per cent per annum except in the core of the CBD and at the city edge where the rate of increase has been rather higher (Lever, 1973a).

Land costs as an element in the locational or relocational decision have played an important role whether they have taken the form of a once-and-for-all payment for the purchase of land or they have formed a persistent recurrent charge in the form of rents for leased land. Perhaps the strongest expression of their importance has been made by Logan (1966) in his study of the movement of manufacturing firms in Sydney. Of 72 manufacturing plants relocating in 1962–1963, 19 said that the major reason was lack of space for expansion, 12 said that the current high costs of their existing sites were causing problems and three of the older plants in the city centre had decided to capitalize on their valuable sites and move to cheaper sites in the suburbs.

It is now possible to create a hypothesis in which firms in industries which are relatively dependent upon either land or labour or both are most likely to be moving away from the city centre where such factors are known to be relatively expensive to suburban sites which in the recent past and in the foreseeable future, are likely to be at an increasing cost advantage and which therefore represent a way of reducing operating costs measured in constant terms. This hypothesis is clearly based upon the assumption that firms in industries with a known high dependence upon labour and/or land and located close to city centres cannot resolve their rising cost problems by substituting between factors of production and making greater use of factors such as capital which is relatively mobile. This assumption appears to be justified in that the substitution of capital for labour by investing in new plant is rarely achieved on an appreciable scale without increasing the firm's demand for space to enable the expensive new capital plant to be operated at maximum efficiency. At the same time it seems that the more intense use of expensive land by increasing the floorspace per acre does not offer a remedy for increasing land costs as either planning controls in the form of plot ratio controls intervene or the increase in the floorspace ratio necessitates heavy capital expenditure on rebuilding and often the use of multi-storey premises reduces the efficiency of the manufacturing process.

The Census of Production for 1963 (Board of Trade, 1969) provides data for each of 119 sectors of manufacturing industry on operating costs. In order to assess the importance of labour costs to each industry the percentage of net output (here defined as total sales minus total purchases of raw materials and semi-finished components) made up by all payments in the form of wages and salaries was calculated. The percentage ranged from 17·0 in spirits distilling to 87·0 in the manufacture of railway locomotives, the median value being 53·6. In general the industries in which labour costs made up a relatively small proportion of net output were those engaged in the food, drink and tobacco industry and in the chemical industry. The industries in which labour costs made up a relatively large proportion of net output were more diverse but included those processing cheap bulky raw materials (ironcasting, brickmaking, pottery and the manufacture of wooden boxes), those which place a high premium on skilled labour (watches and clocks, men's and women's tailoring, aircraft manufacture and the manufacture of telecommunications equipment) and those engaged in the heavier sectors of engineering (industrial engines and industrial plant). The 119 industries were ranked into quartiles in which the interquartile percentage values were 59·0, 53·6 and 45·7.

It was less easy to derive data from the Census of Production to indicate the importance of space costs. A compromise was reached in which the expenditure in 1963 on purchasing new land and erecting new buildings as a measure of new space expenditure and on rates as a measure of ongoing space costs was regarded as an index of the importance of total space costs. The major inadequacy of this measure is that it fails to take account of rents for leased factory space but as this is included in a ubiquitous 'payments for services' category it is impossible to include it in the assessment of space costs. These space costs were calculated as a percentage of net output and the figure ranged between 1·0 per cent in the tobacco, miscellaneous textiles and weatherproof outwear industries and 10·2 per cent in the brewing industry with the median value being 3·5. Industries in which land costs make up a high proportion of net output include those processing bulky raw materials such as ironcasting, cement and miscellaneous building material manufactures, grain milling and coke ovens, those with highly specialized capital equipment investment such as oil refining and iron and steel manufacture and a number of modern industries with very bulky products such as motor vehicle manufacture, the manufacture of paper and board and of cardboard boxes and plastics moulding and fabricating. Industries in which land costs are relatively unimportant include many of the textile and clothing industries and some engineering and vehicle industries. The 119 industries were again ranked into quartiles in which the interquartile percentage values were 4·4, 3·5 and 2·8.

Table 11.2 places the two rankings together in matrix form with sixteen elements. Industries which are most affected by land and labour costs are in the top left-hand corner of the matrix and those which are least affected are in the bottom right-hand corner. Industries with relatively small labour costs but high land costs are in the top right-hand corner and those in the bottom left-hand corner have high labour costs and low land costs. If the hypothesis that rising land and labour costs in city centres are a reason for outward movement is correct then firms in industries close to the top left-hand corner of Table 11.2 should exhibit higher rates of outward movement than those close to the bottom right-hand corner.

Table 11.3 records the proportion of 'mover' establishments as a proportion of all stayers and movers in industries allocated to the sixteen elements in the matrix. The individual results are far from conclusive but if the sixteen elements are grouped into seven classes by diagonal lines in terms of the hypothetical probability of their relocating to avoid high land and labour cost areas then the results become clearer. Of the establishments in the most probable mover industries 19 per cent moved in the period 1959–1969. The proportions of movers in the other six groups of industries should according to our hypothesis fall as the importance of space and/or labour declines. As Table 11.4 shows, however, there is a gradual rise and then a decline. The reason why firms in industries in which land and labour costs are important are relatively immobile is to be found in the initial distribution of such firms. As Table 11.4 shows firms in industries with a very high dependence upon land and labour inputs were already decentralized in 1959. Only 26 per cent of firms in these industries were located in the inner two zones of Birmingham and Glasgow, as defined below, within roughly three kilometres of the city centres, and the percentages of central firms in the other two groups where demand for land and labour was above average were respectively 37 and 43 in 1959. By contrast the proportions of firms in the two central zones in industries with average or less than average demands for land and/or labour were much higher, between 59 and 63 per cent in 1959. In every sector the proportion of central firms had fallen by 1969 but the most substantial fall and therefore the greatest rate of decentralization was in those sectors of industry with average or slightly higher than average demands for demand and labour.

On this evidence from the Census of Production and on the known movement of manufacturing establishments between 1959 and 1969 in Glasgow and Birmingham it is possible to devise a three-group classification of industries. Those industries such as iron-casting, shipbuilding, iron and steel, motor vehicle manufacture, general mechanical engineering and the manufacture of electrical machinery which have above average demands for land and labour were found to have relatively peripheral locations in 1959 and were relatively immobile in the period 1959–1969. Those industries such as tailoring, the manufacture of industrial engines and plant, machine tool manufacture, many of the food preparing processes and oil refining with

Table 11·2 Labour and land costs, 1963, by industry

Wages + salaries as a percentage of net output

		> 59·0%	59·0 − 53·7%	53·6 − 45·7%	< 45·7%
Land costs as a percentage of net output	> 4·4%	Bricks Iron casting Wooden boxes	Cardboard boxes Explosives Flour/confectionery Iron/steel Miscellaneous wooden goods Motor vehicles Tools	Bacon curing Building material Coke Dyestuffs Paper/board Plastics moulding	Animal food Brewing Cement Cutlery Fruit/vegetables Grain Lubricants Miscellaneous food Oil refining Polish Spirits Sugar refining

	3·5 − 4·4%	Furniture
		Ordnance
		Pottery
		Shipbuilding
		Textile finishing
			Brushes
			General mechanical
			  engineering
			General printing
			Glass
			Non-ferrous metal
			Prams
			Scientific
			  instruments
			Wire goods
				Bedding
				Electrical goods
				Linoleum
				Miscellaneous
				Paper goods
				Stationer's goods
				Wire/cable
					Cocoa
					Fertilizer
					General chemicals
					Margarine
					Paint/ink
					Soft drinks
					Synthetic material

	2·8 − 3·4%	Cotton weaving
		Electrical machinery
		Office machinery
		Railway carriages
		Shopfitting
		Watches
			Cans
			Handling equipment
			Household textiles
			Leather
			Leather goods
			Machine tools
			Metal goods
			Miscellaneous
			  machinery
			Publishing
			Small tools
			Steel tubes
				Agricultural
				  machinery
				Asbestos
				Bolts
				Canvas goods
				Carpets
				Contracting plant
				Domestic electrical
				  goods
				Jewellery
				Miscellaneous
				  clothing
				Radio
				Woollens
					Adhesive
					Gelatine
					Milk products
					Soap/detergent
					Toiletries
					Vegetable fats

	< 2·8%	Aircraft
		Cotton spinning
		Cycles
		Dresses
		Footwear
		Hats
		Industrial
		  engineering
		Industrial plant
		Jute
		Locomotives
		Men's tailoring
		Outerwear
		Overalls
		Telecommunications
		Women's tailoring
			Gloves
			Hosiery
			Textile machinery
				Fur
				Miscellaneous
				  textiles
				Narrow fabrics
				Rope
				Rubber
				Toys
					Biscuits
					Lace
					Pharmaceuticals
					Synthetic fibre
					Tobacco

Table 11.3 Proportion of movers by industries ranked by land/labour costs

| | | | Labour | | |
		High proportion		Low proportion	
Land	High proportion	19%	24%	39%	15%
		26%	24%	41%	19%
		35%	22%	33%	13%
	Low proportion	35%	17%	33%	20%

Table 11.4. Distribution of firms and movers

Labour + land costs		Percentage of 'movers'	Percentage of firms in inner two zones	
Very high	1	19	26	21
	2	25	37	32
	3	26	43	35
Average	4	28	63	51
	5	24	59	55
	6	23	59	54
Very low	7	20	60	56

average demands for land and labour were relatively centralized in 1959 but showed the highest rates of outward movement in the 1959–1969 to escape the rise in costs of both labour and land at the city centre. Finally, those industries such as most chemical manufacturers, radio and electronics, jewellery and a number of the textile industries, which have lower than average demands for land and labour were relatively centralized in 1959 and were able to maintain their central locations between 1959 and 1969 despite the rising costs of these factors.

11.4. External Economies

Moses (1958) and Vernon (1960) and more recently Goldberg (1970) and Bradfield (1971) have attempted to integrate intra-urban manufacturing location theory and the theory of production. Using a neoclassical production function output (q) is a function of several inputs such that

$$q = f(K, L, R, s)$$

where capital (K), labour (L), land (R) and spatial characteristics (s) are substitutable for one another. Up to this point in the analysis it has been assumed that substitution between K, L and R has offered no remedy for the rising costs of L and R in city centres and that only by substitution for s, by changing location, have manufacturing establishments met changes in the costs of the three other factor inputs. By reducing the cost, or slowing the rate of increase in cost, of L and R, the cost of s rises as firms decentralize away from the external economies which are usually available at the city centre. The availability of such externalities in city centres is the reason for the willingness of many firms to bear the higher costs of labour and particularly of land. The importance of such external economies whether they are localization economies external to a firm but internal to an industry, urbanization economies external to an industry or transfer economies arising out of savings in transport costs due to spatial proximity are difficult to measure (Nourse, 1968; Townroe, 1970). Whilst the whole range of external economies covers a wide field including access to such services as data-processing, packaging consultants, entertainment facilities, employment agencies and maintenance services, the core of such economies is to be found in linkages with suppliers of inputs and in linkages to customers which may be other manufacutrers or retail outlets. There is strong evidence that proximity to suppliers and customers is an important locational criterion at the regional or subregional level (Richter, 1969; Streit, 1969; Lever, 1972b) but at the intra-urban level the evidence is less clear-cut. Whilst the report of the South East Joint Planning Team (1971) recorded that 'access to buyers of your product or service' was felt important and essential by almost half of the firms surveyed and 'access to suppliers of goods and materials' was felt important and essential by 29 per cent of firms surveyed other more quantitative studies appear to contradict these findings. Keeble (1969) in his study of north-west London found that decentralization was not impeded by links with central London as firms were prepared to establish a new set of linkages in their new location or to offset higher transport costs to customers and suppliers in central London by their lower land costs. In a study of 24 establishments in Glasgow, Lever (forthcoming a) found that as few as one seventh of all purchases were made from other Glasgow firms. In the American context, Hall (1959) has described how industries which traditionally have been regarded as being tied to the city centre such as tailoring, have under pressure of rising land costs and labour costs decentralized leaving only the measuring and design functions in the city centre. Finally, the suggestion has been made, though it remains unsupported by empirical evidence, that the deliberate creation of peripheral industrial zones in the form of industrial estates or advance factories may create external economies at the city edge and in the suburbs similar to those which used to be found in the city centre (Bredo, 1960).

In order to develop a single quantifiable measure of the importance of access to suppliers to various industries, data from the 1963 Census of Production were used. The ratio between the annual value of purchases and the annual value of sales was calculated on the assumption that firms in industries in which the ratio is low will be less constrained in their locational or relocational decision by the need for proximity to suppliers and accordingly proximity to the city centre with its concentration of potential suppliers and transport termini such as railway freight depots and container depots. The ratio was calculated for each of the 119 industries listed in the Census and ranged from an anomalous 99 per cent in the case of milk products manufacture to 16 per cent in the case of tobacco, with a median value of 52 per cent. Industries engaged in the mass processing of crude raw materials (oil refining, iron and steel, coke ovens, grain milling and sugar refining) and industries such as food and drink, metals manufacture and chemicals form the majority of those industries in which the value of inputs makes up a high proportion of the value of output. At the other extreme industries which place a high premium upon skill (pharmaceuticals, aircraft, scientific instruments, hand tools, jobbing printing, publishing, watches, telecommunications equipment) have a low purchases/sales ratio as do tobacco, spirit distilling and brewing in which industries government tax is added to the value of sales but not to the inputs purchased. The 119 industries were ranked into quartiles so that the interquartile percentage values were 61, 52 and 43.

It is less easy to derive a single quantifiable measure of the importance of access to customers by industry. On the basis of a study of forward linkages of plants in Glasgow which established a strong positive correlation between value per tonne of output and linkage length (Lever, forthcoming a) it was hypothesized that firms in industries whose output was bulky and low value would place the greatest importance on minimizing delivery costs to customers by locating close to them. In some cases it was possible to abstract value per tonne data from the Census of Production and where this was impossible data was drawn from Chinitz's (1960) study of the effect of value and freight rates on industries located in the New York Metropolitan Region. The highest valued goods inevitably were products such as lace and jewellery for which the price per tonne was a near-meaningless figure whilst others with realistically high values were scientific instruments, aircraft, textiles, knitwear and tailored clothing. At the other end of the scale were industries whose products included cement and building materials, timber, coke, refined oil and bricks which, in 1963 prices were valued at less than £18 per tonne. Again the industries were ranked into quartiles so that the median value was £324 per tonne and the interquartile values were £126 per tonne and £900 per tonne.

As with labour and land costs the input and output linkages were formed into a 16-element matrix, shown in Table 11.5. If the hypothesis is correct that firms in industries which are known to have low value/weight products and/or high purchase/sales ratios will be more constrained in the locational or relocational choice, then it is to be expected that firms in the industries in the top left-hand element of the matrix will show the lowest propensity to move and those in the bottom right-hand element will be the most mobile and there should be a regular transition between the two. Table 11.6 broadly confirms the hypothesis with a marked tendency for low values in the top-right elements and high

Table 11.5 External economies, 1963, by industry

Value of product, £ per tonne

	4 – 126	126 – 324	324 – 900	> 900
61 – 99	Animal food Coke Fertilizer Fruit/vegetables Grain Iron/steel Lubricants Margarine Miscellaneous food Oil refining Sugar Timber Vegetable fats Wire goods	Bacon curing Cans Cotton spinning Jute Leather Milk products Motor vehicles Wire/cable	Canvas goods Household textiles Non-ferrous metals Rope	Cotton weaving Jewellery Woollens
53 – 60	Carboard boxes Flour Paper/board Soap/detergent Steel tubes Wooden boxes	Biscuits Carpets Cocoa Gelatine Iron casting Linoleum Miscellaneous paper goods Paint/ink Rubber Synthetic material	Bedding Brushes Contracting plant Miscellaneous textiles	Dresses Fur Gloves Hosiery Lace Leather goods Locomotives Men's tailoring Outerwear Overalls
44 – 52	Building materials Cement Dyestuffs General chemicals Miscellaneous wooden goods Soft drinks	Furniture Industrial plant Miscellaneous metal goods Motor cycles Polishes Prams Stationer's goods	Agricultural machinery Asbestos Domestic electrical goods Electric machinery Industrial engines Miscellaneous electrical goods Miscellaneous manufacturing Narrow fabrics Plastics Synthetic fibre Toys	Bolts Footwear Hats Miscellaneous clothing Radio Women's tailoring
16 – 43	Abrasives Brewing Bricks	General mechanical engineering Mechanical handling equipment Printing/publishing Shopfitting Spirits	Cutlery Engineers tools Explosives General printing Glass Machine tools Miscellaneous machinery Ordnance Textile finishing Textile machinery Tools	Aircraft Office machinery Pharmaceuticals Pottery Railway carriages Scientific instruments Shipbuilding Telecommunications Tobacco Toiletries Watches

Purchases/Sales x 100

Table 11.6. Proportion of movers by industries ranked by linkages

		Value of product			
		Low			High
	High	5%	24%	17%	27%
Purchases		18%	19%	14%	24%
Sales		21%	50%	29%	45%
	Low	16%	19%	29%	34%

valucs in thc bottom-left elements. If, as in the case of Table 11.3 the sixteen results are grouped into seven levels of probability of movemcnt the average values from the expected lowest to the expected highest range successively from 5 per cent to 34 per cent. A rank correlation test yields a value of $r = +0 \cdot 893$ which where $n = 7$ is significant at the 1 per cent level of confidence. There does therefore seem to be strong evidence that in Glasgow and Birmingham in the 1960's at least those manufacturing establishments which were relocating and usually decentralizing were in those industries which are known to be relatively independent of the locations of suppliers of inputs and of customers.

11.5. A Comparison of Glasgow and Birmingham

Up to this point the data on manufacturing establishments in Glasgow and in Birmingham have been used jointly to test hypotheses relating shifts in factor costs and external economies to the production functions of different industries and their resultant propensities to move to accommodate spatial variations in the rates of change of these costs and economies. The final section of this paper now compares the results of these shifts in Glasgow and in Birmingham in order to identify general similarities in the urban industrial structure of the two cities and to identify broad differences in the patterns of industrial relocation changes. Two reasons prompted the selection of Glasgow and Birmingham for comparison—industrial structure and economic growth. Of the six British conurbations excluding Greater London Glasgow's industrial structure is most similar to the national average and Birmingham's is most dissimilar. An index of specialization—s—was devised

$$s = \sum \frac{|Xn_1 - Xc_1|, |Xn_2 - Xc_2| \dots |Xn_n - Xc_n|}{n}$$

where Xn_1 is the proportion of employment in industry 1 in Britain as a whole and Xc_1 is the proportion of employment in industry 1 in the conurbation for which the calculation is made and n is the number of industries (61) over which the comparison is made. Table 11.7 shows that thc valucs of s range from $0 \cdot 93$ for Glasgow to $1 \cdot 52$ for Birmingham. Hypothetically we should expect that

Table 11.7. Industrial structure and unemployment

	Coefficient of specialization	Unemployment rate, July 1969
Birmingham	1·52	1·7%
West Yorkshire	1·37	2·2%
Tyneside	1·34	5·0%
Merseyside	1·14	3·8%
Manchester	0·96	2·0%
Clydeside	0·96	4·4%

industrial movement within the Birmingham conurbation will be less than that in Glasgow as the higher level of specialization there appears to indicate that a particular group of industries have identified a marked comparative advantage there which movement might reduce. As the specialist industries are particularly those of metal and metal goods manufacture the availability of external economies through linkages is likely to be especially great. Both Barbara Smith (1971) and Taylor (1971) have stressed the volume of subcontracting between metal-working plants in the West Midlands and in Birmingham in particular and it is known that subcontracting linkages exert a strong locational pull between manufacturing plants. In a survey of Glasgow plants only 13·3 per cent of input linkages by value were with other Glasgow firms but 66·8 per cent of subcontracting linkages were with other Glasgow firms.

The choice of employment growth as a criterion for selection relates to the relative birth and death rates of manufacturing establishments as the other element in spatial shifts in manufacturing. Table 11.7 shows that, using unemployment rate as a crude measure of economic growth in July 1969 at the end of the survey period Birmingham had the most buoyant conurbation economy whilst Glasgow's unemployment rate was exceeded only by that of Tyneside.

These expectations are largely confirmed by the data presented in Table 11.8. The death rate in Glasgow (2·77% p.a.) was only marginally higher than that in Birmingham (2·70% p.a.) but the latter's birth rate was about 20 per cent higher than the former's. The healthier economy of Birmingham therefore appears to be due to a higher rate of new manufacturing plant establishment, and to the greater rate of increase in existing plants on which we have no information, than to an exceptionally high rate of plant closure in Glasgow. The movement rate which expresses moving firms as a proportion of movers plus stayers is, as hypothesized, higher in Glasgow as the dependence upon external economies particularly in such forms as subcontracting in the metal-working industries keeps Birmingham firms less mobile.

Of the 1,231 plants in the study in existence in 1969, 681 (55·3%) were 'stayers' with the same address in 1959, 248 (20·2%) were 'movers' with a different address in 1959, and 302 (24·5%) were new firms created since 1959. The proportion of stayers was slightly higher in Glasgow than in Birmingham

Table 11.8. Births, deaths and movement 1959–1969

	Glasgow		Birmingham	
	1959	1969	1959	1969
Deaths 59–69	124	—	224	—
Stayers	232	232	449	449
Movers	93	93	155	155
New firms 59–69	—	94	—	208
Total	449	419	828	812
Death rate	2·77% p.a.		2·70% p.a.	
Birth rate	2·09% p.a.		2·52% p.a.	
Mover rate	2·86% p.a.		2·56% p.a.	

(56%, 55% respectively) and the proportion of movers was higher in Glasgow than in Birmingham (22%, 19% respectively). The proportion of new firms in Glasgow was therefore lower in Glasgow than in Birmingham (22%, 26% respectively). Having made this distinction between stayers, movers and new firms their different distributions were used to divide up the two cities into areas with differing industrial location characteristics. Figure 11.3 shows which of the three types was proportionately most important in each of the kilometre squares in which firms were located in 1969. In both Glasgow and Birmingham there appear to be four concentric zones with distinctive industrial locational characteristics. At the city centre there are zones in which stayers are proportionately by far the most significant of the three types though this area of stability is larger in Glasgow than in Birmingham. Surrounding the city centres, usually between two and four kilometres from the land value peak is a second zone in which new firms and migrants tend to outnumber immobile firms. A third zone surrounds this area of new and migrant industry characterized by a high proportion of immobile firms. In the case of Glasgow this appears as a narrow belt one to two kilometres wide all around the city centre except where the area of open land in the south-west intervenes. In the case of Birmingham however this zone varies considerably with width from one to two kilometres north and west of the city centre to seven to eight kilometres in the south-east of the city where it extends along the line of the Coventry road right to the city edge. Finally an outermost zone is to be found comprising the suburban and peripheral areas in which new and migrant industry again predominates. Within this outer zone however are older areas of stable industry such as those at Clydebank and Tollcross in Glasgow associated with shipbuilding and iron and steel manufacture and at Bournville and Stirchley in Birmingham.

The proportions of stayers, movers and new firms in each square were used to allocate the squares into four zones. The grouping process followed a routine which generated zones in which homogeneity of firm type was maximized and in which inter-zone differences were maximized. The only spatial constraint on the process was that only contiguous squares could be joined. The result was a

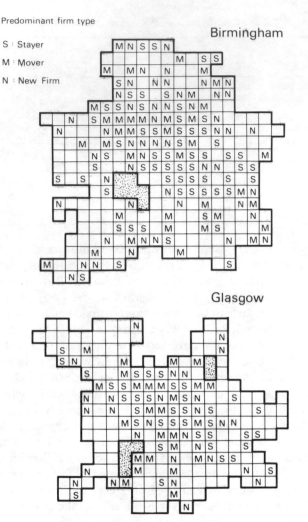

Figure 11.3. Movers, stayers and new firms

set of zones in which no squares, other than those which were blank could be transferred from one zone to another without reducing interzone differences. The results are summarized in Table 11.9 and in Figure 11.4. The data in Table 11.9 shows the remarkable similarity between the industrial patterning of Glasgow and Birmingham. In both cities the percentage of stayers is about 65 in Zone 1, falls to 44 in Zone 2, rises to 66 in Zone 3 and falls to 40 in Zone 4. Conversely the percentages of migrant and new firms are low in Zone 1, rise in Zone 2, fall in Zone 3 and rise again in Zone 4. The major points of difference between the two cities are the fact that the proportion of movers in Glasgow in every zone exceeds that in the corresponding zone of Birmingham, the fact that the proportion of stayers is lower in Glasgow than in Birmingham in every zone

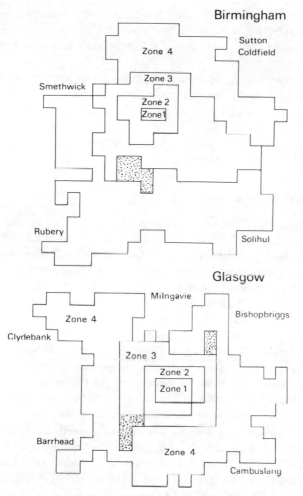

Figure 11.4. Concentric zonal models, Birmingham
and Glasgow

Table 11.9. Types of firm by zone and by city (%)

		Stayers	Movers	New firms
Zone 1	Glasgow	69%	19%	12%
	Birmingham	63%	18%	18%
Zone 2	Glasgow	40%	26%	34%
	Birmingham	47%	21%	32%
Zone 3	Glasgow	66%	17%	17%
	Birmingham	67%	16%	17%
Zone 4	Glasgow	37%	29%	34%
	Birmingham	43%	22%	35%

except the city centre, and the fact that whilst the proportion of new firms is almost identical between the two cities in the three outer zones the rate of new firm creation in the centre of Glasgow falls markedly below that in the centre of Birmingham.

The net gains and losses by zone from intra-urban migration of manufacturing plants again demonstrate the underlying pattern of decentralization. In Glasgow Zone 1 had a net loss of 21 plants, Zone 2 a net loss of 6 plants, Zone 3 a net gain of 7 plants and Zone 4 a net gain of 20 plants. In Birmingham the rather small Zone 1 had a net loss of 11 plants, Zone 2 a net loss of 13 plants, Zone 3 a net loss of 5 plants and Zone 4 a net gain of 29 plants.

11.6. The Markov Chain Model

It is possible to utilize these observed regularities in the processes of manufacturing decentralization as the basis of a predictive and comparative model. Both Harvey (1967) and Hamilton (1967) have suggested that manufacturing location and relocation are probability processes and that in consequence models which seek to describe or simulate them should have a stochastic rather than a deterministic base. Of the range of stochastic models available those based upon the Markov process appear most suitable (Collins, 1972; Lever, 1972a). In this instance therefore the distribution of manufacturing establishments in 1969 is some function of the distribution in 1959 plus some component of change covering the intervening decade. The particular model known as the Markov chain conforms to the general class of Markov processes but has the additional characteristic of stationarity (Kemeny and Snell, 1960, 1962; Bartholomew, 1967) which is met only if the matrix of transition probabilities does not change from one time period to another. There is reason to believe that the process of industrial movement, especially at the intra-urban scale does conform, unlike the process of population movement for example (Anderson, 1954; Brown, 1970) to the condition of stationarity. The attractive force of agglomeration economies is less important at the intra-urban scale than at the national or regional scale so that concentrations of manufacturing within the city such as that at the city centre are unlikely to attract further establishments at an increasing rate (Richardson, 1969). In fact as has been shown above the external economies of the city centre have been devalued both by rising labour and land costs and by the growth of negative externalities such as traffic congestion so that the generation of a steady rate of outmigration of plants from the city centre necessary to meet the condition of stationarity seems to accord with reality. More detailed evidence is presented elsewhere to support the assumption of stationarity, in the short run at least (Lever 1972a).

Brown (1970) rightly points out that Markov chain models are only properly applied to situations of relocation in which the number of units under study, manufacturing establishments in this case, does not change from t_n to t_{n+1}. Where, as in this study, the process is one of spatial change due to both relocation and differences in birth and death rates the Markov chain model has to be modified. Accordingly both a closed system model for relocation and an open system model incorporating births and deaths are run on the data for Birmingham and Glasgow.

On the basis of the data on stayers and movers it is possible to provide values for the two separate transition probability matrices for the closed system Markov model. Thus the numerical matrix for Glasgow:

	To	Zone 1	Zone 2	Zone 3	Zone 4	Total
	Zone 1	118	13	4	14	149
From	Zone 2	6	33	8	6	53
	Zone 3	1	1	68	5	75
	Zone 4	2	0	3	43	48

can be converted into the transitional probability matrix, P_G:

	Z_1	Z_2	Z_3	Z_4
Z_1	0·79	0·09	0·03	0·09
Z_2	0·11	0·63	0·15	0·11
Z_3	0·01	0·01	0·91	0·07
Z_4	0·04	0·00	0·06	0·90

Similarly the numerical matrix for Birmingham:

	To	Zone 1	Zone 2	Zone 3	Zone 4	Total
	Zone 1	58	8	3	4	73
From	Zone 2	3	134	11	15	163
	Zone 3	1	8	245	16	270
	Zone 4	0	2	6	90	98

can be converted into the transitional probability matrix, P_B,:

	Z_1	Z_2	Z_3	Z_4
Z_1	0·79	0·11	0·04	0·06
Z_2	0·02	0·82	0·07	0·09
Z_3	0·01	0·03	0·90	0·06
Z_4	0·00	0·02	0·06	0·92

There appear to be two major differences between P_G and P_B. Firstly, the values along the diagonal which indicate the level of immobility in the system (as hypothesized) are higher in $P_B(0·86)$ than in $P_G(0·81)$. Secondly the mean probability of outward movement in $P_G(0.09)$ is greater than that in $P_B(0.07)$ and the mean probability of inward movement in P_G is greater (0.04) than that in $P_B(0.02)$.

The total columns at the right of the two numerical matrices represent the distributions of the stayers and movers in 1959 and as such can be expressed as probability vectors with the forms

$$\mathbf{p}_G^{(0)} = (0.46, 0.16, 0.23, 0.15) \text{ and}$$

$$\mathbf{p}_B^{(0)} = (0.12, 0.27, 0.45, 0.16)$$

Subsequent successive states of the system are generated by the sequences

$$\mathbf{p}_G^{(1)} = \mathbf{p}_G^{(0)} \cdot P_G ; \mathbf{p}_G^{(2)} = \mathbf{p}_G^{(1)} \cdot P_G ; \quad \text{etc and}$$

$$\mathbf{p}_B^{(1)} = \mathbf{p}_B^{(0)} \cdot P_B ; \mathbf{p}_B^{(2)} = \mathbf{p}_B^{(1)} \cdot P_B ; \quad \text{etc}$$

Table 11.10 shows the predicted distributions of manufacturing plants in Birmingham and Glasgow from t_0 (1959) through t_1 (1969) to t_6 (2019). In both cities the rate of loss of firms from the city centre is about half over the six time

Table 11.10. Predicted distribution of firms (%): closed model

	Glasgow				Birmingham			
	Zone 1	Zone 2	Zone 3	Zone 4	Zone 1	Zone 2	Zone 3	Zone 4
t_0	46	16	23	15	12	27	45	16
t_1	39	14	26	21	10	25	44	21
t_2	33	13	28	26	9	23	43	25
t_3	29	11	30	30	8	22	42	28
t_4	25	10	32	33	7	21	41	31
t_5	23	9	33	35	6	20	41	33
t_6	21	8	34	37	6	19	40	35

periods though inevitably the absolute rate of loss declines with each successive iteration of the model. Losses from Zone 2 appear to be more serious in Glasgow where the proportion of firms falls from 16 per cent in t_0 (1959) to 8 per cent in t_6 than in Birmingham where the proportion falls from 27 per cent to 19. The most significant difference between the two cities occurs in Zone 3 for in Glasgow the percentage of firms rises from 23 at t_0 to 34 at t_6 whilst in Birmingham it falls from 45 at t_0 to 40 at t_6. The difference appears to be explicable in terms of the industrial structure of Birmingham's Zone 2 with its heavy dependence upon metalworking industries which require close contact with one another because of the importance of subcontracting and in terms of the redevelopment process in Glasgow which has created a number of attractive new industrial areas in parts of Zone 3 such as Govan and Rutherglen. Lastly the rates of manufacturing growth in the suburban and peripheral Zone 4 are very similar in Glasgow (+145%) and in Birmingham (+120%).

Up to this point the model has been used to simulate a closed system in which the same firms continue in existence throughout the period t_0 to t_6 and in which spatial shifts in manufacturing take place only through intra-urban movement. Just as important an element in the pattern of manufacturing shifts is the relative birth and death rates of each zone. (Blumen, Kogan and McCarthy, 1955; Hart and Prais, 1956). One solution to the problem of openness is offered by Adelman (1958) who suggests that an additional state be created to act as a reservoir. This state, here termed X in order to distinguish it from Zones 1 to 4, is assumed to lose a firm when one is established in one of the zones and firms which go out of existence are assumed to return to this state. The numerical matrices of firm behaviour can now be extended to take account of births and deaths. The Glasgow matrix has the form:

	Z_1	Z_2	Z_3	Z_4	X
Z_1	118	13	4	14	63
Z_2	6	33	8	6	20
Z_3	1	1	68	5	24
Z_4	2	0	3	43	17
X	17	24	17	36	—

whilst that for Birmingham has the form:

	Z_1	Z_2	Z_3	Z_4	X
Z_1	58	8	3	4	17
Z_2	3	134	11	15	75
Z_3	1	8	245	16	98
Z_4	0	2	6	90	34
X	14	73	54	67	—

The bottom right-hand square in each matrix presents the problem of allocating a meaningful value to the number of firms in X at both t_0 and t_1. Adelman (1958) solves the problem by arbitrarily assigning a large value to X at t_0 and proves that the actual value does not affect the model's predictions of the final stable state. In this case the value 1,000 was assigned to X at t_0 in both matrices and the missing values were therefore 906 in the Glasgow case and 772 in the Birmingham case. The two numerical matrices can now be converted to transition probability matrices as before with the forms:

$$P_G = \begin{matrix} 0\cdot556 & 0\cdot062 & 0\cdot019 & 0\cdot066 & 0\cdot297 \\ 0\cdot082 & 0\cdot452 & 0\cdot110 & 0\cdot082 & 0\cdot274 \\ 0\cdot010 & 0\cdot010 & 0\cdot690 & 0\cdot050 & 0\cdot240 \\ 0\cdot031 & 0\cdot000 & 0\cdot046 & 0\cdot661 & 0\cdot262 \\ 0\cdot017 & 0\cdot024 & 0\cdot017 & 0\cdot036 & 0\cdot906 \end{matrix}$$

and

$$P_B = \begin{matrix} 0\cdot646 & 0\cdot089 & 0\cdot033 & 0\cdot044 & 0\cdot189 \\ 0\cdot013 & 0\cdot563 & 0\cdot046 & 0\cdot063 & 0\cdot315 \\ 0\cdot003 & 0\cdot022 & 0\cdot665 & 0\cdot044 & 0\cdot266 \\ 0\cdot000 & 0\cdot015 & 0\cdot046 & 0\cdot682 & 0\cdot257 \\ 0\cdot014 & 0\cdot073 & 0\cdot054 & 0\cdot067 & 0\cdot792 \end{matrix}$$

The addition of values of 1,000 for X in both cases creates initial probability vectors of $(0\cdot147, 0\cdot050, 0\cdot068, 0\cdot043, 0\cdot692)$ in the case of Glasgow and $(0\cdot049, 0\cdot130, 0\cdot201, 0\cdot072, 0\cdot547)$ in the case of Birmingham.

Again successive states of the system are generated by the repeated multiplication of successive values of p by P_G or P_B. At each time cross-section the value of X can be disregarded as the model is only concerned with those firms in existence at that point in time and these are described in the relative sizes of Z_1, Z_2, Z_3 and Z_4. It is of interest to note however that in both Glasgow and Birmingham the value of X continues to increase as in each time period the number of deaths exceeds the number of births irrespective of their locations within the city.

Table 11.11. Predicted distribution of firms (%); open model

	Glasgow				Birmingham			
	Zone 1	Zone 2	Zone 3	Zone 4	Zone 1	Zone 2	Zone 3	Zone 4
t_0	48	16	22	14	11	29	45	16
t_1	34	16	25	25	10	27	39	24
t_2	27	15	26	32	9	27	36	29
t_3	23	14	28	35	8	27	33	32
t_4	20	14	28	38	8	26	32	34
t_5	19	14	28	39	7	26	31	36
t_6	18	13	29	40	7	26	31	36
t_7	18	12	29	41	7	26	31	37
t_8	18	12	29	41	6	26	31	37

Table 11.11 gives the predicted distributions of firms in Glasgow and Birmingham from t_0 (1959) to t_8 (2039). From the table it is apparent that the rate of change of manufacturing establishment distribution slows rapidly with successive iterations. It is a feature of Markov chain models with their assumption of stationarity that they predict, in most cases, an end state at which stability is reached. This stability does not mean that firms cease to move or to be born or go out of existence but that all flows cancel one another out. This terminal state, p_t, therefore must statisfy the expression.

$$p_t = p_t . P$$

In both the Glasgow and Birmingham cases t_8 is found to be t_t. Criticism has been levelled at predictions based on Markov chain models because of the frequency of examples which require hundreds of iterations, implying the passage of centuries if not millenia, before stability is reached, (Compton, 1969; Lever, forthcoming b). In this case however stability is reached very quickly which is itself an indication of the rapidity of shifts in manufacturing location patterns.

Comparison between Tables 11.10 and 11.11 gives some indication of the relative impact of adding births and deaths into a purely migratory model of intra-urban manufacturing locational shifts. In Glasgow the death rate is relatively uniform within the city at between 2·4 and 2·9 per cent per year but the birth rate is markedly higher in Zones 2 and 4. Consequently in the open model Zones 2 and 4 do rather better than in the closed model whilst Zones 1 and 3 inevitably fare worse. In Birmingham the death rate varies more widely from 1·9 per annum in the city centre to 3·2 in Zone 2 whilst the birth rate is very low in the city centre (1·5%) and Zone 3 (1·5%) and high in Zone 2 (3·1%) and Zone 4 (5·1%). As a result the open model predicts a similar proportion of firms and Zone 1 as the closed model whilst Zones 2 and 4 retain more firms and Zone 3 retains fewer firms in the open model than in the closed model.

11.7. Conclusion

This study has attempted to do two things. The first section relates theories of intra-urban location and relocation of manufacturing establishments to production theory. By examining the structure of input costs and external economies within the framework of a neoclassical production function it was possible to relate the movement of firms in Glasgow and Birmingham to relative shifts in the costs of land and labour and to changes in the value of external economies. As a general rule firms in industries known to have a high dependence upon labour and/or land which are increasingly expensive especially in the centres of cities either located initially away from the city centre or have relocated to suburban and peripheral sites before the start of the period under study, 1959–1969. Firms in industries which are known to have a low level of dependence upon labour and/or land have located in city centres and despite the rising cost of these factors have been able to maintain these central locations. The rate of outward movement has therefore been greatest amongst firms in industries with demands for labour and/or land which are close to the average for all industries. These are the firms which prior to 1959 located close to city centres, drawn by the availability there of external economies unavailable elsewhere, but the rate of increase of costs of land and labour in the city centre is higher than elsewhere and consequently these are the firms which have been forced to substitute a new set of spatial characteristics into their production functions as a result of the rising price of other factor inputs. The importance of external economies, particularly those associated with ease of access to suppliers, subcontractors and customers, is also shown to play an important part in explaining which firms and which industries have shown the highest propensity to move away from the centres of Birmingham and Glasgow in the period 1959–1969. In the final part of the study a general stochastic model has been used to simulate the process of manufacturing decentralization in two British cities with very different industrial structures and growth rates. The model identifies surprisingly similar basic structures for the two cities in terms of the location of mobile, immobile and new manufacturing establishments. Within the framework of a four-zone concentric model of the cities a Markov chain model is developed to predict the most probable end result of the current trends of decentralization of manufacturing industry both by migration and by births and deaths of establishments. Data however is unavailable to add the final dimension to the model—that of growth or decline of employment or output within individual firms—so that the extension of the model to levels comparable with those of Norcliffe (1970) and Collins (1972) is impossible. Nevertheless the predictions for both Birmingham and Glasgow underline the extreme rapidity of manufacturing decentralization with the numbers of manufacturing establishments in the city centre falling by 44 per cent in Glasgow between 1959 and 1979 and falling by 18 per cent in Birmingham which has a much more tightly linked set of manufacturing firms close to the city centre. In contrast the suburban and peripheral areas of the two cities increase their share of manufacturing establishments by 129 per cent and 82 per cent respectively over the same period of time. The size of these shifts in manufacturing location within major British cities cannot but have far-reaching implications for public transport, physical planning, local government finance and the concept of the core-dominated model which has been such a feature of urban research.

References

Adelman, I. G. (1958), A Stochastic Analysis of the Size Distribution of Firms, *Journal, American Statistical Association*, **53**, 893–904.

Anderson, T. W. (1954), Probability Models for Analyzing Time Changes in Attitudes, in Lazarsfeld, P. F. (ed.), *Mathematical Thinking in the Social Sciences*. Glencoe, Ill.: Free Press.

Bartholomew, D. J. (1967), *Stochastic Models for Social Processes*. London: Wiley.

Blumen, I., Kogan, M. and McCarthy, P. J. (1955), *The Industrial Mobility of Labor as a Probability Process*. Ithaca. N.Y.: Cornell University Press.

Board of Trade (1968), *The Movement of Manufacturing Industry in the United Kingdom, 1945–1965*. London: H.M.S.O.

Board of Trade (1969), *Report on the Census of Production, 1963*. London: H.M.S.O.

Boddy, D. (1973), Personal Communication.

Bradfield, M. (1971), A Note on Location and the Theory of Production, *Journal of Regional Science*, **11**, 263–266.

Bredo, W. (1960), *Industrial Estates*. Glencoe, Ill.: Free Press.

Brown, L. A. (1970), On the Use of Markov Chains in Movement Research, *Economic Geography*, *60 (Supplement)*, 393–403.

Cameron, G. C. and Johnson, K. M. (1969), Comprehensive Urban Renewal and Industrial Relocation—the Glasgow Case, in Cullingworth, J. B. and Orr, S. C., (eds.), *Regional and Urban Studies*. London: Allen and Unwin.

Chinitz, B. (1960), *Freight and the Metropolis*. Cambridge, Mass.: Harvard University Press.

Chinitz, B. (1961), Contrasts in Agglomeration: New York and Pittsburgh, *American Economic Review*, **51**, 279–289.

Clark, C. (1967), *Population Growth and Land Use*. London: Macmillan.

Collins, L. (1972), *Industrial Migration in Ontario:* Ottawa: Statistics Canada.

Compton, P. A. (1969), Internal Migration and Population Change in Hungary between 1959 and 1965, *Transactions, Institute of British Geographers*, **47**, 111–130.

Davidson, R. N. (1970), The Pattern of Employment Densities in Glasgow, *Urban Studies*, **7**, 69–75.

Diamond, D. R. (1962), The Central Business District of Glasgow, in Norberg, K. (ed.), *Proceedings of the IGU Symposium in Urban Geography*. Lund: Gleerup.

Firn, J. (1970), The Glasgow University Register of Manufacturing Establishments in the Central Clydeside Conurbation, Glasgow: University of Glasgow, Mimeographed.

Goldberg, M. J. (1970), An Economic Model of Intrametropolitan Industrial Location, *Journal of Regional Science*, **10**, 75–80.

Hague, D. C. and Dunning, J. H. (1954), Costs in Alternative Locations: the Radio Industry, *Review of Economic Studies*, **22**, 203–213.

Hague, D. C. and Newman, P. C. (1952), *Costs in Alternative Locations: the Clothing Industry*. N.I.E.S.R. Occasional Papers No. 15, Cambridge University Press.

Hall, M. E. (ed.) (1959), *Made in New York*. Cambridge, Mass.: Harvard University Press.

Hamilton, F. E. I. (1967), Models of Industrial Location, in Chorley, R. J. and Haggett, P. (eds.), *Models in Geography*. London: Methuen, 361–424.

Hart, P. M. and Prais, S. J. (1956), The Analysis of Business Concentration: a Statistical Approach, *Journal, Royal Statistical Society*, Series A, **119**, 150–175.

Harvey, D. W. (1967), Models of the Evolution of Spatial Patterns in Human Geography in Chorley, R. J. and Haggett, P. (eds.), *Models in Geography*. London: Methuen, 547–608.

Hoover, E. M. and Vernon, R. (1959), *Anatomy of a Metropolis*. Cambridge, Mass.: Harvard University Press.

Keeble, D. E. (1968), Industrial Decentralization and the Metropolis: the North-West London Case, *Transactions, Institute British Geographers*, **44**, 1–54.

Keeble, D. E. (1969), Local Industrial Linkage and Manufacturing Growth in Outer London, *Town Planning Review*, **40**, 163–188.

Kemeny, J. G. and Snell, J. L. (1960), *Finite Markov Chains*. Princeton, N.J.: Van Nostrand.

Kemeny, J. G. and Snell, J. L. (1962), *Mathematical Models in the Social Sciences*. Englewood Cliffs, N.J.: Prentice-Hall.

Knos, D. (1962), *Distribution of Land Values in Topeka, Kansas*. Lawrence, Kansas: Centre for Research in Business, University of Kansas.

Lever, W. F. (1972a), The Intraurban Movement of Manufacturing: a Markov Approach, *Transactions, Institute British Geographers*, **56**, 21–38.

Lever, W. F. (1972b), Industrial Movement, Spatial Association and Functional Linkages, *Regional Studies*, **6**, 371–384.

Lever, W. F. (1973a), Industrial and Office Location: Land Values, Unpublished Paper Prepared for the Conference on the Property Market, April 1973, University of York.

Lever, W. F. (Forthcoming a), Manufacturing Linkages and the Search for Suppliers and Markets, in Hamilton, F. E. I. (ed.), *Locational Decisions and the Industrial Firm*. London: Wiley.

324

Lever, W. F. (Forthcoming b), A Markov Approach to the Optimal Size of Cities in England and Wales, *Urban Studies*, **10.**

Logan, M. I. (1966), Locational Behavior of Manufacturing Firms in Urban Areas, *Annals, Association of American Geographers*, **56,** 451–466.

Luttrell, W. F. (1962), *Factory Location and Industrial Movement.* 2 Vols. London: N.I.E.S.R.

Mackay, D. I. *et al.* (1971), *Labour Markets under Different Employment Conditions.* London: Allen and Unwin.

Moses, L. N. (1958), Location and the theory of Production, *Quarterly Journal of Economics*, **72,** 259–272.

Moses, L. N. and Williamson, H. F. (1967), The Location of Economic Activity in Cities, *American Economic Review*, **57,** 211–222.

National Building Agency (1968), *Land Costs and Housing Development.* London: N.B.A.

Norcliffe, G. B. (1970), Industrial Location Dynamics, unpublished Ph.D. thesis, University of Bristol.

Nourse, H. O. (1968), *Regional Economics.* New York: McGraw-Hill.

Pred, A. R. (1966), *The Spatial Dynamics of U.S. Urban–Industrial Growth, 1800–1914.* Cambridge, Mass.: M.I.T. Press.

Rees, A. and Shultz, G. P. (1970), *Workers and Wages in an Urban Labor Market.* University of Chicago Press.

Richardson, H. W. (1969), *Elements of Regional Economics.* Harmondsworth: Penguin.

Richter, C. E. (1969), The Impact of Industrial Linkages on Geographical Association, *Journal of Regional Science*, **9,** 19–28.

Segal, M. (1960), *Wages in the Metropolis.* Cambridge, Mass: Harvard University Press.

Simon, H. A. (1957), *Models of Man.* New York: Wiley.

Smith, Barbara M. D. (1971), Industrial Movement and Location in the West Midlands, University of Birmingham: Centre for Urban and Regional Studies, Mimeographed.

Smith, D. M. (1971), *Industrial Location: An Economic Geographical Analysis.* New York: Wiley.

South East Joint Planning Team (1971), *Strategic Plan for the South East, Studies Vol. 1 (Population and Employment).* London: H.M.S.O.

Stone, P. A. (1970), *Urban Development in Britain: Standards Costs and Resources, Vol. 1, Population Trends and Housing.* Cambridge University Press.

Streit, M. E. (1969), Spatial Associations and Economic Linkages between Industries, *Journal of Regional Science* **9,** 177–188.

Taylor, M. J. (1971), Spatial Linkage and the West Midlands Ironfounding Industry, unpublished Ph.D. thesis, University of London.

Townroe, P. M. (1970), Industrial Linkage, Agglomeration and External Economies, *Journal, Town Planning Institute.* **56,** 18–20.

Townroe, P. M. (1971), *Industrial Location Decisions: A Study in Management Behavior.* Occasional Paper No. 15, Birmingham: University of Birmingham, Centre for Urban and Regional Studies.

Tulpule, A. H. (1969), Dispersion of Industrial Employment in the Greater London area, *Regional Studies*, **3,** 25–40.

Vernon, R. (1960), *Metropolis, 1985.* Cambridge, Mass.: Harvard University Press.

West Midland Regional Study (1971), *A Developing Strategy for the West Midlands, Technical Appendix 3, Economic Study 3 (Industrial Mobility).* Birmingham: West Midland Regional Study.

12 *Implications of Corporate Strategies and Product Cycle Adjustments for Regional Employment Changes*

GUNTER KRUMME AND ROGER HAYTER

Social scientists have found it traditionally hard to build meaningful bridges between aggregate, macro-scopic concepts and analyses on the one hand, and disaggregated, micro-scopic, behaviouristic methods of research on the other. Seldom is aggregate analysis designed to allow a descension to the level of the individual actor; similarly, behavioural studies seldom go beyond accepting the conditions set by an aggregate environment to an investigation of the mechanisms by which individuals and organizations alter these constraints. In economics, highly homogenous units 'move in more or less given technological and market conditions and try to improve their economic lot *within the constraints of these conditions*' (Rothschild, 1971, p. 7). In spatial economic and location theory, the firm or corporation is equally considered as the abstract 'black box' of production and price theory characterized by Machlup as a 'mental construct' and merely a 'theoretical link helping to explain how one gets from the cause to the effect' (Machlup, 1967, p. 9). As such, the firm's move is supposed to explain prices and locations as automatic outcomes of specific changes in exogenous, environmental conditions and *not* individual behaviour or adjustment strategies, or the influence of accumulated know-how, diversification of product mix or geographic distribution, or, more generally, the influence of size, flexibility and power by which corporations try to alter competitive processes and the constraints of 'equal' conditions. Clearly, within small aggregates, such as within the population of industrial firms in a metropolitan area, heterogenous corporate behaviour and unequal size, power and innovative conditions may be the key element in the explanation of aggregate, regional development patterns.

In general, it is hardly surprising that regional development theorists are still highly unsatisfied with the state of the art claiming, for example, in John Friedmann's (1972, p. 82) words that 'the link between the location of economic activities (microtheory) and the development of a system of regions (macrotheory) is not clearly established'. In fact, regional development problems have in the past been largely disscussed on the macro-level. Frequently, difficulties arose in attempts to reduce the scale of basically national economic concepts and to accommodate the open characteristics of regions and the interaction between a larger number of economic and non-economic variables relevant for explaining economic change in smaller regional aggregates (cf. Lasuen, 1971, p. 171). Increasingly, however, scholars point out the need for more micro-scopic approaches to regional development phenomena as is reflected in Hägerstrand's statement that 'nothing truly general can be said about aggregate regularities until it has been made clear how far they remain invariant with organizational differences at the micro-level' (Hägerstrand, 1970, p. 8). This essay is designed to discuss in a qualitative, non-rigorous fashion a few areas in which micro- and macro-aspects overlap or where the injection of behavioural and organizational considerations is a *sine qua non* for the understanding of the locational dynamics of regional industrial change.

12.1. Structural Change

It has been generally recognized that changes in the structure of the economy represent a prerequisite for, as well as a result of, economic growth processes (Fisher, 1939; Clark, 1940; Fourastié, 1951). Here, 'structure' is defined as a 'set of constant reaction coefficients' which translate external impulses into effects upon economic activities (Machlup, 1958). However, in spite of the extensive literature on the subject of 'structure' and 'structural change', there is very little known about the process which underlies structural change or about criteria which could be used to assess, for example, more or less optimal industrial structures of regions from the point of view of an interregional division of labour.

The motor behind shifts within the (e.g., employment) structure of an economy can be found either on the demand or the supply side—assuming that government influences also work through these channels. Differential development of demand for certain types of goods and services has been traced to such phenomena as *substitution* (between old and new products for a given type of use), physiological *saturation* and, more generally, diminishing marginal utilities (Kneschaurek, 1964, p. 724f.) and has been frequently associated with the empirical work of Engel (1857).

On the supply side, it is the differentiated willingness, ability or pressure to increase productivities, particularly labour productivity, among sectors, industries, regions and firms which, *via* comparative cost reductions, income increases and demand elasticities, result in differentiated patterns of growth, stagnation and decline. Following Baumol (1967, p. 415f.), activities could be broadly classified as either belonging to (a) the technologically progressive ones in which innovation, capital accumulation and scale economies result in cumulative increases in output per man hour, or to (b) those activities which achieve only sporadic productivity increases. Baumol identifies as the major source for differentiation the role which technology assigns to labour. As such, labour represents either a mere instrument for the attainment of the final product or it approaches the role of an end product in itself (such as in the form of the service of a psychiatrist).

Extending the concept of a 'progressive' activity to the regional level and possibly to a less long-run temporal horizon, one would have to soften the technological determinism implied by Baumol and include behavioural and organizational considerations. It seems unreasonable to expect that firms are equally adaptable and follow identical patterns of locating production activities, scouting for new ideas, recognizing potentially prevalent technologies, innovating their own developments, imitating unavoidable progress, and dropping less promising ideas, products, and locations at different stages of their development. Thus, it has been hypothesized, for example, that young firms have little experience in identifying important problems and tend to overestimate instability in their environment, while older firms have created appropriate mechanisms for recognizing and attending to important needs for adaptation (Starbuck, 1965).

One of the most important yet least understood structural tendencies in the industrial sector is the increasing significance of activities which operate in highly 'turbulent environments'. For individual organizations, this tendency is reflected by a gross increase in their 'relevant uncertainty' leading to a variety of organizational adjustments (Emery and Trist, 1965; Steed, 1971). Emery and Trist have traced the emergence of this turbulence to three sets of forces originating in (a) the increasing unpredictability of market developments and competitive responses, (b) the deepening interdependence between economic organizations on the one hand and social and political institutions on the other and (c) the increasing reliance on Research and Development (R & D) activities to gain control over uncertain environments.

Products produced in this expanding sector with its turbulent environment notably space gear, aircrafts, and high-powered computers and their component parts are highly disassociated from direct consumer needs. Due to long R & D lead times and rapid technological change, their future use is often uncertain and speculative. Additional demand instability is based on the capital good characteristics of the products or the political nature of their demand. Frequently, government financed R & D activities require a longer 'lead' than any one government is in office, possibly leading to abrupt discontinuation of projects financed for reasons of political prestige or differently perceived national security needs. Labour and capital goods used for R & D and production activities of these products have generally long development lead periods themselves (e.g., education) and relatively low substitutability for other uses, thus constituting considerable investment risks for corporations and individuals (Kitching, 1972). To avoid rapid depreciation of such highly specialized factors of production due to (a) loss of value during successive stages of research, development and production activities; (b) cancellation or diminished demand; and (c) technological change, projects of similar magnitude and characteristics have to follow in rapid succession leading, in turn, to additional scale economies, large plant sizes, and possibly locally aggravated instability.

Attempts to identify empirically some typical processes leading to, resulting from, or coinciding with employment shifts between aggregate sectors of the economy have led to some desirable disaggregation into sector components, namely, groups of industries, individual branches of industries, groups of products, and firms. Unfortunately, the clarity of the discussion and the interpretation of empirical findings have suffered from the still existing lack of criteria for meaningful or at least consistent disaggregation and definition of an 'industry' or 'product'. Thus, Hoffmann's (1958) 'law', for example, stating very specific characteristics of the relative decline of consumer goods industries in favour of production and capital goods industries has been critically questioned by a number of researchers who, by checking Hoffmann's classification of industries by means of input–output analysis, found that he had inaccurately allocated too many industries (particularly the chemical industry) to the production goods sector thereby inflating his findings (Kuznets, 1967, p. 141f; Lago, 1969). Similarly, Bela Gold was able to disprove Arthur Burns' generalization that 'an industry tends to grow at a declining rate, its rise being eventually followed by a decline' (Burns, 1934, pp. 170–173; Gold, 1964) simply by extending Burns' time series over a longer period of time. Gold suggests that instead of using aggregate industries with variable combinations of products, products themselves may be a more fruitful focus of 'micro growth theories' warning, however, that in spite of 'intuitive urgings to the contrary' single product series do not widely support Burns' expectations either (Gold, 1964, p. 64; Thomas, 1972).

One would have to add to Gold's statement that, on the regional level, any particular industry may have a unique product mix and that a specific organization which possibly could operate in more than one industry or more than one region may play a very significant role within the region's total economic base. Thus, any simplistic analysis may lead to still more confusion on the regional level and it seems appropriate to analyze the role of at least certain types of products and the significance of their life patterns for regional development in the context of their embeddedness within corporate organizations rather than aggregate industrial categories classified purely for statistical purposes (Krumme, 1966, p. 277).

Regional and Organizational Systems

In any study of economic change in relatively small and open regions we encounter the problem of having to deal with a variety of ties and functional relationships which components of the region maintain with other regions. Many of these ties are trade and communication flows between independent organizational units and, thus, represent 'external' environmental relations for the organization as well as for the region. Market, location and comparative cost principles assist in accounting for many of these interregional interdependencies. However, many, and it seems an increasing number of, other ties and flows which cross regional boundaries represent internal relationships and exchanges of other subsystems of the national or global economy. These other systems which cut across regional or local boundaries may be temporary or permanent organizations or formal or informal arrangements involving subsidiaries, branch plants, subcontractors, and partners in joint ventures of industrial corporations, all held together by legal contracts, systems of threats, power, control, and commitments or by technological dependence and the need for information and know-how. For such organizations, the existence of regional boundaries and local economic concerns may be almost incidental, and the regional and local economic planner may merely be a 'provincial trouble-maker'.

Corporate and Regional Planning

In addition to their differences in goals and organizational structure, regional and corporate planners face different spatial constraints imposed upon their selection of planning strategies. For the regional planner and policy maker, the restrictions resulting from the existence of established regional boundaries often lead to an overemphasis of intra-regional location considerations and relationships and a neglect of the characteristics of the region as an open system. Thus, the planning and policy emphasis on *physical* location, for example, institutionalized in part by the property tax system, neglects the firm's location within a network of economic, social, and ecological relationships inside and across regional boundaries. From this point of view, a specific economic activity located outside an established planning region may be vital and beneficial to the region's well-being, possibly *because* it is located outside the region. The search for new or specific resources needed in the region, the scanning for potential new firms, technologies or products cannot be accomplished only by focusing on specific places or regions (Leven, 1966, p. 91f.). The prevalent planning orientation toward direct employment and tax revenue effects, often representing justified short-run planning targets, may nevertheless barricade the path toward a more efficient interregional distribution of linked industries. Similarly, the problem of the national planner who tries to regionalize economic growth 'does not seem solvable if (he) begins with a focus on the individual region' (Lasuen, 1971, p. 170).

The corporate planner, on the other hand, tends to exploit the spatial constraints of regional authorities utilizing his own intra-corporate, interregional mobility of capital, know-how, personnel, and economic power derived from the size, diversity and status of his national and international activities, possibly neglecting regional concerns about a socially desirable utilization of resources.

'The Seattle-based Boeing Company recently threatened to move part of its newly organized "Boeing Computer Service, Inc." out of the state, after the Governor had vetoed a legislative bill that would have exempted the firm from $1·2 million in business and occupation taxes. An executive was quoted to say, "... the tax environment for expansion in other states is more favorable than anything we see in Washington . . . this veto will not result in any new revenues for the state, because B.C.S. will be reorganized to eliminate this unfair penalty." ' (*Seattle Times*, 1971a.).

The flexibility, fluidity and bargaining power of multi-regional corporations then tends to cause regional authorities to concentrate their regulative and revenue-generating energies unduly on those activities which lack this spatial flexibility or make concessions to those which possess it. In most Western countries, corporate power has been subjected to certain restrictions. Anti-trust legislation, however, differs widely between countries and is generally limited to the undesirable domination of output markets, measured on the national rather than regional level.

'IBM's 70% share of the US computer market has long been a thorn in the eyes of Justice Department lawyers. Most recently, they asked that the corporation be broken up into an unspecified number of "independent and competitively balanced entities." However, in addition to IBM's well developed political connections, "the sheer size and complexity of IBM and the computer industry pose a formidable challenge to the Government's legal resources." ' (*Time*, 1972.).

Specialized, technology-oriented corporations like IBM are in a strong position to extend their influence and power derived from their position on the markets for their outputs to other spheres, particularly the market for highly skilled and specialized labour. The IBM situation may have been an extreme example where employees were asked to 'cut their hair, wear a certain dress, or sit in a certain chair' (Reich, 1971. p. 121). But here, as well as, for example, in parts of the aerospace industry, the almost monopolistic control of the labour market for skilled personnel is real and reinforced by the experience of the few who, after leaving IBM for one of the few much smaller competitors (for example, RCA), are laid off due to the termination of the specialized division, or due to the unpredictable failure of the company to win an expected government contract. The inter-corporate mobility of highly skilled employees can be further impaired by their 'personal' possession of protected corporate know-how:

'In its suit against Memorex, a competitor who allegedly employed almost 200 ex-IBM men, IBM charged that trade secrets from these employees were being used competitively against IBM and asked that Memorex be enjoined for 2–1/2 years from marketing certain products made with these trade secrets.' (*Wall Street Journal*, 1971a).

Power exerted by corporations on the local and regional level, particularly on land and labour markets, is constrained by few and ill-coordinated checks. In fact, translating Galbraith's (1967) thesis about the role of the technostructure and the military-industrial complex into a spatial, interregional context, his arguments become stronger and more concrete: the technostructure is increasingly extending its influence *beyond* its 'state-within-the-state' status. Important implications of economic concentration evade the regulating influence of local, state and national governments without an equal reduction of corporate influence on those respective levels (Krumme, 1970, p. 318).

'In Hanover, Germany, IBM announced in July 1971 that it would not build its long-planned plant for semi-conductors which was supposed to have employed 5,000 highly qualified workers and engineers. The city of Hanover, hoping for a decisive improvement of its industrial structure, had already made considerable concessions to IBM including the costly relocation of the city's famous horse race track in order to free the site for IBM's plant. As a reason for the breach in contract IBM merely stated that due to technological change it preferred to expand existing plants rather than build a new one.' (FAZ, 1971).

Clearly, a local plant's status within a corporate system affects the economic structure of the region and as such not merely the region's growth and development potential but also its sensitivity to economic recessions. General employment 'cut-backs' tend to be very unevenly distributed among individual plants of multi-plant corporations. Often the opportunity is used to close plants which are marginal, possibly, however, only from an intra-corporate point of view (Gerlach and Liepmann, 1972). At times, neither employees nor regional planning authorities are notified of impending closures in advance, nor are serious attempts made to sell such plants to competitive corporations with a more suitable spatial or organizational structure or a more appropriate 'temporal composition' of their product mix.

In industries with comparatively mobile and short-lived capital goods (such as the clothing industry), the only function of such marginal plants may have been to accommodate temporary peak production during a preceding economic boom or a period of overlapping product-cycle stages. While corporations tend to store 'matter-energy inputs' (such as alternative products) in anticipation of such stress situations, they will tend to limit such preparation to areas where alternative adjustments (closure, layoff) are impossible or costly during a recession or slack season, on the one hand, or during periods of peak demand, on the other (Miller, 1972, p. 96).

Thus, the short-notice hiring and firing of personnel is a particularly popular adjustment method in the United States where employees are comparatively unprotected in their status as members of a corporate system.

'In 1971, when RCA terminated its computer production, thousands of employees were laid off with a few days notice, many of them having either just been transferred to new facilities in Marlboro (Mass.) from other RCA locations, or persuaded to leave their jobs with other computer corporations.' (Wall Street Journal, 1971b).

The growth of plants can be equally abrupt in the large-multi-product and multi-plant corporation able to shift resources more or less at will or raise external capital at short notice due to its relatively wide range of locational and technological alternatives, a diversified stock of human and capital resources, and an extensive field of external contracts. Any organizational re-arrangement, any rebundling of knowledge, people, and materials at different or new locations for new or old but manipulated projects may involve very drastic changes in the status, production objectives and characteristics, employment composition and growth potential for the individual plant and, via a variety of linkage effects, for the local community and the regional environment. These qualitative and quantitative changes may, in many ways, be 'abnormal' or 'out of proportion' relative to the size and importance of the individual plant or relative to the change attainable at the level of the firm.

In the past, there has been comparatively little concern about the negative repercussions which too rapid change, particularly rapid growth imposes upon the community, its fiscal and environmental budget and its planning efforts. It appears now that, even in the United States, industrial corporations are being forced to recognize certain social and environmental constraints and have lost part of their traditional freedom to expand, contract or change their local employment demands without regard to the social and economic repercussions. Society, *via* political authorities at local, regional and national levels, is gradually beginning to encourage a broadening of the concept of social responsibility to encompass not merely tax deductible contributions to local charity and social activities but also the incorporation of 'welfare' criteria into corporate decision-making and planning (Stabler, 1971). The effects of adjustments of existing productive capacities with respect to production technology, range and characteristics of the product mix, and the stages of a product life cycle performed at any one plant are widely dispersed. Although the abandonment of a product line, for example, does in large corporations generally not lead to the closure of the plant but merely to the replacement of the product (Berry, 1967, p. 419), it does affect many of the plant's external relations, particularly in terms of 'the firm's responsibility to its employees, its customers, its suppliers and the communities in which it operates' (Berenson, 1971, p. 217).

Regional and Corporate Product Cycles

The corporate as well as the regional system maintains the structure of its roles and functions within a flow of continuously changing components: the regional population and industrial employment are subject to demographic cycles, in- and out-migration, intra-regional occupational mobility, and reorganization of the population of firms and plants. The corporate system survives by regenerating employment, reallocating capital and other resources, and rejuvenating technological and organizational know-how, industrial processes, and final products, adjusting them to changes in internal and external requirements, in short, by arresting and counteracting a variety of entropic processes (Katz, 1966). In the search for regularities in the evolution of corporate environments, the concept of product life cycle has been related to the interplay of changes in technology and market demand. Products pass through a variety of stages, from post-invention stages (innovation, imitation) *via* early production stages to stages of maturity (mass production), market saturation and decline, at each phase entering into specific and symptomatic exchange relationships with the environment. The way in which individual industrial corporations or specific regions participate along the path of such 'global' product cycles will depend on the organizational and spatial locale of the innovation and the characteristics of the diffusion process. The course of a product cycle in any one corporation, for example, can be described by its changing impact on one region or a system of regions, i.e., in terms of input–output linkages, skill requirements, or income and quantitative employment multipliers. In this context, it has been postulated that skill requirements tend to decrease in the course of a product life cycle due to the gradual increase in the application of proven, automated production and routine management and marketing techniques (Hirsch, 1967, Ch. 2).

> 'For the Boeing Company, "average employment during 1968 varied little in numbers from the previous years ... There were, however, changes in the composition of the work force. As tooling was completed on major products, there was a shift to greater requirements for production skills." ' (Boeing, 1968, p. 29).

A regional skill niveau and relative per-capita income can, in turn, and, *ceteris paribus*, be maintained only by a more or less continuous introduction of new products and technologies.

Briefly, then, the following region-product relationships can be identified:

(1) A product passes through all stages within any one region, i.e., the regional factors of production adjust to the changing requirements of the product cycle.

    (a) There is the mono-product region which is faced with factor adjustment frictions, potential structural deterioration and absolute decline unless adjustments are made in due time.

    (b) At the other end of the spectrum, there is the well-diversified multi-product region which, at any one point in time, is able to distribute its capital and human resources optimally among the different product stages of different products.

(2) A product changes its regional environment while passing through different stages, a situation which corresponds to the individual region specializing in a specific stage of product life cycles for many products (for example, localities in California or Massachusetts specializing in innovative R. & D activities or various depressed rural areas attracting low-skill, labour intensive assembly work for 'mature' consumer goods).

12.2. Products: Missions, Roles, Strategies, and Life Cycles

The product concept as used in this paper shall be distinguished from that of the familiar abstract commodity-type 'product' of price and production theory. While the latter appears to be mainly defined in terms of its physical attributes, the 'product' is interpreted here as a more complex phenomenon, emphasizing its functions or missions, its alternative uses, its market status, its ties to competitive and complementary products, its technology and technological spillovers to product 'derivatives' or subsequent product developments, its backward linkages to inputs, know-how and investments, and last but not least, its roles within industrial corporations and regions.

In micro-economic theory, the product as a variable has more or less shared the fate of space as a dimensional phenomenon at the periphery of price competition. Chamberlin has been one of the few who have discussed the problem of product determination and the relationships between products which would best satisfy customers' preferences and those actually offered: 'The economic problem of "products", like that of prices, is simply to discover and elaborate the principles that determine which of the many potential products (prices) become, or tend to become, actual' (Chamberlin, 1953, p. 12). Extensively discussing various analogies between product and spatial competition à la Hotelling, Chamberlin also turns to new products: 'Thus in a world whose technology is constantly creating new products, it should not be surprising to find that a part of the whole process is the deterioration of other products in order to make room for the new ones at the mass level where the population is concentrated.' (Chamberlin, 1953, p. 23).

Products perform 'missions' through their potential or actual uses as final consumption goods, investment goods, or as components of such goods in addition to some more specialized uses such as those of the military. Any one product may have a variety of uses at any one point in time or through time. Frequently, products are initially developed for a specific purpose which is supplemented or replaced by other uses as specific characteristics of the product emerge during its development, as the information about such characteristics spreads, or as the cost of production sufficiently declines to make different uses feasible. In a spatial sense, distinction has been made between products with 'mondial', 'continental', 'national', 'regional' and 'local' missions either in terms of the product's direct markets or in terms of their final demand markets taking their indirect, forward linkages into account (Tinbergen, 1965; Sakai, 1972).

Supposedly, products result from needs or technical possibilities perceived by manufacturers or powerful customers, are then designed or developed, efficiently produced and channelled to the customer to fulfil the identified mission (Johnson, 1963, p. 120). Such a mission may consist of satisfying some consumer demand or of filling some gap in the retaliatory defense shield of a nation. In addition to this initial mission and subsequent uses of the product, there are other roles which a product may perform once it is perceived, designed and allocated to specific production facilities, once workers have been hired and subcontractors selected and once the product is in use and performs its mission in a more or less adequate way. In fact, there are as many roles as there are private and public plans which are affected by the development, production and use of the product. These may be the plans or budgets of individual households, manufacturing firms, service and financing activities, regional planning agencies, labour unions and governments. To whatever extent, the idea of a potential product or the product itself may create expectations as to its performance, its impact on competing products, its direct and indirect environmental and employment repercussions, and thus may cause changes in plans and initiate a variety of economic, social and political commitments, many of them with a locational or regional dimension.

'The fact that large portions of a metropolitan population can identify with a single, admittedly not minor, product was demonstrated by a civic bumper-sticker campaign

("SST—Seattle Stands Tall") before and after the Senate withdrawal of project funding for the Supersonic transport plane from the Boeing Company in Seattle.'

Clearly, the production and diffusion of such relatively recent inventions or developments as the rotary-type Wankel engine, the radial tyre, the PAL colour television system, the vertical take-off plane or the Concorde are not merely conditioned (i.e., encouraged, delayed or terminated) by the expected mission performance but, in addition, by the products' many roles and more or less powerful lobbies which pave or barricade their development and life cycle paths.

The Lockheed Company's serious financial problems in 1971 caused in part by the heavy financial engagements in the development of the Tristar Airbus were 'solved' by the US Government's loan guarantee for an additional $250 million credit. In its 'anatomy' of the crucial US Senate vote, the Wall Street Journal pointed out:

'On an economic issue that will have a direct plus or minus impact back home, a Senator naturally votes the interest of the folks who elected him. Thus California's two liberal Democratic Senators . . . voted for Lockheed. So did (the) Senators . . . of Georgia, another state where Lockheed employment is large. A Senator from Washington State who was running for president leaned toward opposing the bill, because Lockheed is a competitor of Boeing Co., his own state's biggest employer . . . Lockheed has thousands of subcontractors, and many of them are sufficiently large so that the effect of a Lockheed failure would give a Senator pause. Avco Corp., for example, has a big contract to build wing assemblies for Lockheed's Tristar Airbus in Nashville. Not surprisingly, Tennessee's two . . . Senators voted for the measure . . . General Electric, whose plant that makes aircraft engine parts (for the Tristar's competitors) in Albuquerque gives it some clout in little-industrialized New Mexico, snatched that state's two Senators . . . out of the Lockheed column. . . .' (Zimmerman, 1971).

Whether the implications of this 'anatomy' are totally justified or not, it does point out that governments may not always be entirely mission-oriented in their motivation when deciding on or influencing product developments (see also Melman, 1970, p. 175).

Moreover, there is no reason to believe that within large, possibly highly decentralized organizations such as governments or multi-divisional industrial corporations, there is a clearly articulated understanding about the actual mission of the product, either in terms of corporate goals or in terms of eventual use of the product. After one gives up the assumption of the corporation being an 'organism single-mindedly devoted to maximizing profits' and accepts it as a 'group of cooperating semi-independent forces with distinguishably different goals . . . each will resist having its own functions cut back or obliterated in the interest of the firm as a whole' (Vernon, 1969, p. 115f.), one may expect differences in the identification of a product mission or in the definition of design and performance standards or in the setting of overall priorities to develop between departments which are responsible for different product-related functions or which are competing for scarce resources in the corporation.

Product Spaces and Corporate Strategies

For purposes of differentiating spatially significant elements of corporate strategies, such as strategies of expansion, vertical integration, diversification, or consolidation, the distinction between spatial or locational adjustments and adjustments of primarily non-spatial parameters *at given* locations has been frequently used in discussions of corporate geography and locational decision-making (Stafford, 1969, p. 142f.; Krumme, 1966, p. 28f.). Relocation decisions and decisions to locate new establishments belong to the first group and are, at the same time, generally rather long term decisions, while quantitative and qualitative capacity adjustments, not directly involving location decisions *per se*, exemplify short- or medium-run in-site decisions (Krumme, 1969). In such cases, the comparative attributes of a given location will have an impact on the determination of optimal or satisfactory levels of production, product mix, production processes and inputs (Dicken, 1971, p. 427).

The distinction appears blurred, however, whenever decisions include spatial and non-spatial aspects as is unavoidably the case in multi-plant, multi-regional, and multi-product industrial corporations. Here, the decision to restructure or diversify the production programme, or enter the next stage of the development path of a particular product, generally also implies the locationally discriminating decision to convert, expand, or reduce existing capacities at specific locations within the corporate organization.

The use of product or location related action parameters can be assumed to be embedded within the general corporate growth or development strategy and, thus, be triggered by the reaching of critical thresholds of growth rates (sales) or profitability. In the definition of such control points, the firm will have to consider the lead times for new product developments or the construction and tooling of new capacities presumably differing for old vis-à-vis new and unfamiliar locations or types of products. Unavoidable uncertainty about the success of R & D activities or about the emerging qualities of a new location and the market potential for the new products and capacities will additionally influence the identification of such thresholds (Albach, 1965, p. 58ff.).

Large and/or multi-plant locations are often able to reduce the effective time horizon implied by locational commitments or new product decisions. They may be in the position to shift capacity increments between existing locations, to finance facilities at new locations out of current depreciations, to charge current development costs for new products against current rather than future earnings, or to strive for maximum economies of plant specialization while, at the same time, effectively diversify overall corporate activities. Thus, such corporations may be able to maintain a diversified locational structure, a wide range of products, and a smooth distribution of products along their respective life cycles. Any new location or new product decision possibly represents a major strategic step for a relatively small firm but only an incremental affair for the large corporation in relation to its total product mix or total corporate assets.

Product Strategies

Following Ansoff (1963) there are four basic product related strategies available to the entrepreneur. These strategies are differentiated by their reference to (a) products and (b) missions and markets.

(1) *Market penetration* represents a strategy to increase sales of a present product 'at home or abroad' without changes in the product or its mission. Thus, either the penetration will 'deepen' the product's use in present geographical markets or the markets will be geographically extended. Wood-roofe (1968) an executive officer of Unilever, points out that:

'Today, the advantages of geographic expansion are only too obvious. Many national markets throughout the world are becoming similar as trade flows across frontiers and as consumer tastes move towards a common pattern ... geographic expansion helps to cover the calculated risk which lurks in every research project ... some products can be truly international as Sunlight soap was, and still is, while others need to be tailored to national tastes. . . .' (p. 180).

(2) *Market development* refers to the search for new missions of an existing product or product line (usually with some alterations of the product adapting to new missions). These new missions may be sought in new or already established geographic markets. Under the pressure of increasing competition, threatening market saturation and a flattening out of the corporate sales curve for the particular product, the firm may encroach upon sales-acceleration or life extension policies which may involve attempts to tune the product specification more precisely to the customers' procurement specifications. Further analysis may necessitate a disaggregation of the 'product' into components and attributes in order to specify the life patterns of the latter. Certain aspects of products may be 'sticky', i.e., they do not change over a long period of time, possibly the total length of the product's life, whereas other characteristics are frequently 'unfrozen' and adapted due to technological improvements or due to the fact that competitive pressures have zeroed in on such specific characteristics while creating rigidities in the variability of other product attributes (Chamberlin, 1953, p. 12f.). The many commercial airplane derivatives ('stretch', 'quick-change', 'all-cargo', 'wide-body-look', etc.) offered to airlines a short time after the first introduction of the initial model are appropriate examples. An additional impetus for product differentiation seems to have emerged from the geographical widening of markets by multi-regional and particularly by multi-national firms faced with a demand which is less homogenous—even for their mature products—and can be less easily manipulated than the demand in domestic markets. This additional demand therefore imposes more constraints upon the freedom of the entrepreneur to design his products solely on the basis of technological and mass production requirements (Rosenberg, 1972, p. 49f.).

(3) *A product development* strategy assumes that the firm identifies with a given mission and tries to develop new products with different and improving characteristics. Since the characteristics of the mission may change through

338

time due to general structural change in the environment, the product's characteristics and performance may have to adjust to this change. Mission requirement may also vary between geographic markets.

(4) *Diversification*, according to Ansoff (1963, p. 312), is characterized by the 'simultaneous departure from the present product line and the present market structure'. Thus, a firm 'diversifies its productive activities whenever, without entirely abandoning its old lines of product, it embarks upon the production of new products, including intermediate products, which are sufficiently different from the other products it produces to imply some significant difference in the firm's production and distribution programmes' (Penrose, 1959, p. 108f.). In general it seems that, although primarily market oriented, diversification strategies would tend to require major organizational adjustments, new know-how and skills, and possibly new facilities and locations, particularly if the strategic change is not just an incremental one. Typically, the diversification of the product mix will be accompanied by a diversification of research activities. Although efforts will be made to exploit to the utmost the existing scientific know-how, additional expertise may have to be acquired for the new products which may feed back beneficially to the older areas, draw in new scientific disciplines and may more generally contribute to the development of 'a whole complex of scientific know-how for the variety of product areas' (Woodroofe, 1968, p. 181).

The following local and regional environmental factors have been listed as particularly significant for the development of new, science-based products (US Dept. of Commerce, 1967a, p. 37f.): (a) the availability of capital being critical at all stages of the innovative process; (b) the availability of sufficiently skilled labour willing and capable to adapt to new technology; (c) the presence of administrative and entrepreneurial skills; (d) a relative lack of market or technological uncertainties or constraints imposed by powerful customers; (e) the ability to obtain the cooperation of interested or affected groups, such as labour unions; (f) existence of a sufficiently large market.

Most of these conditions change in their relative significance during the 'incubation' period. These relative shifts in external requirements which the product's life cycle imposes on its environment inside and outside the firm continue during succeeding stages, i.e., once the product is being produced and has been introduced into the market place. In other words, labour and other input requirements as well as production processes, the locational and organizational pattern of production, marketing strategies and markets tend to change due to a variety of processes inside (learning, internal growth) or outside (market satiation, competitive responses, technological change) the specific organization or region. Thus, a product is positioned in a multi-dimensional product environment which conditions its life path, and which in turn may be affected by it. The extent of the strain imposed upon the local labour market, for example, will depend on the magnitude of the changes in local labour requirements associated with any one product production cycle and on possible adaptive responses related to job mobility or the willingness or ability of employers to counteract negative impacts by spacing the stages for different products in order to minimize local employment reductions other than by attrition or voluntary transfers to other locations (Mansfield, 1968, p. 144). A more positive interpretation would emphasize the propulsive effect of changing product cycle requirements. If certain skills and risk-seeking capital have been assembled in a specific region and are being partially set free periodically, new activities may be attracted to utilize these factors. Since scientists tend to prefer locations which offer a variety of employment opportunities between which they can move with a minimum of inconvenience 'a region or community which has been successful in developing science-based activity finds itself in a stronger competitive position for further development' (US Dept. of Commerce, 1967b, p. 33).

The Product Life Cycle Concept

It appears that the roots of the product life cycle concept have to be traced through an extensive literature in marketing back to an article by Kuznets (1929), although many descriptive references to the life cycle of particular products can be found in earlier writings (see, e.g., Bücher, 1918, p. 125).

In the marketing literature, product life cycle paths have been associated with the changing markets to which products tend to address themselves during their lifetime and the consequences such changes have for the entrepreneur in terms of the need for adjusting product characteristics, changing advertising strategies, exploring new markets and new uses for the product and searching for new products to replace the old (for example, Patton, 1959; Levitt, 1965).

In the more production-oriented sphere, the concept has been used in operations research and project management. Here, it is supposed to provide a better understanding of the 'anatomy and physiology' of R & D projects, particularly with respect to assessing the total length of a project, the technical manpower requirements, and the scheduling of individual tasks for various R & D stages (Norden, 1970, p. 71). As such, recognized regularities in research and development processes permit more accurate estimation of 'expected behaviour' of these and other requirements and a more sensitive monitoring of significant departures from the expected pattern. For the manufacturing of complex areospace or weapon systems, for example, the life-cycle concept is often used as a broad organizing concept encompassing and coordinating more detailed and specific scheduling techniques throughout the life of a project. The initial specification of a weapon-system life cycle, for example, would include (a) the *conceptual stage* for specifying performance characteristics, (b) a *definition stage* for identifying hardware configurations, (c) a *development phase* in which the design, fabrication and testing of prototypes generally represent the major work, (d) the *production operations stage*, and finally, (e) the operation of the system itself lasting until the system is obsolete (Holtz, 1969, p. 318).

The more explanatory research on technological innovation processes dominated by the work of Mansfield (1968, 1971) provides extensive analytical discussions and empirical information about a variety of time, cost and other characteristics of new products as they move between successive research and development stages. The following stages have been used in this context for analytical purposes: (a) applied research, involving experimentation, data collection, and testing of hypotheses primarily by scientific professionals; (b) preparation of project requirements and basic specifications; (c) prototype or pilot-plant design, construction and testing; (d) production planning, tooling, construction, and installation of manufacturing facilities; (e) manufacturing start-up; and (f) marketing start-up (Rapoport, 1971, p. 112ff.).

Finally, and maybe most importantly, we find extensive reference to the product life cycle concept in the more recent literature on international trade and investment, represented mainly by the research of Raymond Vernon and his students, emerging out of attempts to offer another explanation for the 'Leontief Paradox' as it deviates from the Heckscher–Ohlin theory of comparative advantage (Moroney and Walker, 1966; Vernon, 1966). One of the central questions of the research done by the 'Vernon-School' is 'To what extent are the international trade flows of an industry associated with the technological aspects of the industry, and how do these associations vary according to the countries of origin and destination of the trade flows?' (Gruber and Vernon, 1970, p. 235). The specific model which emerged from the ensuing investigations by Hirsch (1967), Stobaugh (1968), Wells (1969), Adler (1970) and others assumes that a product innovation originates in one of the technologically most advanced countries—i.e., the United States for all practical purposes occupying the peak of the technological and economic development pyramid. In the first phase of the product cycle, when communication needs are high and the product is not yet standardized, all production takes place in the high-income, large-market country (United States) which is thus also the only country exporting the product, mainly to second-ranked countries in Europe. It is here where production will begin in the second phase while exports from the US to these countries will decline. In the third phase, the US faces increasing competition in its remaining markets of less developed countries from those newly exporting countries (which may still depend on US know-how and US subsidiaries). With the US being entirely displaced as an exporting country, European countries will begin exporting to the US in the fourth phase, while in the fifth phase, when technology and the product have been sufficiently standardized for the use of low-skill labour the less developed countries will assume total responsibility for production and exports (Wells, 1972).

Earlier literature had already contributed to the explanation of the timing in this sequence of phases. Every step leading to further diffusion of the product's exports and foreign production is conditioned by forces trying to gain maximum benefits for the innovating source by extending foreign markets, forces trying to find successively lower-cost locations for production, and forces trying to stem against the disruptive introduction of new products. These forces then create what Posner (1961) calls 'reaction lags' referring to the time between production in the innovating country and production in an imitating country. The entrepreneurial reaction lag is complemented by a demand related lag which considers the time needed for a new product to be accepted in a new market as a substitute for an older product. The reaction lag consists of three components, namely, the 'foreign reaction lag' (l_1) which measures the time which elapses until the first foreign firm tries to produce the product, the domestic reaction lag (l_2) which covers the periods until other domestic competitors imitate the first, and the learning period (l_3), a technical concept describing the time needed to adapt to the new technology (Findlay, 1970, p. 82). The period (N) over which an innovating exporter can successfully market his new product abroad is, moreover, shortened by the 'demand lag' (λ) which is the period needed for convincing the foreign consumer that the new product is superior to the old one. Thus, the total imitation lag consists of $L = l_1 + l_2 + l_3$ and the net lag after deduction of the demand lag (λ) of $N = L - \lambda$. Posner (1961) formulated his model initially for the intra-national, interregional trade situation spelling out the condition under which a 'southern' firm would imitate an innovating 'northern' firm or would recede from the contested market and persue alternative lines of production.

Reviewing these and other uses of the product life cycle concept leads to the conclusion that the concept is still very much in the early phases of its growth stage itself, i.e., most of its notions, except its most basic ones, still await empirical verification. Wells (1972, p. 26) reviewed a few empirical studies validating the 'Vernon et al. model', but had to admit that they 'examine only part of the model and treat only a few products, a single industry, or the trade of a single country.' Nevertheless, it seems that, although less compelling for products than for mammals, the existence of life cycles is more plausible for products than either for organizations or for whole industries, and one can hardly argue with Levitt (1965, p. 81) who stated that 'the life story of most successful products is a history of their passing through recognizable stages'. Furthermore, comparing the evidence in the extensive literature on technological innovation and diffusion (for example, Mansfield, 1968, 1971) as indicative for early life stages with the evidence in the marketing and international trade literature for the more 'mature' stages, it seems that the life of the product during the incubation and introduction stages is, in a stochastic sense, much more predictable following a regular pattern suggested by the life cycle concept than in subsequent stages.

As we decrease the size of the region within which we try to find product cycle regularities or as we increase the organizational complexity of industrial corporations we would expect to have to introduce more behavioural interpretations of the product cycle concept. This would apply particularly for those types of production, often referred to as 'footloose', for which the regional comparative advantage is principally conditioned by internal, organizational characteristics rather than by regional advantages external to the individual firm. In such situations the way in which a regional product cycle emerges from the life patterns of the product on a global or national scale may be largely determined by the strategies of one or a few corporations.

Product Development Thresholds

In view of the above discussion and the presumably resulting differences in length of regional and corporate product cycles and their individual stages, the analysis of such patterns will be greatly enhanced by the recognition of thresholds, 'checkpoints' or 'milestones' which have to be passed before a specific stage ends or a new one begins and which serve as temporal yardsticks for measuring the rate of development (Lynn, 1966, p. 101). These 'gates' may vary greatly in significance and origin.

> 'The most significant are termed "major milestones" usually representing the completion of an important group of activities. . . . Events of lesser significance are often called "footstones" and "inchstones" at least in conversation if not in the formal literature.' (Holtz, 1969, p. 329).

They may emerge conveniently as a result of significant changes in labour force requirements, external linkages, or internal organization necessitated by the changing characteristics of the advancing life cycle. They may be internally determined by the unique set-up of the firm and may possibly differ from project to project. For example, periodic checks may be designed to ensure continued coordination between the engineering and marketing efforts on behalf of any one product. Alternatively, the firm may accept general, industry-wide conventions for such thresholds. Certain checkpoints are imposed upon the industry or the specific firm by regulative agencies (e.g., the Federal Aviation Administration) or by customers who are opting for opportunities to receive progress reports, to reconsider their commitments, to compare progress on various programmes at certain intervals and/or to make performance checks and perform contract controls against specified benchmarks or 'baselines' (e.g., 'design requirements baseline' or 'product configuration baseline' as used in military procurement contracts) (Morrison, 1967). Thus, in addition to all other changes occurring at such checkpoints or during such milestone-episodes the composition and characteristics of the uncertainty attached to the product or project may significantly change. For example, uncertainty may be reduced resulting from the conclusion of an initial performance test market survey; on the other hand, the decision to go ahead with the next stage and to commit additional resources to the project may compound the significance of uncertainty attached to the remaining stages of the cycle.

For more complex products, the sequence of more or less decisive thresholds forming a long queue of episodes during the various stages of the project's development cycle may be similar to the ones of the SST-Supersonic Transport plane developed by the Boeing Company (authors' research files):

Initiation of design studies (1952); Project status of engineering efforts (1958); Entering of FAA design competition (1963); Submission of Phase I design proposal (Jan. 1964); Boeing declared one of two finalists (1964); Formation of SST Division (1966); Display 'mock-up' unveiled (mid-1966); Submission of Phase II design proposal (Sept. 1966); Award of contract for design, construction and flight testing for two prototypes (Dec. 1966); Major subcontractors selected (by 1967); Complete restudy of all design possibilities leading to submission of new design proposal to FAA (1968); Production-mock-up of fuselage completed (mid-1970); Start of drawing release, tool design and tool fabrication and procurement phase (2nd half of 1970); Manpower build-up for construction of main assembly tools (early 1971); beginning of structural assembly work (June 1971, planned); Structural drawing release completed and first 'body joining' (late 1971); Start of final assembly of prototype (April 1972); Roll-out and first test flight of prototype (late 1972); Start of production (late 1973); First commercial flight (1976/1978). The project's unusually late termination in March 1971 directly affected the jobs of more than 4,400 people on the programme and 1,800 in supporting organizations in Seattle alone. The mock-up was sold in 1972.

Some of such thresholds are known for their high 'product-mortality' rates; others are generally more easily passed although they may imply organizational and locational changes. Still others provide an opportunity to reconsider the timing of the future stages including the possibility to stall and to wait for external encouragement (demand change, competitors' strategy), or to lay the project 'on ice' as a contingency.

If the status of a project or product is promoted to the next stage not all functions which have been performed for the former stage are necessarily suddenly terminated while the new stage may also have been prepared in advance. In fact, one would expect considerable overlap of activity for and periods of transition between stages of any one product (Mansfield, 1971, p. 145ff.). In terms of manpower requirements, for example, one would expect to be able to identify cycle curves for individual stages such as planning, design, etc., each of them having its own particular shape and skill composition.

Go-ahead or cut-off decisions are made at checkpoints in the face of uncertainty (about competitors and markets) which has to be judged against past commitments. Corporations will differ with respect to how the subjective evaluation of this uncertainty will influence the termination decision due to differences in ability and willingness to face such risks. But, there seems to be a tendency of the weight of accumulated investments to favour a continuation as long as the corporation is financially strong enough to absorb the potential losses. In this context, Schon introduced two new 'gates'. As R & D managers climb the slope of the product-related investment curve, 'they rather quickly reach what appears to be a point of no return. "We have put in so much. We may as well put in a little more and find out whether the investment is worthwhile" ' (Schon, 1969, p. 127). Following such a threshold, Schon claims, the development would soon reach a point where, should a mistake have been recognized, it would be too big to be admitted without losing personal or corporate face (Schon, 1967, p. 35). Efforts will then have to be made to minimize losses and to make the product appear successful. Firms which have a policy to go about their research and product development quietly and to depreciate all related outlays as instant costs will be in a much better position to either drop the product at any particular point or to feign subsequent profitability than firms which have invested heavily in public relations activities and have capitalized all R & D related outlays which then will have to be depreciated in the future.

Organizational Adjustments to Product Cycles

The recognition of the organizational and technological implications of product life cycles and the fast turnover of projects and products in many growth industries has led to the emergence of a new form of organization. 'Project management' is supposed to have the flexibility necessary for organizational adaptation to product cycle change, a flexibility which would run counter to the long-run objectives and necessities of traditional forms of organizing corporate divisions based on locational aspects, manufacturing processes, or product groups. Under 'project management', corporations form within their existing divisions or across divisional lines special teams or project groups, i.e., non-routine organizations of varying size and composition which are assigned special tasks related to the development or production of a project or product, generally on a temporarily limited basis working within the existing organizational and locational system. In Alvin Toffler's (1971, p. 135) words these 'throw-away organizations, ad hoc teams or committees, do not necessarily replace permanent structures, but they change them beyond recognition, draining them of both people and power . . . (and) spring up in their midst and disappear . . . people . . . move back and forth at a high rate of speed (but) often retain their "home base" '.

Such efforts are directed and coordinated by a project manager who, generally with a limited staff of 'accountants, control clerks, and perhaps a few engineers' would be in charge of the project on a corporate or divisional, often multi-plant basis for the whole or for certain stages of the project life (Litterer, 1969, p. 152).

'The Boeing Company in trying to find new functions and outlets for its at least temporarily "sticky" product, the "747-Superjet", announced in 1971 that it "has formed a joint Aerospace Group-Commercial Airplane Group team to tailor the 747 for military assignments. D.E.G. has been named general manager . . . the new organization will be responsible for development and marketing of the 747 for such military roles as an advanced airborne command post, aerial tanker, logistics and troop transport, air-launched missile platform and surveillance systems" '. (*Seattle Times*, 1971b).

In the early stages of a project when the corporation prepares a bid for a larger development or production order, or when it simply explores the possibilities for using a certain technology for a certain commercial end, a 'study programme manager' may be in charge, while in later stages, when the project reaches the stage of technological maturity, full responsibility may be handed over to the production division. The product manager has a variety of functions, not all of which can be listed here. An important coordinating role that he often has to assume is (in response, e.g., to competitive pressures) to shorten the lead time of the product by continuously trying to conduct the development of major components in a concurrent rather than in serial fashion

(Litterer, 1969, p. 152). Another important function often consists of playing the product's advocate inside or outside the corporation.

'To (the) Minuteman ballistic-missile-program manager for the Boeing Co.'s Aerospace Group, the intercontinental Minuteman "is the big stick that keeps the peace." . . . "I can see a Boeing Minuteman program as far ahead as I can look," (he) said suggesting there would be a Boeing manager for the missile project in 1980, just as there is today. . . . "Over the past four years, there has been a fairly constant level of Boeing effort," he added, forecasting the firm's 5,000-member Minuteman work force will continue at that level at least through 1973.' (Interview with *Seattle Times*, 1972).

Many principles govern the intra-corporate *location* decision process with regard to any one product or project. A detailed discussion would go beyond the scope of this essay. However, certain locational repercussions of the functional transfers between departments, particularly R & D and production departments, during the product cycle should be noted. Communications requirements, particularly the fine tuning of technological detail and the solving of technical problems which may arise will promote proximity. In addition, a 'firm's R & D and production facilities, if not located in the same plant, are often close together, and since a technological advance is often a refinement of extension of existing operations, the new activity will be located close to the old' (US Dept. of Commerce, 1967b, p. 33). On the other hand, there may be forces which would favour separation. Existing regional comparative advantages (factor price differentials) for research vis-à-vis production activities may be a strong inducement for separation. Another factor may be that separation may facilitate control over the type of communication flowing between parts of the system. Thus, it has been pointed out by a Bell Telephone research executive, for example, that:

'. . . if I allow the feedback loop from design or manufacturing to basic research to get very strong, the feedback will stop the basic research. And it won't be long before I've lost my research and perhaps my research people. So we purposely put a barrier between manufacture and basic research—either a space barrier or an organizational barrier, maybe both.' (Morton, 1969, p. 219.)

12.3. Case Study: The Boeing Company

This essay had three highly interdependent objectives. On the most general level, an attempt was made to exemplify one mechanism for the relationship between individual behaviour and aggregate patterns of change. Second, and more specifically, some of the implications of corporate development strategies for employment changes on the local and regional level were discussed. Finally, we introduced the 'product' as an explanatory variable for the employment repercussions of corporate strategies. Due to rather obvious constraints, the following case study can illustrate only a selection of the arguments presented earlier. The particular corporation (The Boeing Company) was chosen not merely for geographical convenience, but primarily because of its industrial and technological characteristics, its rather dominating position in the regional economy (Seattle Metropolitan Area), and its remarkable employment fluctuations in recent years (Figure 12.1).

Firms in the industry aerospace tend to belong to one of three categories: (a) there are a few, large corporations serving primarily as 'prime contractors',

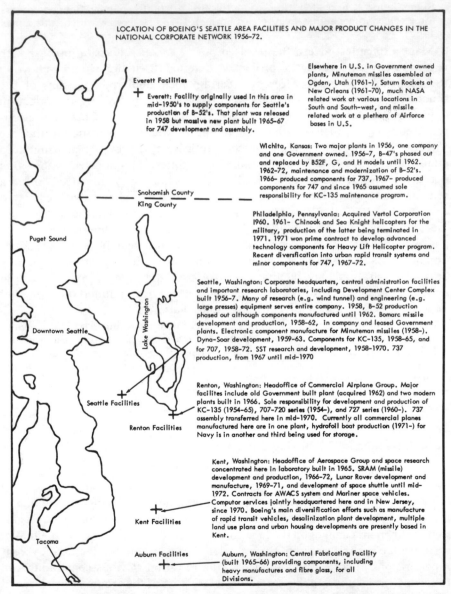

Figure 12.1. Location of Boeing's Seattle area facilities and major product changes in the national corporate network 1956–1972

such as Boeing, Lockheed, McDonnell-Douglas, North American-Rockwell and General Dynamics; (b) generally smaller firms employed as subcontractors and (c) relatively small firms supplying standardized parts and assemblies (Boness, 1972, p. 121). Given a strong general concentration of R & D activities in the first group of prime contractors, there are additional differences in the type of R & D activities performed by the different kinds of firms. Thus, basic research being most removed from the final product tends to be most strongly represented in the large corporation, while subcontractors and small suppliers tend to be more involved in applied research and development work, as a percentage of their total R & D budgets (Boness, 1972, p. 122).

Processes of commercial product development generally start with a search process which is designed to identify potentially feasible additions to the corporation's product line (Pessemier, 1966, p. 10). Whether the initial idea for a potential product is prompted by some exogenous stimulus, such as the plans of rivals or specific consumer need, or internally in the company's own laboratories, the potential product is likely to be related in terms of scientific and engineering skills to the existing corporate product mix. Many 'potential products' are shelved or eliminated, but for those given encouragement R & D work proceeds to a preliminary design for consumer evaluation. If the company's initial market evaluation is sufficiently favourable, the product will be promoted to 'project status', a significant threshold decision signalling increasing research efforts and expectations for future growth. Generally this development work retains its location within existing research facilities.

While an aeroplane only rarely reaches project status without some competitive response (unless it is itself prompted by a competitor's lead) behaviour of rivals and consumers becomes increasingly important during the next stage. The critical decision to commit the project for production depends on close scrutiny of the market and, in view of competition and high tooling cost, some commitment by major customers. In addition, the production of the initial model (for certification) is preceded by the plant allocation decision, generally heavy capital investments, and the build-up of the production work force leading to some temporary overlap of large-scale engineering and production employment.

The production and testing of the prototype or the establishment of the production line tends to be accomplished under pressure to be the first on the market, as it is easier to sell an available and certified, rather than just a projected, aeroplane. Completion of the first model signals the award or confirmation of subcontracts and the locational allocation of component production within the corporation, neither of which need necessarily be at or near the final assembly plant.

As engineering and development problems are ironed out, there tends to be a decline in the labour input per unit of production commonly referred to as the 'learning curve effect' (cf. Rapoport, 1971, p. 100f.; Hartley, 1965). Ultimately, production employment and the subsequent shape of the product life cycle will depend upon the nature of the market, the timing of its penetration and

TABLE 12.1. Product development stages

Aircraft model	707	727	737	747	SST
Potential product	1949	1956			1952
Project status	1951	1959	1964		1958
Production 'go ahead'	1952	1960	1965	1966	1963*
Initial model	1954†	1963	1967	1969	1966
Mass production	1958	1963	1967	1969	—
Delivery of 1st plane	1958	1964	1967	1970	

* Stage 3 for the SST represents a decision to go ahead for Government 'tender' and stage 4 the award of the prime contract (terminated in 1971).

† Prototype model; for the other planes, stage 4 represents FAA certification.

Sources: Bowers, 1968; and authors' research files.

saturation, and the market shares obtained by rivals, the first target threshold being the 'break-even' number of sold planes needed for covering development and tooling costs.

Boeing's postwar commercial jet production path consists of a small number of distinct models (Table 12.1) and a significantly larger number of product 'derivatives'. Derivatives can be described as sub-models designed to adjust the product to additional, smaller market segments, thereby extending the product's market and its total life time, possibly avoiding or at least delaying new product developments. While derivatives of any one product model have basically identical designs, different models are distinguished by major design changes, although the development of successive planes has been highly interrelated. Aeroplanes developed within a relatively short time period cannot represent genuine innovations; rather they are based on combinations of unchanged, extended and innovative principles. In Boeing's case, this communality went beyond the sharing of technological principles with other commercial and military planes and included extensive joint use of equipment, components and even whole sections of planes (e.g., 707 vis-à-vis 727 and 727 vis-à-vis 737). The development of the substantially larger 747-Jumbo Jet was aided by the fact that no major breakthroughs were required in the structural field or in aerodynamics, and that the design still could rely on principles of the 707 which itself was patterned after the B-47 bomber and conquered German WWII design (Bowers, 1968, p. 326). At the same time, a ready-made development team and basic developmental work could be taken over from the terminated C-5A military transport project. The SST development project, officially terminated but still having many characteristics of a merely dormant project, was no doubt the most innovative of all recent commercial developments, although it also benefited from the past military design experience.

Changes in Product Mix and Locational Adaptation

Differentiated demand fluctuations for a corporation's products results in fairly automatic relative shifts within its product mix and its locational structure, and possibly leads to less automatic, strategic adjustment measures designed to counteract negative or reinforce beneficial repercussions. The decline of Boeing's commercial aircraft sector not only led to an overall decline of Boeing's activities, but also to automatic 'diversification' in the sense that other products and projects were gaining relative significance. Although Boeing consistently attempted to retain some degree of balance between its different Government and commercial markets, broad market specialization has remained high after the early 1960's. The company's present more deliberate drive to compensate for losses in the aircraft field by utilizing the firm's broad technological base for new product developments is generally still in its infant stage, and for most products still a long way from production stages. This diversification policy, which includes projects and products ranging from hydrofoil boats and urban transit system developments to residential housing construction and agricultural rehabilitation schemes suffers from long development lead periods as well as, of course, from the already quite visible recovery of the commercial aeroplane market.

Corporate diversification efforts do not necessarily lead to an equal degree of regional diversification of a corporation's activities. While Boeing's production plants outside the Seattle area have been heavily specialized in military and NASA work only occasionally and temporarily 'diversified' by the production and sub-assembly of components for Seattle-based products, Boeing achieved in Seattle through its multi-plant presence and its concentration of R & D work and new commercial products a limited degree of effective regional diversification in spite of its high level of specialization on the plant level. Because a large part of Boeing's employees are able to reside within reasonable commuting distances from all Seattle area plants and because there is a significant differentiation of the employment cycles of products and plants, a degree of adaptability has been attained in the general context of overspecialization. The proximity of the plants has also facilitated the mutual exchange of free capacities between plants and projects aiding, for example, the consolidation of the 707/727/737 production lines under one roof during the recent recession. However, the intra-regional labour mobility and capacity flexibility in the Seattle region and the interregional coordination of capacities at the corporate level could not prevent massive transfers of production workers from Boeing's Wichita plant to Seattle and Everett in support of the 747 production build-up in 1966/1967.

Local Employment Patterns

Boeing's total employment and Seattle's economic performance have been intimately related in the past (Figure 12.2). Three times since 1958, the influence of Boeing's employment pattern has reversed national growth or decline trends for the Seattle area. Twice, in 1959–1960 and 1963–1964, declines in Boeing's fortunes created minor recessions in Seattle during periods of general national prosperity, while Boeing's expansion in 1966–1967 reversed a nationwide recession for the Seattle area. Three times over the past

AEROSPACE EMPLOYMENT IN THE SEATTLE METROPOLITAN AREA AND BOEING'S PRODUCT
CHANGES AND SALES TRENDS (1956 - 1972)

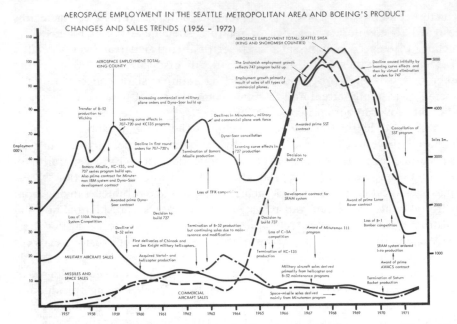

Figure 12.2. Aerospace employment in the Seattle metropolitan area and Boeing's product changes and sales trends (1956–1972)

fifteen years, Boeing's local employment dropped by over 20 per cent. During 1966 alone, on the other hand, it grew from 64,000 to about 92,000. It seems that this unprecedented upswing was largely the result of maladjusted product cycle stages in combination with too optimistic growth expectations, misinterpreted acceleration processes, and a remarkable dose of nonchalance with which management was able to impose this employment avalanche upon the community.

During this whole period of rapid expansion and reduction, absolute employment changes were accompanied by high rates of intra-corporate labour migration, reassignments, and rapid promotions. Even at the height of the wave, this internal mobility and change in the employment structure did not cease. 'Average employment during 1968 varied little in numbers from the previous year . . . there were, however, changes in the composition of the work force. As tooling was completed on major projects, there was a shift to greater requirement for production skills. The result was a steady skill interchange, accomplished by retraining, transfer and hiring' (Boeing, 1968, p. 29). Only a short time later, between mid-1968 to October 1971, Boeing's employment in Seattle fell again from its all-time high of about 101,500 to 37,200. Boeing's payroll declined from $958 million in 1969 to $515 million in 1971, while Seattle area unemployment increased from 21,200 (3·2 per cent) in mid-1968 to 98,200 (15 per cent) in mid-1971. It was estimated that the total direct, indirect and induced employment impact, 'after all accommodations have been made, would be at least 100,000 jobs lost, and an income decline of at least $1·4 billion' (Bourque, 1971, p. 20).

While the underlying initiation of this local downturn can be easily traced to the national recession, airline demand and the tight money markets, it nevertheless was strongly reinforced by the preceding expansion decisions, a fact which was eventually acknowledged by Boeing management. Thus, a Seattle newspaper, publishing year-end interviews with Boeing executives, reported that:

'Boullioun (president of Boeing Commercial Airplane & Co.) stressed that the company, while striving to avoid the peaks and valleys of recent years, nonetheless is determined to grow.' (*Seattle Times*, 1973).

and quoted the president of the Boeing Corporation, Stamper, 'We intend to do everything we can to keep the company and the community from going through another boom-and-bust cycle'.

12.4. Conclusions

Certain problems which arise from the multi-regional or multi-product characteristics or merely from the relative size of large industrial corporations were of particular concern in this essay. Spatially separated subsidiaries and branch plants or corporations and greatly diverse products of a corporate product mix tend to be parts of subsystem structures of different regions or industrial (employment) categories. However, due to their characteristics as subsystems of the corporation, their boundary constraints differ from those of political or economic regions or industrial categories, respectively (Miller, 1972, p. 20f.). Corporate and regional systems and subsystems maintain themselves and grow by exchanges of matter energy and information with their respective environments inside or outside the region or corporation. The ability to use their own presence in many regions and in many fields of operation to their maximum benefit and to shift resources between components makes many types of exchanges between a plant and the region within which it is located potentially unstable and uncertain, adding to the uncertainty which originates outside the corporation (e.g., product markets). Thus it places a burden on other decision-makers in the region whose behaviour may possibly be more predictable, especially households, small dependent industrial activities, and regional planning agencies responsible for coordinating and projecting the region's economic and social development.

In the field of locational dynamics, one important link between industrial expansion and decline and their spatial manifestations is provided by the analysis of product developments and changes at the corporate and regional level. Research and development activities, innovation, growth, stagnation, decline and possibly 'death' of product markets constitute, together with many additional 'episodes' along the development and life path of a product, specific explanatory connections between corporate and regional development patterns. Some of the repercussions of product changes and changing local environmental requirements during product cycles were discussed in the context of corporate development focusing particularly on the Boeing Company in the Seattle Metropolitan Area during the past fifteen years. While it was found that the organizational and industrial characteristics of Seattle's economic base had significant impacts on employment developments in the region (as they differed from national or industry-wide more aggregate employment fluctuations), many of the sharp employment increases, declines, and qualitative changes could be related more specifically to the influence of product cycle mechanisms. With these regional repercussions of corporate decision-making in mind, it seems appropriate to suggest that future research on product life cycles and locational impacts might benefit from a more thorough analysis of the decision-making processes involved. Decisions to research, innovate, modify, expand, consolidate and withdraw products are predicated upon a corporate decision maker's judgments as to future consumer needs, competitor behaviour, technological change, factor inputs required and the competitive abilities of the firm. Such judgments, which may be successively revised on the basis of new information and experience, represent a qualitative expression of subjective probabilities as to the likelihood of particular product development paths. Expectations frequently play an important role in decisions which, for example, commit a product to future production. A subjective probability framework would allow the incorporation of judgmental assessments of external developments and chance events together with relevant internal parameters into the analysis of location and product decision-making processes, which in combination with other types of analysis would greatly facilitate the improvement of our tools for regional employment analysis and forecasting, particularly for regions which are dominated by a small number of employers.

Acknowledgements

The authors wish to acknowledge the partial support of the research underlying this essay through the National Science Foundation and the Graduate School of the University of Washington. Mr. Hayter's responsibility for this essay is limited to the co-authorship of the Boeing Company case study. However, he has extensively commented on the remainder of the paper.

References

Alder, F. M. (1970), The Relationship Between the Income and Price Elasticities of Demand for United States Exports, *Review of Economics and Statistics*, **52**, 313–319.

Albach, H. (1965), Zur Theorie des wachsenden Unternehmens, *Theorien des einzelwirtschaftlichen und des gesamtwirtschaftlichen Wachstums*, Schriften des Vereins fur Socialpolitik, Band **34**, Duncker & Humblot, Berlin, 9–97.

Ansoff, H. I. (1963), Strategies for Diversification, in Bursk, E. C. and Chapman, J. F. (eds.), *New Decision-Making Tools for Managers*. New York: Mentor Books, 309–333.

Baumol, W. J. (1967), Macroeconomics of Unbalanced Growth: The Anatomy of Urban Crisis, *The American Economic Review*, **57**, 415–426.

Berenson, C. (1971), Pruning the Product Line, in Lawrence, R. J. and Thomas, M. J. (eds.), *Modern Marketing Management*. Penguin Books, 208–220.

Berry, C. H. (1967), Corporate Bigness and Diversification in Manufacturing, *Ohio State Law Journal*, **28**, 402–426.

Boeing (1968), *Annual Report*,, Seattle.

Boness, A. J. (1972), *Capital Budgeting*. New York: Praeger, Chap. 7.

Bourque, P. J. (1971), An Input–Output Analysis of Economic Change in Washington State, *University of Washington Business Review*, **30**, 5–22.

Bowers, P. M. (1968), *Boeing Aircraft Since 1916*. Second Edition, New York: Funk and Wagnalls.

Bücher, K. (1918), *Die Entstehung der Vokswirtschaft*. Zweite Sammlung, Tubingen Laupp.

Burns, A. F. (1934), *Production Trends in the United States Since 1870*. New York: National Bureau of Economic Research.

Chamberlin, E. H. (1953), The Product as an Economic Variable, *Quarterly Journal of Economics*, **67**, 1–29.

Clark, C. (1940), *The Conditions of Economic Progress*. London: Macmillan.

Dicken, P. (1971), Some Aspects of the Decision Making Behaviour of Business Organizations, *Economic Geography*, **47**, 426–437.

Emery, F. E. and Trist, E. L. (1965), The Causal Texture of Organizational Environments, *Human Relations*, **18**, 21–31.

Engel, E. (1857), Die Produktions- und Consumptionsverhaltnisse des Konigreichs Sachsen, *Zeitschrift d. Stat. Bureaus d. Konigl. Sachsischen Minist. d. Innern*, Nos. 8 and 9 November; reprinted in *Bull. of the Int. Inst. of Stat.*, **9** (1895), p. 1.

Findlay, R. (1970), *Trade and Specialization*. Harmondsworth: Penguin Books.

Fisher, A. G. B. (1939), Production, Primary, Secondary, and Tertiary, *Economic Record*, **15**, 24–38.

Fourastié, J. (1951), *Machinisme et Bien-Etre*. Second Edition, Paris: Editions de Minuit.

FAZ-Frankfurter Allgemeine Zeitung (1971), July 16.

Freidmann, J. (1972), A General Theory of Polarized Development, in Hansen, N. (ed.), *Growth Centers in Regional Economic Development*. New York: Free Press, 82–107.

Galbraith, J. K. (1967), *The New Industrial State*. Boston: Houghton Miflin.

Gerlach, K. and Liepmann, P. (1972), Konjunkturelle Aspekte der Industrialisierund peripherer Regionen, *Jahrb. f. Nationalok. u. Stat.*, **187**, 1–21.

Gold, B. (1964), Industry Growth Patterns: Theory and Empirical Results, *Journal of Industrial Economics*, **13**, 53–73.

Gruber, W. H. and Vernon, R. (1970), The Technology Factor in a World Trade Matrix, in Vernon, R. (ed.), *The Technology Factor in International Trade*. New York: National Bureau of Economic Research, 233–272.

Hägerstrand, T. (1970, What About People in Regional Science?, *Papers and Proceedings, Regional Science Association*, **24**, 7–21.

Hartley, K. (1965), The Learning Curve and its Application to the Aircraft Industry, *Journal of Industrial Economics*, **13**, 122–128.

Hirsch, S. (1967), *Location of Industry and International Competitiveness*. Oxford: Clarendon Press.

Hoffmann, W. G. (1958), *The Growth of Industrial Economies*. Manchester University Press.

Holtz, J. (1969), An Analysis of Major Scheduling Techniques in the Defense Systems Environment, in Cleland, D. I. and King, W. R. (eds.), *Systems, Organizations, Analysis Management*. New York: McGraw-Hill, 317–355.

Jenner, R. A. (1966), An Information Version of Pure Competition, *Economic Journal*, **76**, 786–805.

Johnson, R. A., Kast, F. E. and Rosenzweig, J. E. (1963), *The Theory and Management of Systems*. New York: McGraw-Hill.

Katz, D. and Kahn, R. L. (1966), *The Social Psychology of Organizations*. New York: Wiley, Chap. 2.

Kitching, B. (1972), Real 'Crowding Out' as a Factor in the American Inflation-Recession, *Zeitschrift fur Nationalokonomie*, **32**, 289–303.

Kneschaurek, F. (1964), Wachstumsbedingte Wandlungen der Beschaftigungsstruktur im industriellen Produktionssektor, *Strukturwandlungen einer wachsenden Wirtschaft*, Schriften des Vereins fur Socialpolitik, Band **30/II**. Berlin: Duncker & Humblot, 720–739.

Krumme, G. (1966), Theoretical and Empirical Analyses of Patterns of Industrial Change and Entrepreneurial Adjustments: The Munich Region, unpublished Ph.D. dissertation, University of Washington, Seattle.

Krumme, G. (1969), Notes on Locational Adjustment Patterns in Industrial Geography, *Geografiska Annaler*, **51B**, 15–19.

Krumme, G. (1970), The Interregional Corporation and the Region: A Case Study of Siemens' Growth Characteristics and Response Patterns in Munich, West Germany, *Tijdschrift voor Econ. en Soc. Geografie*, **61**, 318–333.

Kuznets, S. (1929), Retardation of Industrial Growth, *Journal of Economic and Business History*, **1**, 534–560.

Kuznets, S. (1967), *Modern Economic Growth*. New Haven: Yale University Press.

Lago, A. M. (1969), The Hoffmann Industrial Growth Development Path: An International Comparison, *Weltwirtschaftliches Archiv*, **103**, 41–56.

Lasuen, J. R. (1971), Multi-Regional Economic Development: An Open-System Approach, in Hägerstrand, T. and Kuklinski, A. R. (eds.), *Information Systems for Regional Development*. Lund: C. W. K. Gleerup, 169–211.

Leven, C. L. (1966), The Economic Base and Regional Growth, *Research and Education for Regional and Area Development*. Iowa: Iowa State University Center for Agricultural and Economic Development, University Press, 79–94.

Levitt, T. (1965), Exploit the Product Life-Cycle, *Harvard Business Review*, **43**, 81–94.

Litterer, J. A. (1969), Program Management: Organizing for Stability and Flexibility, in Litterer, J. A. (ed.), *Organizations: Structure and Behaviour*, Vol. **1**, Second Edition. New York: Wiley, 150–156.

Lynn, F. (1966), The Rate of Development and Diffusion of Technology, in Bowen, H. R. and Magnum, G. L. (eds.), *Automation and Economic Progress*. Englewood Cliffs, New Jersey: Prentice-Hall, 99–113.

Machlup, F. (1958), Structure and Structural Change: Weaselwords and Jargon, *Zeitschrift fur Nationalokonomie*, **18**, 280–298.

Machlup, F. (1967), Theories of the Firm: Marginalist, Behavioural, Managerial, *American Economic Review*, **57**, 1–33.

Mansfield, E. (1968), *The Economics of Technological Change*. New York: Norton.

Mansfield, E. et al. (1971), *Research and Innovation in the Modern Corporation*. New York: Norton.

Melman, S. (1970), *Pentagon Capitalism: The Political Economy of War*. New York: McGraw-Hill.

Miller, J. G. (1972), Living Systems: The Organization, *Behavioural Science*, **17**, 1–182.

Moroney, J. R. and Walker, J. M. (1966), A Regional Test of the Hechscher—Ohlin Hypothesis, *Journal of Political Economy*, **74**, 573–586.

Morrison, E. J. (1967), Defense Systems Management: The 375 Series, *California Management Review*, **9**(4), 17–26.

355

Morton, J. (1969), From Research to Technology, in Allison, D. (ed.), *The R & D Game*. Cambridge: M.I.T. Press.

Norden, P. V. (1970), Useful Tools for Project Management, in Starr, M. K. (ed.), *Management of Production*. Harmondsworth: Penguin Books, 71–101.

Patton, A. (1959), Top Management's Stake in the Product Life Cycle, *Management Review*, **48**, 9–79.

Penrose, E. (1959), *The Theory of the Growth of the Firm*. Oxford: Blackwell.

Pessemier, E. A. (1966), *New-Product Decisions*. New York: McGraw-Hill.

Posner, M. V. (1961), International Trade and Technical Change, *Oxford Economic Papers*, **13**, 323–341.

Rapoport, J. (1971), The Anatomy of the Product-Innovation Process: Cost and Time, in Mansfield, E., *et al.* (eds.), *Research and Innovation in the Modern Corporation*. New York: Norton, Chap. 6.

Reich, C. A. (1971), *The Greening of America*. New York: Bantam Books.

Rosenberg, N. (1972), *Technology and American Economic Growth*. New York: Harper and Row.

Rothschild, K. W. (ed.) (1971), *Power in Economics*. Harmondsworth: Penguin Books, 7–17.

Sakai, H. (1972), The Center-Periphery Dichotomy in the Japanese Economy: A Study in Distance and Spatial Interaction, unpublished Ph.D. dissertation, Columbia University, New York.

Schon, D. (1967), *Technology and Change*. New York: Delacorte Press.

Schon, D. (1969), The Fear of Innovation, in Allison, D. (ed.), *The R & D Game*. Cambridge: M.I.T. Press.

Seattle Times (1971a), May 23.

Seattle Times (1971b), December 5.

Seattle Times (1972), December 3.

Seattle Times (1973), January 14.

Stabler, C. (1971), Changing Times: Many Corporations Make Social Goals a Major Concern, *Wall Street Journal*, October 26, 1 and 14.

Stafford, H. A. (1969), An Industrial Location Decision Model, *Proceedings, Association of American Geographers*, **1**, 141–145.

Starbuck, W. H. (1965), Organizational Growth and Development, in *Handbook of Organizations*. Chicago: Rand McNally, 451–522.

Steed, G. P. F. (1971), Plant Adaptation, Firm Environments and Location Analysis, *Professional Geographer*, **23**, 324–328.

Stobaugh, R. B. (1968), The Product Life Cycle, U.S. Exports, and International Investment, unpublished D.B.A. dissertation, Harvard Business School. Cambridge.

Thomas, M. D. (1972), Growth Pole Theory: An Examination of Some of its Basic Concepts, in Hansen, N. M. (ed.), *Growth Centers in Regional Economic Development*. New York: Free Press, 50–81.

Time (1972), October 30, 94.

Tinbergen, J. (1965), Eine Neue Raumwirtschaftslehre, *Zeitschrift fur die gesamte Staatswissenschaft*, **121**, 625–632.

Toffler, A. (1971), *Future Shock*. New York: Bantam Books.

U.S. Dept. of Commerce (1967a), *Regional Effects of Government Procurement and Related Policies*. Washington, D.C.: U.S. Govt. Printing Office.

U.S. Dept. of Commerce (1967b), *Impact of Science and Technology of Regional Development*. Washington, D.C.: U.S. Govt. Printing Office.

Vernon, R. (1966), International Investment and International Trade in the Product Cycle, *Quarterly Journal of Economics*, **80**, 190–207.

Vernon, R. (1969), The Role of U.S. Enterprise Abroad, *Daedalus*, **98**, 113–133.

Wall Street Journal (1971a), February 4, 26.

Wall Street Journal (1971b), September 30.

356

Wells, L. T. (1969), Test of a Product Cycle Model of International Trade: U.S. Exports of Consumer Variables, *Quarterly Journal of Economics*, **83,** 152–162.

Wells, L. T. (ed.) (1972), *The Product Life Cycle and International Trade*. Boston: Graduate School of Business Administration, Harvard University.

Woodroofe, E. G. (1968), Science in the Market Place, *Progress: The Unilever Quarterly*, **52,** 179–186.

Zimmerman, F. L. (1971), Anatomy of a Vote, *Wall Street Journal*, August 5, 1 and 17.

13 The Market Area of a Firm

H. D. WATTS

'Adequate investigations on this subject are none too numerous.' August Lösch, 1954, p. 403

'There has been surprisingly little research on the identification of market areas in an industrial context.' David M. Smith, 1971, p. 305

Despite the extensive discussions of market areas in the major works on location (Hoover, 1948, pp. 47–66; Lösch, 1954, pp. 105–137; Greenhut, 1956, pp. 23–83; Isard, 1956, pp. 105–137) students of industrial locations have made only a few efforts to identify the market areas of manufacturing firms. The study of market areas has played an important part in the empirical analysis of central places (Carter, 1955; Rowley, 1971), but the most thorough discussion of a firm's market area is still that of Lösch (1954, pp. 395–430). Yet, he considers only briefly the way in which a firm's market area can change over time. This essay has a very small body of complementary studies on which to draw and, inevitably, it is exploratory in character and its findings are tentative in nature.

In this account the terms plant and firm are synonymous. Attention is concentrated on the manufacturing firm with one or, at the most, two plants. As far as possible the market area of a firm is considered in isolation; such isolation is necessary because the role of a market area in the dynamics of manufacturing activity is not yet clarified. The description of market areas which follows illustrates the use of some possible data sources, and analyses features of market areas which are thought to be important on either intuitive or *a priori* grounds. Thus, the focus of the essay is the spatial character of the market area of a single plant firm.

It may be possible, in some future work, to extend the analysis to include the consequences of market area variations upon other spatial phenomena. For example, the relationship of the market area to location patterns will be of primary importance. The spacing of plants is related to the size of market areas especially in industries where an element of spatial monopoly is present (Smith, 1971, p. 305). Secondly, it could be suggested that, in the long run, survival of a firm will depend, *ceteris paribus,* on its ability to extend or intensify its market area. Thirdly, some attempt will have to be made to relate the market area to other economic aspects of a firm's activities. Fourthly, the inter-action of the market areas of different firms will need to be considered and, finally, the analysis will have to be elaborated to include multi-plant firms.

In the present context, some preliminary considerations lead to the conclusion that the market area of a manufacturing firm is defined best as the area in which a firm sells its products. A geographical analysis of market areas necessitates measurement of their size and their internal characteristics; the latter relating to the pattern of sales within the market area, and to the distribution system necessary to meet the market's demands. The discussion is in three parts. First, market areas are considered as static phenomena and this permits the identification of market area characteristics which might be expected to change in response to changing economic circumstances. The dynamics of market areas are examined by considering the extension of a market area in a diffusion framework, whilst major changes in a distribution system are analysed within a market area of fixed limits.

13.1. Preliminary Considerations

It is evident that market areas can exist at various scales, from a very local area (a neighbourhood bakery) to a world market (IBM). The cases presented here are drawn from the United Kingdom, and none have a radius greater than 550 km. The consequences of distance may be less well marked than at a continental scale, and the consideration of the growth and development of international market areas (McNee, 1961; Steed, 1971) is excluded.

Where international market areas are excluded from discussion, the limits of the market areas of many firms will be the boundary of the political unit in which they are set. At this level, the market area is simply the political unit, i.e. the market area of a Danish firm is Denmark. Market areas which are smaller than the territory of major political units can be detected most readily where two conditions are met. First, where the firm serves a market of numerous dispersed points, and second where the friction of distance has an effect upon the distribution of a firm's outputs. These outputs can be either information or material flows.

A firm producing goods for the consumer market is most likely to meet the first condition. It supplies goods, at a uniform delivered price, to consumers dispersed over the possible market area. If this market area is divided into a set of zones within each zone the volume of sales may tend to remain constant in the short-run, although there might be variations in the behaviour of individual buyers. In contrast, the firm producing semi-manufactures may sell to only a small number of points, each point of sale representing a carefully negotiated contract. The points served will change as contracts are won or lost, and because the firm serves a series of widely separated points it is not particularly meaningful to talk of its market area.

There is little evidence relating to distance-decay in the information flows from a firm; perhaps the closest parallel that can be found is the pattern of telephone calls from towns (Davies and Lewis, 1970) or office contact studies (Goddard, 1971). Information flows in the present context encompass all the organizational problems of marketing, receiving orders, despatching orders, billing customers and receiving the final payment. It is expected that these information flows will be especially sensitive to the friction of distance in the early stages of a firm's growth, and particularly so in the pre-electronic age (Pred, 1971a and 1971b).

Identification of consumer industries with important distribution costs can be attempted by using Census of Production data and by expressing transport costs as a percentage of net output plus payments for purchased transport. For example, in most food and drink industries transport costs represent over 10 per cent of net output; and for some (bread and milk products) the percentage rises to over twenty. Admittedly, there is some difficulty in separating material assembly costs from distribution costs, but these values should be compared with those identified by Chisholm for broader industrial groups. Outside the food and drink, and the brick, pottery and glass industries percentage values ranged from 6·6 per cent to 1·1 per cent (Chisholm, 1971, p. 230). Some industries, notably those with potentially high transport costs, may be under-represented by these data especially if their production facilities are dispersed to help reduce transport costs. Nevertheless, it seems reasonable to conclude that in firms in industries where transport costs exceed 6·6 per cent of net output distance-decay in output flows will be readily apparent.

Although it is possible to suggest the kind of industries where market areas are recognizable it is difficult to obtain the relevant data. This is not surprising. Sales are the basis of a firm's existence, and the publication of a detailed geographic analysis of sales figures may weaken its competitive position. Some current information can be obtained but this is usually of little value for inter-firm comparison. An interview sample survey of a number of buyers has to be rejected for all but the most local of firms, so there seem to be two ways round the data problem if the discussion of the market areas of firms is to proceed. Firstly, non-current data can be analysed; when looking for evidence of general patterns there can be little objection to using 'historical' sources. Unfortunately few firms keep such records, and to find a time series would be an extremely fortunate occurrence. Secondly, where a firm controls some or all of its retail outlets, the distribution and sales of these outlets can provide an approximate indication of a firm's market area. Both possibilities have been used to provide evidence in this essay.

13.2. Static Features

Lösch (1954, pp. 402–420) suggests that a market area can be analysed in terms of its size, shape, and structure. Only size and structure are considered here, and they present a number of problems. The most fundamental one is that operational definitions of the term market area are difficult to formulate. theoretically it is the area in which the spatial monopolist sells all his products;

and a closely related operational definition is that it is the area where a firm has a monopoly—thus allowing for areas of indifference and competition between firms at the limits of their sales areas. However, except in a few negotiated environments spatial monopolists are rare. An alternative approach, suggested for example by Beckmann (1971, p. 7), is that 'the market area of a . . . (firm is) . . . that region where the . . . (firm's) . . . market share is dominant i.e. larger than that of any other . . . (firm).' To work on this basis, detailed knowledge of the market shares of all firms in all areas would be needed, unless one firm had over 50 per cent of the market. Even if this case occurred problems would still arise, because given this definition a plant might be separated from its 'market area' by a distance of several kilometres. For the study of the market areas of manufacturing firms, it is necessary to fall back on a series of measures related to the firm itself and to define the market area as the area in which a firm sells its goods.

Size

The size of a market area differs from industry to industry, and from firm to firm in the same industry; these variations are outlined before discussing the nature of the market area of one firm.

Table 13.1. Movement of four selected industrial products in the U.K.

Product	Distance (km)			
	40·25	40·25–80·49	80·50–161·00	161·00
	per cent of *consignments* by all transport 1966–1967			
1. Processed foods	57	23	6	14
2. Engineering and electrical goods	8	23	18	51
	per cent of *tonnes* carried by road, 1962			
3. Beverages	63	25	7	5
4. Electrical and non-electrical machinery: transport equipment	46	17	18	19

Source: Bayliss and Edwards, 1968, p. 74; Ministry of Transport, 1966, p. 98.

Table 13.1 illustrates the distance over which products in two contrasting industries are marketed. The extensive nature of the market areas of the engineering industry is clear—51 per cent of consignments, and 19 per cent of tonnes carried travel over 161 km. The contrasting figures for the two 'food and drink' industries—14 per cent, and 5 per cent—speak for themselves. Similarly, the mean haul for category four was 70·4 km, which may be compared with 47·9 km for category three.

Variations between firms in the same industry are difficult to discover, but Gleave (1965) shows that these variations can be related to both differences in output levels and differences in products. In the United Kingdom, brick-making industry plants vary in size from very small ones to those with annual outputs of over 650 million bricks each. The large plants (and related larger firms) serve the whole of the U.K. and despite transport costs, economies of large scale production mean that their bricks can be supplied to most places at a rate cheaper than that of local producers. However, in general this reduces the cost of an average house by only 0·1 per cent, and only purchasers of large quantities of bricks find the savings worthwhile; other users rely on local brickworks whose selling and distribution system is more flexible in their response to local needs. Even at this local level common bricks have a smaller market area than facing bricks: 'the facing brick which commands a higher market price than the common brick is . . . able to stand higher transportation costs and is sold in a wider area than its cheaper counterpart' (Gleave, 1965, p. 59).

In the analysis of the market area of individual firms, it is possible to move away from the high level of aggregation used in examining variations between and within industries. Examples are drawn principally from one small brewing firm, supplemented by references to some other small firms in the same industry. The choice of firms was dictated by the need to deal initially with firms with a simple history and by the availability of records.

The size of a firm's market area can be measured in a number of ways—the maximum sales range, the mean sales range or the radius of a circle which incorporates a percentage of total sales. The use of these measures is illustrated by applying them to the market area of the firm shown in Figure 13.1.

Figure 13.1 depicts the market area of Aberbeeg brewery in South Wales in 1936. This is the only year for which complete records are available, and even then the sales in each settlement have to be represented by value of deliveries. The main roads to the principal groups of sales outlets are shown because this is a district of broken relief. The firm had a maximum sales range of 28 km. The mean sales range probably provides a better indication of the size of the market area. It can be based on either mean distance to outlets (used here) or mean distance to settlements served (used in section on Market Area Extension). The market area shown has a mean sales range of 8·9 km. Both the mean and maximum sales range can give undue emphasis to a few more distant places, and a more appropriate measure may be the distance within which 50 per cent or 75 per cent of the firms products are sold. The percentage cut-off point has to be chosen arbitrarily, but there are parallels in central place studies (Rowley, 1971). In Figure 13.1, 50 per cent of the sales are made within 4·5 km; and 75 per cent within 7·5 km. The 75 per cent limit is represented by the pecked line which has been adjusted to allow for major surface irregularities.

In practice it is not possible to use all these measures because the necessary data are just not available. Brewing firms in England and Wales sell their

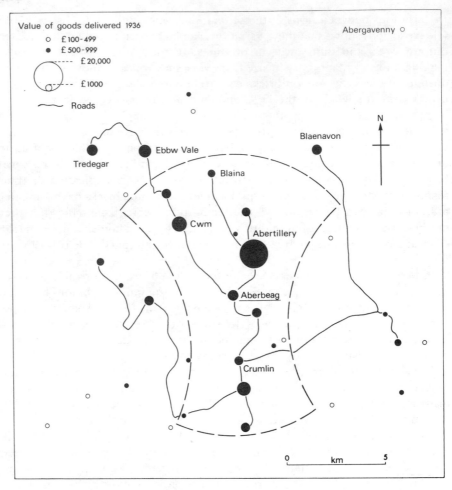

Figure 13.1. The market area of a firm: Webbs (Aberbeeg) Ltd, 1936
Source: Monmouthshire Record Office, D886.78

production through 'tied' outlets which have to purchase the majority of their supplies from the brewery to which they are tied. Breweries also supply 'free' outlets which can purchase beers from the breweries of their own choice. Very often only records of the tied trade are available, and usually only a list of outlets, with no indication of sales, is provided.

The mean range of the tied trade (7·6 km) in Figure 13.1 is less than that for all outlets (8.9 km). For two other breweries operating in the same area in the 1930's the mean range for the tied trade is higher 9·7 km (Pentre brewery) and 13·4 km (Fernvale brewery) despite the fact they controlled only half as many tied outlets as the Aberbeeg firm. Where less data are available the 75 per cent sales measure can be adapted and 75 per cent of tied outlets can be used in its place. This gives a 75 per cent 'sales' radius of 9 km in Figure 13.1, 10 km for Pentre and 15 km for Fernvale. If one is interested only in the rank-size of different market areas these three examples suggest either mean range or 75 per cent of outlets could be used as both give the same result.

Any of these measures can be calculated for a firm at different years in its life to study the growth in the size of its market area, but discussion of any changes should proceed with care. In the first part of this section it is shown that market areas differ between industries and between products within an industry. A change in a firm's market area can be a result of diversification into other industries, or the introduction of a different product mix.

Structure

The structure of a market area can be analysed in at least two ways. First, the spatial pattern of the consumers can be examined, and second, the distribution system for meeting consumer demand can be considered. The two approaches are, of course, inter-related.

An interpretation of customer-plant relationships in a distance decay framework is presented in Figure 13.2. Sales outlets are used as an indication of the location of consumers, and all outlets in these examples are supplied direct from the production unit without any intermediate depots.

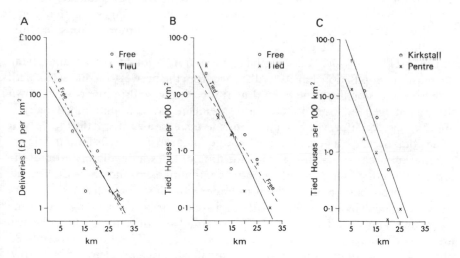

Figure 13.2. The structure of a market area—1
Sources: Monmouthshire Record Office, D886.78; Glamorgan Record Office, D/D XCu 14/7, D/D XCu 13 Anon (1949) *150 years of the house of Dutton*

Using the data shown in Figure 13.1 it is possible to plot the decline in the mean value of sales per km² in each of six distance bands. The mean value falls from £435 per km² (in the area less than 5 km from the plant) to £1 in the area between 25 and 30 km from the plant. It was argued that, in measuring size, tied outlets were a reasonable surrogate measure of total sales. In Figure 13.2A and 13.2B separate regression lines are presented for the tied and free trade; in both cases they show similar trends. The analysis can therefore proceed using data relating to tied outlets only.

It is necessary to use the density of tied outlets per 100 km^2 where sales and free trade data are absent. Figure 13.2B shows that the density of tied outlets per 100 km^2 falls from 32·0 (in the first 5 km) to 0·1 (in the last 5 km). The similarity between the trends in tied sales and tied outlets is examined by calculating the two correlation coefficients between logarithmically transformed density data and the six distance bands from 0 to 30 km. There is a correlation of −0·93 between density of sales and distance, and a correlation of −0·92 between density of outlets and distance. It seems reasonable to accept the latter as an efficient surrogate measure of the former. Regrettably, no further data were available to establish whether tied outlets are always a reasonable measure of market area characteristics in this industry; intuitively, one suspects this may not be the case.

The extent to which these distance-decay features of the tied trade are typical of other brewing firms can be judged by examining two further examples. Figure 13.2C represents another South Wales brewery (Pentre) and a brewery in the city of Leeds (Kirkstall); the latter is in an area where the population is at a higher density than the parts of South Wales considered. The similarity between the two trends is most striking, suggesting that some consistent spatial regularities might be established if a more extensive study than this was to be undertaken.

The processes which may explain these trends might reflect underlying decreases in population density as distance from the brewery increases; indeed, if these regression lines had been drawn for a brewing firm in a country town this might well be true. in the cases depicted here, population density is approximately uniform or has a tendency to *increase* away from the brewery. It seems that here, for a given level of production, transport costs limit the size of the market area, and assure a concentration of sales immediately around the production point. The market share of competing firms increases as distance from the production point of the firm under consideration increases.

No detailed evidence of the way these distance-decay rates change over time was found. However if Figure 13.2C is regarded as representing a hypothetical firm at two stages of growth—Pentre controlled 21 outlets; Kirkstall 83 outlets—it is possible to recognize two ways in which a market area might grow. First, it can grow by market area *intensification,* that is an increase in the density of outlets. Second, it can grow by market area *extension,* that is by an increase in the maximum sales range of the market area. This however assumes infinite extension of the market area; in general some barrier may be reached (e.g. a national boundary), so that extension across it may present different problems, for example new languages, or new marketing techniques (Steed, 1971). Once a barrier is reached market area extension may halt temporarily, but intensification will continue until some saturation level is achieved. The latter stage of the process is considered more fully in the next section.

The second part of this discussion of the structure of market areas is concerned with the analysis of distribution systems. In larger and more complex firms than those examined in the previous paragraphs sales outlets are supplied *via* intermediate depots and not directly from the point of production. The distribution systems of firms have attracted little attention in geographical literature, despite the extensive development of models of distribution systems by operational research teams. These models are reviewed in Eilon (1971) and hints of the elaborate structure of distribution systems have been provided by Warren (1971) and Gleave (1965).

It is usual to break the factory-to-customer flow into at least two stages. The first stage, known as trunking, ships the goods in bulk to some point where they are transferred, either directly or indirectly, to a different vehicle for the second, or delivery stage. This leads to the development of a hierarchical

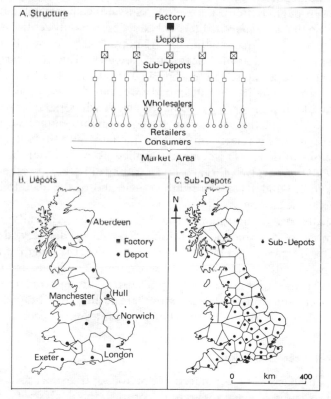

Figures 13.3. The structure of a market area—2
Source: After Sussams (1968) 'Some problems associated
with the distribution of consumer products' *Operational
Research Quarterly*, 19, 161–174

distribution system Figure 13.3A, the firm controlling depots and sub-depots—the high order stages of the system. The logic of the system is quite simple. Trunking vehicles operate at a lower cost per tonne than delivery vehicles because of their larger size, while for delivery purposes a firm uses the smallest vehicle which can give a sufficient pay load to fill a driver's day. Points of exchange between trunk and delivery vehicles may be transfer points or stock-holding sites. In any particular system the relative costs of trunking, delivery and depots will guide the character of the distribution system. The kind of pattern that can result from these considerations for a hypothetical firm, is illustrated in Figure 13.3B and 13.3A. The firm has two factories, each making a different product. One factory is located in London, the other in Manchester; both factories function also as depots. A system of stock-holding depots is set up so that all sub-depots (non-stockholding) can be supplied within 24 hours of receiving an order. The best network of depots to achieve this, using road transport, is shown in Figure 13.3B. The Aberdeen, Hull, Norwich and Exeter depots are included principally because of the time constraint. The depot areas on 13.3B have been interpolated by the present author. The sub-depot pattern suggested by Sussams is shown in Figure 13.3C; it is designed so that as far as possible, a sub-depot is not only central to the area it supplies but also central in relation to surrounding sub-depots. This pattern, of course, approaches that of a hexagonal network. The boundaries of the sub-depot areas are set up so that each delivery vehicle can reach the edge of the delivery area, and deliver its full load in a working day. As far as possible no sub-depot should be more than a working day from a depot, but for some of the more remote parts of the country such requirements cannot be met. The number of sub-depots is related not only to demand, but also to the minimum efficient size of sub-depot. The demand supplied from the latter should be the exact equivalent of one, two, three or more trunk vehicles. Any other demand level results in the under use of a trunk vehicle and/or the need to introduce warehousing at the sub-depot site.

The physical distribution system of a market area reflects a firm's response to a wide number of variables in addition to trunking, delivery, depot, and sub-depot costs. Examples of these other variables are the length of the driver day, average speeds, delivery/trunk vehicle ratio, and customer density. Change in any one of the variables, perhaps resulting from market area extension and/or intensification, may stimulate rethinking of the distribution system and a desire to modify the market area's internal structure.

13.3. Market Area Extension

Hitherto, emphasis has been placed on the role of transport costs in guiding the size and structure of a market area. In contrast, this analysis of market area extension considers firms where constraints on the flow of information hinder the process of growth; here transport costs play only a minor role and for purposes of discussion they can be ignored. The information flows are those exchanges of information which are necessary to organize a market area efficiently. Where information flows are important to the growth of a market area, then an approach using diffusion concepts seems to be relevant. The diffusion discussed here envisages the spread of information in the way shown below;

A, B, C, and D are adjacent places or different levels of a hierarchy. This is the kind of process that would be expected in the growth of a market area as a 'self-interested propagator' (the firm) sets up 'innovation agencies' (new outlets). The outlets are established first where risk is minimized; that is, in the towns closest to the propagator (i.e. the most well known) or in the largest towns (i.e. those offering the largest potential market).

The process of diffusion envisaged here is, of course, different from that described in most diffusion studies (Brown and Moore, 1970). Brown and Cox (1971) stress that a theory of the diffusion of 'innovation agencies' by a 'self-interested propagator' is unlikely to be valid for the diffusion of innovations themselves. This is because 'inter-personal communication plays a critical role in the adaption of innovations, whereas its relevance in the establishment of innovation agencies is marginal at best' (Brown and Cox, 1971, p. 556).

The organizational and information problems faced by a self-interested propagator would be large especially where a firm controls its retail outlets. For example, to build up a successful group of outlets requires a careful and accurate selection of sites; supervision of staffs and quality of service in all outlets; receipt of cash from sales and despatch of salaries and wages; as well as the supply of goods to the outlets from the principal manufacturing site. During the pre-electronic era there would be a tendency for these organizational difficulties to limit the size of a firm's market area; whether they apply with equal force today is difficult to establish.

This examination of the diffusion of a firm's market area, focuses attention on a firm's selection of towns in which to establish a sales outlet. A small sample of firms controlling their sales outlets could form the basis for an exploratory study of the value of this approach. One example of an industry characterized by forward integration into retailing has been discussed previously (brewing); similar forward integration into retailing is found in the United Kingdom in the baking, clothing and footwear industries. A pilot survey based on these three industries would have to include most of the firms that would be needed in a full scale study. Instead of approaching firms twice, the diffusion concepts are tested by a detailed study of one firm. The firm chosen for this study met two conditions. First, it was outside the sectors where forward integration into retailing by manufacturers was well established, thus leaving those sectors available for a detailed analysis if the preliminary study was found to be rewarding. Second, some details of its evolution were contained in published sources (Wells, 1966) and in manuscript form (Daniels, 1956). A detailed history of the firm is to be published shortly (Chapman, 1973).

Data provided by The Boots Company Ltd form the basis of the analysis of diffusion presented below. In 1924 this firm manufactured a wide range of pharmaceutical goods in Nottingham and owned 665 retail outlets. There are no published records of the proportion of the firms output being sold through its own outlets, but by 1924 about two-thirds of the firm's turnover came from the sale of pharmaceutical preparations, and about one third of those were the firm's own products.

The firm was set up in Nottingham in 1849, but did not begin manufacturing until the 1880's. The move into manufacturing was accompanied by the extension of the market area. By 1884 outlets had been established in Sheffield, Grimsby and Lincoln. The 33 outlets of 1892 had increased to 289 a decade later, and to 444 in 1913. The firm grew in three ways; by the opening of new chemists shops, by purchasing existing single shop firms, and by the acquisition of rival chains of shops. The position of the decision to purchase in the decision sequence is not known, and it is assumed that the decision to purchase a new sales outlet in a town not formerly served would be made by the Nottingham head office; it has also to be assumed that this policy was constant throughout the time period under discussion. Some confirmation of the validity of this assumption is provided by Wells (1966, p. 409) who notes 'the administration of the retailing side of the business remained centred in Nottingham.'

The time period utilized (1892 to 1924) reflects the survival in the firm's archives of copies of either *Boots Scribbling Diary* or *Boots Home Diary and Ladies Notebook*. These provided lists of branches for 1898 (t_2), 1905 (t_3); 1914 (t_4) and 1924 (t_5). Daniels (1956) lists the branches operating in 1892 (t_1). The data are analysed by examining the date on which the first outlet was established in a specific town in England and Wales. The spread of outlets is depicted in Figure 13.4. The isolines show the maximum extent of the outlets at t_1, t_2, and t_3; by t_3 only relatively isolated areas such as the extreme south-west of the south-west peninsula and West Cumberland were still outside the market area. If the measures of market size discussed earlier are applied in this case, it can be shown that the mean sales range increased from 49 km at t_1 to 71·8 km at t_2 and 151 km at t_3—there was little change subsequently in the mean sales range. On the other hand, the maximum sales range increased from 93 km (t_1) to 200 km (t_2); then through 288 km (t_3) to 355 km (t_4). There seems then to be strong evidence here of market area extension.

Although the maximum sales range gives an indication of market area extension, the mean sales range evidence is less clear cut. A detailed analysis of the data permits more accurate statements to be made about the role of distance in market area extension, and at the same time it allows the examination of the role of town size in guiding the diffusion of outlets. A systematic unaligned sample identified 114 urban areas with populations of over 3,500 inhabitants in 1901. Statements about all towns, and about the contrasts between large and small towns are taken from this sample. A second data set based on the total enumeration of large towns of over 25,000 inhabitants is used to make statements about large towns. It is assumed that

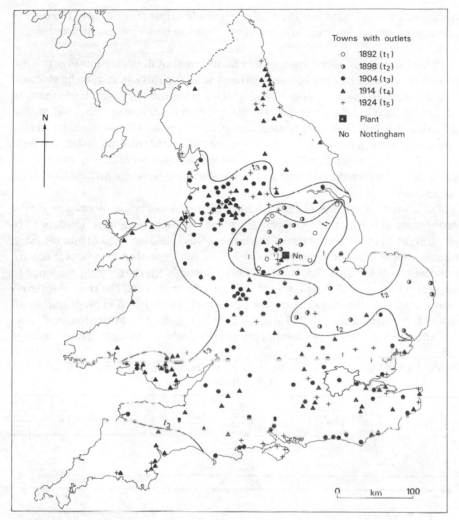

Figure 13.4. Market area extension: The Boots Company Ltd, 1892–1924
Sources: *Boots Scribbling Diary*, 1898 and 1924; *Boots Home Diary and Ladies Notebook*, 1905 and 1914; Daniels M. (1956) *Jesse Boot*. Unpublished manuscript

population size was constant at the 1901 level from t_1 to t_5; this does not appear to be unduly restrictive as most of the discussion is based on only two town size categories.

The proportion of all towns with outlets rose from 7·8 per cent (+/−5·0 per cent) at t_2 to 44·7 per cent (+/−9·3 per cent) at t_5. At first the proportion with outlets rose slowly; this was followed by a phase of very rapid increase, and then a return to the original slower rate. This is in marked contrast to the almost steady increase in the number of outlets. The characteristic S-shaped curve for the proportion of towns with branches is encouraging not only because this is the logistic curve found in other diffusion studies, but also because the period selected by chance survival of documents seems to be a reasonably meaningful one.

Detailed analysis of the apparently chaotic pattern illustrated in Figure 13.4 provides evidence of both hierarchical and spatial diffusion. It must be stressed that although the *patterns* of diffusion which are identified are similar to those in other diffusion studies the *process* is completely different. The pattern of diffusion is a function of the inter-action of three variables—time, town size and distance from Nottingham. In the investigation that follows distance is held constant and the town size/time relationships considered, and then, as a second stage, town size is held constant and the relationship between distance and time is examined.

The search for evidence of hierarchical diffusion can begin by examining the proportion of towns with outlets in the two town-size categories. Outlets were present (at t_5) in 90·7 per cent of the large towns (i.e. over 25,000 inhabitants), but they were present in only 33·0 (+/−9·7) per cent of small towns (i.e. with populations between 3,500 and 25,000). Certainly there is strong evidence to suggest that town size did play a role in attracting a branch. The time element is introduced by examining the number of outlets established in large and small towns before and after 1910 (Table 13.2). The two distributions are significantly different ($p < 0.01$), and this reflects the early arrival of outlets in large

Table 13.2. Number of outlets by date of establishment and town size: all towns (sample data)

(a) Town population (1901)	t_1-t_3 Number of outlets	t_4-t_5
⩾ 25,000	16	6
< 25,000	8	21

(b) Town population (1901)	t_1-t_2	t_3	t_4	t_5
⩾ 25,000	5	11	6	0
< 25,000*	4	2	10	6

* Row total reduced to same number of observations as previous row by the random elimination of seven observations.
Source: The Boots Co. Ltd.; Census of Population 1901.

towns. Thus, in all towns there is strong evidence to suggest that hierarchical diffusion did take place because there is a marked distinction between the time of the introduction of outlets into towns of the two different size classes (Table 13.2a). The pattern for a fourfold time division (t_1/t_2, t_3, t_4, t_5) is examined in Table 13.2b. The evidence points in the same direction but although acceptable statistically ($p < 0.05$) it is less conclusive.

The search for evidence of hierarchical diffusion is focused next on the large towns only, as they make up a more limited central place system than all towns. The assumption is made that if any difference did occur within this group it would be apparent in the data for towns with populations of above and below 75,000 inhabitants. There was no significant difference for a 2×2 (or 4×2) contingency table and it is possible to conclude that the firm was not hierarchically selective in the establishment of outlets within the set of large towns.

An alternative approach is to assume that if the firm is hierarchically selective then the mean size of towns receiving an outlet will decrease from t_1 to t_5. The skewed distributions of the data prevent this approach to the sample, but there is a marked decrease in the mean size of large towns receiving an outlet from t_3 (102,000) through t_4 (58,000) to t_5 (48,000). This appears to contradict the evidence in the previous paragraph but in the first stage of development (t_1/t_2) smaller towns were being served (88,000), and it may be that these smaller towns gained an outlet because of their relative proximity to Nottingham. This is the first confirmation of the spatial diffusion suggested by the mean and maximum sales range.

For tests of spatial diffusion, 150 km is chosen as the critical limit. The Plymouth shop, 355 km from Nottingham, is the firm's most distant outlet located in a large town. Only one per cent of the towns with outlets are further than 200 km from Nottingham so 150 km is towards the most distant end of the range of observations, and it is most likely that the consequences of distance will be identified more readily than over shorter distances. Table 13.3 shows the data for all towns; there is no significant difference between these two distributions. This confirms the earlier view that for all towns, hierarchical diffusion is more important than spatial diffusion in the growth of a firm's market area.

Table 13.3. Number of outlets by date of establishment and distance from Nottingham: all towns (sample)

Kilometres	t_1-t_3	t_4-t_5
	Number of outlets	
≤ 150	15	11
> 150	9	16

Source: The Boots Co. Ltd.

The relationship between hierarchical and spatial diffusion has been clarified by Brown (1968, pp. 31–32). In a system containing central places of contrasting order there will be a tendency for hierarchical diffusion to operate; whereas in a system containing central places of nearly the same order spatial diffusion may occur. Therefore, if all towns show no evidence of spatial diffusion it seems appropriate to consider large and small towns separately.

Table 13.4. Number of outlets by date of establishment and distance from Nottingham: large towns (full enumeration)

(a) Kilometres	t_1-t_3	t_4-t_5
	Number of outlets	
⩽ 150	58	18
> 150	24	24

(b) Kilometres	t_1-t_2	t_3	t_4	t_5
	Number of outlets			
⩽ 150	15	43	12	6
> 150	4	20	22	2

Source: The Boots Co. Ltd.

There is no evidence for a spatial diffusion in small towns. Table 13.4a presents data for large towns. Most towns within 150 km of Nottingham had outlets by 1910; whereas only half the towns more than 150 km distant had outlets by 1910. The two distributions are significantly different ($p < 0.01$) and this suggests proximity to Nottingham was important for large towns before 1910. A four-stage table (13.4b) also indicates a significant difference but at a lower level of probability ($p < 0.05$). It could be argued that the interpretation of the 2×2 table is open to doubt and further tests showed there is no difference (after 1910) in the frequency of outlets established over and under 150 km from Nottingham; but there is a difference before 1910 ($p < 0.01$). It seems that in large towns the spatial element in the diffusion of outlets was most obvious in the period before 1910. It is therefore appropriate to identify the passage of diffusion wave across the potential market area.

The diffusion wave for large towns is illustrated in Figure 13.5. Each wave depicts the proportion of new outlets at each time period in each distance zone. The distance to the crest of the wave from Nottingham increases through time: 0–50 km (t_1), 50–100 (t_2), 100–150 (t_3) and 200–250 (t_4). The foot of the wave shows also a consistent outward movement from 100–150 km (t_1), through 250–300 (t_2), 300–350 (t_3) and to over 350 km (t_4). Despite the irregularities introduced by t_2 the height of each wave decreases from 60 per cent (t_1) through 40 per cent (t_3) to 30 per cent (t_4). The irregularities in the wave possibly reflect the hierarchical diffusion examined earlier, but the general pattern indicates the process of market area extension.

In conclusion, these data show that elements of both hierarchical and spatial diffusion are present in the diffusion of innovation agencies by a self-interested propagator, spatial diffusion being more important in the early stages. Extending the conclusion beyond the present case is probably unwise for the pattern may be unique to both time and firm. In particular it is doubtful whether this approach would work as well in industries with high distribution costs, in which case alternative approaches based on the relationship of transport costs and

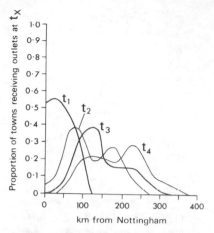

Figure 13.5. Market area extension: diffusion waves: The Boots Company Ltd, 1892–1914
Sources: Boots Scribbling Diary, 1898; *Boots Home Diary and Ladies Notebook,* 1905 and 1914; Daniels M. (1956) *Jesse Boot.* Unpublished manuscript

economies of scale, might be more appropriate. At best, it is possible to argue that distance considerations seem to play some part in the growth of a firm's market area, and the results obtained here would seem to justify a full-scale study over those industries where forward integration into retailing is common.

13.4. Structural change

The extension of the market area discussed in the previous section was accompanied by changes in its internal structure. Firstly, by changes in the proportion of towns served, and secondly by changes in the firm's distribution system.

The increase in the proportion of towns over 25,000 with outlets is shown in Figure 13.6. The market area, in this case, is regarded as ending at 300 km; only two potential sites occured beyond this point, whilst all other 50 km bands had at least seven potential sites. Whilst market area extension can be seen from t_1 to t_2, the principal value of this diagram is the illustration of the process of market area intensification. Over time the proportion of potential sites with outlets increases steadily until at t_3 all large towns within 50 km have outlets; a decreasing proportion have outlets, as distance from Nottingham increases. At t_4 intensification is further advanced but is not complete, except in the first and last distance bands; a number of intermediate towns are not served. The trough between these two bands is a reflection of the greater number of towns to be served in this middle distance, these 'towns' often being part of major urban

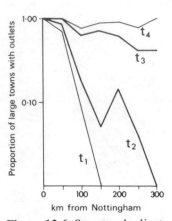

Figure 13.6. Structural adjustment of a market area—1: Intensification

Sources: *Boots Scribbling Diary*, 1898; *Boots Home Diary and Ladies Notebook*, 1905 and 1914; Daniels M. (1956) *Jesse Boot*. Unpublished manuscript

areas enjoying a distinct administrative status. In sum, Figure 13.6 shows the twin processes of market area extension and intensification postulated in the second section above, and confirms that when market area extension is complete, the process of intensification continues.

The need by the firm under consideration to serve a larger area and a greater demand, resulted in the establishment of depots in Manchester and London. In firms where transport costs are more significant market area growth depends on the development of an improved distribution system. It is not feasible to study the interaction of market area extension with changes in the distribution system. Instead, change in a distribution is considered within static market limits; market area extension has been completed, and changes in a distribution system are examined as the intensity of sales per unit area rises and then falls.

The variables affecting the distribution system of a market area, and the general relationships of trunking, delivery and depot costs were outlined earlier. The discussion which follows considers two major structural changes within the United Kingdom market area of the confectionery group of a major firm. The first change involved the setting up of a distribution system with depots; the second change involved the elimination of some of these depots, and the introduction of sub-depots.

Although the distribution system of a market area is the focus of this section, the structure of the system must inevitably be affected by the needs of the production division (supply) and the requests of the marketing and sales divisions (demand). The development of the internal structure of a market area must be read with this general qualification constantly in mind.

The confectionery group (of Cadbury Schweppes) is the present day descendent of the chocolate confectionery operations of two firms (Fry and Cadbury). The final product plants of the group are in the Bristol (Somerdale) area, and the Birmingham (Bournville) area; at the present time there is a tendency for the two plants to specialize in different types of confectionery. The two firms merged in 1918, and throughout the 1920's and 1930's, their operations were integrated gradually. In essence, the development of Cadbury's distribution system, is also the development of the Cadbury–Fry distribution system.

The distribution system discussed in the next section developed during a period of marked increase in demand for confectionery, and thus an increase in sales per unit area. Total consumption averaged 0·11 kg per caput in 1920, and had risen to 0·20 kg per caput in 1938 (Crane, 1969, p. 45). The firm's increase in output (measured in tonnes) was even greater; it doubled between 1922 and 1933 and doubled again between 1933 and 1938 (Cadbury Brothers, 1945, p. 59). The rationalization in 1970 (discussed below) was stimulated by a 25 per cent fall in depot throughput when the firm transferred its much expanded food products division to a separate distribution system. This resulted in a net decrease in sales per unit area for the confectionery division; it, of course, made no difference to total sales.

(1) *Establishment of a Depot System.* Cadbury's began chocolate manufacture in 1831. National distribution was achieved in 1881 (Williams, 1931, p. 30). Up until 1920 all orders were received at the factory and the products despatched by rail in the amounts required by each customer.

By 1920 the difficulties of this system for serving the United Kingdom market were becoming apparent. First, there was a delay between order and receipt of goods, especially for more distant customers. Not only was this a disadvantage to the customer, but clearly delays of this nature could affect the firm's sales. Second, the handling and despatching of goods in small lots to a variety of destinations, meant that many of the possible economies of scale in a large organization were not being achieved. Finally, increasing demands were being placed on an already overcrowded production site. By moving stockholding depots to other sites, land could be freed for alternative uses. Such was the pressure for land that some of the early or ancillary stages of production were moved away from Birmingham in 1923.

A change in the internal structure of the market area would offer possibilities of better services for customers, transport cost savings in distribution, and the release of land for production purposes. Williams (1931, p. 248) notes that relief 'of congestion at Bournville was one of the reasons for the establishment of transport depots'. The distribution system set up in the 1920's and 1930's was based on rail transport for trunking and road transport for delivery. The depots in the system by 1936 were being served by two train loads of 35 to 40 wagons per day. The choice of a rail based system was encouraged by the concessionary rail rates which the firm obtained. The areas served by road from

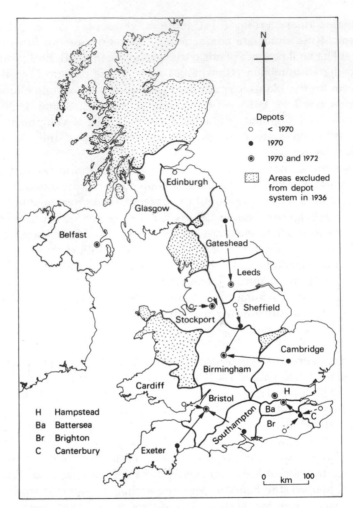

Figure 13.7. Structural adjustment of a market area—2. Depots and delivery areas of a confectionery firm, 1935, together with depot closures and 1970 rationalization scheme Sources: Cadbury Schweppes Ltd; Cadbury Bros (1945) *Industrial Record 1919–1939*, Cadbury, Bournville, 57–59; Williams I. A. (1931) *The firm of Cadbury, 1831–1931*. Constable, London. p. 245

each depot are illustrated in Figure 13.7, and, if the factory depot at Birmingham is typical, road vehicles moved products up to approximately 100 km. This was exceeded for areas where demand was small; generally these were the stippled areas in Figure 13.7. These areas, accounted for only about five per cent of sales (Anon, 1936).

The attractions of this new system were obvious; the depots could provide a convenient and more flexible system for customers; space at Birmingham was freed, and the advantage of low cost rail trunk haulage could be realized. The change over to separate depots was eased by the introduction of hand trolleys and the ability to move products on platforms from factory floor to rail wagon to depot without break of bulk. By shipping in bulk lots, packing costs were cut from 14 per cent of total distribution costs to only five per cent between 1927 and 1937. A company history records 'the main advantage of the depot system is that by sending out loads from the factory in bulk containers, the cost of carriage and freight, and particularly of packing and packing cases has been reduced' (Cadbury Brothers, 1945, p. 59). Overall distribution costs fell by 50 per cent between 1922 and 1938.

The published literature on the timing, size and location of depots in this particular case is sparse, and reasons for the observed pattern can be suggested only by examining the pattern itself. All 'large centres of population' (Rogers, 1931, p. 78) had received a depot by 1930; and a Spearman's Rank correlation coefficient of $+0.89$ between date of opening and population size shows a strong relationship between the two variables. This can be illustrated by inspection of the data; the first depot was established in London in 1922, and the last in Exeter and Cambridge in 1930 (Figure 13.7). Traffic congestion in London seems to have encouraged the establishment of two depots—one to the north and one to the south of the Thames. The reasons for the choice of certain smaller centres, like Cambridge instead of Peterborough, are not known. The majority of depots adjoined a railway, and had direct access to sidings (Williams, 1931, p. 245). At first, the system did not offer much saving for with the expansion of the number of depots '. . . the economies in carriage and freight from the factory failed to offset the increasing cost of the depots' (Cadbury Brothers, 1945, p. 59). However as depot throughput rose the depot system was justified fully.

(2) *Rationalization.* The modifications introduced before 1970 were small. Two schemes involved concentration at one site. The Manchester and Liverpool depots were replaced by Stockport in 1929 and Paddock Wood replaced Canterbury and Brighton in 1968. The Sheffield depot was replaced by one near Nottingham in 1961 and with improved road communications resulting from the Severn Bridge, the Cardiff depot was closed and the area served from Bristol. These changes indicate a continuing careful study of distribution costs, and a readiness to make changes where economies seemed possible.

The 1970 rationalization scheme differed from these earlier adjustments in that it involved a major review of the total distribution system, and the implementation of a rationalization programme after a major operations research exercise. The two principal spatial changes resulting from the rationalization plan were, first, the number of stockholding depots was reduced from 14 to eight, and second, a number of sub-depots (non-stockholding) were set up. This change made the distribution system similar to the hierarchical system shown in Figure 13.2a. The objective of the change was to reduce the operating costs, and the operations research survey sought to find the minimum operation cost which would maintain customer service at a pre-specified level, that is to offer customers a regular service. The service levels required at the present time are these; for orders to be delivered on a scheduled day in a stockholding depot delivery area the orders must be at the stockholding depot 48 hours before the scheduled day; for orders to be delivered on a schedule day in a non-stockholding depot area, the order must be at the parent stockholding depot 72 hours before the scheduled day. Depot cost curves were estimated from average conditions, except in London where local site costs were utilized.

The transportation problem was concerned with finding the best balance between 'trunking' and 'delivery'. In general, a trunk vehicle carried three times the load of a delivery vehicle at about half the cost. For example, use of trunk vehicles between Glasgow and Edinburgh reduced costs per 1,000 'outers' by 42 per cent. The analysis of trunking, delivery and warehouse costs, suggested a wide use of sub-depots and trunk vehicles with delivery sequenced loads. The advantage of this new system is that it increases trunk vehicle mileage and decreases the use of 'delivery' vehicles on trunking operations, without an increase in depot costs. For example, before 1970, delivery vans ran daily from Glasgow to Edinburgh, this meant that vans spent as long trunking as they did delivering. By basing the vans in Edinburgh, and trunking from Glasgow, transport costs between Glasgow and Edinburgh were reduced, the number of deliveries per van per day rose, and the number of delivery vehicles was reduced.

The rationalization scheme is shown in Figure 13.7 by arrows; the rationalized distribution system is shown in detail in Figure 13.8. The new combination of depots is only one of 11! (factorial) possible combinations if it is assumed that the 'factory' depots and Belfast would be kept anyway—the latter because of the need to keep separate stocks in areas supplied by water. It seems the depots closed were the smallest ones. The system of sub-depots is made up of points in the general vicinity of earlier depots (e.g. Nottingham, Gateshead, Exeter), and by a number of new sites (e.g. Northampton and Swansea). In the selection of these sites some 80 points were fed into the calculation. The sub-depots are served by road trunk units; whereas approximately 25 per cent of the goods arriving at the depots come in by rail.

It is interesting to compare the rationalized pattern of depots and depot capacity with an optimal pattern for a nationally distributed consumer product (Table 13.5). The two 'factory' depots have larger capacity than Sussams suggests, and in the north two medium-sized depots have replaced one large and one small depot. If allowance is made for the individual circumstances of this company, the rationalized pattern is close to the suggestions provided by Sussams.

This section has shown the kind of change that occurs within market areas as sales intensity rises and then falls. Certainly it is possible to see increasing sophistication in the control of a market area's structure as increased knowledge of the inter-relationships of distributions costs becomes available. It now seems possible to provide an optimal solution to distribution problems in a

Table 13.5. Allocation of depot capacity for a seven-depot system to serve U.K. market: 'optimal' and actual

	Birmingham	London*	Glasgow	Bristol	Manchester	Newcastle	Leeds
				Per cent of total capacity			
'Optimal'	16	33	11	12	12	6	—
Confectionery group	26	24	10	17	13	—	10

Source: Sussams, 1968; Cadbury Schweppes Ltd.
*The two London depots are considered as one unit in this table.

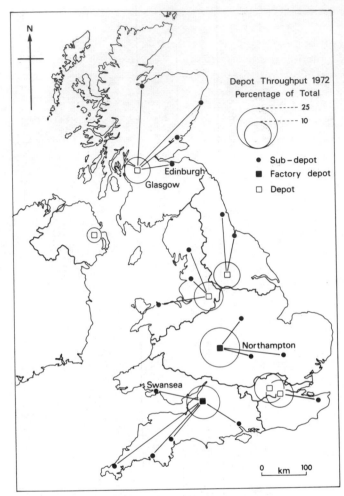

Figure 13.8. The rationalized distribution system, 1972. Depots, delivery areas and sub-depots of the confectionery division of a food and drink firm
Source: Cadbury Schweppes Limited

market area; a solution encompassing a continuously expanding market area is more elusive but in the long-run an optimal spatial adjustment pattern for market area growth may emerge.

13.5. Concluding Comments

The firms discussed in this chapter all produce goods which can be purchased by consumers at retail outlets, and where these outlets are owned by manufacturers they provide a useful measure of market area characteristics. Their value is indicated in the study of firms in the brewing and pharmaceutical industries.

In some firms the market area characteristics of size and structure are guided by high distribution costs—in the confectionery and brewing industries these costs represent between 6·8 and 10·5 per cent of net output. In other firms, such as those in the pharmaceutical industry, organizational needs rather than distribution costs limit initially the size and structure of a firm's market area. Certainly it does seem possible to identify the market areas of manufacturing firms, and to assess their spatial features; this at least is a move forward from the situation observed by both Lösch and Smith.

The size of a market area is the least difficult item to measure, but some might dispute the definition of a market area used here. To these, one asks whether a better operational definition can be reached, which can also be related to the kind of data which manufacturing industry makes available. Change in the size of market area is measured by the mean sales range or the 75 per cent sales radius.

Analysis of structural changes requires the measurement of two features; first, the rate at which the density of sales decreases with increased distance from the production point, and second, the pattern of depots, sub-depots and associated regionalization of the market area. An increase in a firm's market is accompanied by market area extension and/or market area intensification; such extension and intensification is paralleled, usually, by adaptation of the distribution system.

A detailed study of the process of market area extension is made by utilizing concepts from diffusion studies. However, it is stressed that while the terms hierarchical and spatial diffusion are used, the processes guiding the spread of retail outlets (innovation agencies) are different from the processes which lie at the core of most diffusion work. The analysis of one firm suggests that elements of both hierarchical and spatial diffusion are present. Spatial diffusion is most apparent during the early stages of market area extension through a limited central place system made up of only large towns. The study deals principally with the pre-electronic age, and it is necessary to proceed with caution if attempting to extend the conclusions to the present time. Perhaps the major limitation of the diffusion approach is that it is probably most appropriate to firms where distribution costs are low; where they are high, diffusion concepts will be less important and some transport based model may have to be developed.

The process of intensification, which accompanies market area extension is shown to continue after market area extension is complete. At the same time as extension and intensification is taking place it is necessary to adjust the distribution system. Unfortunately it is not possible to treat extension and structural change together; instead structural change is examined where a firm already serves the whole United Kingdom and has to adjust its distribution system to increases and decreases in density of sales per unit area. It is shown that within a period of only fifty years, there are marked variations in the hierarchical structure of a distribution system and in the regionalization of a firm's market area. The firm discussed is probably atypical both in its early

(1921) recognition of the value of road transport for short journeys, and in its early (for the United Kingdom) use of operational research procedures to help solve locational problems.

One implicit assumption underlying the analysis needs challenging at this point. Most of the essay assumes that market areas grow and firms increase their market shares. Undoubtedly market areas can contract, and it is unlikely that this will be simply the extension and intensification processes run in reverse. This point is discussed briefly in Lösch (1954, pp. 401–402), and is not elaborated further here.

Throughout this essay an attempt has been made to isolate the market area of a firm engaged in manufacturing activities, and to study the way in which it changes. Clearly, no claim is made to have presented the conclusive study of market areas of manufacturing firms. Spatial features of market areas worthy of consideration have been identified, and the dynamics of these features have been identified, and the dynamics of these features have been discussed for firms for which fragmentary evidence is available. Hopefully, some ideas may be developed further, and the direction of these possible developments is considered in the conclusions to the volume.

Acknowledgements

The author is indebted to The Boots Co. Ltd. and Cadbury Schweppes Ltd. for making available some of the information used in this chapter. The author's interpretation of this material does not necessarily reflect the views of the firms concerned.

References

Anon. (1936), Industrial Transport Organisation: Cadbury Brothers' Distribution Scheme, *Modern Transport,* **35,** No. 897, no pagination.

Anon. (1949), *150 Years of the House of Dutton.* Blackburn: Dutton.

Bayliss, B. T. and Edwards, S. L. (1970), *Industrial Demand for Transport.* London: H.M.S.O.

Beckmann, M. J. (1971), Market Share, Distance and Potential, *Regional and Urban Economics',* 3–18.

Brown, L. A. (1968), *Diffusion Dynamics: A Review and Revision of the Quantitative Theory of the Spatial Diffusion of Innovation.* Lund Studies in Geography, Series B, No. 28, Lund: C. W. K. Gleerup.

Brown, L. A. (1969), Diffusion Research in Geography a Perspective, in Board C. *et. al.* (eds.), *Progress in Geography,* **1.** London: Arnold. 119–157.

Brown, L. A. and Cox, K. R. (1971), Empirical Regularities in the Diffusion of Innovation, *Annals, Association of American Geographers,* **61,** 551–559.

Brown, L. A. and Moore, E. G. (1970), The Intra-urban Migration Process: A Perspective, *Geografiska Annaler,* Series B, **52,** 1–13.

Cadbury Brothers (1945), *Industrial Record, 1919–1939.* Bournville: Cadbury.

Carter, H. (1955), Urban Grades and Spheres of Influence in South-West Wales, *Scottish Geographical Magazine,* **71,** 43–58.

Chapman, S. D. (1973), *Jesse Boot of Boots the Chemist*. London: Hodder and Stoughton.

Chisholm, M. (1971), Freight Transport Costs, Industrial Location and Regional Development, in Chisholm, M. and Manners G. (eds.), *Spatial Policy of the British Economy*. Cambridge University Press, 213–244.

Crane, M. (1969), *Sweet Encounter*. London: MacMillan.

Daniels, M. (1956), Jesse Boot, unpublished manuscript, Nottingham: Boots Research Library.

Davies, W. K. D. and Lewis, C. R. (1970) The Nodal Structure of Wales, in Carter, H. and Davies, W. K. D. (eds.), *Urban Essays*. London: Longman, 24–31.

Eilon, S., Watson-Gandy, C. D. T. and Christofides, N. (1971), *Distribution Management: Mathematical Modelling and Practical Analysis*. London: Griffin.

Glamorgan Record Office. David John (Pentre) D/D XCu 13.

Glamorgan Record Office. Fern Vale Brewery Co. Ltd. (Pontygwaith) D/D XCu 14.

Gleave, M. B. (1965), Some Contrasts in the English Brick-making Industry, *Tijdschrift Voor. Econ. Soc. Geografie*, **56**, 54–62.

Goddard, J. B. (1971), Office Communications and Office Locations: A Review of Current Research, *Regional Studies*, **5**, 263–289.

Greenhut, M. L. (1956), *Plant Location in Theory and Practise*. Chapel Hill: University of North Carolina Press.

Hoover, E. M. (1948), *The Location of Economic Activity*. New York: McGraw-Hill.

Isard, W. (1956), *Location and Space Economy*. Cambridge, Mass.: M.I.T. Press.

Lösch, A. (1954), *The Economics of Location*. New Haven: Yale University Press.

Ministry of Transport (1966), *Survey of Road Goods Transport, 1962. Final Results: Geographical Analysis*. London: H.M.S.O.

McNee, R. B. (1961), Centrifugal and Centripetal Forces in International Petroleum Company Regions, *Annals, Association of American Geographers*, **51**, 124–138.

Monmouthshire Record Office. Webbs (Aberbeeg) Ltd. D 886.

Pred, A. R. (1971a), Large City Interdependence and the Pre-electronic Diffusion of Innovations in the United States, *Geographical Analysis*, **3**, 165–181.

Pred, A. R. (1971b), Urban Systems Development and the Long Distance Flow of Information through Pre-electronic U.S. Newspapers, *Economic Geography*, **47**, 498–524.

Rogers, T. B. (1931), *A Century of Progress, 1831–1931*. Bournville: Cadbury.

Rowley, G, (1971), Central Places in Rural Wales, *Annals, Association of American Geographers*, **61**, 537–550.

Smith, D. M. (1971), *Industrial Location: An Economic Geographical Analysis*. New York: Wiley.

Steed, G. P. F. (1971), Forms of Corporate Environmental Adaptation, *Tijdschrift Voor Econ. Soc. Geografie*, **62**, 90–94.

Sussams, J. E. (1968), Some Problems Associated with the Distribution of Consumer Products, *Operational Research Quarterly*, **19**, 161–174.

Warren, K. (1971), Growth, Technical Change, and Planning Problems in Heavy Industry with Special Reference to the Chemical Industry, in Chisholm, M. and Manners, G. (eds.), *Spatial Policy Problems of the British Economy*. Cambridge University Press, 180–212.

Wells, F. A. (1966), Industrial Structure, in Edwards, K. C. (ed.), *Nottingham and its Region*. Nottingham: British Association, 405–415.

Williams, I. A. (1931), *The Firm of Cadbury, 1831–1931*. London: Constable.

Prospects: A Summary of Possible Avenues of Future Research An Editorial Synopsis of Contributors' Comments

The preceding essays illustrate the variety of approaches to the study of the locational dynamics of manufacturing activity. The spectrum of approach includes: attempts to develop theoretical and conceptual constructs which can be used as frameworks for analysing changes in the location of manufacturing activity at the urban, regional and national levels; the adoption and application of methodologies and statistical procedures for describing, analysing and forecasting aggregate changes in manufacturing activity; detailed studies of particular areas illustrating historical trends and the evolution of new patterns; and the micro-study of individual firms to show how decision making processes lead to changes in the structure and spatial pattern of manufacturing activity. Perhaps one of the most important common elements of these essays is their emphasis on current and ongoing research so that most of the essays raise questions which remain unanswered and which require further investigation and commentary.

Most of the calls for further research relate to the fact that there is inadequate evidence about so many aspects of locational dynamics. Frequently we are in the dark not only about the future but also about the past. There is, for example, a need for a more complete examination of many important *relationships.* In his essay Norcliffe uses, in addition to his own empirical observations of the Bristol region, supportive evidence of research conducted in Australia, the United States and Canada. Yet he stresses that this empirical evidence is still too fragmentary for building a general theory and he calls for more detailed case studies of 'the relationships between plant size and city size, between plant function and city size, and between industrial composition and city size.' Undoubtedly the main difficulty in studying these relationships will be lack of suitably disaggregated data. But among the many interesting questions that can be investigated, especially with respect to plant size, is the importance of achieving a balanced industrial size structure as well as a diversified one for developing urban areas.

385

As in the Norcliffe essay, the call for more empirical studies to test existing theoretical models is echoed throughout Feller's essay on Invention, Diffusion and Industrial Location. Feller recognizes that 'Webber's latest contribution is a significant theoretical advance over, for example, Pred's earlier work in integrating the location of inventive activity, the diffusion of innovations and regional growth. Webber's model, however, still remains to be formally tested.' In terms of extending his own research Feller feels that 'it would be interesting in a study of the ways in which diffusion affects location to assess how differential rates of adoption by region influence the geographic distribution of output. Moreover, there is a need to investigate further the relationship between composition of inventive activity and composition of economic activity. Additional empirical studies are required to estimate the importance of technological change relative to other factors in industrial location and the assumption that the ties between location and invention underwent a structural change after 1901 has yet to be tested.' The general tenor of Feller's work then is that more attention be paid to the role of technology in developing general theories and conceptual models of locational change.

Another way of examining relationships may be by means of computer experiments. Walker suggests that a simulation model could be used to examine the effect of different types of decision-making on locational patterns over a series of time periods. Walker's model, and others of a similar type, should allow experimentation which will explore the consequences of relationships established empirically and allow evaluation of alternative futures. Admittedly, much has to be done before there are similar models of specific areas, but the line of research looks promising.

Another research avenue which holds promise is the *extension of approaches and concepts*. Gilmour, for example, recognizes that the concept of the export region is unlikely to have the same value as a theoretical framework for the future analysis of as yet undeveloped areas, but he does suggest that the model still has partial relevance. It would be appropriate, for example, to adapt the concept 'to the study of developing Third World economies if allowance is made for changing technological, political and economic factors'. As well, Gilmour indicates that this approach 'may have value for studying extant export-base regions such as British Columbia which was settled late in the spatial economic expansion of Western industrial society'.

It would seem in fact that much of what we know about industrial location needs testing in a variety of cultural and political contexts. Although some work has been completed on socialist economies most theory and empirical evidence is based on advanced western economies. Bater hints at this when he notes that his findings on nineteenth-century St. Petersburg contrast with those of some other studies. He suggests that this could partly be attributable to the fact that Russian cities had some different characteristics from those in the West. This would suggest the potential importance of cultural and political factors in the design of cities, a topic that has been little studied, especially in relation to industrial location.

The political climate is becoming increasingly important as governments take an active interest in industrial location and economic development. Cannon's essay discusses the difficulty of assessing the impact of a particular Canadian policy and in so doing introduces an area in which prediction of future locational patterns may be very troublesome. He notes that, 'incentive programmes are being practised at such a large scale that their effect on the growth performance of manufacturing cannot be ignored'. But which programmes will a particular government use in the future? Even if that question could be answered, there is still relatively little evidence to help in the assessment of the impact of past programmes or that of those to be used in the future.

An *extension of application* may also be expected in the realm of quantitatively-based methodologies and statistical techniques. These are becoming increasingly popular in the analysis of industrial location. The simulation model, an example of which is discussed by Walker, is capable of far more varied use. Koenig, Lewis and Ray introduce allometry to the study of manufacturing activity for the first time and it is clear that much more work will be needed before it can be fully appreciated. The authors define allometry as being 'concerned with the relative growth of the components of a system rather than with the absolute growth-in-time of these components or of the system itself, mathematically allometry is simply a ratio of two specific growth rates.' Although the data used by Koenig, Lewis and Ray is too coarse for the application of allometry to the Canadian manufacturing hierarchy to be statistically convincing, further research is strongly advocated. In particular 'the deduction of size-required proportional adjustments needs detailed elaboration and further improvements in the measurement of allometries are necessary.'

In his essay Cant elaborates three-mode factor analysis which he considers to be 'a useful alternative to the singular decomposition of matrices used by Koenig, Lewis and Ray to examine the system structure in the second stage of their mathematical methodology. Koenig, Lewis and Ray, for example, indicate that the choice of alternatives will depend on the quality of the available data and on the judgement of the researcher concerned.' The methodology outlined in the Cant essay helps to clarify some of the issues involved in such decisions. Cant's essay is the second of two studies which use factor analysis to investigate changes in the location of manufacturing in New Zealand. Although Cant revealed 'a number of operational problems in the first study the research reported in his essay here establishes the utility of the method for geographical analysis.' Cant now suggests, therefore, 'that the immediate need is for a wider range of empirical experience both within and beyond industrial geography. Only in this way can we move beyond a preoccupation with the actual technique to the point where we can link up the results with ongoing world of research and the development of theory.'

Whereas Norcliffe posits a partial equilibrium theory which emphasizes the relationships between size of manufacturing plant and urban area, Collins outlines a statistical procedure for analysing and predicting not only changes in the aggregate size distribution of plants in an urban area but also changes in the spatial distribution of plants through time. These two facets of change are examined here in two separate models but Collins suggests that the two could be combined to provide a single three dimensional construct in which it would be possible to determine the probability of a plant's change in size consequent upon its relocation from one spatial state to another. One of the main obstacles to the more widespread use of Markov models, especially at the individual urban or metropolitan scale is the dearth of suitably disaggregated data for estimating the transition probabilities; this problem is also emphasized by Lever. If the data can be obtained then the outlined procedure applied to a wide selection of individual urban areas may provide the sort of empirical evidence required for further theoretical developments outlined by Norcliffe.

If we are to understand fully the existing patterns of industrial location in the world's major *urban areas* we require more *empirical studies* of the sort presented by Bater, Bastié and Lever. The study of industrial linkages in a historical setting is the theme of Bater's essay. Bater concludes that, in later nineteenth-century St. Petersburg, small plants did not have a great tendency to localize. He calls for further research of 'factors such as land cost, rent, zoning, and labour availability and immobility . . . in order that the process of nineteenth-century intra-urban industrial location be better comprehended.'

Although Bastié recognizes the difficulty of undertaking detailed studies of small areas outside the main industrial concentrations, it is important that many studies be commissioned if the impact of planned decentralization is to be fully appreciated. Such studies would be essential, not only for assessing, *via* questionnaires, the effects of decentralization on industrial linkages within the agglomeration and hence on economies of scale, but also for assessing the total effect on the surrounding landscape in terms of the loss of agricultural land and the requirement of new facilities, waste disposal, roads and residential demands. If industry is to be decentralized to new town developments what sort of industry mix and size structure would be most viable and at what scale?

Just as we lack adequate information related to intra-urban location of industry, there is also a need for more *empirical studies of the spatial behaviour of the firm*. Krumme and Hayter, for example, feel that 'although it seems that we are already or almost at the stage where we can analyse certain aspects of aggregate industrial patterns *via* stochastic techniques, there is a continuing need for case studies of individual or groups of firms and for finding new perspectives for the understanding of corporate behaviour'. In their essay, the authors stress the significance of particular behavioural constraints related to product life cycles. This research direction appears to gain importance in a world where industrial activity is becoming increasingly controlled by large and complex multi-functional and multi-locational organizations which can have a dominating influence over industrial location patterns at a variety of scales. Krumme and Hayter would like to see 'the application of statistical (time series) techniques for the study of a small number of corporations which exhibit appropriate similarities and differences, for example, in their market and investment expansion paths and locational response patterns'.

Watts' discussion of individual firm's market areas stresses its exploratory character, but it seems to open up a number of new lines of enquiry in a formerly neglected field. The necessarily restricted scale of the case studies obviously raises questions as to whether similar patterns emerge at continental level, and to what extent international market areas differ from those discussed.

From limited evidence Watts suggests using 'the distribution of retail outlets as a surrogate measure of the distribution of sales', but he recognizes that 'while this seems valid for the cases presented, more needs to be known about the relationship between outlets and sales before the measure can be widely accepted. The decline in sales density as distance from production point increases shows an interesting regularity and if similar regularities do emerge readily from other studies, then it is possible to advance from description to an understanding of the processes which underly the observed trends. A further possibility is to undertake a detailed analysis of the relationship between a firm's growth, its sales density and its market area size. It may even be feasible to build up more complex models of variations in the sales density of multi-plant firms.

'Perhaps an important distinction in the analysis of the dynamics of market areas is the distinction between market area extension and market area intensification. The inter-relationships of extension and intensification can only be suggested in the essay, and the relationships of the two elements with each other and with distribution systems remain to be developed. The study of distribution systems seems to lie somewhere between the geography of manufacturing and wholesaling, in a kind of no-man's land. The basic elements guiding the form of these systems are well-known, but the patterns of spatial change that result from them still require further investigation

'The study of the growth of one firm's market area seems to gain in a different framework; although the patterns of the diffusion of "innovation agencies" are similar to those of the diffusion of "innovations", the processes at work are different. The mixture of spatial and hierarchical features studied will need further attention and the influence of one upon the other has to be clarified. It will be important also to examine the effect of the pre-existing urban hierarchy on the diffusion of the agencies and the extent to which the diffusion is influenced by the technological environment.' It should not be forgotten that Watts deals essentially with the pre-electronic age, and he stresses that 'the diffusion approach may not be appropriate where distribution costs make up a high proportion of net output.'

While it is possible to provide a detailed study of market area extension, 'the study of structural change pays brief attention to intensification, before focusing principally on the adjustment of a distribution system. The rationalization of a distribution system depended on the use of operational research techniques and it would be useful to know the extent to which these techniques are used in solving distribution problems in other firms and industries. Further questions raised by the concluding section of the study of market areas are the nature of variations in distribution systems as firms and industries grow, and the correlation between expected and existing distribution systems.'

The volume has brought together a number of studies concerned with the locational dynamics of manufacturing activity. The aim has been to emphasize the wide spectrum of research interest that is currently being focused on the variety of approaches to the study of changing manufacturing patterns. Recent research published elsewhere has demonstrated the enormous scale of these changes in most Western countries. The essays presented here have explored ways of analysing the processes of change both in terms of theory and practice at different geographic scales ranging from local to national for selected industries, but with a major emphasis on the behaviour of industrial regions or agglomerations and of individual firms. It is hoped that the numerous research questions that have been posed and which remain unanswered will be pursued in continuing studies designed for developing and expanding the study of industrial location.

Author Index

Subject Index